Neil Munro
The Biography

Neil Munro

The Biography

Lesley Lendrum

Air son gach còmhnuidh 'sam faighte 'n aoigheachd,
Tha'n larach dhuaichnidh - o! uaigh na féileachd!

To K.B.

British Library Cataloguing in Publication Data
A catalogue record of this book is available from the British Library

ISBN 1 899863 91 5

© Lesley Lendrum, 2004

The publisher acknowledges the financial assistance of the Scottish Arts Council

Typeset by XL Publishing Services, Tiverton
Printed in Great Britain
by SRP Ltd, Exeter
for House of Lochar
Isle of Colonsay, Argyll PA61 7YR

Contents

Introduction:
The beginnings of things are to be well considered   vii

1.	The oe from Ladyfield	1
2.	Those lovely, unperplexed and simple days	7
3.	Blythe were the seasons	10
4.	The key of the street and the freedom of the seashore and the forest	16
5.	My earliest impressions of a prison	18
6.	A burgh most large and wonderful	21
7.	This roaring city of our exile	27
8.	An awfu' peely-wally yin!	34
9.	All alone on Greenock quay	39
10.	The jawbox of journalism	45
11.	I believe I know the heart of the Highland people	53
12.	The said Celtic glamour	62
13.	Aora mo chridh tha mi seoladh	67
14.	First day in the house as a Literary Man!	72
15.	The happy manner with Romance	81
16.	I burned my journalistic boats	90
17.	A regard for the manner of his message	93
18.	The slave of two serials	98
19.	I got about 2 doz trout	105
20.	The pause of the morning, when time stands	110
21.	They are saying the old wife is gone!	116
22.	I could see Inveraray – if it weren't for the mountains in between	124
23.	I hope to finish this yarn by April	133
24.	Not in the kailyard, but up tenement closes	140
25.	The bugles of the mind	149
26.	Blythmeat and breadberry... in the house of Daniel Dyce	156
27.	Ailie's geese	164
28.	It's a sair fecht, a faim'ly!	168
29.	My own folk are pleased with me	175
30.	Or I'm a soused gannet	180

31. Jolly decent imaginative work 186
32. By the old ways north 191
33. War! Inveraray Post Office open day and night 195
34. We went for you to the yetts o' hell 202
35. That strange French countryside war-battered 215
36. This is the house for me! 221
37. My imaginative faculty has been lying fallow 227
38. Inveraray is as gorgeous as ever 235
39. A soul imprisoned! 241
40. Startles me like a hare 248
41. I miss my Swiss 253
42. No more hack work for me 259
43. And this becomes a lonely house 265
44. Cha Till Mi Tuilidh 273

Munro in Print 279
Genealogical tables
  The Forebears of Neil Munro 281
  The Descendants of Neil Munro 282
References 283
Index 295

The photographs, located between pages 152 and 153, have been provided for the most part by the author. The pictures of the 8th Duke of Argyll and the Marquis of Lorne with Princess Louise are in the Inveraray Collection, while that of Lord Archibald Campbell is in the collection of Ian Anstruther.

Introduction:
The beginnings of things are to be well considered

NEIL Munro loved the rain – so my mother, fifth of his seven children, used to tell me. His native Argyll has a high rainfall, and much water has flowed down the river Aray and into Loch Fyne since he was buried in Kilmalieu more than half a century ago. At that time – December 1930 – an anonymous leader writer in the *Glasgow Herald* declared: 'It may be many a day before Scotland finds a writer who can hold the attention and charm the minds of his own people as Munro did from 1896 to 1918.'

Those are the years when his first and last books, *The Lost Pibroch* and *Jaunty Jock*, were published: they also span a period that falls between the death of Robert Louis Stevenson and the emergence of Hugh MacDiarmid. In 1935, when a new collected edition of Neil Munro's novels and stories was published, the *Times Literary Supplement*, echoing the *Glasgow Herald*, said: 'In the scanty annals of Scottish literature during the generation between Stevenson and the nineteen-twenties, the name of Neil Munro stands out substantial.'[1]

Stevenson was only 44 when he died. It is fascinating, if idle, to speculate as to the difference it might have made to Scottish letters if Stevenson and George Douglas Brown (1869–1902) had lived out their allotted spans. Neil Munro, born thirteen years after Stevenson, was already achieving success with short stories written 'in a Highland manner' when Stevenson died in 1894, and would live on for another 36 years.

All but three of the chapter headings in this biography come from Neil Munro's own writings. The Gaelic lines on the title page are by Evan MacColl (1808–98), the Loch Fyne bard, and have been translated by Marion Campbell of Kilberry:

In place of each house that gave a welcome
Are crippled ruins – o, graves of bounty!

vii

Acknowledgements

My best thanks go to my husband, Kenneth Bratton, who rashly suggested my undertaking this biography. Neil Munro himself died before I was born, alas, but I was lucky enough to have close early associations with all his surviving family and with Inveraray and Glasgow. Naturally my late mother's memories have contributed greatly to this book. My uncle the late Neil Munro junior was especially helpful, as were my sister Finella Wilson and her husband David. I should also like to thank four other kinsfolk – Daisy Renfrew, Ian Munro, Eoin McArthur and Duncan Beaton.

Thanks are also due to Georgina Hobhouse at House of Lochar and to my editor, Jeremy Hodges, who has been so patient and understanding.

When I started to collect material, nothing was further from my mind than a veritable Munro revival, yet this has indeed occurred independently of myself with the founding of the Neil Munro Society in 1996 and the re-publication of nearly all of his fiction. My fellow committee members in the Society have all been very supportive, in particular Ronald W. Renton. Others for whose help I am grateful would include the late Donald Mackechnie, Hermann Völkel, Beata Kohlbek and Euan Robson.

CHAPTER ONE

The oe from Ladyfield

THE Inveraray of Victorian days was capital of a little kingdom more than three thousand miles square, with a seaboard of two thousand miles if islands be included. Its population was then about a thousand, with seven hundred more in the landward parts of the parish. There were frequent and varied events: the comings and goings of the Duke of Argyll and his family, the court sessions, the coaches and steamers, the herring drifters and cargo boats and ferries. For one born and bred there, those were the familiar extras to the staple diet – the small white-walled town, the sea loch, the hills and moor lochs, the forest, rivers and burns, the warmth and affection of a simple home, the school-fellows known since memory began. To spend his first years there, where all knew of his circumstances, was not the worst beginning in life for Neil Munro.

He was born on 3 June 1863, towards ten o'clock in the evening. He had a twin sister who was stillborn, but no other brothers or sisters. His mother, Ann, was thirty-three, and she was unmarried. The identity of Neil's father is unknown: to my certain knowledge, he never spoke of the matter to any of his own children.

His birthplace was the little Inveraray tenement called Crombie's Land, but that seems to have been only a fleeting abode. His mother, who gave her occupation as 'kitchenmaid' when she registered his birth, had to go back to work as soon as she could. She was not able to nurse her new baby and entrusted him to a foster mother, her friend Jane MacKellar, wife of a garden labourer, whose own son was a few months younger than Neil.

Two years before Neil was born, the 1861 Census recorded an Ann Munro (not necessarily Neil's mother) working at the Manse in Inveraray as a nursery maid. There is also a family tradition that she worked at Inveraray Castle, but when and for how long is unknown.

In his book *The Highland Clans* (1967) the late Sir Iain Moncreiffe of that Ilk mentioned 'Neil Munro (so closely related, we are told, to the ducal house of Argyll)'. In reply to a letter from myself querying this, he wrote 'in my opinion your grandfather Neil Munro was almost certainly a natural son of the 8th Duke of Argyll' and cited 'the constant rumours to this effect and that Duke's well-known fecundity', also the fact that he was 'a skilled and prolific writer'. Sir Iain also wrote to his friend the 11th Duke, who replied: 'All I can say is that Niall [his uncle, the 10th Duke] and, more strongly, his sister Elspeth, were apt to consider Neil M. as a by-blow of my great-great-grandfather.' Sir Iain concluded his letter to me: 'I feel that the relationship was too close for him [Neil Munro] to wish to disclose it in his own time; but that he would see such things very differently nowadays... what is known or very strongly surmised should be set down for posterity.'[1]

The earliest photograph of Neil shows him aged four or five, wearing the kilt. He is standing beside his mother, who is sitting on a chair, with her right arm round him: his left hand rests confidingly on her skirt, his right holds a bonnet that looks much too large for him. Although a kind woman, his mother was given to strong personal dislikes, which she did not bother to hide. She was very superstitious, and in a thunderstorm she would cover all the mirrors in the house. Yet despite her Gaelic belief in the supernatural, Ann Munro was an intelligent woman. Neil's younger son and namesake, who looked extremely like his father, remembered visiting his grandmother in Inveraray when she lived in a flat of four small rooms on the ground floor of Arkland, nearest the church. It was very full of furniture 'probably including a large piano'. He recalled she was 'well educated, articulate, a player of the piano (which she did sometimes at Inveraray Castle gatherings) and given to long political discussions with the [8th] Duke [of Argyll]'.[2]

Neil and his mother shared a one-roomed dwelling with her widowed mother in McVicar's Land (now Arkland II). Ann was the youngest daughter and there may well have been an assumption in the family that she would give up marriage prospects in order to be her mother's companion. In later life Neil would describe 'a room in McVicar's Land, with a wooden floor, and a fire on the side of the wall with a built-in chimney, and other gentilities besides... McVicar's Land was full of smells – of sweating flesh and dirty water, of fish and the rotting airs of sunless holes...'[3] But within all this the one room that was his grandmother's house was a haven of happy domesticity, and Neil would long remember 'the interior, that would have been dull and mean but for the brilliant delf upon the dresser rack and the cleanliness of all things and the smiling faces...'[4]

Nevertheless, it was far from an ideal start in life. When Neil himself was almost sixty, he said in a letter: 'I fancy I shall never write the story of my own childhood, though there were tragic and pathetic elements in it which would make a dozen novels of the

grimy sort now in vogue. I sought escape from them in the imagination for so long, and so ardently, that I couldn't help becoming a
romancer in the end.'[5]

Yet it was never in his nature to repine, and he makes few references elsewhere to these negative aspects of his childhood. Against
them must be set the happier elements to be gleaned from what is
known of his early days, from his constant choice of Argyll as the
setting for his fiction, from the lifelong connections he cherished
with Inveraray. His mother is said to have been an extremely kind
woman: a loving family compensated for fatherlessness and poverty,
and he spent his first eighteen years within the small yet intricate
society of Inveraray on its crowded, sealoch-girt promontory.

There was little money in the one-roomed house. Oatmeal,
whether as porridge or oatcakes, was a staple food and, as a change
from home-made scones, there were the baker's rolls and bread as a
treat, 'town bread, and sugar on its butter'. Then, of course, there
was a cheap and plentiful supply of herring from Inveraray's own
fleet. Some of the townsfolk, including Neil's mother at one time,
had milch cows which a lad known as the town herd took to the
Common Muir each day, bringing them back in the evening. Water
was drawn from iron wells, one of which was set into a wall near
McVicar's Land, and carried into the house in wooden buckets
known as 'stoups'.

It is certain that Neil's grandmother had a good deal to do with
his upbringing. She had five sons of her own, forbye three stepsons,
so she had plenty of experience with boys of all ages. Neil's love for
her ran deep, 'indeed he had loved the old shrunk woman, brown as
a nut, with a love that our race makes no parade of, but feels to the
very core'.[6]

He was the only child and the only male in a house of talkative,
sociable women. Luckily for young Neil, he was always a good
listener: 'When I sit and look at people without saying anything, I
am reading them far in'.[7] These words seem especially to portray
Neil as a boy, drinking in the conversation of his mother and grandmother, and of his many aunts, uncles and cousins who would come
and go about the house.

Among them was Aunt Bell, his grandmother's unmarried sister
Isabella McArthur, on whom he would model Miss Mary, the elderly
spinster who looks after Gilian and with whom he experiences 'the
kind air of fond companionship'. Neil describes her as 'A dear fond
heart, a darling hypocrite, a foolish bounteous mother-soul without
chick or child of her own, and yet with tenement for the loves of a

3

large family.'⁸ The first thing Miss Mary gives Gilian is a cup of cream, and he gets soup and 'the tenderest portions of the hen' and cheese that is not 'the plain skim-milk curd cheese of Ladyfield', known otherwise as crowdie.

At home the conversation was in Gaelic, the first language Neil heard and learned – 'the natural tongue, friendly Gaelic' – in which he was liable to be addressed as '*Laochain! Balachan ban!*' (little hero, fair-haired fellow). Years later Ann Munro would address Neil's younger son Neil, who looked very like him, in the same way, and on Sundays would take him up to the nursery and read to him from some religious book.

Although English had been spoken at Inveraray, capital of Argyll, since before 1700, Neil grew up bilingual, and from early childhood would unconsciously start to associate Gaelic with the old ways, on which a door was slowly closing forever. He was fully conscious of the divide between two cultures, summed up perfectly by John Francis Campbell of Islay in his preface to *Popular Tales of the West Highlands*: 'The shoals of herrings that enter Loch Fyne know as much as the dun deer on the hill-side, as Londoners and Highland peasants know of each other... the want of a common language, here as elsewhere, keeps Highlands and Lowlands, Celt and Saxon, as clearly separate as oil and water in the same glass.'

Inveraray, partly from its very nearness to the Lowlands, partly from its being county town of Argyll (a county so large that 'capital' seems an apter name) and seat of the then still prominent Duke of Argyll, was in many ways a border town, where the old ways came in contact with the new and were gradually absorbed by them. But Neil's mother and his grandmother were both born and brought up on farms in 'real Argyll' – that land between Loch Fyne and Loch Awe – and it was from them he chiefly got his insight into 'the old, darling, foolish Highlands in us'.⁹

Neil's mother was fourteenth of the fifteen children of John Munro, a shepherd, grieve of the small farm of Ladyfield (Lecknamban) in Glen Aray. Perhaps he was one of the shepherds overheard by John Keats as the poet walked from Inveraray to Loch Awe in July 1818. Keats wrote to his brother: 'I forgot to tell you that when we came through Glenside it was early morning and we were pleased with the noise of Shepherds, Sheep and dogs in the misty heights close above us – we saw none of them for some time, till two came in sight creeping among the Crags like Emmets, yet their voices came quite plainly to us.'¹⁰

Keats must have passed near the small farm of Ladyfield at the top of Glen Aray, where John Munro had been grieve since 1812. In 1815 his first wife, Lillias Bell, had died, leaving him with six children to bring up. In April 1818, shortly before Keats passed by, the minister of the Gaelic-speaking part of the parish had come up to Ladyfield to marry John to his second wife, Ann McArthur – the grandmother who was to have such an important part in Neil's upbringing.

For the first 15 years of Neil's life 'the goodwife of Ladyfield' would be a constant presence. Ann McArthur has been described as 'a redoubtable woman from Lochaweside'.[11] When she married John Munro he was 44 and she was 25, only eleven years older than his oldest child, Mary. Ann was to have nine children of her own, the second last being Neil's mother. When the first official Census was taken in 1841, husband and wife were listed there at the farm, with four children still at home – Duncan, 20, Peter, 14, Ann, 11 and Dugald, 9.

John, who gave his occupation as 'agricultural labourer', was then about 67. As he grew older, the likelihood is that Ann took over much of the running of Ladyfield. On his death, she did her best to keep the farm going. As the Sergeant More observes in *Gilian the Dreamer*: 'Many a time I wondered that the widow did so well in the farm for Captain Campbell, with no man to help her, the sowing and the shearing, the dipping and the clipping, ploughmen and herds to keep an eye on, and bargains to make with wool merchants and drovers. Oh! she was a clever woman, your grandmother.'[12]

Again, the Sergeant More calls her 'the best woman in the three parishes and the cleverest'. His words are surely based on family recollections directly learnt by Neil: 'Is that not wonderful? The first time I saw her was at a wedding in Kames, Lochow, and she was the handsomest woman in the room, and there were sixty people at the wedding from all parts, and sixty-nine roasted hens at the supper.'[13]

Ann McArthur was not only clever and handsome. Born in 1793, she grew up with the blood of Highland chieftains in her veins. Both her parents were McArthurs. Her mother Lilly was the daughter of Patrick McArthur of Inistrynich, described by Neil in his diary as 'last chief of the sept'.[14] His carved oak bedstead was handed down as far as Ann McArthur's generation, and she and one of her sisters gave it to the 7th Duke of Argyll for safekeeping. The bed is still in Inveraray Castle.

The story would often have been recited in Neil's presence at McVicar's Land, and for his reaction to it one need look no further than young Elrigmore's rather ambivalent words in Neil's novel *John*

5

Splendid: 'And so we went into all this perplexity of Highland pedigree like old wives at a waulking... I think I was cool, for I was never a person that cared a bodle about my history bye the second generation. They might be lairds or they might be lackeys for all the differ it made to me. Not that there were any lackeys among them. My grandfather was the grandson of Tormaid Mor, who held the whole east side of Lochow from Ford to Sonachan, and we have at home the four-posted bed that Tormaid slept on when the heads of the house of Argile were lying on white hay or chaff.'[15]

For all Neil's professed indifference to the status of lairds and lackeys, it seems he took secret satisfaction in thinking that his mother's ancestors had once outranked the Duke's. Certainly he felt no inhibition when roaming through the great forest around Inveraray which contained more than two million trees, planted by Dukes of Argyll during the 18th century.

As a man Neil would write of 'that great territory of ancient trees', the haunt of red and fallow deer, and recall his early childhood there: 'I think, on the whole, I prefer my forest in spring. It is then children venture into the less bewildering borders for white hay – the bleached bog-grass... This hay abounds in pine roots... It [has] an odour of the open air, clean rain, chaste snow. The children pluck the grass and put it in little sacks to take it home for bedding... I remember once of a child straying away from his fellows on such a Spring expedition... a fawn running behind a thicket of young oaks conveyed an invitation to the chase. To some children the forest must be full of beckonings... So, expecting and yet apprehending, this little fellow went further into the forest. Before he had accustomed himself to the solitude, the glade and its familiars were lost. A moment ago he saw his companions, their hair golden in the sun, and heard their cheerful cries; now they seemed to have deserted him on a sudden whim... by-and-bye the silence and his own footsteps among the pine-needles struck him as something dreadful, and of a sudden the forest seemed a place he had never been in before and full of unseen eyes. He was found, hours after, asleep among anemones, and has told me since that it must have been then, for all his fears, the passion for the wood came to him, to remain with him for the rest of his life...'[16]

CHAPTER TWO
Those lovely, unperplexed and simple days

A T the age of five or six Neil was sent to the Parish School, almost next door to his home. It stood between the Parish Church and the avenue of ancient beeches: a long, three-storey building, then already a century old, and of the same plain, white-washed style as the rest of the town. It also housed the schoolmaster, Henry Dunn Smith, and his ever-expanding family.

When Neil started school, Mr Smith, the only teacher, was in his early thirties. He came from Banffshire and was an M.A. of Aberdeen. His wife Lillias was a certificated teacher. He had come to Inveraray in 1854, not long married, and stayed in the same post for half a century. He was long remembered as a sound scholar, an excellent teacher and a disciplinarian (perhaps on that account his nickname was 'Old Skull'). He would march up and down with his strap over his shoulder. To generations of Inveraray children, Mr Smith, the 8th Duke and Queen Victoria must have seemed an eternal triumvirate.

A sound basic education was given – reading, writing and arithmetic ('bills of parcels', etc.) – as well as some Latin and Euclid, geography, the Bible and Shorter Catechism. Mr Smith was keen on singing – he wrote a song called 'O, Land of the Free' – and a huge chart known as a modulator was used to demonstrate the tunic sol-fa scales. He also wrote *An English Grammar Simplified*, which ran to three editions. As late as 1893, H.M. Inspector recorded that Mr Smith's school was 'conducted with exceptional vigour and skill'.

The Parish Church in Inveraray was built with a Gaelic half and an English half, and until the 1930s Gaelic services were held. But this egalitarian attitude to the two languages was not shared by the dominie. Being a Lowlander, Mr Smith did not have the Gaelic, and any child caught speaking that language either in classroom or playground was punished. Some attributed this to the master's determination to know what was going on, but in fact the discouragement of Gaelic, to us so deplorable, was the general rule then. A generation earlier, at Kenmore just down the loch, children who had heard no English till they started school were punished for speaking Gaelic in class with blows and a horse's skull hung round the neck.

An entry in Mr Smith's logbook records that a Neil Munro was put out of the school for disobedience. This was, I suspect, my grandfather, although both 'Neil' and 'Munro' were very common names about Inveraray then. When there were two children with the same name, Mr Smith sometimes bestowed a nickname, though it is not known who first gave Neil his two nicknames of 'Neilie Ro' and 'Moose Lugs'. If Neil was in fact put out of the Parish School for persistently speaking Gaelic, this may explain how he came to be a pupil for a while at Glen Aray School in the Gaelic-speaking hinterland where his family had its roots.

Some of the town children would walk to Glen Aray to join the glen children, perhaps because the schoolmaster, John MacArthur, taught the children to read from the Gaelic Bible. The school's pastoral setting on the Aray near Stronmagachan appealed to Neil, as did the fact that his mother and her brothers and sisters had gone there from Ladyfield. In their day, the dominie had granted a holiday on Candlemas Day and Handsel Monday and there were cock-fights on the schoolroom floor. By Neil's day, the cock-fights had been abandoned but the children still brought 'oblations' of money for the dominie and scrambled for sweets scattered across the floor.

The children loved snowy weather 'when we had to put on an extra waistcoat and carry a peat through the drifts to old John MacArthur's school. Nobody grudged a peat per day in winter time, not even the boy who had to carry them three miles up the glen to school to feed the grandest hearth in Mid-Argyll, for the children themselves had helped to cut and garner the peats, and so had a personal claim to their little share of them... one could, moreover, get a wondrous amount of pure delight in stuffing a pinch or two of gunpowder in a peat's interior, and witnessing the explosion which ensued later in the day, when, perhaps, the geography class was, in its turn, warming its toes on the hearth-stone. There was, too, a curious pride in the sight of one's own personal peat in the communal fire. It could, for a time, be identified, perhaps, by the absence of a corner portion lost in a melee two miles down the glen at the Three Bridges.'[1]

Eventually, however, Neil returned to the Parish School in Inveraray and submitted to the discipline of being taught in what was his second tongue. One of the textbooks Mr Smith used for English contained 'elegant extracts' from Shakespeare, Milton, Addison and Macaulay, through which Neil 'acquired an abhorrence of these writers which it took many years to overcome... and in the case of the essayists... will never be eradicated... Macaulay's studied phrase will ever be a task, and the heart that (I am told on good authority) should stir to the martial pomp of the lays will never respond to their trumpet call by a fillip of so much as the hundredth part of a second. On the contrary, to see them in type is again to be unbreeched, and a boy of ten is alone in the dingy schoolroom telling himself over and over again that Lars Porsena of Clusium by the Nine Gods he swore, and that if he had Willie Young, who "clyped" about the interruption during prayer, he would punch his nose.'²

Once Neil removed himself, this time of his own accord, to the small Free Church school in the Newton. His defection lasted only a week or two. When he re-appeared in his old place, Mr Smith merely remarked: 'I see Neil has come back to us.' Perhaps this was before Neil was nine, when school became compulsory. Certainly he had no other option from the age of eleven, when the Free Church school was closed and its pupils transferred to the Parish School, swelling its numbers to 159. Mr Smith applied for an assistant but was refused. By then some of his own sons were pupil-teachers under him, while their sisters taught the infants and gave needlework lessons. Despite having twelve children of their own, the Smiths sacrificed bedrooms so that the classroom where the older pupils were taught could be heightened. At one end of this room was a gallery known as the 'big end', rising in tiers with forms on them, where younger pupils could also sit for morning prayers.

There was great rivalry between the two schools in the town and once, after a heavy fall of snow, the Parish School boys snowballed the children going to the Newton school. Mr Smith tolerated this for a while, then strapped every boy coming into the classroom. Neil put this episode into his song 'Dae ye mind o' Auld Lang Syne?'

On the whole, Neil's schooldays were happy and he looked back on them as 'those lovely, unperplexed and simple days, when I deliberately refused to learn anything and yet, in some mysterious way, was learning all that was to be of use to me in after life'.³ In later years Mr Smith, when questioned about his former pupil, would say he was not a brilliant scholar but had 'a remarkable head'. Certainly Neil's head was remarkably large – and a great deal was going on inside it.

CHAPTER THREE

Blythe were the seasons

NEIL'S greatest friend was Charlie Maitland, who followed his father into the plumbing trade and was the first and only Pipe Major of the pipe band raised by Lord Archie, the Duke's second son, in the 1890s. Charlie also sang and played the violin in the dance band known as the 'Bumbee Band' (Henry Dunn Smith's daughter Lilias was its pianist).

Other friends were Bob Fraser, who became Parish Registrar and had a newsagent-cum-chemist's shop; Neil's foster-brother Archie MacKellar; Robert Clark, latterly of the George Hotel; and Colin McPhail, who went to sea and whose names would be misappropriated for Colin the Tar and Macphail the long-suffering engineer of Para Handy's *Vital Spark*. These were to be lifelong friendships: indeed, as George Blake wrote, 'two of them helped to carry him to his grave in Kilmalieu'.[1]

Once Charlie and Neil experimented with a telephone system made out of lidless cocoa tins and eighty feet of 'grocer's twine'. Neil stood at the Temperance Corner (then the north end of Arkland), while Charlie walked across the street and into Maggie Kelly's Close, as far as the string would allow. Neil shouted into his cocoa tin: 'Do you hear me?' 'Not bad,' came the reply. 'But I could hear you better if you kept your face away from the tinny.'

Earlier playthings included 'dabbities' (transfers), pea-slings (catapults) and the 'dallan', sheepskin stretched over a hoop, used to beat and make a noise by guisers at Hallowe'en and Hogmanay. 'Sells', or tricks, were played on the guileless glen child, who was invited to 'rattle two stones into one' or was given 'the bumbee's bite' by having the back of his hand rubbed by the trickster's thumb till blood was drawn. And if this resulted in punishment by the dominie, a horsehair on the palm was held to ruin the tawse when it descended upon one's hand...

In summertime, two or three four-in-hand coaches came to Inveraray. The boys used to polish the horses' bridle-bits and chains with syver sand, thus earning 'the opportunity of riding the horses bare-backed out into the sea or slowly round the church, to cool them after their run of five-and-twenty-miles... we rode the froth-flecked horses belly deep along the edges of the tide... The post-horn of the guard gave the daily passage of the coach a superbly romantic character'.[2]

A relation of Neil's kept a posting-horse, a skittish roan called Judy. There was little demand for her services, and one winter Neil was allowed to ride her bare-back to the water-trough at Second Cromalt, a mile down the loch. On the way there she ambled along, but as soon as she had taken a drink from the trough she bolted for her stable. Neil had the presence of mind to duck under the lintel as they went in. This went on all that winter, with Judy running away each time. Neil was given no riding lessons, let alone a saddle.

Once, as he often did, Neil was playing with other children in the square beside the church. But this time the castle carriage stopped and the coachman asked which was Neil Munro. On going forward Neil was handed a flat parcel and told to take it home to his mother. (This incident was related to me by Mrs Rae MacGregor, Inveraray, whose great-grandfather Charlie MacLaren was one of Neil's playmates.)

One summer *Northumbria*, a big steam-yacht, anchored off Inveraray. In the evening a silver band played on deck under a furled awning. Neil and a few other boys went out in a punt (rowing-boat) with very little freeboard and lay in the dark, listening. It is likely this was about the time of his seventh birthday: Robert Louis Stevenson recorded that in 1870, on the way to Iona to visit the lighthouse his father was building on Dubh-heartach, he sculled round *Northumbria* in the dark of Oban harbour to listen to the band.

Though of necessity a strict disciplinarian, Mr Smith the dominie had time for extra-curricular activities. Looking back, Neil would write: 'I bless my stars that my first school teacher was a sportsman poacher! A considerable part of my old dominie's summer vacation was spent with his family – a great and gallant one – on the moor-lochs of Mid Argyll. Young and old, male and female, they slept under bivouacs on the verges of the small lochs strung almost like beads along the high backbone of the lands belonging to MacCailein and Poltalloch. They actually lived for a week or two at a time on the fish they caught and their own baking.

'It was from the old dominie I got my first lesson in striking camp and quenching fires – "Never leave stick or paper! Of old our people never left an ash, but all of Gaeldom's grey with their smothered fires!" It was not concealment of his poaching he was thinking of, but cleanliness and decency... he loved the wilds like an altar and would keep them spotless.'[3]

At least once Neil also fished the moor lochs with Mr Smith, an initiation into what would be his chief outdoor pastime. His favourite place was the Balantyre burn, tributary of the Aray: 'In less than a mile it runs over half-a-dozen cataracts and high falls, at the bottom of which are unplumbed pools, where sea trout and salmon come in late September. As boys we fished there so constantly that it might be said to have been for weeks on end our habitat. Every boulder was an old companion; there is no aspect of the stream and the high cliffs round it that we cannot now restore to the inward eye at any time... As we lay on ledges watching the baited lines, the roar of the linns, the scent of the flowers, and the look of all things, filled the cells of memory...'[4]

Neil and his friends fished the Douglas Water as well, new territory at first, but 'when its broken delta, combing through little isles of sea-grass and pinks and thickets of whin and broom, its sandy spits, its wooded terraces, its ancient bridge and stoney sites of abandoned cottages, and its traditional tales became a little more familiar, it, also, took our hearts.'[5]

Hallowe'en was more fun than Christmas for most Scottish children in those days. They scooped out turnip lanterns with knife or mussel-shell, dooked for apples in a tub of water, ate their way through mounds of mashed potato in search of hidden silver trinkets. Best of all were 'the guizards...black-faced, garmented as for a masque, each thumping a sheepskin stretched on a barrel-hoop – the thing we call a dallan'.[6]

Christmas, on the other hand, was scarcely celebrated then in Scotland: 'It was a glorious, far-off foreign affair, like prairies, crossing the line and Viking fights. Two or three times we came, in a curious way, on the edge, as it were, of Christmas... but I felt then, and I know now, it was not, even there and then, the real Christmas... In our neighbourhood there was a great castle to which the people used to come for Christmas. There was a Christmas tree for the children of the castle, and it was the privilege of the school to which I went to go to the castle the night before Christmas Eve and see the tree. Our teacher led us in procession to the castle; the great fir tree, laden with candles and toys and apples of silver and gold, filled one end of a huge hall, and we were ranged up in front of it, while all its candles were lit that we might see it in its glory. Only for a few minutes were they lit; then they were snuffed out quickly, for it was simply a dress rehearsal. We got an orange each, sang "Let us with a gladsome mind, Praise the Lord for He is kind," and marched home...

'I came much closer on the Christmas spirit of my dreams one January in the forest. There was an abandoned little quarry... a great place for adventure on Saturdays... This Saturday in January we found in it the Castle Christmas tree that we had seen, poor dears! with gladsome mind. The stumps of tapers, the tinsel cords, some broken balls were still on it. For a moment we stood and stared, like the alleged Cortez and his men, "silent upon a peak in Darien", and ever since I know how it feels to come upon the treasure of the pirate's isle. How it should be so I know not, but that discarded tree in the little quarry roused the true sentiment of Christmas more than anything I have known before or since.'[7]

New Year, like Hallowe'en, was a jollier time than Christmas for the Inveraray children. Guisers came round on the evening of Hogmanay, then on New Year's morning, as soon as the town's bell had rung at six o'clock, a fife and drum band went through the streets playing such tunes as 'Hey, Johnnie Cope, are ye waukin' yet?' There was shortbread, ham and eggs for breakfast instead of porridge, and later on the day would bring more delights including a treacly sweet they called 'Black Man'. At mid-day the band marched out again and the children followed to a field in the Avenue where brass ball shooting took place, then up to the Winterton (a stretch of grass near the castle) to watch the shinty match between Inveraray and Furnace. Then there was generally another match to look forward to on Old New Year's Day, 12 January.

A more sedate diversion was provided by the Duke: 'For our good, his Grace gave lectures in the old pavilion, where there shall never be any dancing or lecturing any more. They were wonderful lectures, but mostly we did not understand them, though that did not prevent us from eagerly handling the star-fish and fossils as they were passed round the audience by old Tarry, the forester, or James Ferguson, Clerk of Works. It seemed an amiable, inexplicable idiosyncracy, this talking about stones and shell-fish, but refreshments were considerately provided for such as had far to come from the glens, and the audiences were invariably large and appreciative.'[8]

The 'pavilion' was a large wooden building put up in 1871 as a ballroom for the festivities when Lord Lorne, the Duke's heir, brought home his new wife, Queen Victoria's daughter Princess Louise. They arrived on an August day that the Duke described as 'one of the most violent days both of rain and wind I ever saw, the river in a torrent, yet the poor people stood out in it all as patient and good-humoured as possible'.[9] One of Lord Lorne's sisters, Lady Victoria Campbell, then fifteen, described the scene in a letter to an aunt: 'The awful day is over, and it went off very well. The people were arranged pretty well. There were a few police. The Volunteers were to line the road from the approach by Frew's Bridge. On the Bridge the people were to unharness the horses, and drag the carriage to the Castle.

'We had not been long in the turret, when the firing from the yachts began. My father thought it was their arrival. He thought the people were being kept too far back, and instead of whispering it to the police he said it in a loud voice, so the geese at once rushed... The people swarmed upon him like bees, cheering tremendously... The carriage looked as if it were just ploughing through people, and such a noise as sounded! There was a total lack of order, but people comforted themselves with the enthusiasm which was shown... By means of the police, and Volunteers, the crowd was pushed back. The women were dreadfully obstreperous, and also nasty little boys...'[10]

Neil, then eight, was almost certainly there, but could not remember it in after years. For a few years more, Lord Lorne would remain in Neil's mind 'a dazzling abstraction'.

Long before Neil's mother was born, the first steam-boat had come from the Clyde to Inveraray, and by 1820 three steamers were plying the route. MacBrayne's *Mary Jane*, which came three times a week from the Broomielaw, was the first steamer Neil knew. The route was taken over by the *Inveraray Castle* (third of that name) when he was in Standard IV, then by the first *Lord of the Isles* in 1877.

At the Glasgow Fair each July when Neil was a boy, Inveraray 'used to be taken possession of by hordes of hooligans, male and female... They arrived in a steamer that took twelve hours to come from the Broomielaw; they came whooping, and more or less intoxicated, to the quay; whooping and decidedly intoxicated they took their departure. While they remained they were a nuisance to all others who had come to the country for quietness; their odour... was something we boys used to rather like... imagining it was the odour of the active outer world of cities, discovering in it... suggestions of rich streets, theatres, brass bands, shops, and old-time companions gone from us to Glasgow and "getting on"... possibly it was compounded of not too well-washed garments, of herring breakfasts, stale whisky, chewed tobacco, and dulse...

'When the Glasgow Fair tripper landed in the 'seventies, he and his wife and children first sampled the local public houses until it struck 11 p.m., and then they sallied forth with the tin box to look for lodgings, and when the morning dawned the air was thick with the odour of frying herrings. It was marvellous that a fish diet could sustain the visitors in the arduous recreations of the succeeding days. For they had to tramp through the woods and wantonly break down young trees, despoil the hedge-rows, plunder every flower in all the gardens, steal small-boats, make miserable the life of the local police, and in general maintain at all costs the reputation of Glasgow as a place whence came fellows who knew what "life" was... we had to take in our signboards and sit up at night to guard the church bells. Organised gangs of young men came year after year to parade the roads day after day and night after night in grotesque habiliments, bawling discordant melodies, and meddling with every peaceful passer-by, keeping an eye intently open for every opportunity of doing some mischief or other. Half of them never found lodgings anywhere, but seemed to sleep in the plantations, true reversions of type, temporarily as savage in their walk and conversation as in their sylvan domesticity. The men bathed from the quay, and the women joyously waded all along the shore, high kilted, in pursuit of the crab or the cockle, while their children, recklessly "oaring" in punts, were being rescued from watery graves.

'If it was wet weather, the squalor of the experience was increased a hundredfold; the Glasgow odour was so potent that it disillusioned even us. The local authorities, in pity for the poor wretches trudging about with no shelter, had often to open up the churches and schools in wet weather, turning these edifices temporarily into model lodging-houses. Wull went to church and school, sometimes no doubt for the first time in his life; I have seen him and his melodeon camped for several days in the choir seats, and his pals making a travesty of preaching from the precentor's box. For weeks after, the churches retained the odour of the Wee Doo Hill, and parents who were very particular did not send their children to school. Even the police cells... were sometimes let for a night to people who desired a little more seclusion and privacy than the churches and school-rooms afforded.'[11]

So, merely by remaining in his native place, Neil could observe at first hand both aristocrats and Glasgow keelies. In September 1875 this social rainbow gained a regal tint: Queen Victoria herself came to stay at the castle, which she had first visited with Prince Albert in 1847. It was a private visit, so she was rarely visible, but the Inveraray air was full of the royal presence.

CHAPTER FOUR

The key of the street and the freedom of the seashore and the forest

NEIL told his own children that he used to play truant and hide under his mother's bed to read. On winter evenings he would read by the light of a crusie lamp filled with saithe or herring oil. Peter Macintyre, an older schoolmate, used to recall that Neil was not keen on school and could be found at times reading on the outside rampart of the old prison wall or wandering in the forest.

Books, not the usual delight of truants, were part of the escape he sought in his imagination from the 'tragic and pathetic elements' in his life. Even as a child, he struggled inwardly with the distinction between books and lessons on the one hand and 'life' on the other. In his tale 'Boboon's Children', a father asks his son if he has had a lesson. The boy replies: 'I was too busy living.' In *Gilian The Dreamer* a boy called Young Islay comes upon the truant Gilian reading 'stretched on dry bracken' and says contemptuously: 'It's not a school-book, there's not a picture in it, it's full of talking – fancy being here with that rubbish, when you might be fishing with me!' But Gilian's strengths lie elsewhere, in imaginative love and perception, and Old Brooks the schoolmaster early diagnoses him as being 'of the dream nature'.

By the time of Neil's boyhood there was a new sort of reading material that was not scorned by his schoolmates – the 'Penny Bloods' and 'Threepenny Indians and Pirates' which he devoured at the rate of two a day. Sometimes recourse was had to girl-books such as *Jessica's First Prayer* or Ellen Montgomery's *The Wide, Wide World*: 'I was half ashamed to admit that there was any charm in these for me... No shooting, no sailing, no comic negro cooks! and yet somehow that wretched *Wide, Wide World* had a fascination...'[1]

Then one day, in the Sunday School library in the church steeple, Neil discovered 'the Magician' – R.M. Ballantyne. There, too, he came upon some bound volumes of *Blackwood's Magazine*. The 'yarns' in them so delighted him that he managed to get hold of copies of *Tales From Blackwood*. One essay, on the evolution of the sword, was especially fascinating because the sentences seemed to sing themselves to him, though he had then no idea of literary style. Bunyan's *Holy War* held no interest, but the illustrations for Charles Dickens's *Pickwick Papers* appealed: 'We used to lie on the floor and look over the pictures by Phiz... Jimmie and I must have got the whole spirit of the story through these illustrations long before we were able to read the letterpress with understanding. Then, somehow, it grew upon us that Bloods were not the last word in English Literature.'[2]

Neil and 'Jimmie' (perhaps an amalgam of his boyhood friends Charlie Maitland and Archie MacKellar) began reading Surtees and Smollett. 'Nobody took the slightest trouble to select reading for Jimmie and me; if Scott came our way, I do not recall him, and for years he was merely a name on the back of a file of sixpenny reprints in the druggist's shop where we bought H.D. Smith's Grammar, and the senna for ourselves... but a time came when we profited by the literary counsel of a lady who sold tea and tobacco and hair-oil, and conducted the funniest kind of circulating library.'[3]

This curious establishment, which rejoiced under the name of Miss Macleod's Italian Warehouse, was run in fact by three genteel sisters who reputedly shared one wig, and was kept open late on Saturday evenings for their literary customers. There were two or three hundred books in their 'eighteenth-centuryish' collection, and when Neil was 13 he exhausted it in a single winter. The first books he borrowed were *The Castle Of Otranto* by Horace Walpole and *The Monk* by Matthew Gregor Lewis. The latter, he was excited to learn, had been written at Inveraray Castle.

He began to keep a record of his reading. In one fortnight he read Mrs Radcliffe's *Mysteries Of Udolpho* and *The Italian*, Smollett's *Roderick Random*, Le Sage's *Gil Blas*, Godwin's *Caleb*, Shelley's *St Irvyne* and Mary Shelley's *Frankenstein*. Fenimore Cooper, Jules Verne and *The Swiss Family Robinson* (much favoured) were also somehow acquired.

'The days were long, but not long enough for us as we read in the byre, the stable, the wash-house, or the wood. Two special days stand out pure golden – that one when Grant's *Romance of War* (without covers) came with the noise of bugles and pipes, and that other when the *Boy's Own Paper* Part I came full of beautiful things. There was the *Weekly Citizen* also, giving lovely vistas of another world of letters, and *Cassell's Magazine*; but Jimmie and I were then in trousers, and virtually our golden age was done.'[4]

In his forties, Neil still had two books which had belonged to his grandmother: *Magazin Des Enfans: Or the Young Misses' Magazine*, and *Mornings Improved*. Then there was 'Sunday reading' – books and magazines such as *The Christian Treasury* and *Good Words*. 'Dear old familiars! We look afar off at their sturdy, honest old backs, recalling that we kept our white mice behind them, and how Boston jammed in our perspiring hurry to conceal the Queen's Birthday cartridges behind him before Aunt Jane came into the room, and how exquisite (but precarious) was our delight in *Tomahawk Joey* with his edges cut down so that he might fit neatly and unobtrusively within the leaves of Queachy, that Communion Sunday, when, as on all Communion Sundays, the adults of the household felt it incumbent on them to sit in ghastly meditation and a silence broken only by Aunt Jane's unaccountable sobs.'[5]

CHAPTER FIVE
My earliest impressions of a prison

NEIL's twelfth birthday fell on 3 June, 1875. Later that month he went to Glasgow for the first time in his life, not on holiday, but for his mother's wedding. The fact that she took Neil with her suggests a sympathetic handling of the situation. He was old enough to comprehend that changes were afoot, young enough to accept them almost as a matter of course, at least outwardly. Besides, the bridegroom was no stranger to Neil – he was Malcom Thomson, retired Governor of Inveraray jail – and it is safe to say that Ann Munro, who did not hide strong personal dislikes, would never have married a man she found unpleasant.

The relationship between Neil and his stepfather seems to have been straightforward and amicable, so far as it went. In terms of age it was more a grandfather than a stepfather that he was acquiring. Malcom Thomson was then seventy. His first wife had died just after his retirement. He came from Ardchattan in Argyll, and had been a prison warder in Glasgow before coming to Inveraray, where his task was to reform the prison and he at once made new rules, such as: 'Feet to be washed once a week.'

For Neil the journey to Glasgow was a real excitement: to

Greenock on the *Inveraray Castle,* and then by the first train he had
ever set eyes on! From Central Station it was not far to the house
near George Square where the wedding was to take place. Ann's
oldest full brother, Neil's namesake, had long lived in Glasgow, and
it was most likely his house.

While the wedding party was in Glasgow, Malcom Thomson took
Neil for a long walk through the streets. The details of that walk
lingered in Neil's memory. They saw Duke Street Jail and public
houses once so notorious that they had caused Thomson to turn
teetotal. Not having been there for many years, the retired Governor
was startled to find how far west of Hope Street the city had spread
behind his back.

Neil would recall: 'It was in Jamaica Street his eye caught sight of
a man lounging along the pavement with his gaze intently fixed on
a shop across the street, where two or three loafers were looking in
at the merchandise. "Look! look!" he said to me hurriedly. "There's
a thief-catcher!" And I knew it was a thief-catcher, though never
hitherto had I heard of such a bird. The Governor's eyes had lit with
expectant eagerness, as if in another moment he hoped to see the
men at the window pounced on. And they were! This was something
like a holiday! When I got home a day or two after, I was the envy of
my young companions... I was in great demand for the narrative
of my adventures, which became more sensational with every
repetition.'[1]

'Home' now meant his new stepfather's house, only a few steps
from his grandmother's. On retiring from his Highland bastille two
years before, Malcom Thomson had rented the end of Arkland
nearest the church. He lived in the four small rooms on the ground
floor, while the flats above were run as a temperance hotel. His son
Maikie used one of the front rooms on the street as his baker's shop,
the bakery being in the lane behind. Malcom's daughter Susan was
already married, as was his son John, burgh chamberlain of
Inveraray for over half a century.

Neil once wrote: 'My earliest impressions of a prison were got,
innocently enough, from the inside. A bedroom window looked out
on the exercise yard...'[2] He does not say '*my* bedroom window'.
Since Malcom Thomson had retired before his second marriage, the
inference would seem to be that Ann Munro had worked for the
Thomsons in the Court House, part of which was made into living
quarters when they first came to Inveraray. Although the 1871
Census shows Neil and his mother still living in McVicar's Land, the
one-room house must have been increasingly awkward. Neil was

growing big, and his grandmother was in her eighties. It could be that he and his mother slept in the Court House, or that he had the run of it when his mother was at work. He never dwelt on aspects of his life that veered anywhere near the 'tragic and pathetic', having early acquired the knack of sublimation.

From the bedroom window, however it was he came to be there, Neil observed the prisoners walking round and round in an iron cage: 'I cannot recollect being ever pitiful or touched by the spectacle. Life, even for a fairly good child, is so often spent in cages! Liberty is a luxury only the more fortunate among grown-ups can hope for. It was a prison for generations notorious over the West and the Inner Hebrides... Yet, knowing something of the life within these granite walls... it seemed to me by no means an unkindly institution. The cells, I admit, were ugly and cruel-looking, even to a child permitted only to glance in at cleaning-up hours, but I missed their tragedy, being too little to reach up to the peep-holes and see the solitary occupants at other hours... A garrulous old parrot at the open kitchen window scolded the exercising prisoners in a voice most ludicrously like the Governor's... Those thieves, infanticides, murderers – for sometimes there were at least man-slaughterers – looked to the unsophisticated eye of childhood in no particular different from men and women outside. They smiled to the child at the window; whistled to him sometimes; they seemed, on the whole, gentle and more friendly than the big, black-bearded fishermen on the quay.

'Besides, they were not always in cells or in the exercise cage. The men... made furniture... They made clothing, baskets (if some of them were tinkers)... As for the women, they seemed really to be in the cells only when they slept there. They were always in the washing-houses or laundry, cracking jokes with the maids, busy with knitting-needles or sewing... The story went that at times the Governor would sit to a game of draughts with a prisoner... and I know with certainty old guests of his came back in after years, as free men, to play him at the dambrod...'³

In those days the Court House and the castle were the twin nerve centres of Inveraray, capital of Argyll. Perhaps Neil would sometimes steal on his own into the silent courtroom, a great semi-circle of classical proportions with tall windows looking over Loch Fyne, surely one of the finest courtrooms in the world. The Court House accommodated the Town Council and the Commissioners of Supply as well as three different courts.

When the High Court came to Inveraray, the children got a

holiday from school and took part in their own way in the proceedings. The judge rode all the way from Edinburgh in a semi-state coach with trumpeters, red-coated postilions and out-riders. The trumpeters blew a fanfare when the judge left the Argyll Arms to walk to the Court House behind two old halberdiers in scarlet cloaks. Neil always noticed particularly how the judge's white-and-red silk gown trailed along the sandy pavement, and how his wigged head was bare, while he carried in one hand the black tricorne that he might later don in court for a certain fatal purpose. Behind the judge came a goodly procession, with the provost, bailies and councillors in full fig. The trumpeters played over and over again a tune familiar to the children, who had their own words to it:

> Pity be on poor prisoners, pity be on them;
> Pity be on poor prisoners, if they come back again.

CHAPTER SIX

A burgh most large and wonderful

BEFORE another year had passed, Neil's schooldays were over. There seemed no prospect but to knuckle under and learn how to herd sheep, harvest and thin turnips for the Duke – in other words, to work for one of His Grace's tenant farmers, most likely one of Neil's own uncles. It would seem, from a later reminiscence of atypical disillusionment, that he had been partly broken-in already during the school holidays:

'As a lad I spent long periods each year about farms of about 1,000 sheep; the experience may have been profitable, but I look back on it with no very pleasant memories. The old type of sheep-farmer whom I used to know was a good man, and exceeding pious between drams, but though his knowledge impressed me at the time, looking back on him I cannot think now that he was either very bright, or even a very good business man. There were notable exceptions, of course... I know that this is heresy, that there is still much talk about the strong character of the old type, and I used to hold the conventional view myself, but now I am convinced it was a great mistake…

'The homes were miserably squalid, the life in them narrow and unwholesome for body or mind. The farmers had settled into a state of bovine stupidity… They fed roughly if plentifully… but they clad themselves and housed themselves as if it were the 18th century. There was nothing Arcadian in their lives; I recall the boy rising at evening from painful household prayers in Gaelic and English on the stone flags of the kitchens, and, his whole being in revolt against laughterless days, planning to end them all by a dash at night through the woods to any place where the meaning of life was better understood.'[1]

But Neil did keep an idyllic memory of making hay on hot summer days beside a little tributary of the Aray. The reapers kept their milk-bottles cool in it and spent the meal-hour among the wild flowers on its banks: 'Voles, water-hens, wagtails, dragon-flies, swifts and weasels seemed to come to it then, too, and it shared like a living thing in the camaraderie of that hour.'[2]

Neil was lucky. Release from rustic drudgery came after a year or two through the influence of one of the local ministers, probably Gilbert Meikle of the United Presbyterian church, the 'beloved pastor' of James Chalmers the martyr-missionary (1841–1901). Neil had attended Meikle's Sunday School, which drew children from far and wide, quite out of proportion to the small church roll. When Meikle died in 1908, Neil wrote: 'He was gentle, tolerant, unwearied and unostentatious in well-doing, simple as a child, high-spirited and fearless as a soldier.'[3]

Clearly someone in Inveraray had Neil's best interests at heart, although at the time he was not altogether appreciative of strings being pulled on his behalf. Later he would recall 'being insinuated, without any regard for my own desires, into a country lawyer's office'. His new employer was William Douglas, a solicitor, in whose office Mr Meikle's previous *protégé* James Chalmers, son of a stone-mason, had once worked also. Neil never did get to like the law, but the three or four years he spent in Douglas's office compensated for his lack of secondary education. It was fine, also, to have his own place and function in Inveraray, at the very age when a boy can ride free to the world and yet be acutely observant.

William Douglas came from Inverness-shire and was a bachelor, then in his early fifties: a kindly man, with a quaint, eighteenth-century manner. Once, watching some Tiree crofters being marched to prison, Douglas said to a woman standing next him, 'The Duke should think shame to send decent men like that to jail,' and gave her money to get help for them. Douglas fitted well into Neil's little pantheon of benign father-figures.

Neil's work in the solicitor's office was chiefly drafting and 'enlarging' leases, dispositions and so on. The Table of Fees showed that in half a day's work he could earn more for his employer than the £5 per annum he earned as a clerk. He and the other clerk were supposed to study the law or brush up their scanty Latin in spare moments, but often they played a card game called 'catch-the-ten' behind a desk flap which they could close if Mr Douglas appeared. This pastime helped to make Neil's job tolerable.

Another part of his duties had a bearing on his later career. He had to attend the courts, and one day he noticed a reporter from a Glasgow newspaper writing shorthand. Impressed, Neil wrote away for a textbook and taught himself Pitman's system rapidly, by dint of skipping the elementary stages. Soon he was jotting down the sermon verbatim on Sundays, to amaze and amuse his friends.

Sometimes Mr Douglas detailed the two clerks to exercise his dog, Footles. One snowy evening, Footles was nowhere to be found and they went up to search for him in the dark forest. In Easachosain glen they met a tall stranger, who did not reply when they spoke to him. More eerily still, the gates in the high deer fence made no sound when he passed through, though usually they made a loud clang. This episode Neil considered his only real Inveraray adventure, but there were other memorable moments.

Once, for instance, he got as far afield as Carradale. Despite a thick mist, Neil and another boy 'borrowed' a boat and rowed out into Kilbrennan Sound, trusting in a new sixpenny compass. But they lost their bearings entirely and had to shout and whistle. A steam siren responded: they rowed towards it, found that it belonged to a herring-buyer's boat and that they had three miles to row back along the shore to Carradale – where they soon learned that the owner of the boat they had taken was a handy man with a rope end.

On an October night in 1877, when the Duke and his family were in residence, a great storm broke over Inveraray. A young fisherman called John McNab ('Jocka Nab'), woken by the noise of the storm, rose to go and see to the mooring of his boat. As he came out into the open, he saw great tongues of fire leaping from the roof of the castle. He ran to the Porter Lodge and wakened the Clerk of Works. They ran the short distance to the castle, followed by many of the townsfolk – including Neil – roused by Jocka's shouts. Everyone in the castle escaped safely, but the damage was great. It would have been even worse had Princess Louise not suggested to Henry Dunn Smith the schoolmaster that a human chain be formed to get buckets of water from the Aray.

It was then that Neil first got a real glimpse of the Duke's heir, the Marquis of Lorne. Lord Lorne 'took concrete shape to my mind as something more than a dazzling abstraction only when I saw him in a shirt and trousers, with a locket round his neck, battling with the fire... while we heaved out the library's contents into the fosse. The slimness and the youth of him were what most impressed; having seen him in his shirt-sleeves I could never be afraid of him – at least not seriously – again.'[4]

Next morning the hen-wife who lived at the foot of Dunchuach set out with the eggs for the castle breakfast. Seeing the plenishings lying about on the ground, she turned homewards, thinking 'the Duke and Lord Lorne were maybe having a tirrivee, and it wasna for the likes of me to be looking at them'.[5]

The Duchess's failing health could not withstand the shock of the fire, and she died in May 1878. Neil, in his first hard hat, was taken to her funeral at Kilmun on the Holy Loch. There he saw Gladstone walking in the funeral procession and was told that this was 'the champion speaker of the world'. For years he longed to hear him orate – a wish that would come true.

Three months after the Duchess's funeral, there was a bye-election in Argyll. Neil's employer, William Douglas, was the agent of the Liberal candidate Lord Colin Campbell, a younger son of the Duke. To cover Lord Colin's campaign expenses, Neil was sent to lodge cheques for thousands of pounds in a local bank. The Liberal posters proclaimed:

Cuinichibh agus Cuidichibh
Cailein Og
Mac Mhic Chailein Mhor!
('Remember and help young Colin, son of the son of great Colin')

The Tory candidate was John Wingfield Malcolm, Younger of Poltalloch. Looking back in 1906, Neil would write: 'Even a quarter of a century ago... there still survived in the counties a popular impression that an election was a huge festival, or was it that we were young enough to see only its farcical elements? We were in those days emphatically radical; I forget exactly why, but I think it was because the landlord of the place employed most of us, and it was his son who was standing in the Liberal interest.'[6]

The Tory posters were torn down systematically. The candidates went about in steam-yachts and had pipers to play down heckling. The Argyll Arms was the Liberal headquarters, while the Tories in the George were besieged by Lord Colin's younger supporters, including Neil. The blue banners were torn down and all the George's windows broken. The few Tories resident in the town woke one morning to find fishing boats jutting into their front halls – apart from one Tory whose house was invaded by the pole of a 'junker', a device for transporting timber.

On polling-day no pretence at work was made. Both candidates brought supporters in steamers, and when these craft departed there was a free fight on the quay, using potatoes and herrings conveniently awaiting transport. At one wild moment a paper bag of peasemeal thrown by Neil at the Tory steamer burst on the whiskers of a Lochgilphead lawyer: 'There are worse political arguments than a good Lochfyne herring. Then nobody would let go of the Tory steamer's ropes... for the seven native Conservative householders dared not show their faces that day. But the daughter of one of them – as intrepid as she was handsome – came to the relief of her party, and with her own hands threw the ropes off the pawls.'[7]

Lord Colin won the election. At Neil's old school, the dominie found it hard to get the children to settle after all the excitement. Neil himself, for his exertions on the election trail, was given £5 by Lord Colin for 'overtime' – a sum it would take him a year to earn as an apprentice lawyer's clerk.

That September must have been the most lawless month in Neil's life. One of the great ancient beeches in the avenue blew down in the night, damaging the school. Neil was out before breakfast with an axe to get firewood for the grandmaternal coal cellar. Next day 'Tarry' – John Stewart, the Duke's forester – brought a dozen of the more zealous stick-gatherers, including Neil, before a bailie. They were let off with a reprimand and dismissed... and Neil went home to saw up the wood.

Five months later his grandmother, that 'redoubtable woman from Lochaweside', died at the age of 86. Neil felt the loss of his second mother deeply and his mind dwelt, like that of Gilian, on 'the little brown wrinkled dame, no more to be bustling about the kitchen, of her wheel silent, of her foot no more upon the blue flag-stones of the milk-house, of her voice no more in the chamber where they had so often known her hospitality'.[9]

With the old tie dissolved, Neil went with his mother and step-father on a trip to Glasgow by a new route just established. They crossed Loch Fyne in the ferry, then went by coach through Hell's Glen to Lochgoilhead. From there the new paddle steamer *Edinburgh Castle* took them to Greenock and the train to Glasgow. There, among other things, Neil saw his first non-cocoa-tin telephone. 'It was in St Vincent Street I first saw a man, apparently with all his wits about him, conversing with a tea-caddy...'

Once he was sixteen, Neil was able to enrol in the 'delightfully casual' Inveraray rural volunteer company, where he put in two years of drill and class-firing. At first the company captain was the Sheriff-Substitute, then Henry Dunn Smith took over, both of them devils for drill. Neil was a private, but the only doublet in the armoury stores that fitted him had a lance-corporal's chevrons, while his kilt was of an obsolete Campbell tartan with a red stripe. The duties expected of a volunteer were many and various, from scouring the parish for escaped prisoners to digging the great new sewer in the Main Street.

About this time Neil began to keep a scrap book whose contents gave some indication of his adolescent state of mind: 'wan, anaemic verse' from American magazines, cuttings from spiritualist organs, details of cheap emigration rates to New Zealand, chunks of Schopenhauer – and a cutting stating that he himself had, 'at a well attended meeting of the Mutual Improvement Society... read a very lengthy and admirable essay on "The Decay of Friendship"'.[10]

As a member of this society for young men, founded in 1874, Neil also submitted an article on the Inveraray fishing fleet to the manuscript magazine – the alternative being to take part in a debate, from which his lifelong horror of public speaking caused him to recoil in horror. He had never been out with the fleet, but his piece was good enough to make a local bank teller, meeting him one day on the quay, ask why he did not go in for journalism. According to the *Oban Times*, the article was 'afterwards published in a weekly contemporary', making it Neil's first printed work.

When he was seventeen there was 'that marvellous winter on Loch Fyne, when even the stags went skating'.[11] Neil, too, skated, day and night, for weeks – or so memory told him. He and his fellow clerk, it is said, meddled nefariously with the gas supply in Douglas's office until it became too cold (or dark) to work and they were free to skate.

The salt waters of the loch were so thickly frozen that a shinty match was played on the ice between the pier and the mouth of the Aray: 'Ten miles of Loch Fyne at its head was frozen from shore to shore; we cruised on its jet-black polished surface as the Finns on any winter may cruise through the Aland isles in the Gulf of Bothnia... It was an experience never to be repeated; only twice has Loch Fyne seen such stringent frost in over two hundred years.'[12]

And it was part of Neil's last complete year at Inveraray.

CHAPTER SEVEN

This roaring city of our exile

TWO days before his eighteenth birthday, Neil Munro set off, in Sunday clothes and Glengarry bonnet, to seek his fortune in Glasgow. Like Bud in *The Daft Days*, he surely felt 'if I lived here always I'd not grow any more' – but he has left no explanation of his departure from Inveraray beyond the remark that he had 'arrived at years of discretion and revolt'. In any case it was commonplace for Highland youths to emigrate to Glasgow or the colonies.

The 1881 Census, taken earlier that year, shows him living with his eighty-year-old great-aunt Bell – Isabella McArthur, a spinster. Was this an assertion of independence? Also in 1881, William Douglas succeeded Scipio Mactaggart as Sheriff Clerk, a change which could have brought home to Neil that he really did not want to be a solicitor. With his mother now married, he would not be leaving her alone, although Malcom Thomson was now 77.

Neil's companion on the venture was his old friend and foster-brother, Archie MacKellar. How secret were the plans they laid together before leaving Inveraray at mid-day on a Saturday? 'Perhaps the most anguished hour I ever spent in my life was one day when it seemed not unlikely that I might never be back... I stood on the 1st of June on the deck of the first *Lord of the Isles* and saw all that was precious to me at the moment fall rapidly astern... for the first time I realised that I was hopelessly in love with these hills and glens that I had looked at every day with indifference from my infancy.'[1]

The steamer reached the Broomielaw in Glasgow towards eight o'clock that evening, and Neil and Archie found lodgings in Shamrock Street, near St George's Cross, above a bank at the gusset of New City Road (since obliterated by a motorway). For months Neil was 'homesick to the very marrow' and 'pathetically eager to see all that was really worth seeing... before bolting home again'.

He would claim later that no sooner was he off the steamer – was it really so late on his very first Saturday, and without Archie? – than he saw in Glassford Street some placards advertising a hypnotist and phrenologist called Coates. The name was familiar to him from Argyllshire ploughing matches, so he paid 'the incredible entrance fee of eighteenpence' and went in. When Coates invited him to join the volunteers who were having their bumps read, Neil went forward, thinking to himself: 'Well, here am I, a newcomer to Glasgow a couple of hours ago; there is unlikely to be a single person in the audience who knows me, and I have on my Sunday clothes. If I make an ass of myself it doesn't matter. I haven't the slightest idea what I'm going to do in Glasgow, nor what I'm fit for, but now's the chance to find out!

'Unlike all the others who had responded to the Professor's lurings and mounted the platform shamefaced and sniggering, I went up with a high head and chest well out, a perfect figure of calm and self-assurance though my heart was thumping. There was, I fancy, a touch of swank, all-informing for Professor Coates.'

Neil's bumps were left to the last, all the other volunteers having been found to possess Firmness, Constructiveness, Ideality and so on. 'Coates now turned with cheerful expectancy to the last of his victims. "This," he said, as he pawed through my stubble, "is a somewhat unusual skull... Dolichocephalic... One of those long-shaped skulls in which the transverse diameter of width from side to side bears a less proportion to the longitudinal diameter of width from front to back, than 8 to 10... It usually indicates conceit and vanity... Ah, yes, here where my finger is, on the very crown of the head, I find Self-esteem well developed.

'"In the temporal region, exceptionally shaded in this case by the ears, I find Constructiveness somewhat weak in relation to Ideality... The frontal organs of Form, Size, Colour, Language and Individuality are normal... Here, in the rear of the eyes, there is a marked depression where we expect to find the well-filled area of Calculation... So far as you know, have I been right?" he concluded hopefully, no doubt expecting a violent contradiction as a relief to the cheerful acceptance of my predecessors.

'"Absolutely right," I responded heartily, "just as we agreed upon," and he was staggered. The audience laughed louder than ever as I hurried from the platform. I had saved my face... But for months I had agonies of humiliation; whatever Self-esteem I had was shrivelled to the size of a nut. A large V-shaped cloud of inferiority complex settled down on me, and is still responsible for my terror of platforms.'[2]

Still feeling 'exceedingly young, verdant, homesick, with not even the customary stimulant of ambition and hope', Neil sought help from one of the three uncles he had in Glasgow. Donald Munro, his mother's youngest half-brother, had come far since his precarious infancy at Ladyfield, and was now partner in Anderson & Munro, electrical engineers and window-blind makers. He and his son John – 'one of innumerable cousins John' – were kind and helpful. John wrote out a letter of introduction and spent a day taking Neil round offices, but nothing came of it.

He ended up as a clerk with a firm of potato merchants, Greenlees Bros, in Hanover Street. He worked there for about two years, then moved to a job as cashier in an ironmongery in the Trongate, the eastward continuation of Argyle Street – that thoroughfare where, in Gaelic tradition, 'you saw Life'. The proprietors of the ironmongery, Mr MacHaffie and Mr Colquhoun, were survivors of the age when ironmongers wore hats and frock-coats behind the counter. Forty years on, Neil would commemorate them, under fictitious names:

'The dustiness of everything pertaining to the business of Macaulay and Buchanan, Wholesale and Retail (Established 1821) was what most impressed me when I made their first acquaintance... Even then they seemed effete, and early doomed to that extinction that awaits on men and long-established businesses... Nobody seemed to patronise their shop except the very old, and the sight of a bright young lady standing before their counter with her purse in her hand prepared to purchase and pay for anything would have driven Macaulay and Buchanan silly. They never opened a new account; they thought the supply of customers you could trust implicitly had been utterly exhausted shortly after 1821.

'Not knowing at the time how searching is the dust, and how it is first in the mind and heart and on the eyes before it comes into the shop, I used to wish I was old enough to take Macaulay and Buchanan, walk them round the town, and show them things, and finally introduce them to each other over a bit of lunch and a little bottle. Now, I know that nothing would have come of it. Mounds of dust were between them...

'I never heard them say so little as "good day" to one another in the way of human intercourse. The world outside was full of lovely thrilling things... but the partners never knew. At all events, they never spoke of them; never spoke of anything but the business, to grumble at a discount, or to snap a surly question as to where the Irish porter was...

'The shop had a window looking to a court behind, where once a week, on Friday, Syverina, an itinerant penny whistler, came and played on the summer afternoons. He played entrancingly, a maimed old Orpheus – how many thousand tired hearts he must have lightened with his jigging measures! Then the dingy premises of Macaulay and Buchanan (Established 1821) seemed for a little almost pleasant. Buchanan, with his tremulous hands on the grimy ledger pages, stared straight before him at the wall; Macaulay looked through the cleft of narrow doorway from the sombre shadow of the shop into the street and to the sunshine splashing on the further pavement... A trance came on us all when Syverina whistled. Had he played longer, had he played on for ever, he might have blown away the dust from Macaulay and Buchanan, dispelled the influence of years and disillusion, given back the hope, the energy, the enterprise their fathers knew in 1821.'[3]

Uncommunicative as they were, the two ironmongers used to repair together at noon to 'Pie Smith's' next door for that perennial Scottish delicacy, hot mutton pies, which they consumed standing, with porter, as a 'perpendicular lunch'. Neil himself favoured a tavern called The Institution, an eighteenth-century building in King Street, where he would lunch on a slice of silverside and a flagon of draught ale. Its largely genteel clientèle included, at times, junior members of the Scottish Bar.

Other dinner-hours were spent in Stirling's Library, where Neil discovered Alexander Smith's *Dreamthorp*, which solaced his homesickness with the thought that he, too, 'might yet go back to some visionary haven of serenity and silence and content'.[4] Many hours more were spent in Stirling's Library, chiefly reading non-fiction. Cheap secondhand books could be found on the book-barrows near the Albert Bridge, and on Fridays he could glean Lochfyneside news of home from the *Oban Times*, bought at the Paperelia in St Enoch Square.

Thenadays the fastest vehicles in Argyle Street and the Trongate were the horse trams. 'It was not suicidal... to step off the pavement without deliberating to cross the street at any part, or emerge from St Enoch Square on a Friday, abstracted and engrossed in the *Oban Times*, bought that moment in the Paperelia, and regardless of anything but the fact that you had missed, last week, a jolly fine wedding at Cairndow...'[5]

On occasional Sundays, Neil went to St Columba Gaelic Church, at the foot of Hope Street (below Central Station). Another ploy to alleviate homesickness was hiring a boat on St Vincent Pond (between St Vincent Crescent and the Clyde, long since filled in). There a rowing-boat or a canoe with a small sail could be had for 6d, and in winter there was the possibility of skating.

He found also that by dint of leaving Glasgow at 4 o'clock on Saturday afternoon, after work, he could reach Inveraray by midnight. To get back in time for work he had to cross by the 3 a.m. ferry to St Catherines on the Monday morning, then walk the ten miles to Lochgoilhead to catch the *Lord of the Isles*. Not kind on the shoe-leather, and not a frequent exploit, presumably.

Gradually he found a foothold in the city and could look about him. There was plenty to see. Glasgow was then in the throes of phenomenal expansion and would soon become 'Second City of the Empire'. In the fifty years from 1871 the population doubled to a million. The missionary James Chalmers described how, in the 1860s, 'apart from cannibalism, even New Guinea presented no sights more terrible for degradation and impurity than Glasgow'.[6] By the 1880s, thousands of the old houses in the Wynds had already been demolished, leaving an enclave containing hundreds of brothels and shebeens.

Shipbuilding on the Clyde was enjoying a resurgence. In 1880, the Grand Duke Alexis of Russia, at the launch of the huge circular 'steam yacht' *Livadia* (more like a floating fort and built for the Tsar), publicly referred to Glasgow as 'the centre of the intelligence of England'.[7] There was a regular passenger service to New York. Railway locomotives and chemicals were two of Glasgow's chief products. Much of the city was pervaded by foul odours, and the Clyde was an open *cloaca maxima*.

In their first digs together, Neil and Archie (who appear in the following passages as Bill and Tod) were introduced by Mr Weir, their landlord, 'to the mysteries of table-turning… When we had any visitors, he took the liberty of intruding with a kind offer to act as medium for any communications we might like to make with the other world. "No trouble at all… I am only too glad to be the vehicle of disseminating the Eternal Truth; just the small what-not or the window table, and the hour may be Blessed for us." We had many experiences with the other world under these circumstances.'[8]

Once, when they were sitting round a table with Mr and Mrs Weir, Neil found himself 'in touch – by special request – with my grandmother, who had died at the age of eighty-six many years before'. (Her age at death is right, but it was in fact only three years or so since she had died.)

'All that followed took place in the brightest gas-light, and with reverent decorum. Nothing to be seriously regarded as abnormal happened till I asked my grandmother her maiden name, which had not been mentioned, and could not possibly be known to the Weirs. The response was immediate and correct. I asked her where she died, and was correctly answered without a moment's hesitation. An inquiry as to the place of her birth disclosed that she had forgotten, for which I made every allowance in a lady of such age; the place she had named had been only an intermediate home of hers on earth.

'Beyond that, I could think of nothing else to ask in the English language and in the presence of strangers. To a Gaelic grandmother one must be scrupulously considerate, not too inquisitive, and I feared I had already intruded far enough on her privacy. Mr Weir was anxious to carry on with such interrogations as would naturally occur to a City Missionary, but I closed the seance there and then. Our host, the medium, having given the Benediction, shook hands fervently with someone under the table, blessed her specifically as his "dear sister," and invited me to feel how cold his hand had become... I refrained with inexpressible feelings.

'Left to ourselves, Tod and I looked at each other somewhat dazed. He was pallid, and I was not feeling very well myself. We examined the table minutely. Quite a human tea-table of the circular variety! There was nothing on earth that could account for its lifting a leg and rapping in this extraordinary way.

'"With all respect to the Weirs," I said at last, "I'm certain there's a catch of some sort in the performance. Let's try the table between us, and if I get you at any shenaniken I'll break your blessed neck."

'Grandma came back, and made her identity more emphatically clear than ever. I asked her whom I was sitting with at the moment and she told me right off. Tod was watching me like a hawk, and I, on my part, kept his feet and knees under the closest scrutiny, as he did mine. It seemed to both of us impossible that, with cuffs turned back, bare wrists, and open hands on the centre of the table, any leverage of ours could make it move.

'This seance was very short, however. I soon discovered that my old school-friend was quite unconsciously supplying all the answers to my questions by the almost imperceptible suction and thrust of his flattened hands. He had the advantage of knowing my family history as fully as I did myself, and was honestly surprised when I proved to him that he was deputising for my grandmother.'[9]

Interesting though life with the Weirs might be, the Spartan cooking left much to be desired: 'Our good landlady's idea of fruit never swerved from – lettuce! She looked on lettuce as a rare and precious product of the hot-house, at its best when rubbed with salt.' Eventually Archie, who shared digs with Neil for several years, insisted on a move.

'I could not tell how many different lodgings we were in during these golden years of experiment, when (simple souls!) we expected sooner or later to come upon the perfect paragon of landladies... Tod had a sympathetic soul, but he was temperamentally incapable of tolerating what he called "the weepist". We might not be more than a day or two in new quarters when he would display his apprehensions. "A weepist, Bill, a weepist for a ducat! Ten to one she lets the tear doon fa'. Let us not stay upon the order of our going, but pad the hoof at once."

'There must be scores of landladies I utterly forget, but the memories of a few abide with me. It was Mrs Grant (North Portland Street, doubtless) who gave Tod his great distaste for the maudlin landlady... where we were most wounded in our aesthetic souls was in her collection of *In Memoriam* cards... They were framed and hung about the walls of our sitting rooms...

'"Our home is on the mountain wave, our march is on the deep," said Tod, after a fair trial of Mrs Grant. "Bill, it necessitates that we fold our tents like the justly celebrated Arabs and silently hire a cab. The milk gets waterier and waterier every morning; it's plain that Mrs Grant's memories of the past are chronic, and that she sheds the tears of unavailing regret into our lacteal nourishment by means of a filler."

'"But, Lord! we cannot shift again, Tod," I would protest, sick of packing a trunk that seemed to shrink miraculously with each removal. "Leave it to me," Tod always answered generously. "Lean on yours truly and all will yet be well," and he would straightway start to cram his copy of Shakespeare and his alarm clock into his trunk. Later in life, when the restraining influence of my presence was gone... he had copies of the Immortal Bard and alarm clocks in nine different abandoned lodgings in various parts of Glasgow, but at this time it was different; all the solicitude attending our removals centred on Tod's Shakespeare and alarm clock, both, it must be confessed, merely an evidence of good intentions on the part of Tod... he never paid any attention to the alarm of his clock, which he always put outside the window so that it would not disturb his dreams.

'The clock, I remember, played a humorous part in lodgings we had for a while in a house whose windows looked out on the ground of Grafton Square. It was my wish always to have a domicile with a view – however humble and circumscribed – of nature... We saw a bill out – "Apartments" – we stopped the cab; we entered; Mrs Weir, late "cook to the best families in the West End", received us in the lobby in a flustered and rubicund condition. "All right," said Tod, *"J'y suis, j'y reste*; pay the cabbie, Bill, and lug in the *lares* and *penates*. Mrs Weir, do you, by any chance, let the tear doon fa'?" "Nòt me," said Mrs Weir, when explanations followed, "I'm a cheery wee woman"... It was evening when we prepared for bed; Tod put his alarm clock out on the window sill as usual. Early next morning a policeman came to the door with Tod's 3s 11½d Geneva, which had, miraculously enough, not been stolen by casual passers-by.'[10]

CHAPTER EIGHT
An awfu' peely-wally yin!

ONLY two months after leaving Inveraray, Neil was briefly re-united with some of his old companions: he re-joined 'A' Company, Argyllshire Highland Rifles, for a review in Edinburgh when the volunteer regiments of Scotland paraded before Queen Victoria: 'We were a battalion of widely-scattered companies from as far north as Ballachulish, as far south as Kintyre; it took a day to muster us at Greenock. It was the first time I had seen the regiment as a whole, old Poltalloch – gigantic figure – in command.

'The man who used to make the right sort of brass band marches must be dead, for nowadays [1905] I listen in vain for any brass band march so grand and stirring as that which played us to the station. The air I know, but the name I never knew; no matter, it is enough that the brassy quickstep echoing in the dingy East Quay Lane of Greenock was stimulating and divine.

'It was the first time many of us had seen a train; it was the first time we had seen Edinburgh. It must have taken us hours to get to our destination, for when we de-trained at the end of the journey it was in a dark, cold railway station, with nobody in it but ourselves. The pipe band played us through dark streets to our quarters in Summerhall Brewery on the side of the Meadows, in whose lofts, redolent of malt, we more or less slept two nights on adorable straw palliasses.

'The man on the palliasse next to me smoked on his back all night, and talked of the first Review, which he had taken part in, for he was a 'veteran'; the humour of the Campbeltown companies in the rows behind us found expression in the playful theft of our brown blankets, and in the mimicry of farm animals. Dim smoky lights revealed the recumbent lines through which at intervals all night the officers passed to check too much skylarking. And the morning and the evening was the first day.

'The reveille was sounded at five. We rose and washed in troughs which, rightly or wrongly, I have always assumed since had something to do with the manufacture of beer, and having done so, went down from our lofts to the first parade. So far we had not really seen Edinburgh, only a vague impression of dark, damp, midnight streets on our way from the station; we expected that now the splendour of the Capital would be visible when we got out of the brewery. But we were doomed to disappointment, for our parade-ground gave us a vision of very uninteresting tenements, and a menacing sky gave the first indication that we were in for unpleasant weather.

'At six we had breakfast on one of the flats of the brewery; at seven we had distributed to us the haversacks that had never previously formed part of our equipment. The haversacks, we were apprised, were meant to contain our dinners for the day, but the muddling of the British Army extends even to the auxiliary branches; something went wrong with the commissariat department, and when at seven we marched out to the brigade rendezvous on the Meadows, our haversacks still remained empty. To be done with the ghastly fact, we got no dinner at all that day, and fasted from six in the morning till six or seven at night. To the young recruit it did not seem a serious matter, but oh! how the 'veteran' of the next palliasse cursed!

'It was shortly after the brigade began to move from the rendezvous of the Meadows to the review ground that the rain started. Of that morning the mind retains no impression save that for the very first time we envied other regiments on the way with us their greatcoats. So far as the Argylls were concerned, greatcoats had not yet been invented; we stood out the day in our doublets, sparsely protected by our none too copious plaids, and having taken up our position at the foot of the hill, stood hour after hour soaking in the torrent of the century. It didn't matter very much to the young recruit, for now and then the brass band or the pipers played.

'The whole plain seemed a vessel, designed by nature to catch water. It fell in files, it fell in sections, it fell in companies, battalions, brigades; it fell in army corps; not a gentle drizzle, but with fierce lances that penetrated to the skin. And immoveable we stood 'at ease' there from early in the day till late in the afternoon, for we were late, though far from the last, among the regiments of infantry to pass the saluting base. In all distances, visible through the blur of rain, the citizen army stood or moved in steeping masses, and the multitudes of civilian spectators on the slopes with their waterproofs and umbrellas were not envied, for they had not the young recruit's elation to sustain them.

'There was a momentary sensation in the lines of 'A' Company, I remember, because at dinner-time one man, who must have had a mother or a wife, produced a biscuit from the pocket of his doublet and ate it, to the exasperation of his fellows. Even the adjutant – old Hall – looked hungredly at him. From the flat ground below us, in front of the Royal stand, came the continual thunder of passing bands. First the artillery went past, tearing up the soaking ground with the wheels of their gun carriages, and the hoofs of their horses; then the yeomanry followed, further deepening the slough of despond that was later to swallow us up. Regiment after regiment then, too, deliberately wheeled into position, and went past the Scottish ensign; it took them hours.

'To anybody but a young recruit there would be as little emotional uplift in that dreary spectacle on that dreary day as there might be in the sight of a procession of unemployed, but it roused him to lyrical exultation, and a week later he wrote in a local paper a rhapsodical account of the event that would have been too ecstatic even for the charge of Balaclava.

'The young recruit had on peculiarly inappropriate footwear in the shape of what are, or were, known as Lorne shoes, and by-and-bye he was to realise with agonies how unsuitable even the most elegant Lorne shoes are for marching over a quagmire created by the previous progress of artillery and cavalry. The time came for us to form column (or quarter-column, whichever it was), and display what dressing we could in the march past our Sovereign Lady. We unanimously agreed as a battalion afterwards that the corps kept the best dressing of all the corps that day, which was consoling, but the young recruit was so horribly engrossed in the task of tugging his Lorne shoes out of the mud as he marched, that he carried away no lasting impression of the military precision of the regimental movement. The mud was well over the tops of the shoes, and they would have been wholly lost but for... the straps of the spats that had been as white as pipe-clay could make them that morning. On the rear of the company in front were two little bugle boys... But for the the timely assistance of the sergeant, these boys would have died a dreadful death in the mud, for the regiment had one inflexible purpose – to keep the right formation and come up like a wall. When we got through, and went marching back to Summerhall Brewery, we were a spectacle for gods and men!... With delightful humour the commissariat met us... with the cold Melton Mowbray pies that had been meant for our haversacks...

'We dried our clothing as far as possible at the brewery furnace, and round great braziers lighted in the yard for the purpose, and hied us forth in search of gaiety... Instead, there was still the torrential rain, and the padella lights upon the Castle rocks sputtered feebly... even the young recruit felt a poignant disillusionment. We went back to the brewery twice... and finally left our doublets and plaids there, to come out in one last expedition after gaiety, wrapped in our brown soldier s blankets... At five in the morning the pipes awakened us to take the route for home.'[1]

Undeterred, Neil enlisted in the Glasgow Highlanders and carried a musket in the ranks for five years. It was a good way of obtaining a kilt, a plaid and chequered hose and it gave him the chance to march behind a regimental band, to charge with fixed bayonet on the Flesher's Haugh, to take part in mock battles with blank ammunition. Not least, it brought association with other Gaelic speakers.

He claimed that on his first parade an officer told him: 'I doubt you'll never make a proper Glasgow Highlander – you haven't got the hips for it.'[2] And once, marching along the Trongate, he heard a 'shawly' woman remark, just as he came abreast of her, 'Oh, Mery [Mary]! here's an awfu' peely-wally yin!'[3]

CHAPTER NINE

All alone on Greenock quay

THERE is no record of Neil looking for work on a newspaper when he first came to Glasgow. The daily press was then almost entirely devoted to politics, commerce and the law courts, subjects he found on the whole repellent. But he still kept up his shorthand and submitted verse and short articles to weekly country newspapers, chiefly the *Oban Times* and the *Lennox Herald*. Before he came to Glasgow, a poem addressed to Dunchuach, Inveraray's guardian hill, had appeared in the *Oban Times* – his second published work. In after years he would quote the heroic/romantic verses of this poem in self-mockery.

The *Oban Times* began to accept Neil's work on a weekly basis, treating him as an unofficial correspondent, with plenty of space to report the doings of West Highland exiles in Glasgow. Perhaps because this work was unpaid and Neil a sort of anonymous volunteer, the paper often let him choose subjects that enthralled him personally, such as a sentimental picture entitled 'Comrades' by Robert Gibb, on which he expatiated for two columns. It was all experience of a sort, but 'my pen children went for years wauchlin' through papers that ought to be ashamed of themselves for printing them, they were such hapless dears because I had not a single soul to show me my errors'.

He attended 'natives' gatherings' – Highland re-unions – to gather details for the *Oban Times*. In the tale 'The Natives of Clachnacudden', Erchie describes these soirees before they got 'far ower genteel': 'A' the auld folk frae Clachnacudden in Gleska were at thae swarees, as weel as a' the young folk. Ye were packed in your sates like red herrin' in a barrel... When the tea was bye... the chairman wad stand up on the pletform and mak a speech aboot Clachnacudden. I used to ken that speech by hert; it was the same yin for a' the natives' reunions.'

Neil undeniably found the Inveraray version of these high jinks rather jolly himself. He would record in his diary, each November from 1894 to 1901, attending the Glasgow Inveraray Ball. In 1894 he noted: 'At 4th Annual Conversazione, Inveraray natives in Trades Hall. Inveraray Pipe Band there.' This was Lord Archie's band, with Charlie Maitland its Pipe Major. In 1895 Neil bought new Highland dress for the occasion, 'cost £20 (including sporran £2.15/-)', when his average weekly earnings were just £5.

He continued to read as much as he could. Non-fiction and newspapers absorbed his attention particularly. A Glasgow literary journal, James Hedderwick's *Weekly Citizen*, was a special favourite, 'as intellectually influential as a college course of English literature'.[1] An extract in its pages from *The Silverado Squatters*, for instance, was Neil's first introduction to Robert Louis Stevenson as an essayist.

During those early Glasgow years Neil noticed 'a column or two of gaiety and gossip' beginning to creep into the evening papers. Glasgow had pioneers of this 'new journalism' also in such 'illustrated and flippant week-end organs' as *The Bailie*, *The Chiel* and *Quiz*. This fascinated Neil and had its due influence upon him. *The Bailie*, for instance, had a series written by 'Jeems Kaye', a hypothetical Strathbungo coalman, whose topical humour was highly popular in Glasgow.

Early in 1884 Neil, now twenty, saw in the *Glasgow Herald* an advertisement for two posts on the *Greenock Advertiser*, a 'halfpenny evening paper'. Taking cuttings of his work in the *Oban Times*, etc., he went down to Greenock. He handed the cuttings to the editor, saying he would return in an hour. The editor then offered him a post as junior reporter at 25s a week. Although Neil had been prepared to accept 10s, he coolly asked if the 25s would be increased if his work proved satisfactory. The editor agreed, and Neil took the job.

It is likely he had applied unsuccessfully for newspaper jobs already. Looking back twenty years later, he remarked about journalism: 'When I got into it (broke into it might be the better term, for the act in retrospect seems really burglarious), the only guidance a young man had as to how he should set about going to press, and what he should have to do there, was to be found in a few pages in *David Copperfield*.'[2] Why he 'broke into' journalism just then can only be surmised: perhaps the dusty stagnation of the ironmongery in Argyle Street was no longer to be tholed.

At the beginning of April he was given his first big job on the *Greenock Advertiser*: covering the trial run of a new paddle steamer. The *Jeannie Deans*, destined to be the fastest on the Clyde for some years, reached 17½ knots on trial. At the end of a jolly day at sea, Neil stepped ashore, already drafting a brilliant article in his head, only to be confronted on the quay by a colleague with the bleak news that the *Advertiser* had suspended publication. The last number appeared on 8 April 1884. Neil returned to Glasgow and soon found another post on the *Glasgow News*, a Conservative morning paper edited by Frederick Wicks. Here much of his work consisted of reporting petty cases in the Summary Court Room of the County Buildings, where 'half a reporter's time was occupied in badinage over the wire with the girls at the "Douglas" Telephone Exchange, or with "shilling lawyers".'

But Neil had more on his mind than the girls at the telephone exchange. On his return from Greenock to Glasgow he had found lodgings in the house of Hugh and Effie Adam at 227 North Woodside Road. There is a family tradition that Effie had a friend in Inveraray who had written asking her 'to look after Neil' or 'look out for Neil'. Or the connection may have come through Hugh Adam, who worked in Glasgow as a confectioner's mechanic but had been a coppersmith in the Vale of Leven and probably knew Charles McArthur, a cousin of Neil's mother, who plied the same trade in the area.

Hugh and Effie, who had been a Miss Fortune, came originally from the little weaving town of Kilbarchan in Renfrewshire. They had five children – Jessie, Agnes, Phemie (later known as Effie), Andrew and Hugh – and with the addition of Neil as a lodger the living quarters must have been pretty crowded.

Jessie was nearly 22, eleven months older than Neil, and had already suffered her own misfortune. The man she had been engaged to marry had drowned at sea. Agnes, the next sister, had striking good looks, but she found Neil too 'bookish'. Phemie was then about 15 and the two boys were younger. Neil soon became part of the family, sharing its joys – and sorrows. In the spring of 1885, Effie Adam died. The cause of her death is unknown, but a consequence was that Jessie took over her mother's role in looking after the younger family members.

A family tradition has it that she and Neil first got to know each other at a church social: however it began, they would soon become close as he supported her in her new responsibilities. How he proposed to her is unknown. He simply recorded in his diary, without any preamble, that he married Jessie Ewing Adam on 23 July 1885. The wedding ceremony was performed in the Adams' house by the Rev David Pirret of Burnbank United Presbyterian Church, the witnesses being Jessie's father and Neil's friend and foster brother Archie MacKellar. On the wedding certificate, bride and bridegroom gave the same age – twenty-two – although Jessie's 23rd birthday had fallen a week earlier. The honeymoon began in lodgings above the post office in Strachur, across the loch from Inveraray. About this time Jessie first met her mother-in-law, with whom she always got on extremely well. On their return to Glasgow, Jessie and Neil set up house in New City Road (the northern end, now Maryhill Road), just round the corner from the Adams' house. Like most Scots city-dwellers then, they had a rented, unfurnished flat.

My mother used to say that her parents were not at all like each other, that her mother wanted very little for herself, had few clothes and rarely went out. But Jessie and Neil were both reserved and home-loving. An old friend of Neil's wrote in after-years of 'the great good fortune that gave him so devoted a helpmeet... She was ever at his right hand, careful of his every interest, but vigilant above all of those comforts and amenities which contributed to his physical comfort and to his mental vigour.'³ Another friend wrote that she 'did everything for him except write his books'.⁴

On the other hand, Effie, their second daughter, was inclined to think that her mother spoiled her father, laying out his clothes every morning and putting in his studs and cuff-links. But he was truly appreciative and no doubt made New Year resolutions on the lines of Erchie's resolve 'to flype his ain socks and no' leave his claes reel-rall aboot the hoose at night for his wife Jinnet to lay oot richt in the mornin''. Jessie made all her children's clothes, and Neil at times got annoyed because he thought she knitted too much, once remarking in a letter that she was 'gey and ill to shift from her sewing machine and the youngsters'.⁵

A passage in *The Daft Days* where Ailie Dyce speaks of her sister Bell's beau, 'deep drowned in the Indian Ocean', suggests Bell was modelled partly on Jessie. I can see something of my grandmother (who died when I was nineteen) in Bell Dyce, 'a woman small and soft and sappy', content with her 'celestial grocery' in the kitchen and with her household realm 'that had ever to those who knew it best a soul of peace that is not sometimes found in a cathedral. They felt in it a sanctuary safe from the fret and tempest, the alarums and excursions of the world outbye.'

Neil's spell on the *Glasgow News* lasted for about eighteen months, during which he became dissatisfied with his prospects. He suspected also that the paper was in a critical state financially, and with new responsibilities he needed a secure income. Only four months after the wedding, Neil transferred to the *Falkirk Herald* for a wage of £2 a week, and he and Jessie rented a house at Wellacre, Kerse Lane. Very soon after they had flitted to Falkirk, and just nine months after Effie's death, Jessie's father died of a heart attack. Agnes (who would soon be getting married) and Phemie went to stay with their grandmother, but the two boys really needed a father and Neil and Jessie at once took them into their new home. Neil found Andrew, then thirteen, a job as an apprentice compositor on the *Falkirk Herald* and arranged for nine-year-old Hugh to continue his schooling. Jessie's brothers would prove to be a long-term commitment.

In April 1886 Jessie gave birth to a daughter, called Annie after her paternal grandmother. In less than a year, Neil had gone from the carefree life of a bachelor to being the head of a family of four other people, all dependent on him for their wellbeing. He was still not quite 23, which sheds a certain light on a review he was to write of *Thirteen Stories* by R.B. Cunninghame Graham:

'The sketches in Mr Graham's book are obviously recollections of youth... It is then that things seem most vividly to impress themselves; later we grow fat-headed, as the vulgar say, and put off the day's impressions with our evening clothes. Generally it is the best thing we can do with them... The materials for the ruminations of later life – the poetry, the pathos, philosophy, faith, and love – are all gathered up before the age of 23; after 23 or thereabouts we may learn the import of these things and become able to apply them unto art, but it is the old material alone we must work on all our industrious lives.'[6]

Joseph Conrad wrote of 'a shadow-line warning one that the region of early youth, too, must be left behind'.[7] He considered he had crossed that line at thirty. Yeats held 'that our intellects at twenty contain all the truths we shall ever find'.[8] In Neil's case the 'shadow-line' was crossed abruptly in his early twenties as he took on the complex responsibilities of a householder with a wife, a baby daughter and two juvenile orphan brothers-in-law. His self-reliance and zest saw him through.

Already three of the four elements that developed into a strong framework for his life were there: his family, journalism and Inveraray (with all that implies). Already, too, he was nursing literary hopes. It was clearly himself he was thinking of when he wrote years later: 'As to the value of journalistic experience for literary training, there is no doubt that it offers a practical schooling in the rough elements of composition to those whose education has been meagre, and conversely puts the instinctive recluse of bookish habits into more active relations with all sorts and conditions of men than he would be likely to maintain of his own initiative... Probably most writers would be benefited by some years of journalistic work, very likely many would be injured by continuing at it.'[9]

He found little by way of literary inspiration at the *Falkirk Herald* (the only paper he worked on that still survives). While giving him secure employment, it offered little scope to a young reporter keen to stretch his wings. He was expected to report football matches, but football bored him, so he paid a colleague to do the reports. But he took an unaffected interest in the life of the prosperous town, with its cattle market, iron foundries, and places of alcoholic refreshment:

'Falkirk... was probably the most convivial burgh of any size in Scotland, with its congeries of wynds and lanes behind the High Street, an extraordinary number of little inns and taverns in them, all with a choice of several back-door exits, it seemed as if specially laid-out for decorous drinking after the official closing hour of 11 p.m. It was utterly impossible for Superintendent Macdonald and the police at his disposal to enforce the Forbes Mackenzie Act. His lieutenant, Mr William Gordon, a gentleman of natural culture and earnest character... used to say to me, 'We're getting near the end of bad Old Scotland, and the Fa'kirk Bairns are just a little behind in the movement; you can't trap bees, like blue-bonnets [bluetits] with a riddle.'[10]

There is a tradition that Neil's memories of the commercial travellers who frequented the Crown Hotel in Falkirk, at the corner of the High Street and the Lint Riggs, surfaced again in the Jimmy Swan tales, begun a quarter of a century later. Certainly much of his time was spent reporting police court cases, and once this landed him in a scrape. Wallace Thom, self-styled 'Cough-drop King' of Glasgow, appeared on a charge of travelling on a time-expired railway ticket. He was discharged, but the case was mysteriously reported in the Glasgow and Edinburgh papers as well as locally.

Next day the *Falkirk Herald* received a telegram from Thom, claiming £1,000 for moral damages and announcing that he and his law agent were on their way to collect it. But they reckoned without the resourcefulness of Neil Munro, who intercepted them at Grahamston Station and beguiled them into an inn for a 'snack of luncheon' and reminiscences of the Glasgow Summary Court. After they had eaten, 'suddenly the Cough-drop King uplifted his voice, and with much dramatic feeling sang "The Battle of Stirling Bridge"... the lawyer was then prevailed upon to sing "Scotland the Brave"... I followed with my masterpiece, "The Massacre of the Phairson"... and the rest of the afternoon passed with harmony.'[11]

At length, however, Thom remembered why he had come to

Falkirk. Realising the game was up, Neil then revealed it was he who had written the offending paragraph. Yet on learning this, Thom instantly abandoned his claim to damages, declaring: 'We're not going to spoil a dash fine trio.' The *Falkirk Herald*'s Editor must have been happy to overlook his reporter's long absence, seeing the libel action was averted thereby.

Of all the journalistic tasks at the *Herald*, the Editor prided himself particularly on putting together obituaries of local luminaries, for which he would often be rewarded with a bag of potatoes or a middle of pork. He allowed Neil a certain amount of leeway with his literary style, but drew the line when he put the phrase 'the blind fury with th'abhorred shears' into an obituary of a master tailor. At the newspaper's offices certain pigeon-holes known as the Mortuary held more than a thousand pre-prepared obituaries of men still to be seen walking about in Falkirk High Street.

One day, on hearing that the cattle auctioneer had died, the Editor sent Neil round to the house. There he discovered the auctioneer was still in the land of the living and able to summon the *Herald* reporter to his bedside to inform him he was 'no' for nane o' [the Editor's] maudlin sentiment. I was jist Watty Rigg the cattleman. Put that doon!'

In the end the auctioneer recovered, but Neil had now discerned his editor was old and frail himself and 'to put Providence off the trail of one I loved despite his little disabilities, I carefully prepared his obituary in my lodgings. It was affection, not my taste, that made me load the notice with hackneyed phrases he had used, himself, so often. For weeks I kept it in my desk. "How goes the Mortuary, Neil?" he one day asked me wearily. "I hope you're keepin' it up; we must always send them off like gentlemen," and he read no menace in my furtive eye. But Providence, for once, was not stalled off at the sight of a complete obituary in readiness; a few days later we had to turn the leads for the Editor's memoir in the *Herald*.'[12]

CHAPTER TEN

The jawbox of journalism

THE intuition that had led Neil to leave the *Glasgow News* had been well-founded: matters there were indeed precarious. Nevertheless, when he was invited to return to the *News* after less than two years in Falkirk, he accepted. Again his instinct was proved right. During his first spell on the *News* his abilities had been noticed by James Murray Smith, editor of its sister paper, the *Evening News & Star*. It was through Smith's influence and as part of a campaign of resuscitation that Neil was brought back from Falkirk. His entire career as a writer unfolded as it did largely because of Smith's continuing confidence in him and their relationship of implicit trust.

Smith dedicated himself to building up the *Evening News*. A native of Greenock and formerly a compositor, he was very shy and talked mostly in a gruff bark. But he was a shrewd and ambitious businessman, adept at recognising talent and developing new and popular features. In 1889, for instance, the *News* would start a special football edition, and in 1890 one of the first women journalists in Britain, Marion Elsie Niven, would join the staff – to write on women's topics, needless to say.

The Munro family of five moved back to Glasgow and took a house near Jessie's old home. Hugh changed schools, while Andrew found a job at Hillhead Baths. Neil went back to the *Glasgow News* in April 1887 at the same salary as in Falkirk – £100 a year – but his work was immediately more interesting and varied. In his first month he reported several political meetings (Lord Rosebery, Joseph Chamberlain), wrote special articles on the Harbour Trust failure at Greenock and went to Islay to report the unveiling by the Marquis of Lorne of the memorial to J.F. Campbell, the pioneer collector of Gaelic folk-tales.

In July Neil left Scotland for the first time in his life to report the Wimbledon shooting meeting, putting up for a fortnight at an hotel in the Strand. He greatly enjoyed London and took the opportunity to visit the American Exhibition and Wild West show at Earls Court. Back in Glasgow, his normal duties still included court reporting, and sometimes he hung about the side-doors of the Waterloo Rooms waiting for interviews with 'colliers and railwaymen... or Tait, or Cronin, or Keir Hardie' when strike meetings skailed. In September, attending the golf championship at Prestwick, he met the famous golfer 'old Tom Morris'. While never a great golfer or sporting man himself, Neil enjoyed the characters to be found in sport and the colour and atmosphere of sporting occasions. For a period he wrote essays for the *News*'s companion sports paper, *The Referee*, typically earning for this sort of work 15s a week – a sum not to be sneezed at in those days. In 1887 and 1888, Neil was seconded to go to the races as assistant to Jack Jewel, sporting editor of the *Glasgow News*:

'He specialised in horses, cricket, and boxing, about which I knew as little as the Shah of Persia, and cared less... Heaven knows why he took to me, for I dwelt apart from that hectic world... mainly because I felt the sporting columns of my newspaper were beginning to take up too much valuable space which I could have filled, myself, with more valuable and interesting matter... My part it was to write the Introduction, maintaining an atmosphere to suggest that the eyes of the world that particular day were on Hamilton Park or Ayr, as the case might be; as each race came off to jot down its description 'read-off' by my colleague through field-glasses, and rush the result to the telegraph office.

'Jewel and I went from course to course, sharing each night a double-bedded room, fraternising in the hotels with representatives and notable personages of this strange horsey demi-monde which was more intensely interesting to me than the horses, though I had been practically brought up in a stable. It may not be irrelevant to mention that I never put a penny on a horse throughout my wanderings with Jewel...'[1]

On 13 November 1887, 'Bloody Sunday', Neil was in London again and saw the Life Guards quell 'an attempt by the unemployed and their leaders to exercise quite properly their old right of public demonstration and oratory there... I saw the steel and scarlet squadrons of the Life Guards burst from Whitehall through the riot at the corner of the Strand, and I reached the street in time to discover, even in the tumult, my fellow-countryman [R.B. Cunninghame Graham], with a head, though bloody, still unbowed, with John Burns as his fellow-culprit.'[2]

Back in Glasgow, one of the most important journalistic tasks with which Neil was entrusted was the preparation of the leading article or leader, the considered voice of the paper. His first leader, for which he earned the princely sum of 10s 6d, appeared in the *News* of 9 January 1888. That evening a course of Gaelic classes was to start in the High School, and Neil took this as his cue to expatiate on the rapid decline in Gaelic speaking. (He himself attended Gaelic classes in Glasgow, possibly this very course, feeling himself deficient in the reading and writing of his own native tongue.)

His first leader has signs of the fluency and skill in communicating his own enthusiasm that would characterise his columns. Somewhat surprisingly he says that Gaelic is 'a dying tongue'. This regrettable belief came from the observations of an insider brought up on the receding edge of the *Gaidhealtachd*. The views are those of a 24-year-old, writing a few years before An Comunn Gaidhealach was founded or Geddes and Sharp thought of their Celtic renaissance. Neil would have read a good deal about Gaelic in the *Oban Times*, especially when there was controversy before the first chair of Celtic was established at Edinburgh in 1882.

In his leader, Neil opined: 'Philologically as well as physiologically the law of the survival of the fittest must prevail... When Gaelic is waning in the North, is it likely to survive in cities? The fact is, that for the ordinary run of people proficiency in two languages is difficult... After all, apart from sentimental considerations, what is there to be regretted in the extinction of the Highland tongue? Must the old valour of the race, or its piety and characteristic perseverance, wane with the loss of its language? Shall the wild grandeur... of the North not have the effect on the character of the race which environment always has? Surely! In literature again, Gaelic has little to preserve...'[3]

Just two weeks after being promoted to leader writing, Neil noted in his diary: 'Many ominous changes on the *News*. J. Murray Smith, late Editor *Evening News*, appointed 'Editorial Manager', whatever that is!' Thereafter the diary entries become quietly dramatic:

30 Jan. 1888. J. Shields Stewart left the *Evening News* for London, where he has got an appointment on the *Echo* at £5.5s per week. Saw him off, with Kennedy Jones, who goes to edit a Leicester paper.

1 Feb. Cheques this month are signed for the first time by Grier and Brodie, and stamped 'Scottish Press Company's a/c'.

11 Feb. *Evening News* enlarged to eight pages. Last issue of the *Glasgow News*. Fatal tidings came into sub-editors' room at 2 am. Am told that I am to be retained on evening paper staff.

13 Feb. Started work in sub-editors' room for *Evening News* at 6am. (This turning in at 6am lasted for some time till it was found that as the London morning papers did not arrive till eight or so, there was nothing to do.)

15 Feb. Appointed Chief Reporter of *Evening News* at no advance

47

of salary (£100) while all other members of staff have their salaries reduced.

16 Feb. Began writing a leader a day for *News*.

17 Feb. Shields Stewart already back from London – found incompetent and is going to New York.

1 March. Got rise of £10 p.a. on my salary, which is now £110. In bank £15. Circulation of *Evening News* on a Saturday lately was 77,300.

4 April. Example of week's earnings – Salary £2.2s, Lorgnette (gossip column) 12/6, Contrib. to *Saturday Athletic Journal* 7/6.

These sums add up to £3.2s a week, which may be compared with the average wage around that time of £2.5s. The Munros did not live in luxury, but neither did they want, and Neil could survey his growing family with pride. In April 1888, little Annie had her second birthday, just before the International Exhibition opened at Kelvingrove. That summer Neil, now chief reporter, took a fortnight's leave, and they had their first long family holiday together at Inveraray, where Neil was photographed with 'the boys' – Charlie Maitland, Bob Fraser and Archie MacKellar – at Frew's bridge, near the castle.

When Annie fell ill not long after they returned to the city, it was thought by their doctor to be chicken pox. But at the end of September she was still very unwell and, on 11 October, meningitis was diagnosed. In his desperation Neil called in a young consultant of future eminence. At the time he could not bear to confide more than the bald facts to his diary:

14 Oct. Very ill today. Had in Dr Wm McEwan who thinks the case hopeless.

15 Oct. Annie died at 2.10 p.m. in presence of my wife and myself.

17 Oct. Annie buried in the Western Necropolis at 2 o'clock. A lovely day. With me at the funeral were only Revd John Douglas, John Crawford [husband of Jessie's sister Agnes], Archd MacKellar, Andrew & Hugh Adam.

Many years later, Neil wrote to the wife of a friend and colleague who had lost an infant daughter in the same way: 'I remember the desolation of the experience. She was the only child; it seemed as if life was permanently darkened for us. But there came other children who were spared to grow up to manhood and womanhood, and when they were young her individuality somehow became partly merged in them in a consoling way. Yet Annie – as her name was – now remains for us somewhat more our own than the others...'[4]

With Annie's death, it seemed the light had gone out of the world. The triumphantly successful International Exhibition at Kelvingrove that had brought 'six months' unaccustomed *joie de vivre*' to the city closed its doors that autumn and, as Glasgow slipped into sombre winter, there was little to lighten the lives of the Munros.

Neil's two adopted sons, who had accompanied him to Annie's funeral while Jessie mourned at home, cannot have found this an easy period. Andrew Adam left the Munros to go into lodgings a few months later. The following March, his brother Hugh, now 13, would leave school and start work as a clerk.

Early in 1889, a few months after Annie's death, Jessie spent a fortnight at Inveraray, where she had a consoling talk with the Rev Gilbert Meikle. That year the place of Neil's own birth would give them both solace. In April, Neil rented a flat in Arkland for £4.10s a year, 'for occasional use in summer', instead of crowding into his mother's little house. In Glasgow the Munros gave up the house of Annie's childhood and flitted to a new home at 250 New City Road, up the same close as their first married quarters, though behind a different door. In June, Jessie again spent a fortnight in Inveraray, with Neil paying flying visits. Meanwhile Jessie's brother Andrew went to sea as a steward's boy. In December he left for India as an ordinary seaman, and thereafter he led an independent life, eventually settling in Australia.

Neil, too, would venture overseas. It was the year of the great Paris Exposition for the centenary of the Revolution and he went to the French capital – his first time on the Continent – with a colleague, Alexander Comrie. Their third-class tickets from Cook's cost £5.9s.3d, including four days' hotel bill, etc.

'28 July. Reached Paris 8.30am very tired, after being up on deck of steamer all night and travelling all morning in a narrow, cramped, uncomfortable French compartment... Spent afternoon in the Exhibition and went up the Eiffel Tower.'

Two crammed but delightful days were spent on excursions in Cook's 'Select Personally Conducted Carriage', going all round Paris and out to Versailles. At night they went to the Folies Bergère. The return journey from Paris to Glasgow took exactly 23¾ hours. Next day, Neil went to Inveraray in the *Lord of the Isles* for a further ten days' holiday. These days of leisure were a precious restorative for the Munros.

Back in Glasgow, Neil bought a piano – £35! – and had his first piano lesson. But for much of the time he remained enmeshed in daily journalism, reflected in the laconic diary that was all he had time for to illustrate those brimming years:

1889. 7 Oct. At opening Conversazione of New Municipal Buildings, 700 present.

1 Nov. Storm. Great disaster at Templeton's Carpet Mill, Bridgeton. 29 girls killed and many injured. On the ground shortly after accident happened at 5.15 and had out special edition.

8 Nov. Arran Murder Trial (Laurie). Went to Edinburgh today and did trial with Harvey and Ralston, True [the *News* artist] illustrating.

9 Nov. Laurie sentenced to death (afterwards reprieved). News sold 175,491 copies, biggest on record. Management gave me £2 for extra work at trial, others £1.

15 Nov. With John Harvey did by request special note of lecture by Duke of Argyll before Dialectic Society – charging his Grace £10.10/-.

28 Nov. Daily consultation arranged between J.M. Smith, Farquhar and me.

But the most important event of the year occurred just before Christmas, when Jessie had her second baby. Neil wept for joy when he heard it was another daughter. She was christened Euphemia Fortune, after her maternal grandmother, 'by Rev John Douglas, in our house at night. Crawford, Agnes, & Phemie present'.

A family man once more, Neil returned to his work with renewed energy. He had the good fortune to be recording the life of a city at its Victorian apogee: Glasgow was now Britain's second city, and the Empire's.

1890. 14 Jan. Began to go into office at 8.30. We all do 'Echoes' and J.M.S. edits them.

15 Feb. At first local meeting Institute of Journalists, St Enoch's Hotel, and afterwards had dinner there. 41 present.

4 March. At opening of Forth Bridge by Prince of Wales, with True, our artist. Very windy day and had narrow escape of being killed by a crowbar blown from top of a stone pier on the bridge.

19 April. First smoking concert, Institute of Journalists, in Bath Hotel. Excellent.

20 April. At preliminary trial of S.S. *Normannia* built at Fairfield for Hamburg-America Steampacket Coy.

26 May. Started correspondence for the *Dundee Evening Telegraph* at £30 per annum.

12 June. At presentation of freedom of city to Henry Stanley, explorer.

26 June. At Glasgow Water Commissioners' Annual Waterworks Inspection. Went to Aberfoyle, Duchray and Callander; dined and slept at Callander.

27 June. Went to Loch Vennacher, Loch Katrine, steamer to Invergyle House. Then to Inversnaid, where we dined; home to Glasgow via Balloch. Willock, Shand and Stewart dismissed from News with cheques for 3 months. Paper has gone into the hands of J.M. Smith. Wicks [Editor of *Glasgow News* when Neil started on it] out of it. *Scottish People* stopped.

In the middle of all this uncertainty, Neil still found time for what was truly important. In July he bought a cushion-tyred bicycle and, while Jessie, the baby and her brother Hugh went to Inveraray in the *Lord of the Isles*, Neil took his bicycle by train to Dalmally and cycled the 16 miles to Inveraray, taking nearly three hours. 'Bad roads, very soft, and myself very weak for want of food.'

During the family's stay at Inveraray, he was made an Apprentice Mason of Lodge St John 50. He also cycled to Glendaruel to see his uncle Peter Munro, schoolmaster at Stronafion for many years. Then it was time to go back to Glasgow, where the paper was now lurching from one crisis to the next.

2 Sept. Strike of all compositors on the *News*. Paper got out under great difficulties.

3 Sept. Still the strike, a number of strange compositors introduced. Had to fill up the paper with 'Leader' material i.e. type ready set sent to us from the *Scottish Leader* office, Edinburgh.

7 Sept. Began to report sermons for *Scottish Pulpit* (penny paper) at 15/- each.

12 Sept. Payment for 'Lorgnette' which was stopped resumed.

30 Sept. Rumour current that I am losing my situation and leaving *News*. Ramsay, Chief Reporter, *Citizen* [another Glasgow evening paper], offers me situation.

21 Oct. Reporting Gladstone in the Corn Exchange. Reporting ditto, West Calder.

This was not the first time Neil had heard Gladstone. The longing to hear 'the champion speaker of the world' that he'd had since Gladstone was pointed out in 1878 at the Duchess of Argyll's funeral had been fulfilled during the first Midlothian campaign. Neil had then acted as clock-keeper to a newspaper corps, and was so excited and 'rapt by that sonorous and thrilling voice' that a reporter taking notes had to kick him on the shins, having been given double his turn. Neil would hear Gladstone often again, yet each time he found there was 'a certain falling off'.[5]

There is no doubt that journalism provided Neil with a substitute for the higher education he never had. It is arguable that his originality flourished better in the soil of autodidacticism, and that his years as a reporter were an antidote to bookish habits. But there are clues in his novels that Neil dearly wished he'd had the chance to go to university. There he would have met kindred spirits when there was still the time and freedom to talk and explore the world together. But all his life he was gregarious and rejoiced in many friends, however little time he could spend with them.

At this stage he did not know any literary men beyond journalists. The few Scottish writers then active tended, like William Sharp, to have no fixed abode in Scotland. In any case, Neil had stumbled already into a world far more exciting and congenial to him than the realms of the Kailyarders and Celtic Crepusculars and, miraculously, it was there on his own doorstep!

The open-sesame was his first encounter in 1890 with the artist Macaulay Stevenson, while seeking art stories for the *News*. Neil knew of 'those revolting young fellows who called themselves the Glasgow School of Artists' but did not yet appreciate their work. Stevenson explained to Neil the ideals of the Glasgow Boys, as he preferred to call them, especially George Henry's *Galloway Landscape*, then in the Art Institute. All this was an eye-opener to Neil, who was much struck with Stevenson's strange personality.

Stevenson then took him to his studio-cum-living quarters. The Macaulaypol, as these were known, was then a great meeting-place of the Glasgow Boys, and Stevenson was a regular contributor to their monthly *Scottish Art Review* in which they attacked the 'Gluepots' of the Royal Scottish Academy. Neil met several of them and later went to visit Henry and E.A.Hornel in their dingy studio, where he surprised them loudly singing a wild chant, 'The Black Whale Inn of Askelon', as they painted their large picture *The Druids*.

This was among works by more than a dozen Glasgow Boys that were exhibited in London later that year, after which the paintings proceeded to Munich and cosmopolitan fame. Years later Neil looked back on his own part with quiet satisfaction: 'It was locally in the *Glasgow Evening News* alone that the insurgent group, somewhat difficult to define and classify, was given recognition as something of a national, and even international, portent.'

Neil's friendship with Macaulay Stevenson and Hornel proved lasting. Years later, in 1902, Stevenson's future wife, Stansmore Dean, would paint Neil's portrait. In particular, Neil got on well with Pittendrigh Macgillivray, the only sculptor among the Glasgow

Boys and a fiery 'Glue-pot' baiter. 'Macdevilry', as he was nicknamed, wrote poetry attacking the RSA...

A thing they ca' Academy –

An inartistic, senseless thing...

In Macgillivray, Neil recognised a kindred spirit to whom he would, in coming years, reveal himself with unwonted frankness.

CHAPTER ELEVEN

I believe I know the heart of the Highland people

IN late October 1890 Neil heard that the *News* was 'not in the most satisfactory condition'. He wrote to two London papers, the *Star* and the *Daily News*, enquiring about prospects, but without success. Just then a book called *Liberty and A Living* by Philip G. Herbert, an American, came into Neil's hands. It transformed his ambition overnight: 'A week ago I was all for going to London; today I feel mainly in consequence of reading this book that no other lot on earth is half so happy as that of a man living in his own house in the country, as the author of *Liberty and A Living* does, on a small income of £100 a year.'[1]

Perhaps as a first small step in that direction, Neil tried his hand at a Christmas story for *Scottish Sport*, which took him '6 or 8 hours'. He earned a further 10s by writing a St Andrew's Night speech 'for a gentleman'. At the end of 1890 he noted that his income had fluctuated between £3.15s and £4.10s a week, i.e. about £200 for the year, but to achieve that he had to keep hard at the grindstone of journalism. His dream of living in the country, writing stories for a living, would have to wait.

Fortunately the *News* was not in quite so parlous a state as the previous year's upheavals had suggested. A new Marinoni press, printing 9,000 an hour, was acquired early in 1891, and in April the *News* staff had their first annual dinner: 'Office pays. Capital affair.' With the newspaper game looking up, Neil was able to take a small step towards his rustic idyll by moving his family to Hillfoot Terrace, Bearsden, then a quasi-rural area just outside Glasgow. The idea of freeing himself from journalism that had possessed him since Herbert's book had re-awakened his literary dreams. As he travelled in and out of Glasgow, questions of form, content and style jostled in his head against the arithmetic of the family budget and the material he had to deal with on the *News*.

Early in 1891 a *News* colleague, John Harvey, had become assistant editor of the *Newcastle Weekly Courant*, which journal then obligingly accepted two short stories from Neil – 'How the Jeweller of Alnbury was Duped' and 'Dr Everton Sharp's Experiment'. The titles betray a certain lack of wholeheartedness as to choice of genre, but it was a start.

In May J.M. Smith told Neil his salary was to be increased by 10s to £3.10s – a rise which was inexplicably not implemented till October 1894. Meanwhile, in the August of 1891, Neil agreed to become co-editor of the periodical *Quiz*. 'All I do is to supply paragraphs & little articles.' This he would do for over a year.

That summer Neil and Jessie went to London for four days, leaving Effie with Jessie's sister Agnes. Young Hugh had now entered the world of work, as a compositor on the *News*. On their return, the Munros paid a visit to Inveraray, where there was a Volunteer camp at the Deer Park and Neil 'spent a good deal of time in the lines of A. Coy (Inveraray)'. It was a happy time, with little Effie now approaching her second birthday and able to enjoy being with her grandmother. But the year would close on a sad note. On Christmas Day, 1891, Neil's stepfather Malcom Thomson died. Neil's mother was left just £50, and from that time it can be surmised that Neil supported her. With another dependant on his hands, he must have despaired of ever freeing himself to concentrate on literature.

Early in 1892, with J.M. Smith, Neil designed a specimen copy of a literary weekly, which was set up and printed. But the idea was soon abandoned because a General Election was imminent. By now work had taken precedence also over the impracticable rural idyll at Bearsden, and in February 1892 the Munros moved back into Glasgow and took up residence at 21 Gibson Street (three rooms and kitchen, £23 p.a.). It was near the university, and far handier for Neil's work. That month his mother visited them there, and went to Buffalo Bill's Wild West show with Jessie, Neil and Charlie Maitland!

Now approaching his 30th year, Neil attempted to become involved in the pursuits of a normal, settled family man. About this time he played his first round of golf. Two years earlier he had been raised to the third Degree of Master Mason in Inveraray St John Masonic Lodge. But he was neither an ardent Mason nor a keen golfer, just as his piano playing never progressed.

Since publication of Neil's two short stories in the *Newcastle Weekly Courant*, six months had passed with no word of more fiction in his diary. Then on 25 August 1892, he noted: 'Sent a short sketch in a Highland manner, called "Anapla's Boy", to *Blackwood's Magazine*.' This was clearly a new departure, quite different from the two earlier tales and a further 'sensational' story, 'The Prisoner That Puzzled A Prince' which *Cassell's Saturday Journal* would accept in a letter received the day after 'Anapla's Boy' was posted off to *Blackwood's*.

During September *Cassell's* and *Black & White*, a new art periodical, both accepted pieces of work. Also the *Globe*, a 'penny pink' London evening paper, accepted a humorous article, 'The Garb Of Old Gaul'. Writing such 'turnovers' for the *Globe* was then held to be a first step in literature, and Neil contributed them for a good while. They were printed anonymously, earning him a guinea a time. The editor said his work 'considerably enlivened the column'.

'The formula,' Neil would recall, 'was merely to accept the Cockney assumption that north of the Tweed we were bucolically naive and daft... I wrote in the spirit of burlesque... expecting my London readers to perceive the chaff and irony. They didn't. Finding myself in danger of being regarded as an earnest adherent of the Kailyard school, I switched off.'[2] These London reactions foreshadow 'politically correct' misinterpretation of Harry Lauder's humour a century later.

Neil, still waiting to hear from *Blackwood's* about 'Anapla's Boy', sent a short story in the same vein – 'The Secret Of The Heather-Ale' – to the *Cornhill Magazine*. It was returned immediately. He then sent it to *The Speaker*, where it appeared in the December 1892 number – the first of his truly original work to achieve print. It had been a bold stroke to submit this Argyllshire tale, bristling with unpronounceable Gaelic names and oblique historical references, to London magazines not yet *au fait* with the Celtic renaissance.

In the meantime, having had his elbow politely jogged, William Blackwood had regretfully declined 'Anapla's Boy' as too slight, but Neil's disappointment vanished at the next words in Blackwood's letter: 'Should you again try your hand on a Highland sketch, I shall be very pleased to see it...'[3]

Thus emboldened, Neil opened his heart to the unknown

Blackwood about what he had been aiming for in the rejected story: 'It was a first and tentative effort on the part of a young man to deal with the West Highlands and the West Highland people in a modern way as distinguished from the conventional style where the "local colour" depends simply on bagpipes and bad English... I have taken the liberty of sending herewith the present number of *The Speaker*, which contains a story by me. Apart from any merit it may have, I think it shows that in the West Highlands there is a rich field for the writer that has not yet been fully explored.'[4]

Neil came to think that Blackwood had been right to reject 'Anapla's Boy', yet in it 'there was the first idea of the "Lost Pibroch" manner'. In other words, he had 'found himself', as all artists must. 'How? I don't know. But when it happens he will know it himself, with a gush of gladness at the discovery...'[5]

So far it was clearly impossible to give up journalism. Of Neil's £265 income for 1892, only £12 had come from stories and freelance articles. Yet somehow he had saved £75 (around £3,500 by today's values), presumably towards getting enough together to become independent.

Striking before the anvil cooled, he sent another Highland story to *Blackwood's* early in 1893 – 'Shudderman Soldier.' Also he started a story about a pipers' duet, 'The Lost Pibroch'. Eventually *The Speaker* sent him £4 for 'The Secret Of The Heather-Ale' – more than his week's *News* salary, but the time-lag of four or five months between writing the story and payment was discouraging.

Nevertheless, February 1893 was a banner month for Neil, and not just in literary terms. On 11 February, the day after the cheque from *The Speaker* arrived, Jessie gave birth to their first son, named Hugh Adam after her father. For them both it was a time of great joy.

Although *The Speaker* then rejected 'The Red Hand', Neil submitted it to W.E. Henley's *National Observer*, and it was published, albeit anonymously, in the June number – just in time for his 30th birthday. It was a distinct feather in Munro's cap to have work accepted by Henley. Later that summer, the *National Observer* would carry Yeats's poem 'The Celtic Twilight'. Henley also published Kipling, Hardy, Swinburne and Stevenson. According to H.G. Wells, the *National Observer* was then 'at the height of its career of heroic insistence upon lyrical brevity and a vivid finish',[6] qualities evident in Neil's early work.

At last William Blackwood wrote accepting 'Shudderman Soldier', adding: 'Have you been writing anything since you sent me the MS, and what literary projects have you in mind? I shall be interested in hearing from you.'[7] Neil's prompt response, enclosing a copy of the *National Observer* with 'The Red Hand', shows he was well aware of seed-sowing. It begins by reflecting Blackwood's stately tone, becomes confidential and ends with a flourish in a declaration of intent.

'I am very much gratified by your encouraging letter... and I am particularly gratified by the kind inquiry as to my prospects... To a young man, absolutely without what is – perhaps in a mistaken way – described as "influence", and working without the advice of anyone of literary experience, your expression of interest could hardly fail to be welcome and heartening... I am engaged at present in the capacity of reporter, note-writer, and gossip-in-general to one of the evening papers here, consequently I have little leisure to devote to the more congenial pursuit of story-writing, and my productive power is not very rapid...

'The tales you have seen afford, I think, a fairly good idea of the scope and character of the field in which I am of opinion I ought to work. I am a Highlander by birth and upbringing; I know the language and I believe I know the heart of the Highland people. If I have but the technical ability, I have, I think, the imagination and the material to make good stuff of a style no modern writer is attempting. That being so, it is my ambition to put together a sufficient number of Highland sketches... to make into a book wherewith to test my luck. However far I reach in that direction, I shall not forget the courtesy and sympathy of the Editor of *Maga*. With apologies for so long a personal statement...'[8]

William Blackwood – a very different kettle of fish from Henley – was a bachelor in his late fifties, benevolent autocrat of the bookish empire founded by his grandfather. Other publishing-houses had their magazines, but none was so well-known as *Blackwood's Magazine*, with its familiar nickname. *Maga* serials usually turned into Blackwood books, and Neil was understandably eager to establish an association with the firm. Its very Scottishness was a further advantage in his eyes.

This early correspondence, with its human quirks, led to an association that would outlast both men. Blackwood would shrewdly assess Neil's potential, taking the 'personal statement' with a grain of salt. There were grounds for guarded optimism in his letter enclosing a cheque for eight guineas at the end of August. This advance payment was very heartening. Blackwood explained companionably that 'Shudderman Soldier' would be held over till

October's *Maga*, 'when perhaps its appearance will be more season-able and opportune, as it is more of a winter sketch than a summer one... When you have any more of your Highland sketches for me to examine, it will give me much pleasure to see them, and if I can help you in the publication of a volume by and bye it will give me pleasure to give you the best advice I can in the matter.'⁹

This welcome letter came just after Neil's return from his summer break at Inveraray. Even on holiday with the family, he had not relin-quished his reporter's instincts, which brought him a notable scoop. He heard that a 17-year-old youth called Cecil Hambrough had been killed on 10 August in an alleged shooting accident at Ardlamont House in Cowal. By chance Neil met the Depute Fiscal of Argyll who had just returned from Ardlamont. He suddenly said to Neil that he had grave doubts about the case... then he clammed up.

Before leaving Inveraray Neil asked the local correspondent of the *News* – who was also an official of the County Court! – to wire him at the *News* office if the police took any action. Several days later a succinct telegram came: 'Go to Ardlamont.' He hastened down and got an account of the incident from the factor, who believed Hambrough's death was an accident, although he had not witnessed it. But there might be more to it than that.

As Neil hurried back down to the pier in his hired trap to catch the *Lord of the Isles* on her return journey from Inveraray, he was just in time to see disembarking from her the Chief Constable of Argyll and several Sheriff Court officers. Next day his 'scoop' article 'The Ardlamont Mystery' appeared in the *News* to the consternation of the Crown Authorities in Edinburgh, where the case was still being dismissed as a shooting accident.

Hambrough's tutor Alfred Monson, however, was charged with the murder. At the trial in December (which Neil reported and where Dr Joseph Bell, the original for Sherlock Holmes, appeared as a medical witness) it came out that Monson was in dire financial straits and had insured Hambrough's life for £20,000 – yet the verdict was 'not proven'. Neil earned £19.12s.6d extra from the *Daily Graphic* for his report of the trial.

His literary work, too, was beginning to bear fruit financially. Just after receiving the welcome advance for 'Shudderman Soldier' – 'very generous payment,' he told William Blackwood – Neil was engaged to write a serial story for a magazine called *Quips*. He entitled it 'The Afton Moor Mystery' – 'they say it must be a mystery' – and used the pen name George Gaunt, to dissociate it from more esoteric ventures. For thirteen weekly episodes he was to earn £26.

In September Neil went down to London for a journalists' conference, with Emile Zola attending the dinner at the Crystal Palace. While down south, Neil took the opportunity to call on W.E. Henley at the *National Observer* office near Westminster Abbey. J. Nicol Dunn, the assistant editor, knew Neil and sent him upstairs to see Henley, whom he found 'wearing a white linen jacket, leaning out of the window, taking the air. He was affable, wondered where I got the "style" of my prose, and suggested Macaulay! I didn't see it myself. (It might have been Macaulay's grandfather [once minister of Inveraray] if he wrote, as he probably spoke, Gaelic, and I had happened to see what he wrote.) He advised me to go on with similar tales to "The Red Hand". 'The thing is to build brick on brick,' he said, 'and you'll wonder how you get a whole wall.'[10]

Neil was much affected by the casual words of encouragement. It relieved the isolation of literary effort to imagine being one of 'Henley's young men'. There was further encouragement back in Glasgow that November, when Neil was promoted from being chief reporter 'to do extra special literary work, reviews, leaders, special articles and interviews, and Lorgnette'. His salary, however, remained at £3.10s a week.

On 9 January 1894, Neil wrote in his diary: 'Finished Afton Mystery. (Thank goodness!)' The exercise was too ill-paid and time-consuming to be a substitute for daily journalism, and he did not repeat it. Besides, churning out such stuff unfitted him for more serious writing, and he was still very far from accumulating a book's worth of tales. On the positive side, he started the year with an unprecedented bank balance of £140, his 1893 income from all sources having been £250.

In February, an 'exceedingly kind and encouraging letter' came from William Blackwood. Neil replied, reiterating his intention to supply 'at some early date' enough West Highland stories to make a volume. Again he opened his heart with a touch of bravado: 'I am not the most impartial judge, perhaps, but I have a strong belief, amounting almost to a certainty, that my sketches have something of the stuff of popularity in them. They strike upon a field absolutely untouched for one thing, being purely Celtic in their treatment of the Highland Celt and Highland Scenery, whereas all the men who have dealt with the romance of the Highlands hitherto have been Lowlanders writing from the outside.

'The Barrie-Crockett-Maclaren "boom" has confined itself to the

Lowlands; the stuff they deal with is becoming attenuated and runs to seed. Here – or I am a Dutchman! – is a new vein, rich and untried. It should appeal to English readers even more than the Lowland Scots stories, for it dispenses almost entirely with dialect, at all events a glossary is unnecessary.

'We are having a Scots revival in literature, and now or never is, I recognise, the chance for anyone who would expound the genuine Highland character and direct attention to the illimitable stores of romance and poetry still lying in the old glens. I wish I could, if it never brought me a penny. All this I write to you with what is, for me, unusual freedom and egotism because I am touched by the friendly and generous tone of your letters.'[11]

The term 'Kailyard School' had not yet been invented, hence the reference to 'the Barrie-Crockett-Maclaren "boom"'. Though Neil did not name other Scottish novelists such as Fergus Mackenzie, John Tweeddale and D.S. Meldrum, he was mindful of them, and would have been sad to find their work neglected in future studies of the genre.

It is remarkable that he wrote of 'a Scots revival in literature' just then. He could not know that Stevenson, in Samoa, was writing *Weir of Hermiston*, his unfinished masterpiece. He could not know that 'Fiona Macleod' would publish her first Celtic-crepuscular novel – *Pharais* – in 1894. He could not know that 1894 would one day be described as 'the supreme moment of kailyardism'.[12]

Strangely, after Neil's almost ebullient letter to Blackwood, the relationship languished for many months. In March 1894 Blackwood rejected a story called 'Thumb Hero' and the *National Observer* rejected 'The Sgeul of Black Murdo'. Perhaps disappointed by these setbacks, Neil took a break from his writing desk. In July, he went on his own for a week's sail by S.S. *Claymore*, journeying from Oban by Tobermory, Portree and Lochinver to Stornoway – a first glimpse of the Hebrides. He returned refreshed, and in September he sent off the once-rejected 'Sgeul of Black Murdo' to Blackwood. If Neil was hoping for a prompt response, he would be disappointed: Blackwood did nothing with it for the next five months.

Meanwhile Scotland went through a bitterly cold winter, with the coldest weather for 35 years causing great distress in Glasgow where the temperature fell to 6.6F in February 1895. A relief fund of £8,000 was raised. The Munros, like everyone else, had no water in the house for four weeks and had to use *extempore* street wells. Neil spent two days skating on Loch Lomond with a new friend, his colleague David Hodge, recovering the rapture of his last winter at home in Inveraray when Loch Fyne had frozen over. Then, as if heralding a return to better weather, a letter arrived from William Blackwood. Accepting 'The Sgeul of Black Murdo' for *Maga*, he continued: 'If you will send me everything else you have written beyond what I have accepted for the Magazine, I shall see about publishing the sketches in book form and give you a chance of attracting the attention of the public. Your West Highland stories are unique in their way, and though it is more than doubtful how they might strike English readers, I am willing to undertake the risk of such a volume to sell at say 3s 6d, and should there be any profits I shall divide them equally with you.'[13]

Neil's reactions are not recorded. He was bound to feel joy and relief at the definite proposal. Yet, though he had prated of his indifference to profit from his Highland tales, the implication that there might not be any profit at all was chilling. In fact Blackwood's terms were reasonable for their day – Conrad, for instance, sold the copyright of his first novel outright for £20 in 1894 – and at least Neil was compensated when his tales were in *Maga* and other magazines. Most importantly, he now had a firm offer from Blackwood to publish his first book. He began to spend every spare moment putting together the collection of tales that would become *The Lost Pibroch & Other Shieling Stories*.

As usual there were many other calls on his attention, including assisting his old boyhood friend to get married. In May Neil noted in his diary: 'Sent engagement rings to Chas Maitland to pick one for Kate Lemon!' June and July were spent in lodgings at Canniesburn Toll, near Bearsden. There was drama in July when a mad barber called Petrie caused a shindig in the *News* office: Neil kicked him downstairs. In August, he heard James Chalmers the missionary preach in the Pavilion at Inveraray. (Chalmers, who had been a fellow-passenger of R.L. Stevenson on a voyage from Sydney to Samoa in 1890, was killed by cannibals in New Guinea in 1901.)

That same month there was a fresh journalistic opportunity. On the 22nd Neil noted in his diary 'started the column entitled "Views & Reviews" in the *News* in succession to J. Nicol Dunn.' It was a step in the right direction, into a little kingdom of his own.

CHAPTER TWELVE

The said Celtic glamour

IN the August of 1895, a curious shadow-flyting began. One protagonist, unwittingly so at first, was the mysterious Fiona Macleod, the other the anonymous writer of the column 'Views & Reviews' in the *Glasgow Evening News*, who just happened to be preparing a collection of Highland stories for publication.

Neil found editorial supervision of his new column was of the sketchiest – all he had to do was produce his two thousand words a week regularly – and there is a certain nonchalance about his early reviews. He was enjoying his new fief, developing his own judgments and articulating his reactions to his contemporaries. His second 'Views & Reviews' began:

"'Have you read *The Mountain Lovers* by Fiona MacLeod?" a bookseller asked me the other day, and I confessed I had never heard of them. I straightway procured me a copy. I read two pages and was rewarded with a clamjamfry of fine words! The second chapter fetched me up like a rasper fence, but I found a convenient gateway into the next, and got the length of the middle of the book, where I stuck. *The Mountain Lovers* is one of those feminine indulgences in the fal-lals of language. Mr Grant Allen, however, has been pleased to find in Fiona Macleod "something Ossianic" and "the spirit of the Celtic twilight"... If Fiona Macleod gets on like this she'll find herself famous before she knows where she is. Still, I wish her well, all the more because she has provided me with the text for a brief homily on the abuse of the phrase "Celtic glamour"... the said Celtic glamour, the true Gaelic romance, the mixture of ferocity, elfish fancy, pride, *"infinie délicatesse de sentiment"* which struck M. Renan, have never been expressed in English by any Scots writer since J.F. Campbell of Islay collected and translated his folklore and heroic tales into an English... steeped in Gaelic sentiment... The trick of this seems to have been lost in North Britain [sic] with the death of Campbell, but Ireland has produced at least two Anglo-Celtic writers [Tynan and Yeats] who have made the "glamour" of the Irish Celtic character plain to see even by the phlegmatic Sassenach.'[1]

The sculptor Pittendrigh Macgillivray, who had abandoned Glasgow for Edinburgh, where he was now 'living in respectability and comparative affluence', wrote a few days later, asking if Neil himself was Fiona Macleod. Neil at once denied that he was 'the said Fiona, whom I never heard of till ten days ago'. Even though he had been doing 'extra special literary work' for two years, the volume of new fiction was then so great that it is quite conceivable that he should not have come across Fiona Macleod before. It must have been a considerable jolt at first to think his own field suddenly invaded, yet he quickly recovered his equanimity.

That September, Neil accompanied the Inveraray Pipe Band on a march through Glencoe. There were apprehensions that the band, with its strong Campbell affiliation, would meet with hostility in that glen of sorrow and infamy, but no obstruction was offered and Neil returned unscathed to Glasgow to continue his literary endeavours. Soon he was able at last to note in his diary: 'Sent MS The Lost Pibroch and other Sheeling [sic] Stories to Blackwood.' Four weeks later he heard that William Blackwood (then abroad) would publish the book in the spring of 1896. Two of the tales would be in *Maga* shortly beforehand, 'to push you forward'. And furthermore, the letter ended, 'he hopes you will enable him to follow up the volume with another as good in due course as the most likely way to ensure a lasting success'.[2]

Elated by this confidence in him, Neil soon put the finishing touches to his set of eleven stories and prepared a Gaelic glossary. He even had energy to spare to pen a New Year story for *The Bailie* magazine. Blackwood had baulked at the story 'Jus Primae Noctis' on the grounds that it was 'sufficiently broad to give critics a handle should they want one'.[3] Neil accepted this without comment and wrote two more stories, 'Castle Dark' and 'A Fine Pair of Shoes', to replace it. He was vindicated when Henley published 'Jus Primae Noctis' in his *New Review* in 1897. In 1935 Blackwoods would include it in their Inveraray Edition of his works.

Yet even as Neil was completing his first book, he found the tantalising Fiona Macleod advancing further into Scotland: her new novel, *The Sin-Eater*, was published that autumn by Patrick Geddes, Edinburgh, whereas the earlier two had English publishers. Neil had met Geddes, who had once got him in front of a picture of Rossetti's and expatiated on its spiritual aura: Neil found Rossetti morbid and was unconverted. He reviewed *The Sin-Eater* sternly:

'To anyone who is Gaelic and understands what she is striving for, the shortcomings of the book will no doubt be far more apparent than to such critics as find in her a "new voice", the expression of a race hitherto very much left alone by the writer of fiction... To paint the Scottish Gael as if he were eternally listening to the wail of Ossianic ghosts, looking out for corp-lights and strumming his clarsach to plaintive numbers is to misrepresent a very varied and interesting people. Besides his musings on the hill, he had and has his noisy nights in the change house, and his laugh and song at the ceilidh fire; when he was harrying the adjacent clans there was about him a fine lovable zest for adventure, his songs are often of love and roaming, but rarely of death and ghosts. The Gael Miss Macleod knows, in short, is the Gael who has been made by the Free Kirk – a very different fellow from the Gael who carried pike and hagbut with Gustavus Adolphus – a very different Gael from Allan Breck – who, though imagined by a lowlander, is as highland as Mull...'[4]

Neil, still quite unaware of Fiona Macleod's true identity, alluded to her 'inexperience' and added: 'She will improve; she may, indeed, arrive, and for the sake of *tir nan og* and some other things I hope she shall.'

That November Neil went to Rothie Brisbane near Fyvie, Aberdeenshire, and stayed with Miss Chalmers in order to copy unpublished letters of Gilbert Burns, afterwards printed in the *News*. Two days later he was at the wedding of Charlie Maitland and Kate Lemon in the George Hotel, Inveraray, and the day after that he was at the Glasgow Inveraray Ball, having spent £20 on new Highland dress.

In December, the second number of *The Evergreen*, Geddes's ephemeral 'Celtic revival' quarterly, came out, but Neil was unmoved: 'There is something alluring, I must confess, in the idea of a Scottish magazine or review on pompous lines, but the pomp must be no affair of tinsel, brass sequins and *papier-mâché* mail, which, I regret to say, it is in the case of *The Evergreen*. The prefatory note "gars you grue", so stupidly pretentious is it, with its rocky sentences and sham "culchaw".'[5]

Neil began 1896 with just £70 in the bank, only half the amount he had saved two years before. But matters were progressing well on the literary front: the first proofs of *The Lost Pibroch* arrived on 11 January, while 'The Sgeul of Black Murdo' appeared in February's *Maga*, eliciting from Conan Doyle in Egypt the comment: 'I think it is the finest thing I have read for a long time, with the true Celtic romance touch.'[6]

On the home front, Jessie and Neil's third daughter, Lilian McArthur, was born that February. Yet, despite all the excitement, Neil still found himself confined for much of the time to humdrum journalism. He wrote to his friend Pittendrigh Macgillivray: 'I'm sorry I can't get through to Edinburgh tomorrow; it happens to be one of the days when I have to attend a pestiferous Town Council meeting and write a column of comic "copy" for the following day about the Bailie MacKellars and other mechanical personages of that august body.'[7] Already there is a hint of the disenchantment that led to his nickname for journalism, the 'jawbox' (kitchen sink). He once wrote of someone coming 'unscathed through forty years of active journalism, with all that implies of disillusionment, of futilities, of vain material things'.[8]

In March, 1896, shortly before publication of *The Lost Pibroch*, Neil reviewed the Evergreen Press anthology *Lyra Celtica*. It included eleven pages of Fiona Macleod's poetry (compared with just seven of Duncan Ban Macintyre's), and was edited by Elizabeth Sharp, with a long introduction by William Sharp, her husband, whose writings and journalism were of course known to Neil. The book even looked confoundedly like *The Lost Pibroch*, green with a Celtic motif, and surpassed it insofar as it had an attractively illustrated title-page – Neil had wanted just such a title-page, but Blackwoods said it was not a custom of theirs. Neil's review of *Lyra Celtica* was pugnacious:

'On the whole, it is a very interesting and helpful volume...But it is a volume for the Saxon and not for the Celt. This so-called Celtic Revival in Edinburgh is rather a curious thing. It is engineered very largely, I think, by people of no Celtic pedigree, and perhaps the only Celtic scholar in it is Mr Alexander Carmichael, whose knowledge of Gaelic, of Hebridean folklore and hymnology, is greater than that of any living man. I have an old Parliamentary Blue-Book with the evidence of the Crofters' Commission in which Mr Carmichael contributes casually and off-hand more useful matter to the literature of Celticism than anything that the Edinburgh movement has yet produced. There is a Celtic revival of a far more genuine interest than the Edinburgh one, which the Edinburgh enthusiasts are quite incapable of understanding. It is to be found in the Highlands, and to some extent in Glasgow and London; it is producing valuable and lasting work in MacBean's new Gaelic dictionary and other recent examples of the Gaelic Press, recovering the lost lore of the Highlands, and reviving a Highland interest in the works of the Gaelic bards.'[9]

A week later, Neil went to Edinburgh and had a long interview with Wood of Blackwoods at 45 George Street. He was offered 100 guineas to write a history of Argyll for their County Series. He refused, and recommended that Donald Mackinnon, first Professor of Gaelic at Edinburgh University, should do it. Was the identity of Fiona Macleod also discussed at that meeting in Blackwood's saloon, less than a mile from the Outlook Tower, lair of *The Evergreen*? At any rate, Neil tackled the subject manfully in his 'Views & Reviews' the very next day:

'"Who is Fiona Macleod?" a correspondent asks me. The identity of this interesting protegee of Professor Patrick Geddes has puzzled a good many people, and some odd guesses have been made at the authorship of the quaint volumes which have been lately issued with that name on the title page. The first and natural surmise was that "Fiona Macleod" was a *nom-de-plume*, but this idea was temporarily set aside by a report... that the lady was a daughter of the late Norman MacLeod... the Norman MacLeod connection was believed in till recently, when we were told that the mysterious Fiona was a cousin of Mr William Sharp's wife. She is said to be a native of the Hebrides and an invalid... all business communications... are addressed to Mr Sharp's house in Murrayfield. This, combined with the fact that the fair authoress seems to be inaccessible to anyone, has roused a suspicion in many quarters that the credit for the literary form of *Pharaïs*, *The Sin-Eater* &c is due either to Mr Sharp or his wife, both of whom have some Celtic knowledge and the ability to put it to use. I give this tale of the mystery of Fiona for what it is worth. It may turn out that she has a real flesh and blood existence.'[10]

For the time being, Neil had more important concerns of his own. A few days later, the postman climbed the stone stairs to the Munros' front door at 21 Gibson Street to deliver a copy of his first book, *The Lost Pibroch & Other Sheiling Stories*. He was a published author at last, and there was plenty more taking shape in his fertile imagination. A fortnight later, Neil would begin *John Splendid*, his first novel.

CHAPTER THIRTEEN

Aora mo chridhe tha mi seoladh

SOON after completing the manuscript of *The Lost Pibroch*, Neil had written to Pittendrigh Macgillivray: 'Whether the Tales... will turn out a kirk or a mill, the Lord kens: they are at any rate richt curious to behauld, and wrocht out of mine ain inner bowels the whilk is not to be said of muckle that ye read.'[1]

On publication the book was acclaimed at once by reviewers north and south of the Border. 'To the majority of English readers, so veracious a presentment of Celtic manners and feeling will be little less than a revelation,' wrote the *Athenaeum*'s reviewer, succumbing to the book's authoritative tone. The *Literary World* envisaged Neil 'springing at a bound from the bottom rung of the literary ladder to firm foothold not far from its summit'.

In form and in content, *The Lost Pibroch* was innovative. The short story form, pioneered by Scott and Hogg, was much in favour in the 1890s, but for the Highlands there were only the Rev Norman MacLeod's pious Gaelic fables, of little use to Neil as a model. Fiona Macleod's first Celtic renaissance book, *Pharaïs*, had indeed appeared two years before *The Lost Pibroch*, but several of Neil's tales had been printed even earlier, and he had his 'Highland manner' well established in his own mind before reading *Pharaïs*.

The eponymous first tale of *The Lost Pibroch* opens with the words: 'To the make of a piper go seven years of his own learning and seven generations before.' The book was the fruit of many years dwelling on aspects of Argyll, where Neil's forebears had been settled since time immemorial. The tales seem to rise from moods in which the writer feels still in touch with his boyhood self.

They are all set in or near Inveraray, some before 'the wars that scorched the glens' in 1644, and none much later than 1840. A few sources and influences are casually acknowledged, including Neil's mother (implying his grandmother also), 'the writings of my Lord Archie' and 'the writings of 'Iain Og of Isla'. In his *Records of Argyll* (1885) Lord Archibald Campbell explicitly encourages others 'to treasure up the tales of the past'. But it was the exceptional *Popular Tales of the West Highlands*, collected and translated from the Gaelic by John Francis Campbell of Islay (Iain Og Ile), published in

1860–62 and re-issued in 1890, that impressed Neil more deeply. He treasured its long and thoughtful introduction and the language of the translations, which he described as 'an English which is steeped in Gaelic sentiment'.[2] Campbell's book was a vital support when Neil began to combine his own knowledge of Gaelic with his new-found fictive powers, taking the West Highland past for theme. No more aping Kipling or fabricating detective stories!

The outcome was Neil's half-incantatory 'Lost Pibroch manner', as he called it. Like Campbell, but sparingly, he reproduced Gaelic idioms in English. He also used many Gaelic place-names, unusual Christian names such as Marseli, Ellar and Giorsal, and other linguistic devices. Such a densely allusive text might have been rebarbative, yet it works by giving vivid imagery without impeding the narrative. Nor is it far-fetched to see in *The Lost Pibroch* some reflection of the work of the Glasgow Boys, Neil's painter friends.

Neil's use of language to suggest the Gaelic world has been praised by the scholar Ronald Black, who wrote of his 'following the inherited instincts of a traditional memory for which this reviewer has unbounded respect'.[3]

Often, in fiction, the Highlands seem merely a backdrop to a few isolated figures, but Neil's books from the start give a sense of entering (or re-entering) a living community in real places. Most of the *Lost Pibroch* tales deal with death, or revenge, or separation: men are pushed over a cliff or perish in a snow-storm, a child starves, a woman dies in child-birth. But all through, as counterpoint, are glimpses of simple Gaelic homeliness, as in 'The Fell Sergeant': 'She sat propped up in a box-bed, on pillows, with her face to the open door, and the friendly airs of the country-side came in to stir her… they brought her who was at her end a keen craving for one more summer of the grand world.'

This tale and 'Shudderman Soldier' are set at Lecknamban (Ladyfield), childhood home of Neil's mother, and both tales suggest a base in family lore. In 'The Sea-Fairy of French Foreland' the Sea-Fairy is really an *émigré* who has sailed in the last of the French ships to come to Loch Fyne to trade wine for cured herrings. At that time, about 1798, Neil's grandfather John Munro was actually living at Auchindrain, near French Foreland, and might well have encountered the 'French traffickers'. This interweaving of details familiar to himself would always characterise Neil's work. Kurt Wittig recognised in it 'the genuine Gaelic tradition… as in Alexander Macdonald or in Duncan McIntyre…'[4]

Three of the tales are about the blind piper Paruig Dall. In the first he is persuaded to play the Lost Tune, the *piobaireachd* that 'leaves one hungry at the heart'. As he foretells, it has the same effect as when he heard it in Glen Aray: 'In the morning the weans were without fathers, and Carnus men were scattered about the wide world.' The tale can be read as an allegory for the depopulation of the Highlands.

An underlying motif of *The Lost Pibroch* is a harking-back to a half-mythical golden age in Real Argyll, when 'the two glens were crowded with warm homes... Good stout roads and dry went down the passes to Castle Dark from all airts of Albainn... By sea came gabbarts of far France with wine and drink; by land the carriers brought rich cloths, spices and Italian swords' ('Castle Dark').

This linking of Argyll to the wide world beyond became a recurrent theme in Neil's work. He would develop and grow as a novelist, but his first collection of stories was near-perfect in its own way and could never be outshone. Eighteen years later, John Buchan would write of the 'imaginative height' of *The Lost Pibroch*, and declare: 'Such a pitch can scarcely be reached more than once in a man's life.'[5] Neil was perhaps aware of this when he said of another writer, George Douglas Brown: 'To be hailed as a prodigy and a portent on a first performance I am superstitious enough to regard as a misfortune for any young Scot who aspires to a permanent literary reputation.'[6]

Financially, the first returns from *The Lost Pibroch* were slight, as if to fulfil Neil's wish to expound 'the genuine Highland character... if it never brought me a penny'. A year after publication, Blackwoods would send him a cheque for just £4.13s.4d, his share of the profits. Nevertheless, the book would remain in print almost all his life, bringing in a small but steady income.

It brought him also a letter that Neil would treasure all his life. The writer, William Allan, was I believe a former colleague on the *Falkirk Herald*.

'Son of the Gael – Thro' the kindness of Friend Ford (who spent Sunday last with us here) I have enjoyed a most unexpected and delightful treat – to wit – he sent to my daughter Teenie a copy of *The Lost Pibroch* – I began it and ended it ere I slept – It is a Real Book – writ with an Ossianic pen and truly Highland soul – each story is a prose poem – not like many of the present day Scottish stories that seem dug out of the byre and writ with a spurtle – I cannot waste time over such stuff – Jean (who was brought up in Isla) is now engrossed in the Vol – and mark ye – it is only 9.15AM!!!

'I could not resist expressing to you how much I am pleased to know that we have a truly Highland writer at last – My wish – and hope – is that you will continue – give us more of such work – and we will –

> 'While heather blooms and bluebells grow,
> Long bless the name of Neil Munro.'

In April 1896, a month after *The Lost Pibroch* came out, the Munros moved round the corner from Gibson Street to 1 West Bank Quadrant, poised above the river Kelvin and Kelvingrove Park. In June Neil, writing to his cousin Kate McArthur (whose journalistic aspirations he was fostering), apologised for leaving a letter from her so long unanswered. 'The fact is that the youngsters developed measles a day or two after my last letter and from then till now this household has been more or less standing on its head. Effie is now convalescent, but Hugh has taken her place in bed and was at his worst a day or two ago... The baby so far has escaped, but the poor *mater* is worked off the face of the earth. Great moral lesson for you – Don't get married – unless you feel absolutely bound to.'[7]

This unwonted *cri-de-coeur* betrays how much pressure Neil was under. The novel he had started in March was preying on his mind, but it was hard even to find time and privacy for it, let alone to achieve the right frame of mind. There were diversions, however, and his circle of acquaintances began to widen once *The Lost Pibroch* was published.

Neil's social life was forming into an annual pattern: holidays at Inveraray, the Inveraray ball in Glasgow in November, occasional fishing trips and journeys on *News* business, the autumn outings of the Glasgow Ballad Club which ended with dinner in 'some judicious tavern'. Neil also belonged to the mysterious Thirteen Club, to which he once read a paper on Highland superstitions.

Two other small clubs he joined – the Grumphy and the 693 – were started by a Sasunnach, William Guilford, solely (it would seem) for the members' delectation: razor-fish croquettes, four-year-old sugared mutton, marrow bones, *méringue à la Tour de Babel* and so on. Apart from that, the delight of Glasgow Wednesdays, if it could be managed, was the traditional sheep's head, eaten *à même le crâne*.

> There's a'e thing certain, canna be denied,
> That sheep's-heid Wednesday made the fame o' Clyde.
> ('Rations', 1918)

Neil's mainstay was the Art Club in its splendid Bath Street premises. There one could repair at odd hours, perhaps find a few friends, or land up after a dinner elsewhere: 'Dined at Dr Donald MacLeod's, and afterwards took Sir Henry Jones to the Art Club, where we stayed till 1.20.' In June 1896, Neil noted: 'At supper in Art Club 11 p.m. till 4 a.m. with a party of thirteen including Sir Henry Irving, Mudie (of *Citizen*) my host in chair; Primrose, Bram Stoker [then Irving's manager] and others.'

In August 1896, Neil went to Edinburgh and met William Blackwood for the first time, along with his employee David Storrar Meldrum, a minor novelist who became Neil's first writer friend. Meldrum's own novels, although praised by Neil, have failed the test of time, but he is remembered for his early advocacy of Conrad. A Fife man, Meldrum had joined Blackwoods in 1896 as literary adviser, based in London, where Neil stayed with him more than once. He described Meldrum as 'one of the few men who give me the home feeling in the Strand'.

Another new acquaintance was Lord Archibald Campbell. Perusal of *The Lost Pibroch*, in which he is mentioned, apparently led him to track down the author. On 28 August 1896, Neil noted in his diary: 'Lunch with Lord Archd Campbell at St Catherine's and afterwards went through Inveraray Castle with him.'

Lord Archie, the Duke's second son, was then 50, and had been first President of An Comunn Gaidhealach. He had a house in St Catherine's, across the loch from Inveraray, but mostly lived in London, where he frequented artistic, even bohemian circles and was a junior partner in Coutts's Bank. 'Exactly what his position there was, I never knew,' Neil would recall. 'But he went daily to the office, from which he wrote me many letters on subjects far remote from banking, and he brought me with him to his room in the Bank several times.'

Yet pleasant though such meetings might be, they did not solve the problem of how Neil was to find the space to develop as a writer. There is a revelatory passage in a letter to George Murray of the *Falkirk Herald*, thanking him for his generous notice of *The Lost Pibroch*. Neil asks him, rather rhetorically: 'You don't happen to know of a lodge in some vast wilderness (with a good postal connection) where one could retire from the fret of city life and write masterpieces? I have got several in my head (the masterpieces I mean) but as to the time and requisite seclusion – oh lor! Still, we shall see anon.'[8]

A week later, on the day Effie started school, Neil wrote to sound his old schoolfriend Bob Fraser about 'going to Inveraray for good and taking the Cottage, earning a living by literature alone'. As a result, he applied to the factor for this house, whose location is unknown. But his diary entry of 15 October says cryptically: 'Same refused by the factor, acting for the Duke!'

On the day Neil wrote to the factor, he dined with J.M. Smith and other members of the *News* co-partnery. That evening it was decided to start a satirical paper, *St Mungo*. Neil, prevailed upon to edit it, envisaged 'a playground for all the bright young journalists'. The first issue, on 4 December, sold 20,000 copies, having been well publicised the day before. Mr Barlow, the fireworks manufacturer, was hired to discharge, from the roof of the *News* office at 67 Hope Street, *papier-mâché* bombs which would burst in the air and scatter leaflets. After two discharges from six-inch calibre mortars, so many leaflets had landed on the surrounding streets that the ploy had to be stopped. Neil placated the police in Gaelic.

On Christmas Eve, undaunted, he took up a new interest – riding lessons at the Tramway Company's school.

CHAPTER FOURTEEN

First day in the house as a Literary Man!

WHILE Neil brooded without much progress over the novel that would become *John Splendid*, the Edinburgh-based Celtic Revival was proceeding apace. In seeking to curb its worst excesses, Andrew Lang proved a useful ally, contributing an essay on William Sharp's new edition of *Ossian* to the February 1897 issue of *Maga*. Lang referred to 'the conquering legions who march... through the Promised Land of New Celtic Literature' and advised the Neo-Celts to do 'what Mr Neil Munro has begun to do for the West Highlands'.

To this Neil made a dry response in the *News*: 'I am sufficiently in the confidence of Mr Neil Munro to be able to state that the Evergreen Theory of the Celt is quite beyond his comprehension; that he never had the honour of intercourse with the inventors and projectors of that theory; and that if there is any marching to be done it will certainly not be under the banners of the Neo-Celts he will do it.'[1]

A few weeks later Fiona Macleod herself, whoever she might be, lobbed a missile right into the Munro camp. A small parcel was delivered at West Bank Quadrant. Inside Neil found a book and a hand-written letter:

> c/o Miss Rea,
> The Outlook Tower,
> Castlehill,
> Edinburgh.
> 15 March 1897

Dear Sir,
A friend has given me your address... Soon after you published your Lost Pibroch I meant to send you one of my books in witness of my cordial welcome to so fine a new Highland writer – but refrained when I learned that you were on the staff of the *Glasgow Evening News*: as I feared you might think I was sending to you as a reviewer... I regret that the exigencies of my private life prevent my having the pleasure of asking you to call upon me, for the present at any rate, and the more so as I am now very rarely in Edinburgh, and as it is more than likely that my troublesome health will keep me more and more at home in the very remote place where I spend the greater part of the year.
With cordial interest and regard,
Believe me,
Yours very truly,
FIONA MACLEOD.

If Neil could tweak Sharp's mask, Fiona could insinuate that the author of *The Lost Pibroch* was duplicitous. Neil was amused by the 'ingenuous attempt at mystification'. The only record of the next stage in the campaign consists of two undated letters from Sharp. What seems the earlier, written from Edinburgh, sounds like a request for a parley:

My Dear Mr Munro,
It is very good of you to come into Edinburgh... Probably the best arrangement for us both would be for me to meet you at Princes St Station... at 3.15 (Saturday extra train) – and then I hope you will come with me and have tea and a chat at the Café... failing

my appearance, come on to 9 Upper Coltbridge Terrace
[Murrayfield]. What a ghastly day!
Yours sincerely,
WILLIAM SHARP.

The other letter from Sharp, a sort of smokescreen, came from
Hampstead. The cutting mentioned sounds like Neil's article of 12
March the previous year, which perhaps reached Sharp only after
long delay:

Presumably Miss Macleod – or that other Lady, Circumstances –
will some day make clear what (I admit) is meanwhile a wise &
perhaps in a sense an unavoidable mystery, that is to me, now,
personally, a confounded nuisance. But this only in a badgered
literary way!... Of course, too, there is not a shadow of truth in
the rumour that Mrs Sharp is F.M. I write to you because I
recognise your hand in a cutting from the *Glasgow Evening News*.
Both in conversation in Edinburgh, & here, you are yourself (in
more than one essential point) away from the mark – though in
some respects you are of course (mainly, from what I confided in
you in private) better informed than most speculators... In one
matter I wilfully misled you, as in loyalty bound to do: for, devil
take you, you too were born north of the Highland line, & you
know the saying 'what the heather kens, the ling knows'. I also
write to say how much I like your fresh writing; & to ask if you
think there is any likelihood of your being in London on the 15th.
There is a big 'Vagabonds' dinner that night, & if you would be
my guest it would please
Yours sincerely,
WILLIAM SHARP

Whether or no Neil went to the dinner, he did meet Sharp several
times in Glasgow in the late Nineties, and once dined with Mrs
Sharp in a Glasgow hotel. O, to have overheard those conversations!
Neil certainly attended the 1897 dinner of the Highland Society
in London, as the guest of Lord Archie and his son Niall, who put
him up for two nights at the Metropole, where the dinner was held.
Neil's first afternoon was spent with D.S. Meldrum. He also spent
a day with Lord Archie and his daughter Elspeth at Coombe Hill
Farm near Kingston on Thames, and met Lady Archie briefly. Lord
Archie and his daughter drove back with him into London, parting
at the Princes Skating Club, a great haunt of theirs.

Neil had stayed with Meldrum in Kirkcaldy towards the end of 1896, and he now planned to spend a fortnight that summer in the Netherlands, partly with Meldrum, whose wife was Dutch. It was unprecedented for Neil to spend so long away from the *News* and his family, and only the second time he had been abroad. He sailed from Grangemouth to Rotterdam, where he got rid of pestering touts by addressing them in the Gaelic. At Utrecht he joined Meldrum and they had lunch, tea and dinner with Dutch friends. Next day, Meldrum being at a wedding, Neil took a canal boat to Frieswijk, walked along the Yssel dam, then to Oudewater, and so back to Utrecht – '...the same flat water-chequered country all the way, the same pollarded willows stretching in interminable lines to the same horizon where the windmills of yesterday, today and forever shared the sky-line with the towers of towns unknown... An empty landscape, pensive and brooding in the sunny day, only the storks busy on their pillars...'[2] He made many sketches, though he did not consider himself much of a draughtsman, and stuck a few in his diary.

This was the pattern of his holiday – divided pleasantly between time on his own and going about with Meldrum. They were in Amsterdam, the Hague and Rotterdam, where Neil was envious to learn that the *Rotterdam Courier* paid scant attention to the police-court cases beloved of the British and a great deal to the arts. There were also splendid opportunities for long talks with Meldrum. They discussed Neil's first novel, with which he was then in the throes, and planned an illustrated book on the Glasgow Boys. William Blackwood was interested in this idea, but it came to nothing.

Returning via London, where he stayed with the Meldrums, Neil paused overnight in Glasgow and then went straight on to Inveraray. Almost at once he found himself able to work on his novel with a new fluency after a year's stagnation, and in September he began sending the opening chapters of *John Splendid* to William Blackwood, 'on Meldrum's recommendation'. On 25 September, Blackwood sent a telegram of acceptance and also wrote a long letter from Gogar Mount, his house outside Edinburgh: 'I was so delighted with Chaps XI to XV after reading them this morg [sic] that I could not resist sending you a telegram of congratulation & that I was accepting *John Splendid* for the Magazine, hoping, too, that it would give you a happy Saturday & Sunday.'

Blackwood stressed that he was breaking a rule of *Maga*'s in accepting an incomplete serial. He also wanted an immediate response – 'Wire me on Monday morning'. October's *Maga* was due out that week, and he wished to announce in it that *John Splendid* would open in November – but only if Neil thought that gave him enough time for completion.

Neil wrote back that very day, accepting the challenge. He said he was arranging for two months' leave of absence from the *News* so as to concentrate on the serial, and would send a confirmatory telegram on the Monday. 'In the course of the coming week, I shall send Mr Meldrum another 5 chapters instalment as usual and other instalments up till the end of November. Your letter has been a tremendous encouragement to me; one may write a thing in a state of self-satisfactory exaltation and yet feel at times that he may be on the wrong line, but your letter greatly cheers me and what is yet to be done of the story will be done with confidence.'

He went down to 67 Hope Street that Monday morning little knowing that it was to be his very last week as a regular employee on the *News*. Instead of two months' leave, he ended up arranging with James Murray Smith that he would retire from the staff but continue his two columns and occasional articles 'as an outsider', his weekly pay being reduced from £4.10s to £3, with £1.10s for editing *St Mungo* (till it ended that Christmas). It is not clear whose idea this was. Smith may have been alarmed, imagining he might lose Neil altogether, while the young paterfamilias needed a steady income. Neil would continue to contribute his two columns for three decades. As a future *News* colleague Robins Millar would put it long afterwards 'Smith's great find was an incomparable newspaper man, Neil Munro, whom he made footloose, to write as his fancy led.'[3]

At the end of his last week as a full-time *News* journalist, Neil had a parting glass with Smith and the rest of the staff. A few weeks later the mechanical staff of the *News* presented him with a marble clock and bronze statuettes at a large gathering, with songs and instrumental music. Then in November the Glasgow Press held a presentation dinner, J. Murray Smith presiding. Neil was given a gold hunter watch, a Dutch marquetry bureau and a brooch for his wife. There were many toasts, interspersed with songs – to 'Our Guest' (reply by Neil), the Queen, 'Pictures and Paintings' (reply by Macaulay Stevenson), &c.

Neil was only 34, yet to his fellow journalists it seemed as if he had gone into premature semi-retirement. This general assumption that he had taken an irrecoverable step fairly brought things home. 'First day in the house as a Literary Man! Feel a little queer about it...' he wrote in his diary on Monday October 4 (Sunday did not count). But the self-consciousness soon wore off. The maws of *Maga* had to be supplied, the incessant demands of the jawbox had to be met. Jessie did her utmost to create space and quiet for him, but it was hard for them both in the crowded flat with four children, including a new baby, Moira, born on 19 September.

Neil now had to adjust to writing two weekly columns at home as well as his fiction. An invisible dividing line had to be drawn. For Thursday's 'Views & Reviews' there were always books waiting to be read. For a newly undertaken Monday column called 'The Looker-On', begun in August, he had to scout around for topics, less easy to find now that he was mostly away from the hurly-burly of Hope Street. The two columns would continue for 30 years.

He kicked off his first 'Looker-On' with a threnody entitled 'Exodus of Our Artists'. The once tight-knit group of Glasgow Boys was breaking up and moving away, mostly to London, although Pittendrigh Macgillivray had got no further than Edinburgh, where he occasionally entertained Neil at Ravelston Elms, the house he had designed for himself in Murrayfield. Apart from that, their friendship was sustained by infrequent letters.

To Neil the departure of the Glasgow Boys was a sad loss, which he catalogued in 'The Looker-On': the removal of Walton, Lavery and Guthrie, the rumoured departure of Henry...

'Glasgow seems to be quite unmoved at a most lamentable prospect... the removal to London of the school of artists who have given her a respectable reputation,' Neil lamented. 'To this most dolorous conclusion have we come, and it is ever the way of provincial schools of art. There is, of course, not the slightest reason in the world why a devoted band of conscientious enthusiasts should not hang together in Glasgow, and paint masterpieces, and achieve glory, as great as if they were in Chelsea and the Grove of the Apostle. Everything is here – except the Society of London, which is a poor compensation to an artist for the loss of those unconventional associations that inspire.'[4]

Another painter, George Houston, coming on the scene after the Glasgow Boys, would make up for their defection. Houston, whose beautiful landscapes are almost all of Ayrshire and Argyll, was a friend after Neil's heart, anchored with his large family in Ayrshire and later even taking a house near Inveraray as well. Moreover, he shared Neil's passion for fishing.

It was some time before Neil hit his stride in 'The Looker-On'. At first there was rather much padding and flippancy, but then he got the hang of it. Both 'The Looker-On' and 'Views & Reviews' were sometimes cast in the form of imaginary conversations, a good way of giving several points of view without committing oneself. The device was not original, but it would lead imperceptibly to the creation of Erchie & Co.

No longer obliged to spend his days at 67 Hope Street, Neil now had the time and space to address himself seriously to *John Splendid*, instalments of which had to be sent off regularly to Meldrum. The system of serialising novels before they appeared in book form had an ambivalent effect. Besides the double payment, the monthly commitment was good for Neil in that his rate of production was snail-slow, almost never the standard thousand words a day (though once, that October, the tally was 4,000). The concluding chapters of *John Splendid* were not sent off to Meldrum until May 1898. On the other hand, awareness of deadlines could distort the train of decisions, great and tiny, involved particularly in creative writing. The parcelling into instalments also affected the geology of the work in hand.

In those early days Neil fondly believed significant alterations could be made in a novel before it came out in book form. When William Blackwood sent proofs of the opening instalment, he suggested Neil should 'throw more interest and sparkle into the first chapter'. Neil replied: 'To my mind (at present) the introduction is the finite and inevitable one... Once I have seen the whole of the story in print, however, I may, and probably shall, accentuate the interest of Chapter I.'[5]

But by the time the whole story was in print, there was no time to re-shape the novel as a whole. Blackwoods inexorably brought it out in book form only a month after the final *Maga* instalment. Obviously it was better for author as well as publisher to have a manuscript complete before serialisation even began, but this was never an ideal Neil would attain.

Before the end of his first month as a 'Literary Man', he got a cheque for £35 for the first instalment, and Blackwood confirmed that he would publish *John Splendid* as a book, with royalty of 2d in the shilling on the selling price. The *Maga* payments varied, sometimes only £20. Blackwood also told him that Dodd, Mead & Co. wished to publish *John Splendid* in America, both as book and serial. Neil accepted this offer.

As the last *Maga* instalment of *John Splendid* drew near, Blackwood put out feelers. He was staying in London, and wondered when Neil would be down – 'Meldrum is constantly asking me. We had an interesting meeting with Conrad and Stephen Crane last week.'[6]

But Neil was in the middle of moving house. In the spring of 1898, while *John Splendid* was running in *Maga*, this advertisement had caught his eye:

TO BE LET, WATERFOOT HOUSE

About 6 miles from Glasgow, on the road to Eaglesham, about a Mile from Clarkston Station. The House contains 3 public-rooms, 3 Bed-rooms, Kitchen, Bath-room, W.C., and Washing-house, with good sized productive Garden attached.

Neil found the house, less pretentious than its name, was on the roadside next to a farm and just outside the village of Waterfoot, south of Glasgow, then not much more than a few cottages, a mill and a well. It was not Lochfyneside, but it was on the edge of moorland and still fairly remote. The rent was £35 per annum. Neil took a three years' lease, later extended by a year.

Directly after moving house, Neil had to go to Ireland to report on the famine in Connemara, so he could not go south before Blackwood went abroad on holiday. Baulked of a face-to-face discussion with Meldrum present, Blackwood had to put in writing his wish to have the refusal of Munro's next story. He held out the prospect of 'something on a/c for your new book while it was in progress',[7] and a higher rate than *John Splendid*. All this in parenthesis in his letter!

Neil's bluff was called. He replied: 'I have not yet started a third story, though the scope of it is in my mind, but whenever I have given the idea any tangible form I shall only be too glad to let you know... in any case it shall always be my first desire that your house should publish my books. You have no doubt heard that my second story... is appearing in *Good Words* for 1899. This was an arrangement come to last August when Dr Donald Macleod... made a proposal that in my circumstances was too tempting to be refused.'[8]

In fact, after visiting Dr Macleod at the Gareloch in July, he had received an offer from William Canton of *Good Words* – £250 for serial rights – and had written accepting it only a few days before Blackwood accepted *John Splendid*. One can only speculate why, a year earlier, he had turned down an approach made by a Mr Doubleday of Constables, saying he was 'morally bound to Blackwood'. Over lunch in the Central Hotel, Glasgow, Doubleday had proposed that Neil should write a Highland romance, offering '£100 down and 10% royalty first year, 15% or 20% second'. On these terms, Neil made a start on the *Good Words* serial, *The Paymaster's Boy* (later to become *Gilian the Dreamer*), in May 1898 – a month before the last *John Splendid* instalment appeared in *Maga*.

With four children now – Effie, Hugh, Lilian and Moira – ranging from eight years old down to six months, the house was as busy as a hive of bees. Martha, daughter of their farmer neighbour, came to work with Jessie, and Neil employed a jobbing gardener. He also bought a bicycle for access to Clarkston and trains to Glasgow Central, only a few steps from the *News* building in Hope Street.

It is now that the Munros begin to swim into focus as a family with their own idiom. Partly maybe from observing other boys' fathers and imagining one for himself, partly from the warmth of his own childhood home, Neil was naturally a good father (and he had also had some experience with Jessie's young brothers). He loved the company of young people all his life and was never the domineering Victorian papa, though he could certainly lose his temper and when it came to the bit was rather strait-laced. His phrase for repelling invasive children when he was working was: 'Hook it!' Two more children would be born at Waterfoot: Neil in 1900 and Isobel in 1902.

The river White Cart flows through the fields behind Waterfoot House and joins the Water of Earn nearby (hence the name Waterfoot). In summer the corncrake could be heard. On clear days the wide outlook across the Clyde valley to the distant Highland hills gave 'a sense of companionship with the wide world'. These new surroundings were not only congenial but also conducive to work. The first batch of *The Paymaster's Boy* (*Gilian the Dreamer*) was sent off promptly to *Good Words* in July, then he went away on his own to stay with friends in Mull. There was fishing in the Sound of Mull and sailing in a ten-ton cutter: 'Heavy weather, three reefs.'

In August, the Munro family went to Inveraray for a fortnight – less fun for Jessie than the rest, to judge by a letter of Neil's written 'in very inconvenient Hielan' circumstances'. But then he, too, had no let-up in his pen-pushing: copy for his columns had to be 'wired' up to Hope Street; instalments of *Gilian* kept in mind. He had sent the first batch of manuscript off promptly to *Good Words* in July, and from Inveraray he wrote to brief A.S. Boyd, the artist who was to illustrate *Gilian*, 'a poetic-looking fair-haired boy to begin with – yes that is the idea... Inveraray is the town, though I do not once mention its name'.

That summer Neil had several days' fishing on the Balantyre burn and the moor lochs in the hills above Inveraray. The first time at the moor lochs he caught three trout and camped out all night with his step-nephew Dan Thomson and Henry Smith, son of his old school-master. Another day Henry and his father, not yet retired, fished with him. In his column the following day Neil remarked that a book of fishing flies was the only literature he wanted on holiday.

CHAPTER FIFTEEN

The happy manner with Romance

EARLY in September, just back from Inveraray, Neil received a copy of his first novel, *John Splendid*. Blackwoods had already printed a second impression, the first being almost entirely taken up by booksellers' orders before publication. William Blackwood also sent a special tartan-bound copy for young Hugh, to whom it is dedicated.

The dedication of *John Splendid* is somewhat confusing. We are to read it as 'a picture of times and manners', yet not to expect too much historical veracity: 'That is the happy manner with Romance...' The narrative is in the first person, the narrator a man known as Elrigmore who looks back from a later period to the midwinter of 1644–45 when he was caught up in the 'Little Wars of Lorn and Lochaber' – Montrose's invasion of Argyll, the sacking of Inveraray (Inneraora) and Montrose's victory at Inverlochy.

Elrigmore has been a mercenary in Germany, but his depiction of war is non-heroic and scarcely 'romantic'. Mostly he is on the sidelines with his companion John Splendid, cousin of the Marquis of Argile. He is fascinated by the relationship between these two men, Splendid personifying the old wild Highlands and Argile who declares: 'I would sooner be a cottar... with porridge for my every meal, than constable, chastiser... or whatever I am, of all these vexed Highlands.' Argile has done much to introduce more pacific ways: this is brought out in the opening chapters, based partly on old kirk records. The brawl between Maclachlans and Macnicols (Chapter 4) in fact took place, though in 1711, and involved Provost Brown's

81

house, all of which gave Neil the impetus to start his story off. Like several other Munro novels, *John Splendid* opens with an arrival at Inveraray. 'Many a time, in college or in camp, I had planned the style of my homecoming,' says Elrigmore. That homecoming unlocked the door and released Neil into an Argyll of the mind, corresponding at many points with the real Argyll he loved.

The excellent sales of *John Splendid* suggest *The Lost Pibroch* had made its mark. Reviews of Neil's first novel were on the whole favourable, although several complained of a lack of plot. Neil retorted: 'The plot of a book is for the babes and sucklings.'

In *Black & White*, the reviewer 'M' found that 'Neil Munro has written a fine book... there are some few loose tags, but we forget this in the humanity and knowledge that can make two hundred years ago palpitate as the present. And that is why we look to Neil Munro to give us, in the fullness of time, the story of modern Scots life we are waiting for. Of course, he may not want to do it... But we fancy he will come down the ages... by way of the '15 and the '45, and the early days of this century, to the present...'

J.M.Barrie wrote from Kirriemuir: 'To see a man doing his best always makes me want to fling my hat in the air... A dozen times I have wished R.L.S. could have read it. He would have given them all a holiday in Samoa in its honour... I don't know if you are ever in London but I hope you will never be there for however short a time without letting me know where to find you.'[1]

Donald Mackinnon, first Professor of Celtic at Edinburgh, wrote congratulating Neil on 'a splendid work... which only a Highlander of genius could write'.[2] By way of curious contrast, Neil also received an unexpected letter from a Glasgow address:

Dear Mr Munro,
I am not in the way of thinking well of those who write congratulations to Authors personally unknown to them... I can plead 'extenuating circumstances'. You are a fellow clansman... My father was born in Glenaora at his father's farm of Ladyfield. Are you of Glenshira? Oddly enough I had not read the Legend of Montrose until a few weeks before I read John Splendid. It was a bold stroke of you – worthy of a highlander – to tell the same story... If some yet unmatched qualities be conceded to the older writer... 'Still and on,' I like the new tale best. Scott tells me the story from the outside; you tell it from the inside... Scott viewed Mountain and Glen with the eye of romance; your hills and lochans I know and love with that perfect love which does not cast

out fear... With the wish that you may live long to disprove the adage that 'paper and ink will be the Gael's undoing',
I am, &c.,
JOHN M.M. MUNRO

The writer betrays an inkling that the author of *John Splendid* was the half-cousin for whom he had tried in vain to find a job 17 years previously. John Munro was also something of a pioneer: his firm, Anderson & Munro, claimed to have wired the first house in the world lit solely by electricity – Lord Kelvin's, at the University of Glasgow. His letter to Neil led to a renewed friendship.

By the end of 1898, more than 5,000 copies of *John Splendid* had been sold, bringing royalties of £430 – and *The Lost Pibroch* made £156! With various other payments, Neil's income in the twelve months from September 1897 was roughly £1,400. Since his columns brought him only £150 p.a., it might have been tempting to abandon them at this juncture.

There were mixed motives in his persistence with 'the jawbox': financial prudence, loyalty to James Murray Smith and the *News*, the need to be active in worlds beyond his household, and perhaps not least the sheer enjoyment of using his own skills. There is a certain truth in George Blake's observation that Neil's 'heart and genius were in the writing of romances, and yet his instinct and his talent were for journalism'.[3]

Success as an author enabled Neil to lift some of the domestic burden from Jessie's shoulders. On returning home from Inveraray at the end of August, Neil had consulted the servants' register at the Christian Institute in Glasgow. There he engaged a new maid, Maggie McNiven, an orphan of seventeen, her wages to be £12 a year, 'all found'.

The arrival of Maggie was a red letter day in Munro annals. She was soon absorbed into the family and became the lifelong ally of Jessie, whom she always called 'Mistress Munro' in the old Scottish way. Non-achievement of her own ambition to be a nurse did not embitter her. She also struck up a lifelong friendship with Martha. Only three months later the two of them were left in charge while Jessie went off on an unprecedented jaunt of her own to the Kyles of Bute Hydropathic, there to join Mrs James Murray Smith, whose husband was in America.

Not only did Maggie come to Waterfoot in the week that *John Splendid* was published, she also arrived on Hugh's first day as a schoolboy. He joined Effie at the Misses Gardner's dame school in

Clarkston and soon learned to shout the cryptic phrase 'Cheesie Watson!' across the fields on the mile-long walk.

That same month, September 1898, saw another arrival that was momentous for Neil in a different way. Joseph Conrad came to Glasgow to look for the command of a Scottish ship – preferably a sailing ship – a wild resolve brought on by money worries and his excruciatingly slow creative rate. Conrad, only child of a landless Polish aristocrat and now 41, had gone to sea as a youth, but had not sailed for four years, during which time he had published three novels – *Almayer's Folly*, *An Outcast Of The Islands* and *The Nigger of the 'Narcissus'* – all to critical acclaim. But they had taken eight years to write and were not selling well.

Conrad spent three days trudging round the Glasgow shipping offices. Among some letters of introduction given him by R.B. Cunninghame Graham, not just then in Scotland, was one to Dr John Macintyre, nose and throat specialist and an early pioneer of X-rays. Macintyre duly invited Conrad to dinner, along with one other guest – Neil Munro.

Neil had some idea what to expect as he made his way to 179 Bath Street, next to the Art Club. MacIntyre he already knew as a congenial and unconventional host: Conrad's work he had studied and found superb. Moreover, they had a common friend in D.S. Meldrum. Meeting Conrad now, Neil found he 'looked like his profession – a ship's officer in his shore clothes... Manifestly a "swell", but not even remotely of the hidalgo type of Cunninghame Graham.'[4]

Conrad, one imagines, came hoping only to be mildly distracted. He had soon seen that his old ambition to command a Glasgow ship was unlikely to be fulfilled, and a chastened departure from the city was staring him in the face. 'The fact that I'm notorious as a novel-writer is a handicap on the Clyde, I fear,' he remarked.[5] But MacIntyre and Neil between them redeemed Glasgow in his eyes.

After dinner, MacIntyre played to them his early phonograph recordings, made by himself, of leading opera singers such as Tetrazzini and of musicians and actors who had consulted him – a rare and quite futuristic treat. Then they repaired to the basement where he kept his pioneer Röntgen machine. Neil's memories were still vivid thirty years on: 'I stood in front of a fluorescent machine behind which Conrad and the Doctor contemplated my ribs and back-bone, the more opaque portions of my viscera, my Waterbury watch and what coins were in my pocket.'[6]

'The rest of this promising youth was too diaphanous to be

visible,' wrote Conrad (only five years older than Neil!) in a letter to Edward Garnett.[7] While contemplating Neil's skeleton, he and MacIntyre animatedly discussed 'the secret of the Universe', horizontal waves, the possibility of an infinite number of universes &c. Neil must have stood there an unconscionable time. After a good dinner and whisky it all seemed simple: an eternal something that waves, an eternal force that causes the waves...

'These things I said to the Dr. while Neil Munro stood in front of the Röntgen machine,' Conrad would later recall. 'By virtue of these eternities (the doctor said in a strong final burst) exist that picture by Corot, and that Whistler in the dining room upstairs, and Munro here's writing, and your *Nigger* and Graham's politics and Paderewski's playing, and what more do you want? What we wanted apparently was more whisky... we got it. Mrs MacIntyre went to bed. At one o'clock Munro and I went out into the street. We talked. I had read up *The Lost Pibroch*, which I do think wonderful in a way. We foregathered very much indeed and I believe Munro didn't get back till five in the morning.'[8]

The pair of them – dark Jozef Korzeniowski, fair Niall Mac an Rothaich – must have wandered off course. At one point, in George Square, Neil pointed out the statue of James Oswald M.P. holding out his top hat (birds have been known to nest in it), and mischievously declared that throwing a 'chuckie' stone into it made one an honorary Glaswegian. Conrad went on trying till he landed one.

Neil found Conrad 'delightful'. He told him of his great appreciation of *The Nigger of the 'Narcissus'*, in particular the envoi – 'A gone shipmate...' Conrad was heartened, for H.G. Wells found that final passage too emotive. He spoke of his despair as a writer: he was then struggling with *The Rescue*. It was three o'clock when they parted at the St Enoch Hotel, where Conrad was staying. The last train to Busby was long gone, and it took Neil two hours to walk home to Waterfoot.

Next day, he took Conrad up to the Art Club for lunch, and in the evening it seems they foregathered there again with other members of the club. There was great enthusiasm for *The Nigger of the 'Narcissus'* in Glasgow at that time. 'In the smoke-room, when he became animated, telling any of his experiences, he would rise from his chair and pace up and down as on a quarter-deck... Conrad basked that evening in an atmosphere so cordial and understanding that I doubt if he ever before found a company of strangers more agreeable to him.'[9]

All this mitigated the effect of Conrad's failure to get a command

and sent him on his way in a more sanguine frame of mind. Soon afterwards he started *Heart of Darkness*, and also some collaborations with Ford Madox Ford. On 9 November he wrote to Neil from Pent Farm, near Hythe:[9]

My dear Munro,
I feel like a wretch for not having written to tell you how touched I was by your friendliness. Yet the feeling is abiding and loses no strength by the lapse of time.
My congratulations on the fourth edition of *John Splendid*. How splendid indeed it is. I've no gift of critical expression. I feel the beauty strongly but I cannot liberate my artistic emotion in art terms or any other terms. You must have me on trust. If I had you there, in the room and the book, with us two, then, perhaps thumping the pages out of your own heart and act with your own words I could give you a glimmer of my sensations. And some day I love to think it will be. Remember me when you come south. I look forward to seeing you and seeing you here. We shan't stir from home for months ahead.
Believe me always most faithfully,
Yours JPH. CONRAD

Neil never took advantage of Conrad's hospitality. His visits south were mostly brief journalistic skirmishes to London, and Conrad lived in the country. But I think it was partly that he liked to keep intact the memory of a brief and unrepeatable spree: 'A gone shipmate, like any other man, is gone for ever...'
In January 1899, Conrad won an award of £50 from *The Academy* for his *Tales Of Unrest*. Writing to Neil in July – 'Blessings on your head for your good letter' – he said he had seen the notice of the award in the *News*.

I was immensely touched by what you – for it was you – said '*coram publico*' about my work. Verily you and two or three others for whose word I care would give me a swelled head if I did not save myself from that disease by suspecting you all of a mysterious insanity... I am now writing for *Maga* a long short story [probably *Heart of Darkness*] to complete a vol. of three. I am writing with my teeth set very hard, and yet I will bring shame on all your heads, and my heart will shrivel to the size of a pea.
Affectionately yours
CONRAD

When a literary supplement was started in the *News* in 1905, Neil wrote asking Conrad if he might re-print his article 'The Art of Fiction'. Conrad replied from Capri: 'Of course, with the greatest pleasure... I read you and take delight in you. As to my last book [*Nostromo*] it seems a sort of frost. Yours always, J. Conrad.'

Apart from an encounter in 1923, the two men would not meet again.

At the end of October, Neil made an agreement to write a second serial for *Good Words*, to appear in 1901 and earn him £350. He wrote to Donald Macleod: 'I'm enough of the Highlander to fancy a contract for 1901 might be tempting of Providence to send Atropos at me with the cursed shears.'[10] He had also accepted William Blackwood's proposal to write a second serial for *Maga*, for 1900. The work was stretching out for years ahead, but there was still time for pleasure. November 1898 saw various Inveraray manifestations in Glasgow, beginning with the annual ball. Then Neil received a letter from John Campbell, Sheriff Clerk of Argyll:

> My dear M,
> P. McIntyre was speaking to me, on several occasions, on a subject connected with yourself... I refer to a proposal to present you with the freedom of the Royal Burgh – Let me have your opinion, privately of course... I hear the wee Duke, is not extra – gout – Peter has him lug-marked... I observe and hear that *John Splendid* has had a truly favorble recepn. What do you think of yon squeal, of 'Fiona's'?
> Ta ta
> Yrs faitly
> JOHN CAMPBELL[11]

Neil replied, declining the honour. Shortly afterwards, despite not being 'extra', the 75-year-old Duke came up to Glasgow, presumably for the Celtic Bazaar in St Andrew's Hall. But the day before it opened he was reported 'laid up' in his hotel. Neil, of course, went to the Bazaar and heard the Inveraray Pipe Band playing there. Next day he entertained some of the pipers, including Charlie Maitland, at the Art Club. Did they play there too, one wonders.

Towards the end of November, Neil first met R.B. Cunninghame Graham. After seeing *Tannhäuser* at the Theatre Royal, Glasgow, they dined with some others at the North British Hotel. For years Neil had known Cunninghame Graham, in any case a kenspeckle figure, by sight. As a young reporter he had observed him from afar at a big political meeting in St Andrew's Hall, 'too dandified-looking for his audience, who would hardly listen to him... I laughed at him myself then, but learned in later years to admire and like him greatly'.[12] Cunninghame Graham had then just returned from thirteen years ranching in Argentina. Then in 1887, in London to report a demonstration by the unemployed, Neil had seen him again, 'with a head, though bloody, still unbowed, in the hands of the police'.

Neil seems to have mentioned these sightings to Cunninghame Graham, for the latter wrote in a delightful rambling letter two days later from Gartmore: 'I was very glad indeed to make, or to renew acquaintance with you.' He had been reading *John Splendid* till 2 a.m. the previous night, and now expatiated upon it. His confidence as to what is and is not 'Celtic' is touching:

Yes, you have put a great deal of yourself (not into him) but into the book. Into your world I cannot enter, but that does not stop me from admiring from the gate... You are in every way & in all ways a charming writer, & your view of life has surprised me – You put it out quietly... in your way (I think) you show the futility of life, as well as Conrad & I do.

[Here follow some criticisms of the 'fence & horsemanship' in *John Splendid*.]

To resume, all these things are important, style, philosophy, knowledge of mankind, pathos, fine descriptions of scenery, (& you have them all) come by nature. But a knowledge of fence & horsemanship comes by study. No art is superior to nature... It is the old problem, the Sun & the Rain, you on one side, I on the other. But still I admire the rainbow of the Celtic mind, just lighting up the dark, & seeing further into the mist than anyone can see, where the Sun leaves no mystery.

Adios, thank you for a pleasant evening spent with good men, with whom I ought to have that affinity of thought & feeling, which a foreign upbringing has denied me. I predict that *John Splendid* will be as enduring a figure, as 'Alan Breck' or 'Rob Roy', & this I swear on the 'Grey Stone of Glen Fruin', & by 'Inch Cailleach' & those who sleep there.

[illegible Spanish ending]

R.B. CUNNINGHAME GRAHAM

P.S. I hope you are at work on something else, for it is a curse that Scotland should be judged on the demerits of those damned

Kailyarders (ill put together lowland knowt) when we have such a writer as yourself amongst us.[13]

The inference is clearly that he felt more 'affinity of thought & feeling' with Neil than with their fellow-diners at the North British Hotel. A brief flurry of letters from him survives from that winter. Thanking Neil for copies of parodies published in the *News*, he wrote: 'The parodies are splendid, 'Kipling' is better than himself, because shorter... I am excellent... Conrad is I think the least like the original but then he is hard to catch.'[14]

Two days later, Cunninghame Graham sent Neil a photograph of himself: 'It is I think one of the best I ever had done... The cold is intense this evening, and I think we chose the better part in not going to see the *Midsummer Night's Dream*. So I shall labour on a bit with the 'Gold Fish' & then turn to two of the stories in *The Lost Pibroch* which I have never read.'

Like his friend Conrad, Cunninghame Graham had money worries, but of a different order. Early in the new century he would sell his ancestral estate, Gartmore, and move to Ardoch, near Cardross. He was often in London or South America or North Africa.

For Neil, 1898 closed with one more encounter with a fellow literary talent just beginning to emerge. He noted in his diary: 'Met John Buchan the student novelist at Stuarts', Langside.'

CHAPTER SIXTEEN

I burned my journalistic boats

EARLY in January 1899, Neil found himself on display to the nation at the Royal Scottish Academy, where a bust of him by the Glasgow sculptor William Kellock Brown was exhibited. His sculptor friend Pittendrigh Macgillivray would write from Edinburgh, two months later, describing the bust as 'the snouted kind of thing I saw one day, in stucco, in that muckle building on the Mound of Edinburgh'.[1]

Neil replied, giving his news: 'As you may possibly have learned, I burned my journalistic boats, all but a little punt or so, some time ago, and came out here to grow cabbage and tread The Higher Walks. I am now throng a-treading of 'em, and so far have every reason to be pleased with the change. Of course I whack out a little newspaper work now and then, but I have more time for other things... I opined ye would laugh at my stucco presentment. That was the one thought that cheered me... I have now got the stucco at home and need no watch dog. *Le pauvre Kelloch!'*[2]

Also at the start of January, Neil contributed a poem, 'To Exiles', for *Maga*'s thousandth number. It owes something to the Sun/Rain antithesis that Cunninghame Graham had suggested as between non-Gaels and Gaels:

> Are you not weary in your distant places,
> Far, far from Scotland of the mist and storm,
> In drowsy airs, the sun-smite on your faces...

William Blackwood wrote back promptly, enclosing a cheque for five guineas 'in acknowledgment of your charming poem to *Maga*'s Exiles... You must not allow your talent for clever parody and satire to lie fallow. Your burlesque stories in the *News* [the parodies] were delightful, & I should be greatly pleased if you were to hit out something on somewhat similar lines suitable for *Maga* in prose & verse which you could turn to whenever you felt in the humour & subjects presented themselves... I was glad to see that *Black & White* thought you were more deserving than one of the three selected for the Academy awards.'[3]

Neil replied: 'If I can be of any service to *Maga* in the humorous way now and then, I should be only too pleased to have the chance.'[4] As if he did not have enough writing to do, he had also arranged with the Rev Donald McMillan, Kelvinhaugh Parish Church, to contribute a weekly literary column to the church magazine *Saint Andrew*.

But he did not have to lift a finger to earn still more from serialisation of *The Paymaster's Boy* in America, for which he received a cheque for £90. Then on 28 February Blackwoods, sending a cheque for £279, reported that up to the end of the preceding year, 5,847 copies of *John Splendid* had been sold. Royalties for *The Lost Pibroch* (£35) and various Transatlantic royalties (£113) were also included, and the cheque allowed for the £100 advanced in December.

Despite being a literary man these days, Neil kept in touch with his friends at the *News* office, although the old office itself was demolished that March. While the dust was settling, Neil went down with J.M. Smith to London, where they played golf with fellow newspapermen, took a trip to Brighton and returned to the Savoy to dine in style, before going on to various London clubs. The work element, if there was any, seems to have been to make the final arrangements for state-of-the-art Linotype typesetting machines to be installed in the new building in Glasgow. Neil's diary for 23 March notes: 'First Lynotypes (sic) in *News* office.'

On 25 April Effie Adam, Jessie's youngest sister, married William Craig at Waterfoot. Neil had the invitations printed at the office, but when he brought them home, great was the ire when they were found to read 'Mr and Mrs Neil Munro request the pleasure of —'s company at the marriage of their sister, Euphemia Fortune Adam, at Waterfoot House, Busby, on Tuesday afternoon, &c' - no mention of the bridegroom's name! Neil passed it off jocularly by telling his sister-in-law: 'You can still change your mind...'

That August Neil went to Fasnacloich in Appin as the guest of Charles Stewart. The large fishing party included Lord Lionel Cecil, 'who looked so like his brother Salisbury, though in truth a simple genial English farmer squire, that I never could be at ease with him. A gay party of good souls, quite ready to swop flies or lies, or gaff a salmon for you, but someway I was out of it, since the atmosphere was wholly English and my quest in Appin was the '*genius loci*'... It could be Appin only when I was alone, when I climbed to Ben Mhir na Ceisich, or rambled in the woods, walked over the ruins of old sheilings, or by the otter-haunted river to Loch Creranhead. But even more particularly was it Appin when the little lake in front of Fasnacloich was like a mirror through which the salmon and sea-trout multitudinously crashed all day, tempting and taunting the chagrined angler... But better still, more sane, more spacious, free, and fairy, was the spirit of the evening hour in Fasnacloich, when the yellow badger's moon hung over the scented valley...'[5]

One day the party sailed on a steam yacht, *Kelpie*, round to Duror on Loch Linnhe, whence they walked up Glen Salachan and descended precipitously back down to Fasnacloich. Here surely was the germ of Neil's poem 'Duror of Appin':

Blythe were the seasons when we were in Duror together,
In Appin of stories, and songs of brave old tribulations;
Shores of the sheldrake, hills of the deer, and the nut-woods,
Our hearts like a bird in the bosom!

On another morning, Neil set out early on his own to find Dalness at the top of Glen Etive, the house he had described sight unseen in *John Splendid*. For the first bit he had a guide, Peter McKay, tenant of Glenure, once the house of Colin Campbell the Appin murder victim. Neil then went on alone. He had paid more attention to McKay's highland lore than to his directions, and soon got lost. It was a hot sunny day. After scaling a 'torrent of enormous boulders' and traversing miles of trackless heather and moor he got down to Loch Etive, where a woman working in a field told him he was at Barrs, eight miles south of Dalness.

Neil's diary says: 'Went to a shooting lodge (Murray tenant) then took a rowing boat down to Taynuilt. Train to Connel Ferry and drove to Fasnacloich.' The account he wrote in the 1920s, re-printed in *The Looker-On*, differs slightly: 'I went up to the shooting lodge at Barrs, and was met at the door by a man in evening clothes. "I have walked from Fasnacloich," I remarked, with eloquent simplicity, "and I got lost." "By George, that's fine!" he said, with a kindling eye; "come in and have some dinner. This is the loveliest day! My regiment's just got the route for Africa, and I must flag the boat [the steamer] tomorrow." We flagged the boat on the morrow, and a few months later he was dead on the battlefield.'[6]

On a later steamer, going home from Fasnacloich, Neil recognised Andrew Lang, the writer and folklorist, with whom he had had some correspondence. He introduced himself with the audacity acquired as a reporter and found Lang forthcoming and generous, not at all the stand-offish Oxford man he was said to be. 'He showed me a number of interesting old Highland letters. He said Kipling must be sick of newspaper gush, and that he thought little of "Cruisers" – too much "street walker" in it, as there was in Henley's work.'

Lang, who was travelling with his wife, had been fishing also, in Lochaber, where he had been taken to see the house of a crofter 'through whose roof and walls large stones had been inexplicably "oozing" for many weeks'. Later he sent Neil a long hand-written account of this. (He had been in the habit of sending masses of historical material to R.L. Stevenson.) They never met again, but Lang went on sending Neil 'what he considered good material for Scottish romance'. He also suggested they should collaborate on a novel, but nothing came of this. 'Such an experience makes even the humblest life of letters glorious,' Neil remarked.

When September came, Effie and Hugh went for first time to Busby Public School, Miss Gardner's seminary having now closed up. On 11 September, Neil posted off the last proofs of *Gilian the Dreamer*, and on 29 September he had his first copy of the book in his hand.

CHAPTER SEVENTEEN
A regard for the manner of his message

THE novel serialised in Good Words as *The Paymaster's Boy* had become in book form *Gilian the Dreamer: His Fancy, His Love and Adventure*. Neil sent a copy to William Blackwood, remarking in his covering letter: 'It is in a very different vein from *John Splendid* and I have turned again to old Romance (in a MS I trust to show you soon) with great relief.'[1] The reference is to Neil's next novel, *Doom Castle*, and the implication of his 'great relief' is that he found the writing of *Gilian* much harder than dealing with the remoter past. It is the closest of all his books to self-revelation.

Both Gilian and Neil are fatherless only children, both the grandsons of grieves at Ladyfield. Gilian's plight, however, is the worse: his mother has died in giving birth to him, and the grandmother who brings him up dies when he is twelve (Neil's age when his mother married Malcom Thomson). Gilian has something of the boy Neil who was too blate to speak in a debate, yet he is, too, 'of that gifted nature that at times can treat the most bitter insults with indifference'.[2]

But the confessional element is handled lightly and balanced by many passages which demonstrate why Fionn MacColla described Neil's works as 'irradiated and suffused with the unique flavour of Gaelic life in a way which is totally authentic and beyond praise',[3] for instance the description of the late harvesters in Chapter XXV.

Gilian the Dreamer is set in the 1820s, in the Inveraray Neil's grandmother knew as a young woman. It was a time of marked transition: 'the last of the old Highland burgh and the raw beginnings of the new... real *duaine-uasail*, gentry of ancient family, colloguing with the common merchants whose day was coming in...'[4] It opens with Gilian, an orphan lad of twelve from Glen Aray, coming down to the town to give the news of his grandmother's death, which has left him alone in the world. There is no hint as to why, in that glen then so neighbourly, no adult accompanies him. 'But in truth, as he went sobbing in his loneliness down the river-side, a regard for the manner of his message busied him more than the matter of it...'[5] Already his 'dream nature' is apparent.

The description of his grandmother's funeral in Chapter III was altered radically by Neil from the original in *Good Words*. It was probably the only time he was ever able to make changes between serialisation and book form. From unexplained motives he cut out a long detailed section dealing with the scene at Ladyfield, including this passage about Gilian: 'And as he sat waiting in that silent house, whose solemnity the sisters dare only break in whispers, he felt for the first time the odour of death – that blending of laurel and frost that for ever after came to him in the presence of death itself, or at its approach in others, that gave him the certainty of the Second Sight almost, and filled him with pity when he would perceive it in companies where gaiety reigned.'[6]

Gilian is informally adopted by Captain John Campbell, 'late Paymaster of his Majesty's 46th Foot', a bachelor who shares a house with his two bachelor brothers, all three based on real Inveraray men. The oldest, General Dugald, was severely wounded in the head at Waterloo, while Colin, the Cornal, 'led the Royal Scots at Salamanca, Vittoria, and Waterloo'. Their sister Miss Mary – 'a darling hypocrite, a foolish bounteous mother-soul' – takes Gilian to her heart. Neil's spinster great-aunt Bell Macarthur can be glimpsed in her, and she is an early manifestation of Neil's implicit feminism. She comes to be be Gilian's 'only link between his dreams, his books, and the common life of the day'.

The Paymaster wants Gilian to be a soldier, but the Cornal notices from the start: 'There's no stuff for sodgering here.' In the end Miss Mary brings about his return to Ladyfield to learn the shepherd's trade. Here Neil draws on memories of his own 'laughterless days' on sheep farms. Gilian still loves the old place, but cannot recover the old contentment. An amateurish elopement with Nan Turner of Glen Shira fails after they have stravaiged among the moor-lochs, even though Gilian believes he is entering upon an idyll. He imagines the summers when the moorland shielings were still used. 'Empty, empty, but I see all the old peoples roaming in bands over it, the sun smiting them, the rain drenching, I cannot but be thinking of shealing huts that spotted the levels, of bairns crying about the doors, of nights of ceilidh round peat fires dead and cold now, but yet with the smoke of them hanging somewhere round the universe.'[7] This can be taken as a veiled reference to the Highland clearances, and Ronald Renton has written with insight about this aspect of the novel.

'...Munro sees [the Clearances] as a great watershed in Highland history in terms of the role of the creative artist in modern Highland society. The Clearances complete the dislocation of Highland tradition. Gilian is a very gifted and sensitive young man, but there is now no role for him in Highland society... Throughout the novel Gilian's affinity with the old, rich and stable tradition of the Highlands is very obvious.'[8]

In the last chapter we learn that Gilian has been writing poetry in his Glen Aray solitude – 'the first of those heart-wrung fancies that went to the making of the volume that lies before me as I write'. It is worth noting that Neil heard of the death of Evan MacColl, the Loch Fyne bard, while he was in midst of writing *Gilian the Dreamer*, and wrote an obituary of MacColl in the *News*.[9]

Like Gilian, Neil was a dreamer and, despite his sociable nature and the journalistic skills that let him thrive in the modern world, a part of him perhaps felt out of place in the late 19th century. Hugh MacDiarmid once wrote: 'Had Neil Munro never learned English – and lived quietly in an entirely Gaelic-speaking community – he might have come to his true stature as an artist.'[10] If Neil had been given the choice, perhaps he would have been born in Glen Shira before English pervaded the *Gaidhealtachd*; perhaps he would have been a bard or *seanachaidh*. But he was born in Victorian bilingual

Inveraray, which also had its positive influences. The 8th Duke of Argyll wrote of his friend David Livingstone the missionary, whose forefathers lived in the Isle of Ulva, that he was a man 'with a special gift and a special inspiration, which in all human probability would not have been developed if he had been born in the life passed by the old Sub-tenants in Ulva'. [11] By the same token, Neil's special gifts might never have developed had he lived all his days in a Gaelic-speaking Glen Shira.

His friend D.S. Meldrum would rate *Gilian* above the historical romances, writing 16 years later: 'Its scenery is that of the author's boyhood, and no one can doubt that so is its sentiment. *Gilian* is autobiographic to that extent, and farther in being critical of traits that run in the blood of the author's own race. The historical romances (though the historical in them is disavowed) are picaresque... The story does not always absorb, its circumstance, and not the story itself, having the chief attraction for the author... *Gilian* on the other hand is closer-knit and more consistent... And further – reason for singling it out in so very general an estimate – it displays in largest measure the charming grace, partly traditional, partly personal, that distinguishes all Mr Munro's books. In all his novels Mr Munro enlarges the horizons of the *locus in quo*; how cleverly he does so in *Gilian*, where they are, perhaps, the narrowest of all!

'Partly this is accomplished by a hand working on the wide and full landscape of the Scottish Highlands... And partly it is due to the modern reflective element that is essential in Mr Munro's elaborate style... Mr Munro is the novelist of the Scottish Highlands. He is a Gael, and Sir Walter was not and Stevenson was not. But to be a Gaelic novelist – as it was open to him to be – he has not chosen. He leads no Gaelic movement, in affairs or in letters. The legends of the Gael, his sorrows and imaginings, the pathos of his migrations and emigrations, and homesickness for the croft (touched on in some of the poems), he knows and feels, but except in particular instances of tyranny, of man or circumstance, they do not rouse him to passion. The Highlands with a grievance is not his inspiration. There is no room in his oeuvre for a pamphlet. The Highlands for him, as a separate part of Scotland, are past, and it is with wistful sentiment for the past that he veils their bravery in the novels.'[12]

Towards the end of October 1899, Neil heard from William Blackwood: 'I have been away at Harrowgate for a month's holiday, and now on my return I have the pleasure of finding your letter with the copy of *Gilian the Dreamer*, which I have much pleasure in accepting from yourself. Before leaving home I had given it to be included in the article 'Under the Beard of Buchanan' [*Maga*], & what we say of it there will I hope give you much gratification. I am greatly pleased also to hear that you are so far forward with your new romance, & from what Mr Morton told me you have hit upon a splendid title [*Doom Castle*] for it. You are sure to be at your best in a story so much after your own heart, & the vein should be a particularly happy one for a serial in *Maga*.'[13]

The house at Waterfoot was as busy as ever. In November, Jessie and Neil went to the Inveraray dance in the Trades Hall in Glasgow. On 4 December, Neil was at the launch of a new warship, HMS *Cressy*. He was feeling a little embattled himself just then, as a letter written the following day to his cousin Kate Turner in Lincoln reveals:

My dear Kate,

It is my pleasant habit to let my correspondence accumulate until it has all answered itself so to speak, or until some day occurs when I feel like gamely working my way through it. Your letters do not answer themselves... In the course of the past two months the children have indulged in the customary equinoctial colds and at present they are not at school, owing to an outbreak of scarlet fever which will probably keep them at home for a month or two. I have accordingly to add some scholastic duties to my daily industry and I realise from the brevity of as sweet a temper as ever man was blessed with that I am not constructed internally for the instruction of youth...

Gilian has done very well. Two reviewers I think said he was the utterest idiot ever heard tell on, but the rest were fulsome in his praise, which really does not matter. And in spite of the war I expect the book has done better financially than any of its neighbours. I have started the new opus but it grows very slowly and after creating a character with much skill and pains, his familiar look suggested that he must be stolen from somewhere. I had to read the most of Scott over to learn that my deucedly clever Mungo Boyd was only Caleb Balderstone with an alias. And he had to go, poor man. [He was re-instated.]

I suppose you will be spending your Christmas holiday in Lincoln, poor thing, instead of coming up to the fine Highlands where the New Year is something like, with whisky and oranges and short-cake intil't, and nane o' yer kirk three times wi' the *Adeste Fideles* bummin' a' the time. I'm not sure that I'm going home myself this New Year... Oor gyarden is a waste – a dimnition, dreary, dripping dismal swamp. We are quite giddy, the wife and I this winter, with invitations to dinners and things tripping themselves up at the door and us a-accepting of them like anything. Ah sirs sirs! And I think that is all enoo. Jessie sends her kindest regards and kisses from the baby [Moira], and remember us both to Mr Turner who really ought not to have taken you away from Scotland, and believe me

　　Yours sempiternally
　　NEIL MUNRO
　　(alias Drimdarroch of Doom)[14]

Neil saw out the last old year of the old century in health, wealth and prosperity. At the end of 1899, his bank balance was an impressive £852.10s.6d.

CHAPTER EIGHTEEN

The slave of two serials

O N the first day of 1900, Neil noted in his diary: 'New Year opened with great discussion & dispute as to whether or not it is the beginning of the 20th Century. Lord Kelvin says it is, many others say not, & they are in the majority. National depression on account of several grave reverses to our Army in S. Africa. Reserves & Militia called out; Volunteers & yeomanry in large numbers go to the Front.'

While the Boer War raged on, Neil was battling away on the home front at his third novel. On February 12 he wrote to Alexander Wood of Blackwoods: 'Fine curling weather but I'm having none of it; the slave of duty, and putting in hard days' dargs at *Doom*... I hope the Chief is well.'

As if to encourage such literary diligence, Blackwood replied with a cheque for £67, Neil's 1899 royalties on *The Lost Pibroch* and *John Splendid*. Acknowledging receipt, Neil remarked that the money 'seems to give gratifying evidence that *John Splendid* has got a little life in him yet... I am well forward with my new story, of which I should like to send you in a month or two a good instalment for your consideration. If I am at all qualified to judge, it is the best thing I have done and has much more popular elements than its predecessors...'[1]

March began with general jubilation over the relief of Ladysmith. A few days later, Neil enrolled at the Berlitz school for 30 lessons in French conversation, costing £4.10s. This may have been to help him with the character of Count Victor in *Doom Castle*, but more practically it was good preparation for two forthcoming trips to France, a visit to the Exposition and a cycling holiday with J.M. Smith of the *News*. Despite the infrequency of Neil's visits to the newspaper offices, he remained good friends with Smith and the company, in which he now saw a good opportunity to invest his newfound wealth. He bought 25 of the £10 ordinary shares, then paying a dividend of seven and a half percent, and spent a further £250 on 25 preference shares, paying five percent.

In April his duties as special correspondent for the *News* took him to Ireland, to report on a Royal Visit by the elderly Queen Victoria. Arriving in Dublin in pouring rain, he put up at Wynne's Hotel. Yet the sun shone the following day as the Queen entered Dublin, and on subsequent days as Neil reported her appearances at College Green, at an illumination at Kingstown, and finally in Phoenix Park, where 35,000 children in their Sunday best turned out to meet Her Majesty.

Within a couple of days of returning to Glasgow, Neil was off again to cover the Paris Exposition, putting up at the Hôtel London & New York, St Lazare (Cook's coupons 13/6 a day including dinner & breakfast). J. Nicol Dunn had furnished him with a letter of introduction to Paul Derechef, Paris correspondent of the *Pall Mall Gazette*, with whom he had lunch a couple of times. Neil was not, however, impressed by the customary Parisian diversions for newspapermen away from home, noting in his diary: 'At Notre Dame, Invalides, Moulin Rouge (a fraud), Rat Mort in the Place Pigalle & Café d'Enfer there. Pathetically dull & silly.' He was the more delighted to bump into his neighbours the Hendersons from Busby, with whom he lunched on Easter Day at the Hotel Richmond, 'Rue Helder, near place de l'Opéra. They pay 10 fcs a day for room & double bed, lights &c first floor, with 4 fcs for lunch, 5 fcs for dinner optional'.

Four days after returning to Waterfoot, Neil took Jessie off to Inveraray with Effie and Hugh. Up at the Castle, the Duke of Argyll's health was now failing fast and in the early hours of the morning of 24 April, the Munros were wakened by the tolling of the church bell to mark his passing. They left for Glasgow that day, but Neil returned a week later to see the Duke's body lying in state and to write an article for the London *Daily Express*.

After a few days he went back to Waterfoot, where Moira had gone down with the measles, then returned on 11 May to report on the Duke's funeral, taking Niven the *News* artist with him to Inveraray. Lord Archie's pipe band under its pipe major, Charlie Maitland, playing 'The Flowers of the Forest', led the great procession which accompanied the bier, borne by ten men, from the castle to the parish church. After a brief service the coffin was put into the funeral car to be taken to Kilmun and the Argyll mausoleum.

Neil wrote: 'He left on a day of spring – all that was mortal of him – with the state and ceremony fitting the occasion, and it was to all who had known him for two or three generations as a neighbour as if MacCailein Mor had gone upon another foreign journey differing from many former ones in that there would be no return. We were moved by many incidents; no one with a Highland heart – no one with a heart of any kind – could witness without profound emotion those final honours to the dust of the Chief; but when the bells had ceased to toll, when the mourners had broken their processional order, when the last note of the piper's lament had sounded, the most moving moment of the day had come. The Duke was really gone! We stood, a confused and silent throng, at the boundary of his burgh, at the entrance to his policies, and saw his funeral car diminish in the distance... A day of profound emotions, I have said, and – though it may seem strange – a day not yet to be described except in the terms that to the journalist come mechanically.'[2]

Neil almost seems to taunt the reader by hinting that he could describe the day in other terms, an if he would. He was well aware that – in the West of Scotland at least – many believed he was a son of the late Duke. But he maintained his silence on the subject to the end of his days.

After the funeral he returned to Glasgow, wired a column to the *Daily Express*, and went home to Waterfoot.

Three weeks later, Neil sent Blackwood the first fourteen chapters of *Doom Castle*. A fortnight later, on 30 June, he wrote in his diary: 'Designed complete plot of a new novel, *The Red Shoes of Fortune*.' Minus the 'Red', this was to be the 1901 serial he had agreed to write for *Good Words*. Next day, embarking on fiction in a non-Highland setting for the first time, he wrote the first thousand words. In the midst of multifarious writing commitments he had been mulling over the plot of *Shoes*, otherwise he could not have 'designed' it so masterfully.

The idea had been in his mind since at least 1898, when a letter to Neil from Cunninghame Graham – 'Have you read *The Companions Of Pickle*? If not why not?'[3] – suggests the two of them had been comparing notes on Andrew Lang's earlier *Pickle The Spy* (1896). Both books, based on primary research, deal with espionage in Jacobite times, in particular with Glengarry, who spied for the British Government. Here indubitably was Neil's starting point for *The Shoes of Fortune*. As Ronald Renton has pointed out, the key passage seems to be:

'He admits that he acted as a mouton, or prison spy, and gives a dreadful account of the horrors of Galbanon, where men lay in the dark and dirt for half a lifetime. MacAllester next proses endlessly on the alleged Jesuit connection with Damien's attack on Louis XV, and insists that the Jesuits, nobody knows why, meant to assassinate Prince Charles. He was in very little danger from Jesuits.'[4]

In the January 1898 *Maga* there had been an article entitled 'Queen Oglethorpe' by 'A.S. and A.L. [Andrew Lang]'. It dealt also with Glengarry, and Neil had commented in a letter to William Blackwood: 'I like A.S. and A.L.'s "Queen Oglethorpe" very much too. I suppose I ought to kick, as a Highlander, against A.L.'s short way with the Celt, and his persistent exposure of Glengarry, and the whole of his historical interference with the Jacobite chiefs, but I am one of the few Highlanders who do not misunderstand his attitudes. I am sure he likes the race and I know he loves their romance and his only weakness in this affair seems to be a regard for a virtue called Truth which the common Highland sennachie (being a gentleman of imagination) is not apt to value deeply.'[5]

Yet twelve months later, Neil's ideas for *The Shoes of Fortune* remained inchoate, and it would be 1 July 1900 before he penned the opening paragaph. Now he had to buckle down as never before, and by October fourteen chapters had been sent off to *Good Words*. It would take him exactly a year to complete the book.

Three days after making a start, he felt confident enough to take a day off and went to Edinburgh to lunch at the New Club with D.S. Meldrum, William Blackwood and his nephews. It was arranged that he would be paid £400 for the serial rights of *Doom Castle* and '1s 3d per volume on the first 3,000 books, with increases thereafter'. Serialisation was to begin in the October *Maga*. With two novels now on the go, the phenomenal rate of production precluded a family holiday in Inveraray that summer. At any rate Jessie, who was expecting a baby in September, was spared the upheaval, and Neil found some consolation in postponing the family's first return to Argyll in its new mode. One day towards the end of July, in the middle of Glasgow, Neil's attention was caught by a spectacle he must often have seen before but which now, temporarily exiled from Argyll, he found particularly poignant:

'On Saturday forenoon a woman wheeled a barrow of herrings along Waterloo Street. They were Loch Fyne herrings; they were apparently trawl-caught, somewhat limp and bruised in the boxes. I was not having any. Seven or eight hours ago the fish were probably swimming somewhere north of the spit at Otter. It was a still, cloudy night; the skiffs in pairs crept about the Loch in darkness, sailing, simply with a jib, round the spots where gannets had been seen in the afternoon. Other pairs could be seen dimly on the same pursuit further inshore below the loom of the Cowal hills, and out in the middle of the Loch three or four buyers' screws seemed stationary but for the occasional beat of a propellor. A wonderful stillness held the land and sea, and the fishermen, peering through the night, spoke in the lowest tones. It was two in the morning; Glasgow's breakfast seemed a fading possibility.

'All of a sudden a man reports an "eye" to windward; the jib comes down, the sweeps [oars] go out, in a little the net is round the morning's spoils and the two boats close together haul in the net till they bring the leaden bag of it between them. A couple of torches flare and show the fish a silvery mass of countless numbers, so packed together that they are easily lifted out – in hundreds at a time, struggling a little, piping with a faint shrillness, iridescent, altogether lovely, but doomed for the Saltmarket.

'Eight men sweat at the task of emptying the net; eight men in every other pair of boats with similar luck are doing the same all over the Loch; torches gleam from every side. The buyers' screws promptly wake to life and churn the water, bear down with great staring eyes of green and red upon the torches, and lose little time in chaffering for a price. Very quickly the boxes on their decks are filled, very quickly is the steamer's load made up; before dawn she is ploughing round Ardlamont, with Glasgow's breakfast once more secure. And here's a woman wheeling it through the rain in Waterloo Street, perhaps a little late for breakfast, but still in plenty of time for tea.'

This was part of Neil's 'Looker-On' column on 30 July, under the heading 'The Glasgow Magistrate', a nickname for red herring. Writing it must have brought back memories of that other article, written long ago about the Inveraray fishing fleet, that had been the germ of his whole writing career.

In August Neil left the family behind and set out on a cycling tour with J.M. Smith, the artist Macaulay Stevenson and John Ewing, a school inspector. On reaching London they put up for the night at the Norfolk Hotel and dined in the Gaiety. On the morning of 30 August, with the sun shining, they took the 10 a.m. ferry for Dieppe, where they stayed at the Hôtel Soleil d'Or and took a spin out to see the Château d'Argues.

The cycle journey to Paris was wet, broken for one night at Pont de l'Arche, where they decided to put the bikes on the train to the capital. There they checked into the Hôtel London & New York before going out that evening to view the Exposition. There were further excursions in the next few days to the Bois de Boulogne and Montmartre, before setting off on 5 September for a cycling tour of Normandy. They rode through St Germains and put up for the night at Triel. Next day they lunched at Mantes and arrived that evening at the Hôtel d'Evreux in Gaillon. A third day's ride took them via Andelys, Fleury and Boos to Rouen, but by the time they reached the Hôtel Lisieux J.M. Smith was 'knocked up a little'.

The following day, 8 September, Neil went with Smith on the train while Stevenson and Ewing cycled to Dieppe. There the four friends boarded the ferry together for Newhaven. Before returning to Scotland, Neil enjoyed four nights in London, where he attended a meeting of the Journalists' Institute, lunched with friends at Café Florence and went to see Julie Neilson in *Sweet Nell of Old Drury* at the Haymarket Theatre.

His return home to Waterfoot in the small hours of 13 September was not a minute too soon. Five hours later, Jessie presented him with a second son (Dr Macfarlane and Nurse Grieve attending). According to the traditional naming pattern the Munros had followed hitherto, the baby should have been called after his paternal grandfather. Since this was out of the question he was named Neil.

The following day an elated Neil Munro senior flew through proofs of the first instalment of *Doom Castle* and posted them off to *Maga*. Within three weeks the public was enjoying the new serial and Neil was writing to Blackwood: 'I thank you for your kind note received yesterday, and its cheque for £100. What an author hears of his own work must be taken, I suppose, with some discount, but I am glad to be told by some of the booksellers here that their regular customers are very favourably impressed with the first instalment of *Doom Castle*... I dined with Dr William Wallace [Editor of the

Glasgow Herald] the other evening, and found him tremendously enthusiastic over last month's *Maga* article on 'The Old Golf and the New'. He is a very keen golfer, and just as keen a follower of *Maga*... I shall be sending you some more copy in a few days.'[6]

The income Neil could now command with his pen helped pay for the services of Nurse Grieve for a month to help Jessie back on to her feet. Neil's satisfaction at his own progress was enhanced by seeing new work by an old friend. On 13 October he wrote to Blackwood: 'Many thanks for Conrad's novel... I had read the most of it in the magazine, and liked it well... Of Conrad's genius I am convinced, no writer has more strongly impressed me, and whether *Lord Jim* will do it or not, some work of his will open the eyes of the public to the fact that here's a great man among them...'

Now becoming quite a distinguished figure himself, Neil sat that month for a new oil portrait by Miss Stansmore R.L. Dean, future wife of his artist friend and cycling companion Macaulay Stevenson. But with two serials in progress, Neil could not rest on his laurels. On 22 October he posted off Chapters 8 – 14 of *The Shoes of Fortune* to *Good Words* before greeting his mother who had come on a visit from Inveraray.

Neil's literary success was now viewed covetously by other publishers. Eveleigh Nash, of A. Constable & Co., came to see him and, over lunch, offered a royalty of 27.5 per cent with an advance of £300 or £400 if Neil would put his next novel Constable's way. Although no doubt flattered, Neil decided to stick with Blackwood.

Despite keeping hard at work, Neil found time time to socialise, reading a paper on Highland Superstitions to the Thirteen Club and attending the annual dance of Inveraray 'natives' at the Trades Hall. He also went to see Henry Irving and Ellen Terry in *Olivia* at the Theatre Royal. By the end of November Stansmore Dean had finished Neil's portrait and the household at Waterfoot had grown with the arrival of Neilina McGregor, a distant cousin from Inveraray, to act as nurse to young Neil.

Five days before Christmas, the Munros were invited to a dinner party at the home of J.M. Smith, where the night outside was so stormy that Smith's billiard-room window was blown in. The storms continued through into the New Year, but without putting a dampener on the festivities. Neil and Jessie enjoyed 'Hogmanay High Jinks' at Dr William Wallace's house and drove home at 3.30 a.m. 'in tempestuous weather'.

All in all, Neil had weathered the first year of the new century rather well, ending up with a comfortable bank balance of

£586.11s.9d. He made a practice of noting his financial position in his diary at the end of each year. It was a matter of quiet pride, but also of supreme importance to the father of five children, his lifeline in a lonely world where there were no arts council grants or government hand-outs. So long as he was able to keep enough capital in hand, he could forge ahead as a novelist and steer clear of full-time jawboxery.

CHAPTER NINETEEN

I got about 2 doz trout

AS 1901 got under way, the serialisation of *Doom Castle* in *Maga* proceeded smoothly, but not without incident. A descendant of Lord Kilkerran, one of the two judges who presided at the Appin murder trial, took exception to Neil's treatment of his ancestor. When *Doom Castle* eventually came out in book form, a passage in Chapter Ten would describe Kilkerran as having 'the lack-lustre eye of the passionate mathematician, the studious moralist devoted to midnight oil, a ruddy, tall, sturdy man, well filling the crimson and white silk gown'. But Neil's original description that appeared in *Maga* was somewhat stronger, describing Kilkerran as 'an emeritus roué with a cruelly cynical knowledge of the world' and 'the roving bloodshot eyes of a fast liver'.

Neil had overlooked the fact that although there was no present-day Lord Kilkerran, the title of a Scottish law lord not being heritable, there was in fact a direct descendant in Sir James Fergusson of Kilkerran who took great exception to what he regarded as a slander on his noble forebear. Sir James wrote to *Maga*'s editor: 'I submit, Sir, that when the author of a "Romance" draws a fancy and unpleasing picture of a character, which suits his story, he has no right to attach to it the name of a man of good historical repute, whose lineal descendants may well feel themselves outraged by such a liberty, and I cannot but wonder that an Edinburgh magazine of high standing should admit such a travesty of an Edinburgh worthy of not too long gone by.'

On 8 January, 1901, Neil wrote to Alexander Wood of Blackwood's: 'I'm sorry he should feel hurt at the purely imaginary allusion to his ancestor who figures no further in the story... The name may be altered or the character changed the very little that is necessary, in book form; that, obviously, is all I can do now. If Sir James writes to *The Scotsman*, I fancy I shall not reply there, but shall personally apologise to the Right Honourable Gentleman for a reflection upon his house which was never intended. With all good wishes to "No. 45" for the New Century...'

Oddly Neil seemed unaware that the day before another letter from Sir James had already appeared in *The Scotsman*. It is on the same lines as his letter to *Maga* but refers to Neil as 'Neil Malcolm'. Then, on 19 January, Sir James had a very long letter in the *Spectator* in the same vein, with many details about his ancestor, ending up: 'I submit that these methods are offensive and un-English [sic].' No correspondence in the *Spectator* ensued.

On 22 January, Neil was elected President of the Thirteen Club. A week later, an item in Neil's diary marked the close of an era: 'Queen Victoria died about 7 o'clock this evening at Osborne.' In Glasgow, however, there was the more pressing matter of a small-pox epidemic, against which Neil had himself vaccinated, two days before the Queen's funeral on 2 February. Among the poets who marked the Queen's passing was W.E. Henley, and around this time he wrote to Neil who, it seems, had asked him to write something:

Dear Mr Munro,

I will do something – certainly: if I can. Please give me a date; & I'll do my best to work up to it.

I think I owe to your kindness about the only hand I got in the press for my threnody [on Victoria's death]. In any case, for old sake's sake, I believe you'll like to have my enclosure: if it be only as a piece of printing.

How are you? And when (I ask it in all humility) – when are you going to make me think of you as other than the writer of 'Jus Primae Noctis'?

Yours Ever Sincerely,

W.E.H.

P.S. I have mislaid your letter, & must e'en send this to 'the old friend' in Hope Street.

Neil did not complete *Doom Castle* until 1 March, having in the interim allowed himself to be diverted by a tour of the buildings erected at Kelvingrove in Glasgow for the International Exhibition, due to open at the start of May.

While in Glasgow he called on 'Aunty Chirsty', Christina Munro, widow of his mother's half-brother John. She was finding life hard financially and Neil gave her £1, followed up a week later with a further £1.10s. The newspaper publisher J.M. Smith Ltd was doing well, however, and declared a dividend of 7½ per cent on Neil's ordinary shares. Company profits for 1900 had been £12,000, of which £2,000 was put into a reserve fund and £3,000 carried over.

Neil had not, however, heard the last of Sir James Fergusson of Kilkerran. Sir James continued to complain loudly of Neil's slight on his esteemed ancestor. It seems William Blackwood had written to Sir James, for on 12 March Neil wrote to Alexander Wood: 'Don't you think Sir James ought to be satisfied with Mr Blackwood's assurance that there will be no unpleasant allusions to his ancestor in the work? The worthy baronet did not appeal to me for sympathy but to the public who read the *Spectator* and *The Scotsman* and if I cared to advertise myself I might have followed him there with my explanation but I don't. If he had written to me personally he should have had a prompt and profound apology but I consider that as things went he made himself to me a little ridiculous...'

Yet there was more to life than literature, and living in the past. Neil continued to enjoy his journalism and looking to the future. In 'The Looker-On' for 8 April, after talking at length of American imports such as fountain pens and Heinz products, he observed: 'a stiff neck is the worst feature of insularity and insularity's inevitable consequence. Psychologically, we are a people with old ideas and associations. We carry a load of history and precedent on our backs and cannot rid ourselves of the burden... Age in the nation is like age in the individual – it precludes the acceptance of new ideas and prefers to fulfil an ordered routine. Inertia, complacency, self-satisfaction – call it what you will – overtake every old and especially every successful people. England [sic] has prospered, and lies back in calm assurance that all is well. But is it?'

The Press View of the International Exhibition came more than a week before it was open to the public, and included a trip down the Clyde on the *Columba*. Neil, who could still recall the previous International Exhibition of 1888, now used the occasion to turn his 'Looker-On' column into a 'Letter to a Young Man Abroad', discussing the changes in the intervening years. Among these was the arrival of the new Glasgow School of Art, designed by Charles Rennie Mackintosh and already partially completed by 1901.

Although Mackintosh's major designs for the Exhibition itself were largely rejected, he did design some stands. There was also an 18ft-high statue of Edward VII, the new monarch, by one Albert Hodge.

Among other changes, Neil noted the emergence of 'a new type distinctly in the Art School Girl. She was invented, I fancy, by Mr Newbery [Head of the Art School], and by her hair you shall know her. She looks like a plagiarism on Botticelli and the dames of Alphonse Daudet; she has weird conceptions in evening costumes, is in many respects peculiar to Glasgow, and, on the whole, rather charming...'

There were also changes due to the passage of time: 'No consideration would prevail on me to go arm-and-arm with six others down Gibson Street singing "The Guard Ship" (as I think it was in 1888). I have forgotten the words, I have forgotten the way, and, even if I dared, Kate would say it was a lovely example to set before the children! Thirteen years, Jim! *'Eheu fugaces!'* I own a frock-coat – heaven help me...'

'The tartan of the Clanneries would not be tolerated in 1901: we demand quiet tones and no patterns on the walls; under the new system you stir your tea with a spoon that is unlike any other spoon ever seen on this earth, and butter your bread with a sage-green-handled stiletto...'

'Where we crawled on old tram-cars, covered out and in with advertisements, we dart by electricity in vehicles that are a hundred times superior... The Subway and the Central underground [railway station] have been introduced since 1888, and as a whole we have become more restless people, travelling ten miles where before we travelled one.'[1]

As the first paying public flocked through the doors of the Exhibition on 3 May, Neil and the family went down to Inveraray, where they took up residence for two months in Miss Mary Birrell's flat in Arkland. During his stay he went cycling with John Maitland, newly returned from Japan, to Cuil sale, a house near Dunderave, and to Cumlodden with Maitland, Neil's step-cousin Flora Thomson and Maggie McNiven. Neil also met up with J.M.M. Munro and his family, who were staying at the Post Office at St Catherine's.

While at Inveraray, Neil received a letter from William Blackwood that was gratifying on the bread-and-butter side of things: 'On looking up terms of arrangement for *Doom Castle*'s appearance in Magazine I see another payment was due you on 1st of this month & I am sorry it has been delayed. But I now have pleasure of enclosing your cheque on Coutts & Co for £100... The orders [from booksellers for *Doom Castle* in book form] in London & the English provinces were respectively 769 & 400 = 1169 copies, & in Edinburgh 1125 copies. This last is very good owing to our success with John Menzies & Co who intend making a great push with it and ordered 728 copies. They are to have a Munro window at both Waverley & Caledonian Princes Street Stations & in Glasgow too I expect, as they were taken with your idea. The London trade number was very disappointing but they complained that *Gilian* had done very badly with them being stuck with copies... I have been wondering how you progressed with your idea for a new story & if you think it will be one that is likely to suit the Magazine. If so I shall be glad to arrange with you for its appearance serially & in book form on terms similar to those I proposed to you for *Doom Castle*. Mr Morton told me of his meeting with you last week & I was happy to hear you were enjoying a well earned holiday. Hoping soon to send you more news of *Doom Castle* & with best remembrances from all here...'[2]

Neil replied on 28 May, giving his address as simply 'Inveraray, Argyllshire', accepting these terms. The novel he had in mind was to be *Children of Tempest*, but there was no need to rush into it. There was still time to go fishing the moor-lochs at Killean, a farm between Inveraray and Furnace, with Alister McArthur and John Maitland, after which Neil noted with satisfaction: 'I got about 2 doz trout.'

The extended holiday gave him time also to catch up on personal correspondence. On 3 June he typed a convivial letter to his cousin Kate Turner:

'Impute it not to forgetfulness that you have not sooner heard from my wife or myself in answer to your letters. We are, by nature, children of sin and sloth, we mean well... the day after tomorrow, a common Hiel'n [sic] quality you will sympathise with... May was gloriously fine but now we have rain which I am rather glad to see as it compels me to stay indoors and work. When it is fine, I fish, sail, golf, loaf and meditate – especially meditate. If there's anything in heredity my clan must have been deuced strong in Meditation. Runs into Neil too; he just Meditates and Meditates like anything. Sometimes he greets [cries]. The latter usually at night when I want to sleep... Neilina [McGregor, the nurse] has basely deserted us since we came here... I observe of a Sabbath the Faithful Remnant harmonious as of old at John Turner's Corner lifting their voices in sacred song. Nevertheless the town is unregenerate. But as interesting as ever...

'I am, nominally at least or by intention, very busy. *Doom Castle* came out last week, has been very well reviewed and is selling better than any of its predecessors. *The Shoes of Fortune* are still on my conscience, but I hope to put heels on 'em this month. I am in good health and so are all of us... Thanks for offering to take Effie for a few days. Some time we shall send her for I believe in letting young-sters see as many different places as possible and getting as many different impressions as their heads will hold... My wife has just come in to blow me up for not writing this letter long ago. I had quietened her three weeks since by saying I *had* written to you, and now she has found me out. So I am quite distracted and can say no more...'

CHAPTER TWENTY

The pause of the morning, when time stands

WHILE the Munros were staying at the flat in the Arkland, Neil was invited to lunch with the new Duke of Argyll at Kilcatrine, a house near St Catherine's. Since the House of Argyll featured frequently in his novels, and bearing in mind the reaction of Sir James Fergusson of Kilkerran, Neil may have been a little appre-hensive. But there was nothing to fear, as he reported later to William Blackwood: 'The Argylls, I think, were much annoyed at my treatment of their ancestor in *John Splendid*, but my "Duke" in *Doom Castle* seems to have quite made it up between us; the Duke... said some very handsome things about the latter story.'[1]

The title of *Doom Castle* surely caused the Duke some wry amusement, for while it was being serialised in *Maga* he had let Inveraray Castle to a stranger as part of an economy drive. Hence the move to Kilcatrine, where Lady Victoria Campbell, one of the Duke's sisters, was of the luncheon party, along with Elspeth Campbell, Lord Archie's daughter. The presence of Mr Lowis, who like Sim MacTaggart in *Doom Castle* was Chamberlain of Argyll, appealed perhaps to the Duke's well-known sense of humour. The absence of the Duchess, Princess Louise, was scarcely remarkable. She and the Duke now led semi-detached lives, and she had been much taken up with royal matters since her brother succeeded to the throne in January. The Duke had been at Queen Victoria's death bed and described her as going down 'like a great three-masted ship'. He had been in hot water since then with his brother-in-law, the King, and with the Kaiser as well, for publishing biographical *résumés* of Victoria's life.

The oddness of the Duke's living in a modest house from which his large castle was plainly visible across the loch was somehow mitigated by the overarching novelties of the new century and the new *régimes*, royal and ducal. The Duke himself was unperturbed, if Neil was right about him: 'Everybody knew he really was more unaffected and amiable – more of a plain man's man – than any other in the peerage... a Bohemian of the refined and elegant order... He had the artist's power of being at home and at his ease in any situation... he had the artist's merriment, the artist's tenderness, and he had humility – a strange thing to find in an Argyll!'[2]

Though these impressions are from an article the Duke would never see, he could not but sense Neil's sympathy. 'It may have been to me alone, but there seemed, I have always thought, a kind of pathos in those latter re-visitations to the scenes of childhood – the family scattered, dear voices gone... There are in Inveraray many photographic family groups of the Argyll children that affect one like recaptured gleams, in dreams of a once Arcadian Inveraray where the Campbell bairns would seem to live in a perpetual *fête champêtre*.'

The Duke's marriage was childless, but Neil's own bairns could now enjoy Inveraray's Arcadian propensities while their father went off on little jaunts. On 12 June, he cycled with the Rev D.A. Cameron Reid to Portsonochan and lunched with Miss Campbell on Inischonain, an island in Loch Awe belonging to her brother, Walter Campbell of Blythswood. While there, Neil heard that William Blackwood was at nearby Hayfield, the house that replaced the former MacArthur seat of Tiravadich on the western shore of the loch.

Neil's old friend Pittendrigh Macgillivray, the sculptor, continued to urge him to pay a visit, to which Neil replied from Inveraray: 'Many thanks for your note. It has been in my mind a long while that I should bear down on Ravelston Elms, and somehow the expedition has been postponed from month to month. I am seldom in

Edinburgh – only once, I think, I have been there in the past twelve-month, and when there I cannot get out of reach of 45 George Street where the guids are – I mean Blackwood's. For two months back I and my family have been in Inveraray and we will be here till the end of the month. Thereafter for some weeks – mainly on a business expedition – to Uist and Barra and the Outer Isles generally, so that Murrayfield won't be possible till well on in next month...

'Are you still throng on the *piob mor*? I am here in the midst of a dozen constant players – drums and a' – but mysel' I never finger a chanter. And so the Macskeoch is returning from the wars [South African]? I should like fine to be there to welcome with the rest...'⁴

Macgillivray, who had enjoyed *Doom Castle*, was sure he knew where Neil had found the model for one of the characters, but the author replied: 'No, Mungo Boyd was not your waiter. He was, partly, a tailor in this neighbourhood, who had for obvious reasons to be considerably altered in the outline. I had rather a curious experience with Mungo; the beggar was pretty well written up (I mean mostly completed) and I thought him no that bad ava, when it occurred to me that he seemed completely familiar. I have a wretched memory and I had to read over a half a dozen of Scott's novels to discover – alas! – that I was unconsciously plagiarising Caleb Balderstone [in *The Bride of Lammermoor*]! I had to re-write the character; in spite of that I fear sometimes a little of Caleb lingers, and at least I know my Mungo is not so good as he was in the first draft.'⁵

Good enough, surely. Mungo and Caleb are each the only remaining male retainers of impoverished families, battling to keep up appearances in derelict castles. Their devices have a similar touching risibility. Mungo, for instance, declares: 'There's the end o' a hench o' venison frae Strathlachlan, and twa oors syne, when the tide was oot, there was beef padovies and stoved howtowdies, but I gied them to twa gaun-aboot bodies.'⁶ Like Caleb or the porter in *Macbeth*, Mungo provides pawky light relief in a grim tale. He also, being a Lowlander from Fife, gives piquant contrast to the Highlanders about him, as does the French Count Victor.

Dunderave Castle on its small promontory near the head of Loch Fyne is the prototype for Doom Castle. It was still in ruins when Neil unsuspectingly wrote his romance. The inscription given in Chapter II still exists, though Neil altered it a little, superimposing the word 'Doom'. It was the seat of the MacNachtans, built in the late 16th century when they moved from a small island, now a promontory, in the Dubh Loch at the foot of Glen Shira. This, I think, gave Neil the notion to site *Doom Castle* on a tidal islet. Can there be another instance of an obscure ruined castle suddenly receiving such concentrated attention as did Dunderave between 1899 and 1911, first re-peopled by a novelist, then 'restored' by an architect? Neil felt that by Sir Robert Lorimer's re-modelling 'the spiritual sentiment of Dunderave has been utterly and uselessly destroyed... It was virtually an empty shell... It ministered to the artist's eye alone, and to romantic sentiment. It was a salient and attractive feature of the coast.'[7]

The passage leading from the cell in the fosse of Argyll's castle (Chapter XXXI) has an intriguing source. An early visitor to the castle (1758) mentioned that 'Loaded Carts pass through a Subterraneous Passage, to the Fosse', but according to Ian G. Lindsay and Mary Cosh 'there is no evidence that it was ever completed'.[8] Neil likely knew of the aborted passage by hearsay or boyhood exploration. He has the passage coming out under a bridge, clearly Frew's Bridge, which has odd little underground rooms at either end, certainly known to himself.

Probably many readers enjoy *Doom Castle* as a straightforward story of adventure and romance, with a kaleidoscope of characters. Others will revel in the exuberant piling up of Gothic features, not unconnected with Neil's boyhood delight in 18th-century mystery tales. Yet another aspect is the light sketching-in of that period in the Highlands when the *Gleichschaltung* after Culloden was just beginning to be felt.

There is some ambiguity about the date of the action. The Duke says 'this is '55' – yet the Appin trial is on the go, and it took place in 1752. Then again, the new Inveraray Castle was not completed till 1758, but it is clearly the castle described. The 3rd Duke died in 1761 after a long widowerhood following a childless marriage, while the Duke in *Doom Castle* is happily married and much more like the 4th Duke in every way.

Doom Castle itself embodies all that is ambiguous and obscure, its dusty, half-deserted passages seeming to end in 'the dark backward and abysm of time'. Count Victor arrives from France, seeking revenge on the elusive Drimdarroch, to find 'all his pleasant anticipations of the character of this baronial dwelling utterly erroneous'. We discover it gradually through the eyes of this gallant Frenchman: its baffling internal architecture, its inhabitants whose half-revealed actions puzzle him almost to the end.

The plot can mostly be left to wend its own tortuous way while the reader is engrossed by the cast. The Baron of Doom himself,

Lamond, is a valedictory figure, the last of a long line, 'chastened by years and some unco experiences from a truculent man to one preferring peace except at the last ditch', as he tells Count Victor. Another time he says: 'I've seen the day they were throng enough buzzing about Doom, but that was only so long as honey was to rob... Now that I'm a rooked bird and Doom a herried nest, they never look the road I'm on.' He dresses doucely, rises and goes to bed early – yet secretly wears the proscribed Highland dress and has proscribed weapons. Count Victor first gains insight into Doom's character when the latter, opening the outer door to look at the dimly star-lit hills, remarks: 'For me, that prospect is my evening prayer.'

Important elements in the novel are introduced by tantalising degrees. Lamond's daughter Olivia finally appears on page 121. Argyll's castle and town are not fully revealed till Chapter X – a whole complicated society just round the corner from the desolation of Doom. We see enough of Argyll himself to appreciate his balanced outlook and happy marriage. Then there is his Chamberlain, Sim MacTaggart, and that 'lady of extraordinary beauty', Mrs Kate Petullo, whose intimacy with the Chamberlain is strongly sketched in. Sim is an enigmatic character. 'He had just the history and career and reputation that to men and women, except the very wisest and the somewhat elderly, have an attraction all unreasonable...' He wants to end his affair with Kate, whom he privately holds capable of putting 'rat-bane' in her despised husband's broth.

Kate Petullo has been called a 'small-town Argyllshire Emma Bovary'[9] but she is more mettlesome and unscrupulous than Emma, though of course we do not have a full-length character study of her. In wild despair at losing Sim, she sits all night at the window, 'shuddering with distaste at her cage... For her the flaming east was hell's own vestibule...' Madame Bovary cannot be pictured running out on the ebb-tide shore like Kate when she sees Sim and Victor duelling there. 'Her gown trailed in the pools and flicked up the ooze of weed and sand; a shoulder bared itself; some of her hair took shame and covered it with a veil of dull gold.'

All this found favour with the book-buying public, and at the start of July another cheque for £100 arrived from William Blackwood, who wrote from St Andrews that *Doom Castle* was selling steadily: 'Up to the present I calculate we have sold something like 3850 copies at home and 1000 to the Colonies (Colonial Edition). For the time the book has been out this I think is fairly satisfactory. The reviews too have been very favourable with the exception of one in the *Academy* which was plainly the work of one who did not wish you well, and is not likely to see any good in anything you may write... I shall be much disappointed if you do not come into your own with *Doom Castle*...

'I am sure you must be enjoying your stay at Inveraray in this delightful weather, and I hope your Mother keeps better than she was. I am taking a holiday in St Andrews where I used to go so frequently in past years. But it is a greatly changed place and has not the *bonhomie* about it that it had in my Uncle's, Tulloch's and Shairp's days. All the same there are some pleasant men about and some fine golfers. Have you learned the art yet? It is a most enticing game to all ages of both sexes I see now...'[10]

Neil replied on 2 July from Waterfoot: 'I came back here from Inveraray on a flying visit on Saturday and I'm arranging to go off on a short visit to the Hebrides, which I fancy will conclude my rambling for the summer. My recreation at Inveraray was fishing – principally on the moor lochs where I had occasionally a fair basket. There is a golf course – a very rough and ready one unfortunately – and I tried a practice hand two or three days at the game. My first experience was rather funny. I got up at five in the morning with a friend; we had, by an overlook, only two balls between us... At our first drive we both lost a ball in some long grass and after an hour's ineffectual search had to come away in disgust, consoling ourselves partly by a bathe in Loch Fyne. I do not ask you to believe the drives were of Braid-like ability either.'

A week later, Neil at last finished writing *The Shoes of Fortune* – with what relief can well be imagined – and on 13 July he went to Edinburgh for the much-delayed visit to Pittendrigh Macgillivray's, where the two friends talked long into the night.

CHAPTER TWENTY-ONE

They are saying the old wife is gone!

ALTHOUGH the International Exhibition continued in Glasgow until November, Neil saw very little of it apart from 'the flame of the dome in the sunshine'[1] which was visible, planet-like, from Waterfoot. He did, however, help to arrange a visit by the Inveraray Pipe Band. On 1 August he wrote to Charlie Maitland from the News office: 'I have just had a call from ex-Bailie Simons who proposes to have the Inveraray Pipe Band to the Exhibition before the season is over... I mentioned that the band numbered about fourteen or fifteen men all told, and said I thought there would be no difficulty about getting you to come if Lord Archibald and the Duke were willing, and I feel sure they would have no objections... As to remuneration you should charge for expenses, what it will cost you in hotels, fares, &c at the Bazaar, & a good weekly wage for each man, with specially good fee for yourself, and then slump the whole... P.S. Write to Waterfoot. As a matter of courtesy I am writing to Lord A. in Tiree mentioning that the band is asked for, so that he may arrange with you.'

Two weeks later Neil set off for the Outer Isles. He travelled by train to Oban, joining forces at Dunblane with John T. Ewing, the school inspector who had been one of the cycling party in France the previous year. Ewing was to inspect some of the island schools and welcomed the company of a Gaelic speaker. For Neil the trip was an opportunity to gather material for the new novel he had promised Blackwood. Before setting out for the Hebrides, he had in mind a 'fable based upon the fact that a very large sum of money sent from France in 1746 to assist Prince Charles Edward in his "Rising" was hidden in the Highlands and never found again'.[2] This was 'the Loch Arkaig *ulaidh*' (p.23), which Neil took the liberty of locating in the Isle of Mingulay, south of Barra.

They chanced to arrive in Catholic Barra on the eve of the Feast of the Assumption. Neil noted in his diary: 'Though it is a weekday (Wednesday) it is a period of "obligation" and men and women are to be seen walking up to the church, where I found many kneeling at worship inside and many seated on benches outside. To make up their obligatory number of visits some of them go in four times a day.

[As well as being the eve of the Feast of the Assumption there was a Papal injunction to make sixty visitations in celebration of the new century.] The women all wear a tartan plaid on the shoulders and many of them a tartan plaid on the head. No hats are to be seen.'

Neil's abiding impression was of the church in Castlebay, Our Lady Star of the Sea, especially the interior: 'I never thought... to see Gaels kneel before an image of the Virgin Mary, fingering rosaries; but here they are, and it seems the most natural thing in the world. This church upon the rock, its doors open always, and the prayers of the people to be heard daily in it, seem essentially appropriate. I have seen Protestant churches in the Highlands that by comparison are eyesores and outrages on the name and spirit of Christianity.'

He delighted in the populous aspect of the islands compared with most of the *Gaidhealtachd*, where sheep and deer had long ousted human beings. He was less happy to learn that the teacher in Castlebay, though sharing his 250 pupils' Roman Catholic religion, knew no Gaelic, though the children had virtually no English when starting school.

From Castlebay Neil and Ewing walked to the North Bay Hotel via the head of Loch Na, calling in to inspect Loch Bay School, kept by Mr and Mrs Flannigan from Glasgow. 'When Flannigan first came to the island he was very seasick and exhausted on landing at Castlebay. Mr Smith and Father Chisholm wanted him to stay at Castlebay. "No," he replied, "I'll see it through at once, and just take a cab to North Bay!" He had not realised that Barra was not Glasgow.'

After two days in Barra, Neil and Ewing hired a fishing skiff with a crew of four to take them across to the Isle of Eriskay, where the school was to be inspected. On the way Neil idly asked one of the boatmen what was in a box under a thwart. The boatman disclaimed any knowledge of that, declaring cryptically: '*M'anam fhein cha 'n 'eil fhois agam, 's e rudeigenn a fhuair sinn 'n raoir air son Maighstir Ailean.*'[3] Thus for the first time Neil heard the name of the Eriskay priest, Father Allan MacDonald. Soon afterwards, while he was in the schoolhouse with Ewing, the priest came in, 'a man over six feet, lean, and greatly younger-looking than his age'[4] (four years older than Neil). He took them to the Presbytery House for a lunch of sea-trout – the contents of the box, which the boatmen had brought unasked, for they knew that Father Allan would not have fish to give his visitors, though it was Friday. There was also Spanish wine, favoured by Father Allan who had studied five years in Valladolid.

117

The priest was amused and surprised that the boatmen had agreed to have Neil as a passenger in his suit of tweed dyed brown with crotal (lichen), 'for Barra believes that the crotal ever hankers for the native rock, and whoso wears it in a boat courts sure destruction'. Evidently Father Allan regarded such Gaelic superstitions with amused tolerance and, as Neil noted: 'It did not take long to discover that in this gentle, kindly priest there were many rare and shining qualities. He delighted in his people, he had a passion for his isle, and yet his mind ranged far beyond his office and the limits of his parish.'

Father Allan told them of his work collecting folklore, some of which had been used by Alexander Carmichael in *Carmina Gadelica* (1900). Afterwards, when he showed them his little island, roughly the size of Iona, the affectionate camaraderie of his people was evident everywhere. Here Neil's Gaelic stood him in good stead as he spoke to the islanders about the remote life they led. 'There is only one postal mail per week, and it was nine days after Queen Victoria's death before they learned of it in Eriskay. A fisherman came to Father Allan and said: *'Tha iad a'gradh gum bheil a' chailleach air falbh!'* (They are saying the old wife is gone!) Rents on the island average £1 per annum – poor little 'black houses' they are. The natives consider themselves practically outside of Britain, as nothing is ever done for them by the State. They pay no rates, and have no votes.'

After showing them where the new church of St Michael's was to be built, Father Allan saw them to their boat. He told them that the people knelt on these very sands 'when all that was mortal of each departed islander set out on its final voyage to the burial ground in Uist... The fact aroused, and still arouses, a great and moving mental picture, but I cherish another – of the lonely figure of Father Allan waving his farewell on the sands at Rudha Chliadh, and walking slowly, with bent head, upward to his dwelling, and turning again in the wind, and the cry of the uncomforted sea, and waving one last time as our sails filled and we passed from the isle of his dreams and his devotion into the tumult of the Sound, and into the wise world of towns and cities and men.'[5]

The tour of school inspections continued to the next island, where Neil noted: 'A good part of Berneray has lately been divided up among crofters; there is a population of about 300... Berneray gets all its peat from the island of N. Uist and in exchange the Berneray crofters give five or six days per annum of free labour with a boat. Dog-fish is eaten, indeed a great many of the poorer people in these islands make good use of it. They call it *biorach* in Gaelic and we saw in many places dog-fish cured and drying. It is an oily fish with an unpleasant pungent odour when cured. An ex-schoolmaster at Newton told us that pupils who came to school after a meal of *biorach* were pretty odorous.'

On the next island Neil observed: 'Monach Islanders are all Protestants but very primitive in their manners and customs. Till recently they had a practice called "gainish" in which the young women of the island surrounded any stranger arriving with a rope, and extracted from him, before they would release him, a promise that he would benefit the island in some way – either by a purchase of its home-made tweed (3s to 4s a yard) or otherwise. Westford Inn was built by old Sir John Orde for a doctor; it is an ugly square building with lattice windows and all the fireplaces in the centre of the house for the conservation of heat... When we were there we were attended by... a rather pretty but boorish young woman whose manner was execrable.'

So far they had been blessed with good weather, but Neil's diary entry for 25 August reads: 'The only really wet day we have had since coming to the islands. It rained all day; landscape looked melancholy beyond words.'

He returned to auld claes and parritch at Waterfoot and making the usual infrequent and laconic entries in his diary:

13 Sept. With John Maitland seeing Henry Irving in *The Merchant of Venice* at the Royalty Theatre.
21 Sept. David Hodge came from London for his marriage & remained with us till the 26th at Waterfoot.
24 Sept. Effie started taking piano lessons.
26 Sept. With Jessie at wedding of David Hodge & Lizzie Wallace at Dr Wallace's. [The bride was the daughter of the editor of the *Glasgow Herald*.]

Then, on 28 October, Neil noted simply: '*Shoes of Fortune* published to-day.' There was satisfaction in seeing one's fourth novel safely between hard covers, but it is hard to ignore the author's own verdict that '*The Shoes of Fortune* wants a soul...'[6] It is not irrelevant that in this novel Neil deserted the Highlands for the first time: only in a few short stories would he again use Lowland settings. In Chapter V Paul Greig significantly notices Isobel Fortune 'always looking to the hump of Dungoyne that bars the way to the Hielands' (Dumgoyn, the usual spelling, is a hill at the western end of the

Campsie Fells, near Loch Lomond). Paul also says that the elms round Hazel Den, his home, 'hid the valley of the Clyde and the Highland hills, that at bleaker seasons gave us a sense of companionship with the wide world beyond our infield of stunted crops' (Chap. II). Hazel Den is, in fact, only a few fields away from Waterfoot, where Neil was now living: he liked, if he could, to write of the places he knew best. But he could never know Renfrewshire as well as Argyll, where his growth-points were. France and the Low Countries, where much of *The Shoes of Fortune* takes place, were even less familiar. There is an element of playing the same tune in a different key, never a great novelty at the best of times.

The Shoes of Fortune is probably the most 'Stevensonian' of Neil's novels. Where it is most so (the vivid cameos of Paul's uncle Andy, for instance, or the scenes on board the *Seven Sisters* in the Firth of Forth), it is in conscious homage. When Paul reads his uncle's logbook – 'that memoir of a wild loose life… chronicles of a hundred ports, with boozing dens and raving lazarettos in them; far out isles and cays in nameless oceans…' – and then burns the book, it is a sublimation of the bewitching R.L.S. influence. G.K. Chesterton compared Stevenson's imagery with the black and white of woodcuts, the bright colours of toy theatres.[7] Neil worked in a more diffuse style, with the fine detail of pencil and water colour. His appreciation of Stevenson is evident in several 'Views & Reviews' causeries, in one of which he wrote:

'Stevenson is not imitated because – well, mainly because there is nothing to imitate. It has been the misfortune of R.L.S. to have his name trotted out in season and out of season as that of the supreme and ideal 'stylist', meaning by 'stylist' a writer who is dandified in phrase and perjink about his paragraphs, who would sooner be a coxcomb and obscure than write everyday plain English. Now Stevenson's most common and most popular and most matured manner of writing was in strict accordance with the oldest and most respectable traditions of the English language. His anxiety seems ever to have been to eliminate every equivocal word or clause, to make his most subtle meaning plain to a child's intellect. There may have been some of his early essays in which preciosity's cloven hoof betrayed itself: but who would have them different from what they are?'[8]

The unfortunate overlapping of the writing of *The Shoes of Fortune* with that of *Doom Castle*, which lay much closer to Neil's heart, added to his vague disenchantment with the former. Both, of course, first appeared as serials, and Dr Hermann Völkel suggests that Neil suffered in general from the pressures of serialisation, which led to lack of detailed planning and hasty revision of proofs.

Was it deliberate that *The Shoes of Fortune* is a sort of mirror-image of *Doom Castle*, with which it was written in parallel? Was this at least partly a device to help Neil keep them separate in his mind while he was 'the slave of two serials', both set in the post-1745 era and dealing with espionage? In the former a Lowlander goes to France but returns to marry his Scottish sweetheart; in the latter a Frenchman comes to the Highlands and returns to France with a Highland wife. There is also a great contrast between black-haired Paul Greig, the Lowlander, ready-tongued and ready-fisted, and fair-haired Gilian the Dreamer, the Highlander.

By returning to first-person narrative, as in *John Splendid*, Neil could feel himself into the character of his hero, Paul Greig. Paul relates, purportedly for his grandchildren, how at the age of twenty he inherited from his uncle, the 'loveable rogue', a pair of red shoes that took him on perilous adventures, chiefly in France, where he was unwittingly involved in a Jesuit plot to assassinate Prince Charles Edward.

The Greigs have 'the trick of irony', and shafts of humour relieve the convoluted plot, in which coincidence is over-frequent, yet easily forgotten in the mosaic of people and adventures. Many of the characters are little more than thumb-nail sketches, made vivid in a phrase or two, as when the errant Andy Greig explains his long absence from Hazel Den: 'It was the notion of milk for supper and all that means that kept me from calling...'

Apart from Paul himself, the two we learn most of are Clementina Walkinshaw, mistress of Prince Charles Edward, and Father Hamilton, 'this obese cleric'. Clementina's 'hame-wae' for Scotland is shared by Paul, both dwelling in visions on the home country. As soon as she finds out that Paul is from the Mearns she tells him 'she had often had her May milk in [his] native parish'. In Paul's recollection, forty years later, she is not 'lost and wicked' but 'the very football of fate and a heart of yellow gold'. He still cherishes a memory of her 'attired in a pale primrose-coloured paduasoy, the cuffs and throat embroidered in a pattern of roses and leaves, her hair unpowdered and glossy, wantoning in and out of a neck beyond description'.

Father Hamilton is warm-hearted, garrulous and fond of food and wine. Not till they are together in prison does he reveal to Paul his clumsy half-hearted part in a Jesuit plot to assassinate Charles Edward, calling himself 'a happy murderer failed at his trade'. When they escape and are hiding in Paris Father Hamilton shows he is Franciscan rather than Jesuit, befriending birds and children.

The Shoes of Fortune is a neglected child amongst Neil's novels. A percipient contemporary insight is in a letter to Neil from John Lobban, one of Blackwoods' readers, to whom Neil had sent a copy: 'I do hope that in spite of all the advice of Fleet Street you will stick to Argyllshire... *The Shoes of Fortune* seems to me in some ways a condescension into the crowded arena of popular fiction, but if you will follow *Gilian,* you are absolutely certain of succeeding Stevenson in the hierarchy of Scots fiction...'[9]

Writing almost a century later, Ronald Renton said in a full analysis of *The Shoes of Fortune,* too long to quote here: 'Munro was fully aware of the fact that he was exploiting the devices of coincidence and the red shoes... This approach... sits uneasily with the more important historical judgments at the end of the book... Having said that, there is no doubt that the book is heavily influenced by Stevenson's *Kidnapped* and *Catriona* and, although considerably inferior to them artistically, it nonetheless makes a sharp political statement where *Kidnapped* does not, and, although Paul is much less sharply drawn than the David Balfour of *Catriona,* his decisiveness in going to Pitt and averting invasion is a major advance on Balfour's inaction.'[10]

A few days after *The Shoes of Fortune* came out, Neil heard from Father Allan MacDonald: 'I am glad to think you will be good enough to come and spend some days in Eriskay this winter and that you have the idea of taking the Islands as a background of a story. Nothing can give me greater pleasure than your visit. It will break the neck of the winter's monotony. No Englishman would choose winter for a visit to the Islands... Nature is a pleasure to him only in sunlight. For us of the less sensual temperament the howling wind, the [illegible], the flying sand drift, the isolation and its concomitants are in themselves a pleasure. He cannot understand us and in his innermost heart cannot believe that Highlanders and Islanders live on among their rocks because they cannot go elsewhere... I have not read *Doom Castle* yet as I have been doing some letter work... It is a joy in store for me and I thank you for your hurry in sending me it and the other book...'[11] [The remark that Highlanders and Islanders 'cannot go elsewhere' seems to mean that they do not leave voluntarily.]

Neil did not record going to Eriskay that winter in his diary, and I do not know if he ever again met Father Allan, who died in 1905 and would, by then, have had the pleasure of reading *Children of Tempest.*

The Shoes of Fortune, like *Gilian the Dreamer*, was published not by Blackwoods but by Isbister. It may have been Neil's desire to reinforce his association with Blackwoods that led him to call at their London office while on a flying visit to the capital in November with J.M. Smith, 'partly on business and partly for pleasure (if you can call a dinner that)'. The dinner, at the Hotel Cecil, was 'to Sir Thos. Lipton'. Neil had hoped to surprise his friend D.S. Meldrum but arrived too late to catch him at Blackwoods' office in Paternoster Row. Instead, he wrote to Meldrum from Scotland a few days later and sent him a copy of *The Shoes of Fortune* 'which has done very well, in Scotland at least. It would do much better if Isbister spent a farthing on advertising – which they don't.'

More to the point, Neil had news for Meldrum of his next project: 'I have been busy for some time on

Children of Tempest

A Tale of the Outer Isles?

which I think gets on all right so far. It deals with a place and people quite untouched so far – I mean the Outer Hebrides, and the Roman Catholics there, who are as different from the Scots of other parts as you and I are from Spaniards. Fine stuff, Mr Meldrum, I assure you, if I can get it out, and I'm making a great try... You will hear, Sir, the wild Atlantic rave in it; it will save the Londoner money next autumn to buy a copy of it, and, sitting in Crouch End, get his ozone in unlimited quantities for 4/6 instead of taking the train to Oban. Wm Black's sunsets! Pooh!... I read *The House with the Green Shutters* with great interest and look forward to meeting Brown. With kindest regards to Mrs Meldrum, Yours ever...

'P.S. I hope to finish this yarn by April.'[12]

CHAPTER TWENTY-TWO

I could see Inveraray – if it weren't for the mountains in between

A S Neil listened from the top of the Cross Steeple in Glasgow to the bells ringing-in 1902, he could feel that he had made a good start on his new book, *Children of Tempest*. It is set chiefly in South Uist, c.1795, and Father Ludovick MacNeil, one of the chief characters, is frankly based on Father Allan MacDonald. Curiously, a novel inspired by Father Allan's character – *Heroine in Homespun* by Frederic Breton – had appeared in 1893: I cannot tell if Neil was aware of this.

Before 1902 was a week old, George Douglas Brown returned to Scotland after six years' absence. Since autumn publication of his début novel *The House with the Green Shutters* he 'was being widely hailed in his native land as the first of a new school of Scottish fiction where "realism" was to be the specific note...'[1] as Neil put it long afterwards. On 8 January Brown came out to Waterfoot to make Neil's acquaintance. They had almost met a few years before when Neil, on a visit to London, had been given a letter of introduction to Brown (probably by Meldrum). But he had 'found that at the moment Brown was with a houseboat party up the Thames, which too much suggested a typical Oxford swell for my intrusion. That letter was never presented.'[2]

Meeting Brown now at Waterfoot, Neil took to him immediately. Though Brown was six years younger, like Neil he had grown up in the days of Victorian reticence, and it is virtually certain that neither was then aware of certain resemblances in the hinterlands of their lives: Brown was, in fact, the illegitimate son of a farm-girl and a 'gentleman farmer', had grown up in poverty but won his way to Glasgow University, thence to Oxford.

Neil described the Waterfoot meeting in his retrospective diary in 1904: '[Brown] was a nice, genial, unaffected fellow, quite unlike his book as I told him to his own amusement. It was a very cold day. After sitting over an hour with me over a glass & a cigar he said he had a young lady come out with him to Clarkston station, whose father I might possibly know – Bailie MacLennan of Glasgow. I said

I knew her father well, and should like to have seen her. He said she had someone to call on at Clarkston. When he rose to go I said I would walk to the station with him & he betrayed some embarrassment & said I was not to bother. I insisted, & on going out of the house with him, found the young lady walking up & down outside, blue with cold. "Ah Lizzie!" he said ruefully, "you have poorly backed up my fibbing!" He was, it appeared later, engaged to this young lady, while really in love with a sister of hers who had married another man.'

The three of them then walked the three miles to Cathcart station, all intermediate trains having been missed. 'I should gladly have walked much farther than Cathcart in such congenial company,'[3] Neil wrote. Two days later Neil 'had Brown and Risk to lunch in the Art Club'. He never met Brown again.

Even on such short acquaintance, he had realised that Brown 'was not entirely a happy man He was well aware that great novels are written in love and ecstasy, not in hate – even simulated hate. And here he was, on his first acknowledged essay at fiction, permanently earmarked as the kind of author whose speciality was the depiction of rural life in his native country as a welter of unrelieved squalor!'[4] This insight suggests that the straightforward celebration of goodness in *Children of Tempest* was in some measure a reaction to the pessimism of Brown's book, which remained in the back of Neil's mind as his own work progressed. It would not, however, progress as rapidly as planned, due partly to happy distractions.

His daughter Effie, just turned twelve, had been allowed to spend Christmas in Lincoln with Kate Turner – her first trip alone from home – and Kate had asked if she could extend her stay. Her father wrote back: 'We had no intention that she should stay more than a week or so when she left, but her mother readily falls in with your suggestion... Hugh went back to school to-day. His entire holidays have been devoted to reading the Christmas books & shooting with his new air gun (same which was brought by Santa Claus). Baby [Neil] is now walking all over the shop like anything... We spent a very quiet New Year with nary a visitor, solacing ourselves for the flight of time in the English fashion by eating an unusually large dinner whereof the *pièce de résistance* was ane sonsy bubbly-jock. (There's one for your good-man's bewilderment.) With stuffing till't, and sausages till't, and plum-pudding till't... My wife is well (Santa Claus does not confine himself to Christmas in these quarters), and so are all the bairns...'[5]

The cryptic remark about Santa Claus was maybe a covert

reference to the fact that Jessie was expecting another baby at the end of January. With the family growing steadily, Waterfoot was beginning to feel a little cramped. Yet Neil was now a man of substance. At the end of 1901, he had recorded that his bank balance stood at £1,243 (including £67 advance American royalties on *The Shoes of Fortune* and £112 for serial rights of it in America). This un-Micawberish state of affairs had a particular bearing on a plan he had in mind. On 3 January he had noted in his diary: 'Went to Gourock & looked at "West View" [11 Tower Drive] a house for sale by Mr Geo. Thomson, Registrar, Caley [Caledonian] Railway Co.'

On 14 January, a week after Brown's visit to Waterfoot, Neil noted: 'Visited Gourock house again. It consists of Dining-room, Drawing-room, small parlour, four bedrooms, kitchen, scullery, wash-house, bathroom, small conservatory & garden. Owner wants £950. Offered £800.'

The following day, J.M. Smith gave a dinner to 'old *Glasgow News* survivors' at the Imperial Union Club, 'seven present'. Three days later, surely not as a consequence of this dinner, Neil's young brother-in-law Hugh Adam, who'd had a chequered career on several newspapers, 'finally left *News* staff'.

On 25 January – 'Burns's birthday', Neil noted proudly – Jessie gave birth to a daughter, Isobel, 'at 3.15 this morning. Nurse Cameron there'. Four days later Neil clinched the deal for a new family home, buying West View at Gourock for £875. The following week he went down to Lincoln to collect Effie and stayed with the Turners for a couple of days. On the way back, he and Effie had an hour in York between trains which they spent in the Minster. 'Effie slept a good part of the way and was in Scotland before she knew herself to be near it... I had her primed up to maintain an inflexible English accent from the first moment she met her mother; she did her best – much to her mother's amusement – but subject to some embarrassment, and after her breakfast the following morning little of the Saxon accent – alas! – was to the fore. But now and then I hear her fall into "the English".'[6]

In the middle of all this excitement and upheaval, Neil gave birth to a new creation of his own. On 10 February, in the 'Looker-On' column, Erchie MacPherson slid casually into print: 'On Sundays he is the beadle of our church; at other times he Waits.' Neil had often before used the device of imaginary conversations as a way of dealing with topical events and filling a column. For instance, four years previously in a 'Looker-On' entitled 'Sending-in Day' he had

purported to encounter artists called Megilpeson, Old Gamboge
and Wierdsley.[7] But this time, somewhere within himself, he had
struck a vein of gold: Erchie's 'long pent-up and precious strain of
philosophy'.

On his first appearance Erchie gave his views on the Chief
Constable, the 'new slumming crusade' and other matters of
Glaswegian moment. Duffy the coalman was also introduced, at this
stage patronising the Auld Blue Vaults rather than the Mull of
Kintyre Vaults. The inspiration for Duffy was partly traceable to that
earlier coalman, 'Jeems Kaye' of The Bailie magazine, one of those
'illustrated and flippant week-end organs' that had diverted Neil in
his early Glasgow years. 'Jeems Kaye' issued his articles – in reality
written by Archibald MacMillan, a Glasgow commission agent –
from 'The Coal Ree, Strathbungo'.

Erchie's wife Jinnet had yet to make her début and complete the
triumvirate, though in 'Introductory to an odd character', the tale
with which every Erchie book has opened, Erchie mentions her
several times. Their relationship, slowly built up with tiny details, is
a rare example of the convincing depiction of a happy marriage.

St Kentigern's, the church where Erchie is beadle, I always place
in my imagination somewhere off Great Western Road and near St
George's Cross. It was in that airt Neil had lived in the early years
of marriage: now, from a safe distance, he could enjoy harking back
to those days. Unlike himself, Erchie was a true child of the city,
albeit with a Hielan' grandfather. He revealed himself at once 'an
auld man – fifty years waitin', and paid my taxes a' the time, and ten
o' a family; a flet fit, but a gey warm hert under't'. His pawky
humour and free-ranging imagination were evident from the start:

'There's ae thing I canna thole mysel' – it's to see ony suspeecion
o' a deeviation frae the strict path o' righteousness on the pairt o'
onybody wi' twal' shillins a week mair nor mysel'. Naebody wi'
the reediculous wage o' nine hunder' a year should dae onythin'
to anger Duffy, the coalman.'

'Rather a delicate position, Erchie?' I said.

'At least,' said Erchie, 'he should tak' care an' no' be fun' oot.
You an' me hasna been fun' oot yet.'[8]

Erchie would make his second appearance a fortnight later –
commenting on licensing hours, council housing and 'sparky caurs'
(afterwards more familiar as 'skoosh-caurs') – and by the end of
1902 Neil would have written a dozen 'Erchie' pieces. They were a

popular success and gave Glasgow folk another incentive to keep buying the News, hence bolstering the profits of J.M. Smith Ltd, declared in March at £10,500 (including £3,000 carried forward from the previous year). Once again, Neil's shares brought him a dividend of 7½%.

On 7 March, Neil's brother-in-law announced his plans to the Munros. 'Hugh Adam is going to Natal, to a paper there.' Three weeks later Jessie's brother, who had long been in lodgings, left for South Africa. Neil noted in his diary: "Paid £20 for his passage &c, £11.5/- debts, £3.5/- to tailor. Is due me in all over £40." For 16 years Neil had shouldered paternal responsibilities and with this loan to give the footloose Hugh a new life he must have felt they were at last discharged.

George Douglas Brown wrote to Neil on 14 April from Wood View, Totteridge, Buckinghamshire:

My dear Munro,

I don't need to tell you now that I'm one of the worst corre-spondents Heaven (or the Devil) ever made – I believe it was the Devil. However, I'm always very willing to cry *'mea culpa, mea maxima culpa'* – which, by the way, is a very bad sign of a man. *Pecca fortiter*'s a brave motto. I'm bold enough in my sins, but I spoil 'em by my bland apologetics. Behold me, therefore, on the stool of repentance, and trying to hurt my bum. That part of me was calloused in its youth, however, and I quite enjoy the contrite situation – another very bad sign. You're doubtless thinking that my conscience – the seat of which is the seat in unregenerates – might be startled into life by the application of an urgent toe. But please don't kick me for not writing when we next foregather. The gist of all this nonsense is that I'm sorry I didn't answer your letter sooner.

I wrote to the editor of *Saint Andrew*, refusing, but he's at me again to do a small story. (Were it a big lie, I could oblige him with the greatest ease.) He says the most distinguished Scottish writers, such as Mr Ian Maclaren and Mr Neil Munro, are going to contribute. Don't you squirm at the conjunction? Maclaren has about as much sense of the decency of letters as a lachrymose sow – if you can imagine a pathetic pig.

As to marriage, my friend – the rest is silence!
Yours very truly, G.D. BROWN

Towards the end of April, a new sixpenny edition of *The Lost*

Pibroch came out, with Neil taking a royalty of 10%. Early in May he received a cheque for £320 from Blackwood, royalties on *Doom Castle*. This helped to pay for the new house in Gourock – 'Paid £425 down, & left £450 on existing bond. Transfer & Law expenses, recording &c £9.6s.1d.' Neil also pasted a page from a cashbook into his diary, with details of the cost of flitting, new furniture, blinds, plumbing &c., amounting to about £116. There was also the expense of taking lodgings at Thrush Hill, Gourock, 'while house is in the painters' hands'. At last, on 30 May, the Munros moved into the new house, re-named Carnus after a deserted township at the head of Glen Aray, held by Neil to be the *duthus* of our particular Munro branch. The fact that Waterfoot is also an Inveraray name may have inspired this.

The move to Gourock was Jessie and Neil's tenth flitting in seventeen years of marriage. Now the Munros were to stay put for the next sixteen years, although Carnus was only just big enough to contain them all. The small parlour by the front door was given over to the children and re-named 'the nursery'. Isobel was only four months old then and Effie, the oldest, was twelve and a half.

The edge of Gourock was still very near Tower Drive, at the top end of which was Broadfoot's farm. Carnus has a grand outlook to the north-west, over the rooftops and the Firth of Clyde below, and across to the hills of Cowal at the edge of Argyllshire. The Holy Loch and Loch Long open just opposite. Beside Carnus are a few villas identical to it, all with steps leading up from the road because they are built on ground that slopes very steeply, giving a delicious sense of being poised on the edge of things. Neil described the garden behind Carnus as 'mostly rough coppice on the side of a hill'. When they moved in, cuckoos were calling nearby, and in the evening a sound Neil at first took for a little vessel running out her anchor in the bay turned out to be the chur of a night-jar. Then they found that the little steep wood was full of wild hyacinths, and a tradition began of marking Neil's birthday – 3 June – with a 'bluebell tea'.

There was a good train service between Gourock and Glasgow. One of the Munros' first visitors was Dr W.H. Drummond, a Canadian poet. In summer there was also a direct daily sailing from Gourock to Inveraray on the *Lord of the Isles*, the second Clyde steamer to bear that name, on which Neil took Drummond to see a little of Argyll, young Hugh going with them. Neil then went on for five days' fishing in the Black Mount with J.M. Smith and two other friends, putting up at King's House. They fished Loch na Staing, Loch Ba and the Etive, as well as visiting Glencoe.

That first summer in Carnus Neil was still busy with *Children of Tempest*, due to start as a serial in *Maga* in November, for he had fallen far short of his boast to David Meldrum that he hoped 'to finish this yarn by April'. On 28 August Meldrum came and stayed the night at Carnus, possibly on a mission to find out what had happened to the book, although as a friend he was welcome anyway. That very evening, probably by wire from the *News* office, he and Neil learned the sad news: 'George Douglas Brown died suddenly to-day.'

Thus, barely a year after the little world of Scottish literature had been rocked by the publication of *The House with the Green Shutters*, the remarkable talent that produced it was no more. It was as though a new actor of great promise had stridden on stage in Act One, Scene One of the new century, only to perish off-stage during the next scene. Despite the cheerful tone of his letter to Neil just four months ago, Brown had suffered from recurring symptoms of stress and by August was ill enough to make a will before setting off for a friend's home in London. The friend was away, so Brown called on another. Hours later he was dead, of an unidentified illness, at the age of 33.

The following day Meldrum left Carnus with the first ten chapters of *Children of Tempest*, bound for Blackwoods. The book conceived partly in reaction to Brown's bitter masterpiece was now coming to birth as he was laid to rest. On 1 September, Neil noted in his diary: 'At George Douglas Brown's funeral from St Enoch's Station.'

Ten days later Neil got word from Blackwood that he planned to start *Children of Tempest* in *Maga* in November. Like a good journalist, Neil responded positively to the stimulus of a deadline, replying: 'I am much pleased that what you have seen of *Children of Tempest* meets with your approval, and I think I can safely say that the rest will be "equal to sample". I fancy I have got an interesting story – apart altogether from characters and style, and I have certainly got a district of Scotland and a kind of people hitherto quite untouched in romance... I was sorry to see so little of Meldrum when he visited me, and that poor Brown's death came as such an unexpected blow in the midst of his holidays. I hope, however, to see Meldrum in London next month.'[9]

September saw Effie and Hugh going off to Greenock Academy, where the rest of the family were to follow in due course. It was fortunate that this excellent school, already half a century old, was only a short train journey away from Carnus. The Rector, Alexander Gemmell, appointed in 1893 at the tender age of 28, was a classicist, and 'a great man for exhortation', to quote Hugh's friend and classmate, George Blake. He did not retire till 1930. For exercise, in his earlier days, he would go out riding – 'Here's Neddy Gemmell on his white-washed charger!' rude boys would shout – and once he conducted and won a case in the Court of Session in respect of an araucaria in his front garden.

In after days George Blake confessed himself 'puzzled that so many men of my own writing profession look back on their school-days with horror... My own simple soul is completely free from any hangover of grievance against Greenock Academy. No memories of cruel beatings keep me awake o' nights; no female teacher ever chose me as her Young Woodley and provided me with the subject of a future novel... It is quite firm in my mind that the men and women of my generation were lucky in their school above Nelson Street. And there was always the Rector who rode a white horse and went to law about a monkey puzzle. I cannot believe that even a Provost of Eton ever conferred such a distinction of individuality upon his foundation.'[10]

It took so little time to get from Carnus to school that the Munro children used to come home for mid-day dinner. In very stormy weather they stayed at school all day and bought, from the janitor, barm biscuits (a kind of roll) spread with syrup, costing a ha'penny each. The trick then was to sit on the rolls to make them nice and soggy.

Just before returning proofs of the first instalment of *Children of Tempest* to Blackwoods, Neil went to London with J.M. Smith for a dinner of the Whitefriars Club at which he was guest of the evening and opened a discussion on the Celtic Fringe. He 'deprecated the idea that the Celts were a melancholy people, and asserted that the Celtic gloom existed only in the imagination of English writers... he expressed regret that no one was doing for Scotland what W.B.Yeats, the poet, and others were doing for Ireland. A discussion followed...'[11] J.M. Barrie sat beside Neil at dinner. Though he told Neil he had come specially to meet him, and was very friendly and kind, he said very little. Afterwards Neil went to the Covent Garden fancy dress ball with David Hodge, his friend and colleague on the *News* now working in London. Neil spent the better part of a week in London, staying in hotels and with Meldrum, who was at the Whitefriars dinner.

He returned to Gourock as storms signalled the end of autumn, and 14 October may well have been the first of Effie and Hugh's golden syrup days: their father wrote to William Blackwood 'Winter has fairly opened; to-day I look out on a very stormy Firth of Clyde with white spindrift and waves crashing terrifically on the shore.' By this time he had already mapped out a change of literary course, as he explained in this letter: 'I shall not be content until I make the public a good deal more eager in my pursuit (!) [his punctuation] I fancy a lighter vein of character and a modern theme might do the trick and there is simmering in my mind a story on these lines...'

The story he had in mind would not appear between hard covers for another five years, though he knew its setting intimately and thought about it often as he brooded over his next novel. On a brighter day in December, he wrote to Alexander Wood of Blackwoods: 'To-day's glorious, and I could see Inveraray – if it weren't for the mountains in between.' (A reference to a popular song of the day).

On the last day of 1902 he went once more to Inveraray by the Lochgoilhead route to see his mother and bring in the New Year with its 'daft days' of celebration. Hogmanay proceedings followed an inevitable course, as described by Maimie McGillvray, daughter of Neil's old schoolmate Nicol Macintyre:

'We took in New Year every year in the same way. At 12 o'clock the pipe band with Charlie Maitland's dog, Rhuadh, dancing before, paraded down the Barn Gate then back to the Band house (behind Fern Point) then Charlie and Neil Munro came straight to our house and collected us and we went over to Charlie's house [in the Arkland]. Generally there were others first footing but they did not stay long. There were two brass candlesticks on the mantelpiece lit by gas (but not incandescent). Who called this morning but Duncan McLullich and friend. Charlie requested a song from Duncan. "What will I sing?" "Sing Torwood!" So Duncan started. When he had finished, Munro said "You're not going to stop when you're in such good voice," so Duncan asked what he would sing? "Sing Torwood," said Munro and Duncan began again. Charlie now said, "Surely you'll give us another song." "What will I sing?" "Sing Torwood." This went on till the early hours with Duncan continuing to sing Torwood, encouraged by the two rascals, till Mrs Maitland called us for supper.'[12]

CHAPTER TWENTY-THREE

I hope to finish this yarn by April

JANUARY of 1903 brought its usual crop of pleasant diversions – on the 23rd Neil gave the oration on The Immortal Memory at the Greenock Burns Club supper, and on 6 February he dined with Herbert Storey, principal of Glasgow University. But *Maga*'s insatiable appetite for more chapters of *Children of Tempest* could not be denied and throughout February Neil drove himself at the novel, taking the unusual step of keeping a tally in his diary. On 20 February he did 2,200 words, or the whole of Chapter 20, in a day, and his overall tally for the month was about 10,000 words, exceptional for a writer whose literary output was normally much slower than his journalism. On 6 March he sent another three chapters to *Maga* and bought himself a new Blick typewriter for eight guineas. Four days later he used it to write a letter to his cousin Kate Turner in Lincoln:

'I know you detest the type-writer as a medium of correspondence but you'll have to excuse it for once, as I have been using a pen today till my fingers ache. There's a letter (or aiblins two) of yours long due an answer. We have had sair trials here that account for our silence. First there was the weather – you never saw such weather! – months of it, so that I couldn't get down to the village for the necessary stamp. Then I was ill for some weeks, then (in the order of merit you observe) my wife was ill, then the baby took pneumonia, first as an experiment & then a 2nd time because she seemed to enjoy it; then Lilian, Moira & Neil in rapid succession developed frightful colds, & all was far from gay in Carnus. But now we're all right again, taking our food well…

'Effie & Hugh are plodding on at school & liking it; the former getting a big girl now with perhaps just a little too much interest in her hair, & vexation that her nose is not on classic lines, the latter immersed in scalps, buffaloes, red Injins, scouts & trappers, & armed for general with an arsenal of deadly weapons that fire amorces (if your education includes a knowledge of juvenile ammunition). The baby is now walking, & that – take my word for it – is the end of that lot. I'm throng, with *Children of Tempest* still to finish, drat 'em! Love, quo' she! woman did you see a chapter ca'd "Tir-nan-Og" in the

February number of *Maga*? If that's not the stuff don't tell me you know anything about love. If you want me to take the lassie out & cuddle her afore folk I'll no dae't; I never did it in life & I'll no' dae't in leeterature.

'I wish the weather was better & we were in Inveraray. If any of you are coming north to Dunmore [Loch Fyne] at Easter make Gourock your jumping-off place. It's about time, I fancy, Effie was sending you a letter...'[1]

Toward the end of March there were further distractions, including the funeral in Edinburgh of General Sir Hector Macdonald, from which Neil filed copy for the London *Daily Mail* and *News Chronicle*, and the exciting spectacle of Sir Thomas Lipton's yachts *Shamrock I* and *Shamrock III* racing off Gourock. Then on 6 April Neil noted in his diary: 'Wm. Douglas, Sheriff Clerk at Inveraray, died today – my first employer.'

He pressed on with *Children of Tempest*, sending off another monthly instalment of three chapters to *Maga* on 8 April. On the same day he noted making a loan of £20 to his boyhood friend Colin Macphail 'to help him about a new ship'. He received no I.O.U., receipt or other acknowledgment but would note later in the margin: 'Was repaid with interest afterwards.'

With the onset of summer, Neil's labours at the novel became dilatory, giving Blackwood's an uncomfortably slim margin between arrival of the monthly instalment and publication in *Maga*. On 8 May Neil wrote to George Blackwood: 'For a week or two back I've been dreading the postman lest he should bring a terrible wigging from the gods of '45. Anyway, here's an abject apologist and I'll not be so late again. There are eight more chapters of *Children of Tempest* to go; and you'll have them before the month's end.'

Yet within days of making his promise, Neil was off on a fishing trip to Inveraray with J.M. Smith and another friend, staying at the Argyll Arms. On 18 May they fished the Dhu Loch at the foot of Glen Shira, taking 16 trout and 2 saithe (that wee loch is partly tidal), and two days later they took 140 codling in Loch Fyne. The following day Neil dined with the Duke at the castle.

About this time he arranged to take over, for family holidays, the tenancy of Douglas's house in the Main Street, the rent being doubled to £30 p.a. At the sale of Douglas's furniture Neil bought 'to the value of £65'. But as he put down new roots in the town of his birth, it was time for his mother to leave. She was 73 and he did not feel happy about leaving her on her own any longer. On 2 June

– the eve of his own 40th birthday – he brought her to live with them at Carnus.

The turn of the century, emphasised by Victoria's death, had been marked already for Argyll folk by the 8th Duke's death in 1900 after half a century's incumbency. Yet for Neil perhaps the sense of a long era ending was most keenly felt when his mother's house at Inveraray was broken up.

But he had neither time nor inclination for brooding. The domestic upheavals had made him dangerously late with the next month's instalment of *Children of Tempest*, necessitating another abject letter to George Blackwood: 'For ten days back I have been waiting for a clean copy of several chapters from a Glasgow typewriter, and only on Saturday I learned she was from home on holiday. I have had accordingly to be the typewriter myself and enclose two chapters; another chapter will be sent you without fail tonight. I'm dreadfully late, I know, and it must inconvenience and alarm you, but it won't happen again.'[2]

While Neil laboured to finish his novel, the family in Gourock were preparing to spend their first summer in Douglas's old house at Inveraray. The following letter from Effie to Kate Turner, written on 27 June, sketches the Carnus *mêlée*:

My Dear Mrs Turner,
  Mother and Maggie were upstairs packing and as busy as could be to go to Inveraray; I went up to help them, but found it useless to try and do anything right. Baby is 'stotting' about lifting up lamps, putting down jugs and giving an occasional yell now and then, so you may guess what she's like. Neil [junior] has a hammer and whenever he gets some protectors, pins, nails, he hammers them into the nursery chairs, after having done that, he gives a big sigh of satisfaction. Lilian is sitting sewing babies' feeders as hard as she can, and all the time the baby is crying, Mother is scolding, Maggie is strapping up boxes, and Neil is falling down stairs. Lilian comes coolly up and asks if anyone will kindly turn up this hem for her. (Fancy!) Moira is walking about grumbling, because there's 'nothing' to do. Hugh is sitting in the dining room (the only deserted room in the house) reading adventures among the Indians. Neil went downstairs to the dining room on Monday morning, and the Firth was all covered with mist so that you couldn't see it, 'Oh' said Neil, 'The water is all drank and the boats are in their bed.' (Wasn't that smart.) Moira is the grumbler of the house; she came to me this morning and said,

'Janet's an old monkey, she wouldn't let me play at doll's washing in the sink nor brush the boots, and I've nothing to do.' She hates people one minute and next minute you see her hugging them like anything. I think this will do with the family, won't it! (...) This is the prize-giving day in our school, and I got first prize for English you must get to know what that means, it doesn't mean for speaking English (Bless my soul, no) But for History, Geography, meanings, spelling and grammer [sic]. I go to music to a gentleman called 'Enry Green (English you may guess) he's a bachelor, he's got eyes as big as saucers, fingers as long as from here to Lincoln, a neck as stiff as the towers on Lincoln Cathedral (I don't think its natural though, I think its his collar), and he plays the establish Church organ. I'm not going to sleep in Mr Douglas's bedroom for I'll not be able to sleep, thinking I see spirits and things. Father is going to Canada on August 9. We're going to Inveraray on Tuesday so you'll know we're all quite joyful. How's 'The Englishman' [Mr Turner] is he as fond of that country of his as ever; tell him that it always will be 'Scotland forever' with me but never 'England's the place'...
  Yours truly,
  Effie F. Munro.

The Janet Effie mentions was a local girl engaged to help Jessie and Maggie. Later another local girl, Mary Watt, succeeded her, more permanently. Effie does not mention her grandmother, who had joined the family only a few weeks before and would, with Maggie, be one of the tribe returning to Inveraray that Tuesday. Her presence at Carnus must have complicated sleeping arrangements: there were four bedrooms to accommodate six children and four adults. I suspect the drawing-room, which was upstairs, was turned into a bedroom.

It was likely during her years at Carnus that Neil's mother told Maggie that his father was a ghillie who had come to Inveraray Castle with his master as part of a shooting party. This confidence was passed on to me by Maggie half a century later. Apparently she never told anyone else in the family of it. Learning of it from me for the first time in 1977, Neil junior wrote: 'I would quite believe Maggie's version per se, but the truth of it I would doubt. I should really say Maggie's story – not version. N.M.'s mother would certainly be the last person to want any SCANDAL associated with the Campbell family for which she had great respect and admiration... I would reason that my grandmother's most compelling,

136

urgent and decisive instinct would be to protect the ducal reputation and a family who befriended her: nothing to this end could be more effective than to locate the UNKNOWN seducer... where he would be safely beyond questioning or confrontation and never the source of local garbled "confessions". In 1864 [sic] the real truth about N.M.'s paternity would be known to perhaps six people at most; thereafter through "leaks" and confessions it would become general RUMOUR. All the hearsay evidence that his father was the Duke is quite invalid: but despite the usual propensity to romanticise in all similar circumstances (the Cinderella fixation) I think there is no doubt that the Munro family circle and intimates knew that his father was the Duke.'[3]

On 6 July, a few days after moving into Douglas's old house, Neil at last got free of *Children of Tempest*. He was so late that to get the final proofs back to Blackwood in time he took the early Lochgoil route to Glasgow, took ten minutes to post them at St Enoch Station, then immediately caught the train and turbine boat *King Edward* back to Inveraray, arriving at 1.30pm, his labours done. He had met his deadline by the skin of his teeth: Blackwoods intended to publish *Children of Tempest* in book form on 20 July.

Now there remained only a week for him to enjoy the novel delights of having his own abode in Inveraray. On 14 July (not 8 August as Effie had thought) he was due to sail from Liverpool to Canada in the S.S. *Manitoba*, leaving *Children of Tempest* to be published in his absence. Jessie was fair forfochen what with unfamiliar domestic arrangements and Neil's packing for two months in Canada.

He was travelling 'with a Parliamentary party as a guest of the Canadian government', as he informed William Blackwood. In Montreal a reporter from *The Montreal Daily Herald* interviewed Neil at the house of Dr W.H. Drummond, the poet who had visited him in Gourock. The result was an article on 28 July, entitled 'Mr Neil Munro, the Scottish Novelist, Speaks of His Work':

He is forming acquaintance with Canada for the first time, and he brings with him a great enthusiasm. He will follow in its entirety the programme of the itinerary to the Pacific coast and back, arranged by the Government and Canadian Pacific Railway, but after his return he will remain some time in Eastern Canada in order to study the development of the Scottish and especially Gaelic characteristics in an environment far removed from the cradle of the race.

Mr Munro... looks surprisingly young, when one considers the work he has done, for his was not a sudden burst into the blaze of fame, but rather the evolution of steadily improving effort in a realm of art he has made peculiarly his own.

He is slightly above the medium height, of rather slender build and fair complexion, with light fair moustache and refined, scholarly face, a face with certain strong masculine traits that denote firmness of character and stamp the bearer as a man who has entered into the 'full empire' of his manhood. It is a face that draws you toward it with inevitable charm, and for two reasons. One is a singularly winning smile, a little knowing perhaps, and it may be on occasion a little mocking, and the other the eyes which are of a bluish gray, not the cold glinty gray that is the index to cruelty and craft, but warm and lustrous, suggestive of depths of unfathomable soul life.

Such is the man who by unusual acclaim is held in literature to have struck the bedrock of the Gael, and to have found it gold-bearing quartz of uncommon richness. He wore a gray tweed suit, and by his side, on a balcony chair, was a gray billicock.

These words are copied from a cutting in which the hand of some Munro or other has unaccountably underlined certain fulsome phrases such as 'refined scholarly face' and 'depths of unfathomable soul life'.

On a lake steamer in Canada, Neil met a fellow Scot who delighted him with the remark that being in an Edinburgh land (tenement) on a Saturday night was like 'being inside a bagpipes'. His reaction was very different in a Toronto hotel when another compatriot, wearing the kilt, sat down beside him at table and said: 'Eh, sir, we are a michty people!' 'Not at all, sir, not at all,' Neil replied, then ignored the fellow for the rest of the meal.

At Banff he rode to the top of Sulphur Mountain on a little cayuse pony, suffering 'the most sickening vision of giddy depths' on the narrow track. In Manitoba he discovered a new riding gait – the lope – and with another journalist 'scoured leagues of prairie before we realised there were such things as gopher holes for our mounts to break their legs in'.

In Victoria, British Columbia, he was taken by a new friend, Colonel George Ham of the Canadian Pacific Railway, to visit a Chinese merchant, Lee Mong Kow. He took them to dine at the Garden of the Golden Valley Restaurant, where Neil found chopsticks surprisingly easy to use, and they drank samsui wine. A friend of Lee Mong Kow who was eating with them 'produced from the neighbourhood of his sleeves the utensils for an opium dream. He took a puff or two, refilled the pipe, and passed it round to satisfy our curiosity... The smoke to the palate confirmed my impression that nothing at all of all this was new to me. I had smoked opium a thousand years before I was born... That scent of ancient flowers burned on heathen altars, that fragrant flavour of earth – let me think, when was it? Whose was the garden? What became of her?'[4]

After dinner, though it was late, they went out for a walk through the streets of Little China, accompanied by the captain of police. They visited a shop where opium was prepared for smoking and then went to one or two opium joints, and on to a Chinese theatre and a joss-house. Neil described all this at length in his *News* columns.

On 12 September he sailed from Montreal on the Allan liner *Parisian* for Liverpool, and by 21 September was aboard a train for Gourock. By then Jessie and Maggie had got the family back to Carnus and school. Nine days later Neil and Jessie went back to Inveraray on their own, leaving Maggie in charge. Neil described this short break in at letter to William Blackwood as 'a "retreat" from the mass of correspondence which had accumulated in my absence'. He made the trip also to lunch with the Duke of Argyll at Dalchenna, a house south of Inveraray (demolished, alas, in the 1990s) that had succeeded Kilcatrine as alternative ducal residence. The lunch was a sort of 'de-briefing', for the Duke had been Governor-General of Canada, 1878–83.

After such an active summer, Neil was in no mood to begin another novel. He was of course still committed to his weekly 'Looker-On' and 'Views & Reviews' columns for the *News*. In November he began contributing a fortnightly column, 'Here and There in the Highlands', to the *Oban Times*.

There was no shortage of diversions. On 18 November, Neil noted in his diary: 'William Strang the etcher and painter came down to Carnus & drew my portrait in his "Holbein" manner in three hours.' A couple of days later he was at Greenock Theatre. 'I went with Forrest Niven [*News* artist] behind the scenes after a performance of Rob Roy by Durward Lely and his company. Wm Mackintosh was the "Bailie"... Mackintosh I first saw years ago (in 1888–90) in the Grand Theatre, Glasgow, where he was playing in a pantomime... of which I had done the local allusions and some of the songs... Mackintosh... was very anxious that I should write a play with a character to suit him, and I promised to think it over. He said he would come to Gourock about Christmas & spend a fortnight there giving me the advantage of his "mechanical" knowledge of stage craft, but he never came. I sent him one of my books, but with the natural carelessness of the artist – which I never blame, though I am somewhat more fastidious myself – he did not acknowledge it by a line.'

Financially, there was no great immediate pressure to write another novel. At the end of 1903 Neil had £795 in the bank, a healthy sum in those days. *Shoes of Fortune* royalties contributed £133, while *The Lost Pibroch* was still earning money – £49 royalties from the 6d edition. Yet William Blackwood was keen to follow up success with success. In October he had sent a good report of *Children of Tempest*: reviews so far had been 'most gratifying' and the sales 'satisfactory: 4500 of the Home edition, and 1130 Colonial'. Blackwood also wondered if Neil had 'thought out your next book'. Neil replied promptly that he had a story 'simmering' in his mind. Neither could foresee that, after publishing six books in seven years, it would now be almost three years till the next Munro novel opened in *Maga*.

CHAPTER TWENTY-FOUR

Not in the kailyard, but up tenement closes

ARGUABLY *Children of Tempest* is a sort of culmination, illustrating perhaps better than any of the other novels why Fionn MacColla wrote: 'The works of Neil Munro... are irradiated and suffused with the unique flavour of Gaelic life in a way which is totally authentic and beyond praise.'[1] But Neil had gone as far as he could in that vein and from then on his productive rate slowed down markedly. The remaining four volumes of his *oeuvre* (not counting the Hugh Foulis tales) would take him twice as long to write as the first six, which in 1904 exactly matched his family of six children. Now, with the addition of his mother, there was a household of ten at Carnus, supported solely by his pen.

His desire to create a 'lighter vein of character and a modern theme', confided to Blackwood in 1902, was not easy to achieve.

Moreover, since the death of George Douglas Brown, Neil had been aware of a certain weight of expectation on his own shoulders, that he was the man to write the Great Glasgow Novel. As early as 1900 he had quoted William Wallace's anticipation of 'the rise of a school of fiction dealing exclusively and even realistically with the Scotland of today... The horrors of slum life... will never be thoroughly understood, and no attempt at ending, instead of temporarily making believe to end them, will be initiated until we have a Scottish Zola'.[2]

Neil's comments show that he, too, had already brooded on the idea of a school of Scottish realism: 'No one who has had an intelligent eye to the signs of the times for the past ten years will question the shrewdness of the forecast. The historians and the charter chests have had more than a fair share in the inspiration of modern fiction; in the domain of the idealistic idyll, Mr Barrie seems to have said what is like to be the last word for many a day to come; the local colourist (who, oddly enough, seems to be always rural in his topography) has apparently pegged out claims in every pastoral portion of Scotland, and yet the most vital and potent material for a modern Scottish novel is all untouched or left to the tender mercies of the ladies and gentlemen who purvey serial fiction for the Dundee weekly papers. I am not sure if I ardently desire the Zola system in the treatment of our slums... it would be good to see a novelist with the rare combination of poetry, humour, intensity and charm making the most of the dark but profoundly moving theme which modern Scottish life presents, not in the kailyard, but up tenement closes.'[3]

At the time of writing this, Neil had been aware (via Meldrum) of the existence of George Douglas Brown as one of a group of young Scots in London who 'shared a reviving interest in Scottish fiction' and were in 'reaction against the worst emotional excesses of the Kailyard school'.[4] Many had wondered if Brown would be the Scottish Zola. As it turned out, Brown's idol was not Zola but Balzac and his novel was centred in a little Ayrshire village, not in the Glasgow he had known as a poor student. Of the 'poetry, humour, intensity and charm' Neil had stipulated, only the intensity was much in evidence. Hugh MacDiarmid saw in Brown's novel 'a mere reversal'[5] of the Kailyard, part of 'the whole degrading entanglement' of the Kailyard/anti-Kailyard controversy – yet transcending all that by dint of Brown's genius.

When Neil and Brown eventually met, the latter gave the impression of being horrified at the idea that he should continue 'on the lines of *The House with the Green Shutters*'. Perhaps he did not mention his tentative plans for a satirical novel about the Glasgow bourgeoisie: he certainly did not let on that, in a letter to a friend, he had called *Doom Castle* 'a piece of damned sentimental filigree'.

Had Neil seen this, would it have stung him into a defence of his own work, written 'in the Highland manner'? Or would he have acknowledged an element of truth in Brown's criticism? He was certainly aware of the limitations of his work to date, and that of his fellow Scottish novelists, as an article in the *News*, unsigned but surely from his pen, suggests:

> Let any Scotsman consider for a moment how Scotland of today is actually represented in fiction: he will be appalled by the absolute non-existence of any fiction dealing with our daily life, as the daily life of nearly every other country is dealt with by its writers. If we were to apply the test of international importance, there is, perhaps, only one Scottish writer since Scott who could be spoken of as commanding the ear of Europe. And even if we grant Stevenson that rank, it has to be noted that much of his work, for all his fervid patriotism, had little or no reference to Scotland, and that which had was almost exclusively confined to historical romance... Now, while historical romance has its legit-imate place in fiction, it should hardly be needful to point out that no school of fiction which does not base itself on the life of its own period can have any real root of vitality in it... So far as the present writer can recall, almost the only attempt to deal with modern Scottish life... is the late George Brown's *House with the Green Shutters*. Even that is somewhat doubtful, but it may be allowed to stand as at least approaching modernity, and as a useful correc-tive to the shoddy sentiment of the 'kailyarders'.[6]

Technically Neil was capable of writing a novel about contempo-rary urban Scotland, and his own past would have provided ample raw material. But temperamentally he was not qualified to be the Scottish Zola, and he had enough self-knowledge not to attempt urban realism. The innate reticence of the Gael, and in particular of the Victorian Gael, was early compounded in his case by having to hold his tongue when others spoke of their fathers. What Peter Keating has called the 'vivisective nature of modernism'[7] was alien to him, as was the new theory that art and entertainment should be segregated. Yet he had come to think that his own vein, the histor-ical romance, could not be developed any further.

Neil rarely recorded his inner thoughts. We have only the word of Norman Bruce, a freelance journalist whose brother married Neil's daughter Effie, that in a diary Neil once wrote 'an anathema against those (unspecified) who had encouraged him to adopt the vein he had adopted in his fiction'.[8] The 'anathema' is not in the version of the diary now in the National Library of Scotland, which is clearly in part a 'fair copy' started about 1905, perhaps just in order to prune out traces of self-betrayal, though Neil neglected to destroy the original which was still in existence in the early 1930s but has since vanished without trace.

Bruce saw the 11-year gap between *Children of Tempest* and Neil's last historical novel, *The New Road*, as a 'black period with its lost sense of creative urgency'. His opinions are apparently based on conversations with Neil in the 1920s, for he goes on: 'I know, too, that later still he was able to talk about how he had come to adopt the Highland manner and to do so without expressing regret that he had done so.' (It must be remembered that Bruce was writing 30 years after Neil's death.) It is, putting it mildly, an over-simplification to term as a 'black period' those brief years when Neil produced two contemporary novels and some of the short stories gathered later in *Jaunty Jock*, not to mention the vivid contemporary creations from the pen of 'Hugh Foulis'.

The first of these, Erchie Macpherson, had already caught the fancy of William Blackwood, who had written to Neil the previous October: ' My nephew George is very keen about your publishing the "Erchie sketches" in a popular form if you care to consider such a thing. If you thought it might clash with your more dignified works of fiction, it would always be possible for you to make use of a *nom de plume* or issue anonymously.'[9]

Blackwood was shrewd enough to see Erchie as a useful stopgap until Neil could come up with the new novel. Neil himself had no hesitation about Erchie in book form, replying: 'I have every reason to believe a collection of the philosophical utterances of that gentleman would be secure of a certain degree of popularity...' But he opined that it would be better to wait for the spring of 1904 'as the market for that sort of material is very much glutted at present'.[10] The implied reference is to the recent popularity of *Wee Macgreegor* by J.J. Bell, 'put together' on Neil's suggestion but published at the author's own expense, against Neil's advice.

Although, judging by the catalogue of Blackwoods' books at the back of *Children of Tempest*, it was a pretty new departure for them to publish humorous sketches in the vernacular, William Blackwood threw himself into the project with unwonted vigour. Neil himself was also very active in the promotion of *Erchie*. Plans were already well under way when William Blackwood wrote to Neil on 5 February 1904 of his intention to print 100,000 copies, with a royalty of 20% on the selling price, 1/- net ('13 as 12'). He was confident this first impression would sell, bringing the author about £1,000:

'We are determined that if the book does not attain to the widest popularity it will not be for the want of effort on our part. We shall do everything we can think of to bring it very specially before the public and shall be happy to have any suggestions from you to this end. And as this expense should I think go against the first impression, I propose to pay you a royalty of 25% (3d per copy) on all sold beyond that number.

'We should I think send a copy of the book to every editor and reviewer in the country, and enclose with it a sheet of extracts giving some characteristic passages likely to attract attention and be quoted. We should also send out a good blaze of advertisements at the very outset, and in the repeats and show bills keep introducing continually some topical feature until the desired result is obtained. I hope you will be able to discover a real typical Erchie for the cover as much will depend on this.'

Neil suggested a modification in the terms, which Blackwood accepted: 'I am very pleased that you are to co-operate with us so heartily with regard to affording us every assistance in the advertising and popularising of the book, and that you have many novel ideas on the subject.

'We should be glad to have the portrait of "Erchie" as soon as you are able to send it to us. Our travellers are starting on their journeys and it would be an advantage for them to have a cover to show to the booksellers. But of course it is still more important that you should get the right man... How soon will you be able to let us have the complete copy, soon we hope as the printing alone will take 3 to 4 weeks to turn out nicely, which we wish to do?

'With best wishes for a thumping success for *Erchie*...'[11]

Within two weeks Neil had photographs of his Erchie to send off. His colleague Robert J. MacLennan, an Aberdonian and a popular *raconteur*, sat for them, blacking out one or two front teeth for the purpose. Neil also supplied Blackwoods with the pseudonym he had chosen – Hugh Foulis – casually borrowing his elder son's Christian name and the name of the Munro chief's seat for surname. (Neil's columns in the *News* continued to be unsigned, though in the West of Scotland at least the identity of their author was by now an open secret.) He wrote a number of Erchie sketches specially for the book.

With these arrangements in hand, he and Jessie went down to London for a few days. They went to see Barrie's play *Little Mary* at Wyndham's Theatre.

At the end of March Effie, 14, and Hugh, 11, set off on their own by train to stay with a family friend, Mrs Hereford, in St Albans. She was to meet them at Euston, but by mistake they got out too early, at Willesden. Their father described their misadventure in a letter to Kate Turner, 'how they were lost in London, & how they remembered Hodge's address at the Temple, & how they drove in a hansom there, & how the telegraph wires between St Albans, Euston & Greenock got so red hot they melted through the excessive telegraphing which took place on account of these happenings, & how all ended well...'[12]

In April, Neil was in London again and went to St Albans to see the children, before going off with Jessie, Mr & Mrs J.M. Smith and Mr & Mrs Guthrie (Gourock neighbours) on a jaunt to Italy, duly described by Neil in a piece for the *News*: 'Ah! but Summer was ours at last, her bland caressing breath on our cheek. She came in at dawn by the open window, and stayed, even after the day sank o'er the Eugenean Hills, and the full moon rode over the dark lagoon, and the twang of the serenadeers' mandolins and guitars came from the bowers of Chinese lanterns anchored in the Grand Canal. She spent the day with us while Piero, centaur of the sea, raised on high his dolorous "A-ouie! Sia primi!" and paddled us up tall, commanding streets or into narrow lanes. As in the pictures, veritably, dark Italian girls stood upon balconies of marble and the loveliest iron-work; as in the pictures, wisteria blossom fell in thick festoons from the gateway of the palace to the water; as in the pictures, as in the books, as in our dreams, the night (when Piero was not quite sober and once again a buccaneer beyond control) was full of delicious terrors, for we floated, Summer and we, up cut-throat closes of the sea, and under gloomy, murderous bridges...

'Some day, but a century or two hence, a man will sail up the Adriatic and pass through the Porto di Lido in his yacht, and slide among the nestling grasses of the lagoon into a city desolate and abandoned... in the declining sun he will see the doorways yawn in ruined palaces; the rotten shutters swung in the breeze before unglazed windows; altars washed by the tides, campanili broken, streets silted up with mud and sand. Over all that dead metropolis then will brood silence, except that the water will drop in tears from the blade of the last gondolier, his black craft a hearse, himself Death's emissary, sailing up green sea lanes...'[13]

Leaving Venice, their party went to Verona, Milan, Pavia and Certosa, then home by Paris and London, reaching home on 17 May. After a couple of weeks in Gourock, Neil took another break, noting on 4 June: 'At Inveraray with Macpherson on yacht *Nyke*,' and the following day: 'Drove to Port Sonachan with Macpherson, Peacock, C. Maitland, Fraser & c.'

Two days later, an early copy of *Erchie: My Droll Friend* was in his hands. He wrote to George Blackwood: 'I think *Erchie* excellently produced, certainly good value, mechanically at all events, for the shilling. I hope you have arranged a good pictorial bill for the book-stalls. Menzies's people lay some stress on that as very important. I send here some suggestions for such a bill, which might also be used in newspaper advertising. They do not suffer, you'll observe, from an excess of modesty, but the main thing is to get out of the ordinary formulae in advertising works. A bold, black deeply-shaded block of Erchie's head by Simpson or someone else would make an irre-sistible splash in weekly newspapers. – I think you ought to advertise in the evening papers on Saturday first: it's the day of their biggest circulation; in the case of the *Glasgow News* it would be desirable to repeat on Monday, on the page on which Erchie appears fort-nightly... Don't send a review copy to the *Glasgow Citizen*. The proprietor, who can never forgive me for having associated with any other newspaper than his, has never lost an opportunity of depre-cating me, and *Erchie*, because it has appeared in the rival paper, will worry him more than usually – not into any attack on the work (that would rather please me) but perhaps into personalities.'

That June the new *Who's Who* had for the first time an entry for Neil Munro. Perhaps it was then he supplied the wrong birth-date for himself – 1864 instead of 1863 – an error perpetuated elsewhere. In my opinion it was not done deliberately. He had reached the age of 40 the preceding June, and perhaps someone else subtracted 40 from 1904 instead of 1903. Or perhaps Neil was confusedly thinking of being eleven months younger than his wife.

July and August were spent, as usual, at Inveraray, 'during which the weather was exceptionally good, as we had only seven or eight days' rain all the time'. That year Neil's friend David Hodge with his wife and daughter Winifred (the same age as Isobel Munro) took the Post Office House for three weeks. During the holiday Neil, as a local celebrity, was called on to open a bazaar at Ardrishaig, but mostly his time was his own, though naturally he still had to wire copy for his two weekly columns up to Glasgow. 'For the past month I have been living in the country... I have done without any journal save the *News*... Ordinarily I stand breast high among the billows of paper from which there seems no hope of escape if I am to keep a hold of life about me; to-day I realise that all I need is a single sheet of eight pages, in which I can wrap my lunch before putting it into the fishing basket.

'Then there are the letters – it is glorious to do without them... Having no trains to catch, no particular mail to labour for, no business engagements to keep, a watch would be a useless encumbrance. Besides, I have no waistcoat to put it into. I know it is time I was down for breakfast when I hear the breakfast table being cleared; that it is dinner-time when I am hungry, and that the hour of sleep comes the first moment I yawn over my fly-book in the dusk of the long northern evening. Piscator, who is with me, has a watch, a five-and-sixpenny one which has not gone for weeks, and which, without scruple, he used the other day for a sinker in a sea-loch we were fishing for cod... There is a certain hour of the day when a bottle of lager beer, recovered from the cool depths of a shady pool, is as Imperial Tokay...'[14]

The long delightful summer of Venetian canals and West Highland rivers and sea lochs was interrupted on 24 August when Neil and Jessie had to go to Glasgow. The Institute of Journalists was holding its annual conference there that year and Neil, elected chairman of the Glasgow & West of Scotland branch in January, had a leading role to play, an ordeal for one who so much disliked public speaking. For the retiring Jessie it was no less trying. She and Neil stayed with J.M. Smith and his wife in Bute Gardens, Gilmorehill. The conference included a concert and dance, when Neil and Jessie received 500 guests at the Grand Hotel, a 'Corporation Conversazione to journalists' at the Municipal Buildings, and a more convivial 'supper and smoker to some of the journalists' at the Art Club. After that, Neil and Jessie returned with relief for ten more Inveraray days.

All summer *Erchie* had been earning money for Neil and Blackwoods, but by September William Blackwood reported sales were 'sticking rather'. The book had done well in Scotland, but sales in England had been 'very disappointing'. Neil was undaunted, replying: 'I want to say how much I appreciate the way *Erchie* was pushed and displayed; George Street and Paternoster Row seem to have concentrated every effort in its interest and I see it everywhere.' In the same letter he said that he had made no arrangements for the sale of *Erchie* in America: the publication of the sketches 'serially' in the *News* meant loss of American copyright. He hoped, however, that Blackwoods would make 'a similar agreement in the United States to what you have made in Canada'.[15]

November saw publication of another work by the mysterious Fiona Macleod – *The Winged Destiny*. This gave Neil a last chance to challenge Sharp to come clean. In his review, after a detailed attack on 'Fiona's' Gaelic, Neil threw down the gauntlet in the *News*: 'Miss Fiona Macleod's claim to embody in fiction the inner soul of the Gael obviously depends on her knowledge of the language of the people; she has said as much over and over again... Well, I am prepared to make a sporting offer; I am prepared to give a prize of ten pounds to the Gaelic Mod next year if Miss Fiona Macleod can satisfy any three Gaelic-speaking Highlanders, hereinafter to be decided on, that she can carry on ten minutes' conversation in ordinary colloquial Gaelic, read half a page of Gaelic... or write correctly three submitted simple sentences in the language.'[16]

The challenge was not taken up. Thus ended a long and intermittent controversy, not to be lightly dismissed as a squall in a quaich. William Sharp died the following year.

That November Neil accompanied J.M. Smith and Crawford to Liverpool, visiting Port Sunlight for an evening cinematograph lecture on production of the *Liverpool Post* newspaper. From there they went down to London, where they saw Cyril Maude in W.W. Jacob's *Beauty And The Barge* at the New Theatre. Neil noted: 'Was in London with J.M. Smith, Dr Crawford, Sir John Ure Primrose & Lady Primrose. Put up at De Keyser's Hotel on the Embankment. Tonight we went to a dinner of the London District Institute of Journalists in the Hotel Cecil... Wretched speaking: too much giff-gaff among the Scotsmen. I sat beside Sir Douglas Straight LL.D., editor of the *Pall Mall Gazette* – more man-about-town, it struck me, than journalist, given to risqués a little, Geldermann his favourite champagne...'

The only other entry for 1904 gives Neil's bank balance: £822, with Blackwood royalties amounting to £361.

CHAPTER TWENTY-FIVE

The bugles of the mind

ONE Monday in January 1905, readers of 'The Looker-On' in the *Glasgow Evening News* were in at the genesis of a Scottish 20th-century phenomenon. They were introduced to Peter Macfarlane, skipper of the S.S. *Vital Spark*. Para Handy has sailed on ever since. It was he who would keep Neil Munro's name alive while the historical romances were in partial eclipse and who remains instantly recognisable today. He is still in print a century later, and has been the star of three television series. But none of this could be predicted by Neil, nor the thousands of Glaswegians who opened their copies of the *News* that 16 January and first encountered Para Handy: 'A short, thick-set man, with a red beard, a hard round felt hat, ridiculously out of harmony with a blue pilot jacket and trousers and a seaman's jersey, his hands immersed deeply in those pockets our fathers (and the heroes of Rabelais) used to wear behind a front flap...'

His anonymous creator wrote in a style not easily confused with that of Mr Neil Munro, the established author of serious novels. The Para Handy tales have defied that mysterious law by which styles of humour go out of fashion. Neil's own phrase, 'rowan-jelly humour',[1] seems to fit Para Handy perfectly, 'tart and sweet in such a cunning combination that it tickled every palate and held some natural virtue of the mountain tree'. It is a quiet, independent sort of humour, using irony and understatement, that pervades Para Handy's world: the aficionado can find examples by opening the book at random:

He had wan of them names shed in the middle like Fitz-Gerald or Seton-Kerr; that'll prove it to ye.

He fell and staved his arm on the quay, but still had the sense to throw his bagpipes into the middle o' Loch Tarbert.

A Macfarlane would never put his nose in another man's oar.

The last example is from the very first story, which already contains many of the essential ingredients. The range of the steam puffer is indicated as 'all the seas that lie between Bowling and Stornoway'. Para Handy almost scratches his ear, appeals for corroboration to an absent Dougie, utters the phrase 'chust sublime', slily cadges a dram. He is already recognisable as one of those precious characters (not all fictitious) whose very presence bestows a joyous alibi from the everyday. Escapism, maybe, but not to realms of glamour or high adventure. The crew of a steam puffer had a hard, cramped existence, but on board the *Vital Spark* there are plenty of high jinks and 'baurs', while incidents of splendid variety, often recounted by Para Handy himself, banish tedium.

By the time Neil had finished the third story, his readers had met the complete crew of four. Their characters evolve naturally from the talk between them, supplemented by Para Handy's monologues, rather than by being described. Their creator knows them intimately. When they came together in his imagination, he was supposed to be working on a serious novel for Blackwoods and had plenty of other journalistic tasks to occupy him, not to mention social and family commitments. Yet into the middle of all this, almost uninvited, strolled Para Handy.

His first appearance had been foreshadowed in the 'Looker-On' of the previous week, when Neil wrote: 'I delight in the winter steamer to go down into the fore saloon as dusk comes on and see the glowing stove with dusky forms about it, and hear men talk in the accents of Ardrishaig about hoggs and herrings... There is something compact, friendly, communal about a Clyde steamer; the very purser, no longer gold-braid "from clew to ear-ring" as the sailor says, but human, wet and unaffected, as, oilskin-clad, he bears a hand at a rope; the Captain so much on a plane with us that we feel we may, without offence, call him Duncan and be done with it.'

In fact Neil did know a captain called Duncan: Duncan Newlands of the *Lord of the Isles*, father-in-law of his school-friend Colin McPhail – that same McPhail to whom Neil had lent £20 'to help him about a new ship'. Was this new ship one of the two puffers, the *Gleannshira* and the *Stronshira* (good Inveraray names), whose owner was one Colin McPhail? The coincidence, reinforced by the borrowing of McPhail's surname for the engineer of the *Vital Spark* and his Christian name for The Tar, leaves little doubt that Neil's friend was that very puffer owner, yet the origins of the Master Mariner were well concealed.

'One of the major unsolved problems in Para Handy scholarship is the vexed question of our hero's birth place,' state Brian D.

Osborne and Ronald Armstrong, editors of the 1992 edition.[2] They point out that Para Handy says at one time that he knows Loch Fyne well – 'I wass born all along this loch-side and brocht up wi' an auntie' – and at another that he belongs to Arrochar on Loch Long (MacFarlane clan territory). Was Neil being vague and careless, or deliberately misleading? He knew fine where he had got the name of Para Handy. It was the by-name of a herring fisherman, Peter McArthur, born near Inveraray in 1817. He lived all his life in his birthplace, one of two cottages at Drishaig, near Dunderave: not so very far from Arrochar, after all, yet on the very shores of Loch Fyne. His father's name was Alexander, which is often shortened to 'Sandy', and 'Para Handy' is a simplified version of the Gaelic for 'Sandy's Peter' – *Paruig Shandaidh*. ('Padruig' is more properly 'Patrick'.)

Peter McArthur never married. He had a 'punt' (rowing boat) called the *Dan Tod*, in which he used to row across upper Loch Fyne to the inn – or 'Inns', as his namesake and himself would have said – at Cairndow. The *Dan Tod* was popularly supposed to know her own way home. Sometimes, presumably when the tide happened to be far enough in, the Cairndow folk would carry Peter to the boat, put the oars in his hands and push him off. Together they always found the way safely across. The old boat ended her days in the 1920s on a bonfire when there was a wedding at Ardkinglas. Cairndow (which rhymes with 'too') is mentioned appreciatively by his namesake Para Handy as the place 'where they keep the two New Years'. It is also the place where he acquires his own piper, found 'standin' in front of the Inns with pipes under his oxter'.

There is even a family link: a nephew of Peter McArthur married Neil Munro's second cousin Isabella Munro. One of their daughters was the Kate McArthur (Mrs Turner, Lincoln) with whom Neil corresponded. Furthermore, Neil's colleague in the law office, William Disselduff, was also a nephew of Peter McArthur's. According to Maimie McGillvray: 'Old Willie never forgave Neil Munro for using the name!' But I think she was exaggerating.

Another contender in the Para Handy's birthplace stakes is that small one-storey shop that still stands to the north-west of Inveraray parish church. There Charlie Maitland and his brother Peter had their plumbing business, and Neil junior has told how his father 'would frequently go over there and spend an hour or two gossiping. The only seats in the place were the water closets which were there as samples and they would sit on those and chat for hours telling old stories and making jokes. Charlie Maitland actually was a man with quite an acute sense of humour and slightly sardonic at times. That was what gave my father some of his ideas for Para Handy – some of his humour there was based on the humour of Charlie Maitland.' The debt is subtly acknowledged in the very first tale when Para Handy says 'I will make him swallow the hatchet', a phrase invented by Charlie as a schoolboy.

Ronald Renton has suggested perceptively that Dan MacNeil, skipper of the sloop *Happy Return* in *Children of Tempest*, is 'the figure who corresponds to Para Handy in Munro's serious fiction'.[3] He is indeed 'a man that dearly loved a ploy' – does he not say 'I was aye too jolly when it came to inns'?

The timing of Para Handy's first appearance is interesting. It was only half a year since *Erchie: My Droll Friend* had proved so lucrative, and also in the middle of the three-year gap after *Children of Tempest* when Neil was struggling to change course, away from historical romance. Pursuing the alternative source of income opened up with Erchie was undoubtedly in his mind.

Perhaps the final trigger was seeing W.W. Jacobs's play *Beauty and the Barge* in London in November 1904. Parallels between Para Handy and Jacobs's maritime tales have been drawn before now, as also with the work of Jerome K. Jerome. Indeed, in 1896 Eden Phillpots had asked Neil for help with a '3 act farce in Gaelic' (sic) which he was writing with Jerome. One can imagine Neil's amusement at the conjunction of the Gaelic with the author of *Three Men in a Boat*: was this the very first seed of the Master Mariner? On 20 May 1897 his 'Views & Reviews' was entitled 'Three Men in a Yacht' (a light-hearted interweaving of book criticism with an account of sailing in a cutter from Gourock to Rothesay).

Nor was the emergence of a new, if anonymous, comic talent entirely unpredicted. Ten years before Para Handy, just after *The Lost Pibroch* came out, a perceptive piece in *The Bookman* had observed: 'The Celt, as Mr Munro knows him, is not gloomy at all, though something of a fatalist, and... unwilling to frivol with the large issues of existence which some races make jokes about in the comic papers. In half his moods he is riotously funny, with a vivid sense of the humorous, and the most beautiful zest in his little comforts and casual amusements.'

Yet the birth of Para Handy warranted no mention at all in Neil's diary for 1905, which contains just nine brief entries, six of them about fishing trips. Nor does the diary mention the start of an additional labour for Neil that March in the shape of a weekly two-page supplement in the *News*. This innovative feature, entitled 'Literature

Mother and son: Ann Munro and the boy who would grow up to do her such credit

House of Argyll (clockwise from top left): The 8th Duke, Lord Archie, Lord Lorne and his wife Princess Louise. Was Neil Munro (above left) a relative?

Son of Inveraray: Neil Munro was born at Crombie's Land, right, with the town jail in the background. Inveraray was dominated by the Duke of Argyll, who lived at the Castle, below.

Broad horizons: Steamers linked secluded Inveraray with the wide world, into which Neil ventured just before his 18th birthday

Happy family: Bud, Jessie, Lala, Effie, Hugh, Neil junior, Neil and Moira.
Only Annie, who died as a small child, is missing,

Six in a row: Effie, Bud, Lala, Neil junior, Moira and Hugh

Wife and mother: Jessie Munro, pictured with Hugh as a baby, preferred to stay out of the limelight but gave Neil the stable, happy home life he needed

It's a sair fecht, a faim'ly:
Maggie McNiven, left, was kept busy
with the growing family of Munros

Above: Effie, Bud, Moira, Lala

Below: Bud:, Lala, Moira, Effie

Growing family: Jessie with Lala and Effie,
Neil with Hugh and Neil junior

Totem pole (top down):
Neil junior, Neil, Bud,
Moira, Effie, Lala and
Tua the dog

Final sacrifice: An adventurous if shy boy, Hugh Munro had everything to live for and was training to be a doctor. His name is now one of many on the Inveraray war memorial.

A town at war: Inveraray had seen its young men march off to countless conflicts over the centuries, as in this photograph taken around 1914. Neil went down to Bedford to see Hugh before he embarked for France. This was the last time they were photographed together.

Literati (clockwise from top left): Joseph Conrad, George Douglas Brown, Cunninghame Graham and William Sharp

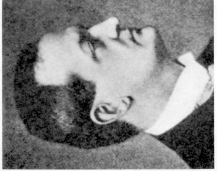

Artists (clockwise from top left): E.A. Hornel, George Houston, Macaulay Stevenson and Pittendrigh Macgillivray

Literary man: Neil with his friend Charlie Maitland, Inveraray plumber extraordinaire, and, above, in later life

Four homes (clockwise from top left): McVicar's Land, Neil's first home in Inveraray; Waterfoot, Cromalt and Carnus

& Life', resuscitated the literary weekly which Neil and J.M. Smith (now editor) had set up and abandoned in 1892 (five years earlier than *The Times* started its weekly periodical, 'Literature'), and claimed 'absolute novelty so far as evening journalism in this country is concerned'. There were to be many book reviews and contributions from well-known writers, all to be solicited and seen through the press by Neil. He also wrote many of the reviews, though these are unsigned. One early contribution was by Joseph Conrad. Offering some recompense for the extra time and energy spent on the supplement, *The Shoes of Fortune* was run as a serial, earning Neil £100.

That year he also took on further work in agreeing to supply the text for *The Clyde: River and Firth*, a large illustrated volume to be published by A. & C. Black in 1907. For this he got '£250 down'. Clearly Neil had plenty of energy but was somehow unwilling, or unable, to focus his attention on the new novel he would call *The Daft Days*. In June, George Blackwood reported his uncle 'much interested in the progress of your new story and delighted at the prospect of its being ready to start in November's *Maga*'.[4] In the same letter he proposed terms for a cheap uniform edition of all Neil's books – to include *The Daft Days*. During 1905, at Neil's instigation, Blackwoods bought the stock of *Gilian the Dreamer* and *The Shoes of Fortune* from Isbister, whose business was to be liquidated.

The two months in Inveraray that year did not give Neil much holiday relief. His increased *News* commitments continued and he intended to make great strides with *The Daft Days*, but in fact made little progress.

It was perhaps that summer that Hugh, now twelve, and his cousin Ion (son of J.M.M. Munro) found in Kilmalieu graveyard part of an old skull, which they bore back to the house as a trophy. Hugh's father 'put it carefully on the sideboard and left the room without a word'. After a night of rain and storm the boys 'noticed that the bit of skull had disappeared'. Neil had taken it back to Kilmalieu during the night and 'buried it back into the sacred ground'.[5]

On a Saturday at the end of August, Neil was invited to go on board Sir Thomas Lipton's steam yacht, just arrived at Inveraray. Lipton's guests were the Prince and Princess Hohenlohe (niece of Edward VII), also Colonel Duncan Neill, a Greenock acquaintance of Neil's:

'I was asked on board the "Erin" this evening – a magnificent ship of between 1300 and 1400 tons, brilliantly lighted by electricity, the state-rooms large and lofty – more like rooms in a house than on a yacht. Lipton, who went to London only 15 years ago and only since then has found his way among the beau monde, showed me, with great pride, over his vessel... I was introduced to the Prince and Princess – young, amiable, interested in Inveraray and the ducal family... A rather comical incident happened to the Princess at Rosncath. While lying with the "'Erin" at Greenock, she expressed to Duncan Neill her desire to see Rosneath, the Scotch home of her aunt Princess Louise, Duchess of Argyll, so he took her over in the yacht's launch, and through an avenue of trees right up to the house. It was late afternoon, and much to her horror, while they were standing close to the house, trespassers really, looking at it, the Princess Louise and a friend came out, and saw them. Without waiting to see if she was recognised the Princess [Hohenlohe] bolted, Duncan Neill after her...

'Lipton. however. is a more curious character than his royal friends. Vain as a peacock, simple as a child in some respects, astounded at his own "success in life". He spoke for an hour at least to me about his intimate friendship with the King and in hushed and rapturous tones about the time when he had thirteen princesses at one time aboard the *Erin*. The only one I can remember... was the Empress Eugenie, whom he took on a trip to Egypt. It was she who opened the Suez Canal, I think: when she went with [Lipton] nobody paid any attention to her, and it was with difficulty she got accommodation.'[6]

This account is from the 'retrospective' diary begun a year earlier (about the time when Neil also made his 'fair copy' diary). Years later he recycled some of the material in the article on Lipton reprinted in *The Brave Days*.

In September Neil was due to go to Edinburgh to report the military review marking the 25th anniversary of the 'Wet Review', in which he had taken part as an eighteen-year-old volunteer. As a curtain-raiser for the event, his 'Looker-On' column for 28 August reminisced about the 1881 review. 'What I know I cannot recall is the zest and happiness of the young recruit, for the first time part of a battalion marching behind a brass band... Ah! that was worth while! I see that those whom they absurdly call the veterans – the men who were reviewed in Edinburgh in '81 – are to be represented on this occasion; but I'm not going. I might put on the old uniform, but I could not resume the old spirit... The young recruit, dear lad! is dead; I know now that his crowded hour of glorious life was a pretty commonplace thing, that his sentiment of glory was very cheaply aroused by an event neither splendid nor important. But what is splendid, or important? Nothing happens but in the mind; there, alone, is glory and its elation, and I have learned the lesson, sometimes bitter, sometimes consoling, that, recruits or veterans, the crowded hours are in ourselves and not external, of no importance to anybody but ourselves, at the best a dream, whether that dream be roused by the sound of a brass band or the bugles of the mind.'

Such moments of self-betrayal were rare indeed, and it is impossible to tell whether this was a fleeting mood of solipsism or a lasting state of mind. It does sound like a quiet *cri de coeur*, curiously emitted in an anonymous column whose author's identity was nevertheless an open secret in the West of Scotland. It accords with a perceptive comment about Neil by John Brandane: 'His reticence about his own writings, his self-effacement on public occasions, are well known: he was, in fact, that type of artist whose sub-conscious, or daimon – to use an older and better word, if we speak of art – was only operative on condition that the other partner in the game, the self-conscious apparition that fronted the world as Neil Munro, should collaborate with his Ariel in secret.'[7]

It is interesting that Neil indulged in this small outburst just when he was making a name for himself as Hugh Foulis and also struggling with his first non-historical novel. The struggle was long drawn out. October came, and the opening chapters of *The Daft Days* were nowhere near ready for serialisation the following month. On 6 October Neil had to beg 'a few months' grace yet before starting the new story... If my delay in apprising you of the situation is likely to put you about I extremely regret it.' William Blackwood, who cannot have been best pleased, replied: 'I must make other arrangements, and fill in the time till you are ready to keep the ball rolling in old *Maga...*'[8]

Eight more months would elapse before even the opening chapters of *The Daft Days* were sent off, but Neil had not been idle and now had something else up his sleeve to placate Blackwood. In the same letter he continued: 'There is another matter I have been going to write to you about for some time. Since the retirement of Erchie I have been fortnightly writing in the *Glasgow News* a series of somewhat analogous articles and stories about the title *The Vital Spark*. They have caught on immensely in the West of Scotland; indeed in an infinitely greater measure than *Erchie*, and I have not the slightest doubt that if you care to undertake their publication this winter in the shilling form of *Erchie* they would exceed that gentleman's popularity.'

William Blackwood swallowed the bait, and on 20 November Neil sent off by parcel post 'the bulk of the *Vital Spark* sketches'.

CHAPTER TWENTY-SIX

Blythmeat and breadberry in the house of Daniel Dyce

THE first days of 1906 found Neil down at Lochgoilhead with his artist friend George Houston, 'white hare shooting' – not bringing in the New Year at Inveraray, as of old. Yet more than ever Neil's imagination would be steeped in the place of his birth all year as *The Daft Days* took shape. As if to signal the change away from historical romance, when he was invited to give the annual April lecture at Stirling's Library, Glasgow, he chose the subject of 'The Modern Novel'.

Set around 1900, the last full year of Victoria's reign, *The Daft Days* would be as modern and contemporary as Neil cared to make it. While deeper and more complex than the rapidly composed work of Hugh Foulis, the novel would shimmer with the same joyous humour found in the Para Handy tales. As if to encourage Neil in the new vein, George Blackwood reported Scottish orders for 15,900 copies of *The Vital Spark and her Queer Crew*, published that April. It was, as Blackwood put it conservatively, 'a fairly good start'.[1]

Three of the twenty-five stories had not appeared beforehand in the *News* but were written specially for the book by Neil, who had also arranged for an artist called Jack Orr to provide a cover and several plates. The readers loved it. Neil once explained Para Handy to a curious English reader, familiar only with his historical romances, as 'humoursome Highland character sketches... written solely for the amusement of West of Scotland sea-board folk...'[2] But Para Handy cast his spell much more widely. For example, Neil

Munro junior writes of Cambridge dons setting themselves 'examination papers on [Para Handy's] voyages and vernacular'.[3] A review at that time, probably by William Power, asked: 'Is it ridiculous to suggest that these Munro tales are literature because they create characters who are bound to live as long as there are readers to enjoy Scottish pawkiness and rich canniness and racy humour, unforced in its essence?... A book designed to aid in the glorious work of cheering us all up.'[4]

Nevertheless, the sum total of serious critical attention to the Para Handy stories would fill few pages. Neil himself would scarcely have been perturbed. Though he himself left no written record of it, there is a strong tradition that he liked to keep a sharp distinction between his novels and his journalism, which of course includes all the humorous tales. *The Glasgow Herald* opined (1957) that the Master Mariner was 'disdained by his creator' who 'had the same feeling for Para Handy as Sullivan had for the music he wrote for Gilbert...' Norman Bruce claimed that 'Munro regarded Para Handy, as he said, in terms of blacking his face and singing in the street'.[5]

But perhaps observers were misled by Neil's casual attitude. He could never have created the crew of the *Vital Spark* in a disdainful mood, even if their escapades did not always stick in his memory. His contemporary Rosslyn Mitchell recalled: 'So much was his writing the expression of his mind that he would forget things he had written himself. One evening in Arran he read aloud a Para Handy sketch, "The Wet Man of Muscadale", and it was so fresh to him that he chuckled and enjoyed it as if he had never seen it before. Indeed, he had to stop because the fun of it was too much for him.'

What is certain is that Neil wrote the Para Handy tales with great fluency, sometimes even slipping into the *News* library to write an episode. A colleague, George Primrose, perhaps racking his brains over a leaderette demanding two more dreadnoughts for the Navy, used to envy the ease with which Neil wrote. That fluency and the author's obvious enjoyment gave the tales a vivid immediacy that has not dimmed.

Yet *The Daft Days* did not come with such fluency. It was not until the end of May, three and a half years since Neil first signalled a change of direction after *Children of Tempest*, that the first twelve chapters of the new novel were despatched at long last to *Maga*. Neil assured George Blackwood that he had the rest 'in draft considerably under way, sufficiently to make it safe for you to start the serial in August or July as you suggest'.

Yet he still evinced an alarming tendency to be distracted. On 13

June he set off on a motor car reliability tour through Scotland, being driven 671 miles in a Darracq. A week later he departed (as stand-in for J.M. Smith) on a fortnight's tour of Sweden with a group of twenty British editors. He learned that 'the *News* consumed each day fully ten acres of an average forest. Being a sentimentalist and a woodsman by nature, and a journalist only by stress of circumstance, the appalling fact created in me very mixed feelings.' They were presented to King Oscar at Stockholm, 'a singularly affable gentleman who was condescending enough personally to show us over his private apartments!'[6] Another 'Engelska Pressmenna', E.C. Bentley, inventor of the clerihew, proved a temporary soulmate.

At the end of June, as always now, the large Munro household removed to Inveraray, a daunting task, what with packing bedlinen, cutlery and other paraphernalia. Usually Neil would even hire a piano from a Glasgow firm – several of these pianos never made the return journey, having been snapped up by Inveraray neighbours. The routine was the same each year, and Neil junior's memories of those days would remain vivid in his eighties, when the following reminiscences were taped: 'We got to Inveraray by travelling on the Clyde steamer the *Lord of the Isles*... We would get to Inveraray about 12 o'clock... We took large quantities of luggage. We actually had... a sort of brake, a thing with high sides, which came up to take our numerous trunks and cases including one or two of those Japanese cane woven basket things which my sisters were very snobbish about – they thought they weren't proper.'

The great pastimes at Inveraray were swimming, walking, fishing and (in later years) golf, with an annual picnic *en famille*. Effie was very good at organising their activities, although the fishing and golf were her brothers' domain. Hugh was friendly with an Inveraray boy called John Macintyre, son of his father's old friend Peter. They often went sea-fishing with Peter in his boat. Neil junior remembered Hugh as 'a very keen fisher... We always chartered a rowing boat every summer, which was tied to a buoy near the pier. My father paid an elderly man – a very elderly chap – to look after this boat and I think he probably paid him something like half a crown a week. It was his great job. He thought it was very important. He used to stop me in the street and talk about the rowing boat and the buoy which was very important to him... [This was Calum Bell, whose sister Mary Ann kept a sweetie shop.] We used this boat for long fishing trips, my brother and myself and sometimes my brother's friend Douglas MacLeod [also known as Willie]... or George Blake...

'I don't recall my father fishing in the loch but he was very keen on salmon fishing or trout fishing. He would go salmon fishing with George Houston the artist who [rented] a house called Cuil further up the loch opposite Cairndow. They would go for long trips fishing and hiring the Argyll Arms hotel car and chauffeur... Once when I was standing down near the Cross – I must have been probably about ten – my father suddenly appeared from the hotel – he'd been away fishing – and as he came up to me he stretched out his hand and showed me that a salmon fly had gone right through the ball of his thumb and because of the barb on it he couldn't remove it and he was going to the doctor, a Dr Stewart who lived somewhere beyond the Coffee House [Fernpoint] and he had to get it cut out of his hand, this hook...

'We fished mainly for... very often it was mackerel, but we caught a good deal of cod, rock cod – we would get it down at the Craigs – the rocky bit beyond the Newtown – and there if you went in close to the rocks you picked up rock cod which had a little beard so far as I remember. But we caught mainly mackerel and sometimes saithe [coalfish] which we didn't think highly of. I can remember once when I was fishing from the rowing boat with Douglas MacLeod and my brother and we ran into a huge shoal of very large fish which I had never seen before. We started bringing them in – I think we caught about two dozen. They told me they were what was called stenlock [large saithe]. I think they must have been very rare in Loch Fyne.

'But of course by that time the great herring fishing industry in Inveraray had died down, although Johnny Dewar – who ran a shoe shop down below us in the Main Street – he went out fishing early every morning and usually had boxes outside the shop on the pavement, a box of mackerel and I think he also had herring... Very often Maggie would go down and bring back several mackerel or herring. Sometimes we had them for breakfast.

'But my great fishing interest apart from that – and also my brother's – was going up to High Ballantyre. It was a burn [tributary of the Aray] running down from a farm up there... where we could catch trout, brown trout. I'm afraid I was a very poor fisherman because I used worm, which of course is not really sporting. Hugh and Douglas MacLeod would also use worm but gradually they started using fly, to cast with fly... But it was rather difficult casting with fly because the banks were covered with small birch trees and bushes and things and you were rather apt to get your gear tangled up in this...

'Our fishing in Ballantyre burn was one of my delights. I didn't like rainy weather then because it spoiled the holiday but it improved the fishing because the water rose after and we got more fish. I sometimes went up there alone to fish and once I remember sitting quietly and noticing on the other bank a white creature with pink eyes, obviously an albino – I think it must have been a weasel or a stoat...

'On another occasion I found on a sort of little sandy island in the middle of one of the reaches of the Ballantyre burn the half body of a salmon which had been gnawed at the head end – the head was not there but there was a great chunk of salmon and then the tail, and when I got back... I described this to my father and he said, "Why didn't you bring it down?" – because, he said, "obviously it had been taken by a weasel or something which had eaten the head end and left the big fleshy tail end. You should have brought it back – it would be quite fresh. You could cut off the jagged bit." So I got on my bike and went back and brought it down in a haversack and we cut off the chewed end and cooked the other end, but the family wouldn't eat it. I ate it and my father ate it and we found it perfectly good.'[7]

The Munros had access to that burn because Donald Macarthur, tenant of High Ballantyre, was married to a second cousin of Neil senior's, Elizabeth Munro. Their swimming place was at First Cromalt, half a mile south of Inveraray, where a burn runs into Loch Fyne at a little sandy bay. In an outhouse of the house nearby they kept a small round-ish striped tent in which the girls could change.

During these idyllic Inveraray summers, there would be intermittent contact with the House of Argyll. The younger Munro children were up in the attic one day when they spied a carriage which had drawn up below, at their door. They pelted it with little apples, only to discover it belonged to the Duke, who had come to call on their father. No serious repercussions are reported. It must have been the 9th Duke, for by the time he was succeeded in 1914 by his nephew Niall the Munro children would have been too grown-up for such an onslaught.

The 10th Duke also used to call on Neil in his summer quarters, though it is most unlikely that he ever came in a carriage. He was 42 when he succeeded, and never married. Neil junior recalled that his own first visit to the castle was in the days of Duke Niall, who was away at the time. He was taken there by Peter Maitland, Charlie's brother, who 'had the sort of freedom of it as he was the official plumber... But what amused me was that in the large dining room the Duke's bicycle was lying up against one of the large sideboards. Evidently he kept it there so that it was always handy – he could just skip out. He always cycled everywhere. He didn't have a car... His visits to us were usually made unfortunately just in the middle of the day, about one o'clock, and we were just sitting down at our main meal... He would come and knock on the brass door knob thing, and my father would take him into what was known as the back parlour, a smallish room at the back of the house looking on to the garden. He also, I remember – the Duke himself – would come down sometimes with a pair of shoes in his hand, and hand them in to Johnny Dewar to have them repaired.'

For the annual family picnic, a trap was hired. The Munros generally went to the Dubh Loch and sometimes further up Glen Shira, to Rob Roy's house. Once or twice, before it was remodelled in 1911, they went to Dunderave Castle. Neil junior remembered it as a ruin: 'There was still a stone stairway and what must have been the large banqueting hall... very uneven floor and dusty.'

In those days, the internal combustion engine being still in its infancy, great peace could be enjoyed in country places. Neil junior recalled 'that even during the summer when there were some holiday visitors in Inveraray the town would go very quiet for long parts of the day when nobody would be in the street. But the great event of the day would be the arrival of the two steamers which came from the Clyde. One was the *Lord of the Isles* and the other was the *King Edward*, a black-and-white steamer belonging to another company. The *King Edward* was a turbine steamer which travelled faster than the *Lord of the Isles* which was a paddle steamer, and the *King Edward* would arrive, drop its passengers and then it would sail out into Loch Shira – it was always known as 'the sheer' and sometimes I and other boys in the town would get on to the *King Edward* and go out just for this short trip... It was always a great event and there would be quite a number of Inveraray people standing waiting for the ships to arrive.

'There were also at that time what were known as German bands on the steamers. I recall "The Little Grey Home in the West" was the first bit of music that I ever became acutely aware of by listening to it on the *Lord of the Isles* when we were on our way from Gourock... The men from the band would come ashore with their instruments and they would start to play in the main street and then go round knocking at doors getting a penny or tuppence in a little bag they handed out...'

At Inveraray the Munros always went to church on Sunday mornings. Neil senior would suddenly get out a small notebook and take the sermon down in shorthand, just as he had done as a lad. At one stage he would always pass along a bag of those large, hard, round peppermints called imperials – once he produced from his pocket an enormous imperial, about four inches across, and handed it wordlessly to Neil junior. The Munros did not go to church in Gourock, but they always went in Inveraray, to keep up a tradition. 'Well, we were not I'm afraid a religious family,' said Neil junior.

On Neil senior's return from Sweden in July 1906 he went straight down to join the rest of the family at Inveraray. There he had still to produce his two weekly articles for the *News*, and this summer there would be little time for rest and relaxation – the first instalment of *The Daft Days* had appeared in July's *Maga* and there could now be no letting up in Neil's literary output. Each day he would labour away for several hours, occasionally going out in search of diversion. Neil junior remembered that his father 'used to see a great deal of his friend Charlie Maitland... and Robert Fraser the chemist who was also a colleague at school...'

Yet that summer could not be an entirely cheerful sojourn, for Neil's mother was very ill. Her memory was failing, and more than once she wandered out into the street in the middle of the night. At the end of August she left Inveraray for the last time when the family returned to Carnus, the children talking scornfully of going back to 'Gourocky-soorocky'. ('Soorocks' is Scottish for sorrel, whose tangy leaves are good to chew.)

Returning to Gourock meant going back to school, but it also meant seeing old friends again. Among these was Arthur Guthrie, a neighbour who was a designer at Templeton's carpet factory in Glasgow and who liked to amuse the Munro children with games and the occasional limerick:

> When you're out in a boat you must know,
> That Lilian bosses the show.
> Moira and Neil
> Are yon two at the wheel,
> And Bud and Effie mun row.

The tasks here are assigned more in the interests of scanning than veracity, and for the same reason Hugh is omitted. The children called their neighbour Uncle Arthur and his wife Aunt Jessie, often shortened to 'U.A.' and 'A.J.' The Guthries' house, Cranford, was just below Carnus. They had no children of their own, and 'U.A.' played a very slightly Lewis Carroll-ish role towards the Munro girls, especially Moira and Lala (as well as to other, non-Munro girls).

When they were away at Inveraray, he would write to them. Here is part of a letter from 'U.A.' to Lala in Inveraray, written that year on Wednesday 22 August:

My dear wee Lilian,
   I am just as proud as Punch, and you know how proud that can be, at getting such a fine long letter from you. I think it is your first letter to me, and I mean to keep it until you have got your hair ever so high up... It must have been great fun at the Bazaar playing at a real shop, and getting real money, and giving back real change... Lord George [Campbell] must be rather a nice sort of Lord, buying you sweeties: I never understood before what Lords were for, but now I know... I suppose you get grand fun even on wet days: the Boat and the Fishing must be spiffin. It is too bad if Moira and you don't get out too, but perhaps mother would be anxious about you... I was expecting your Dad yesterday, and to-day: but perhaps he means to come for the Dunoon Games, & to stay the week-end with us. Love to you all.
   Your loving old Uncle Arthur.

At Christmas time 'U.A.' and 'A.J.' would take them all to the pantomime, where a big box of chocolates was always handed round, and every year they waited for 'U.A.' to say 'Are you happy? Are you glad you came?' He liked to give them books on birthdays and at Christmas, mostly Juliana Horatia Ewing's stories in the Edwardian editions illustrated by M.V. Wheelhouse.

Sadly that Christmas the Munro family circle contracted. On 4 December Neil's mother died at Carnus, aged 77. Her funeral 'from the Parish Church, Inveraray, to Kilmalieu Churchyard' took place two days later.

CHAPTER TWENTY-SEVEN

Ailie's Geese

THROUGHOUT the sad time of his mother's illness and death, Neil continued to send off instalments of *The Daft Days* to *Maga*. To ease his journalistic workload, his 'Views & Reviews' column had been incorporated into the 'Literature & Life' supplement since October, but in March 1907 it returned to its own page. By now the new novel was virtually complete. Just before it came out in book form in May, he wrote to George Blackwood: 'I hope on the matter of advertising you will give the book a fair show, since I am confident it is of a character to be popular if the public first have its humorous nature well impressed on them... I may add that the story in *Maga* brought me a considerable deal of the most flattering correspondence from many parts here and abroad.'[1] One of the Blackwoods (likely George) has written on this letter: 'I hope Jimmy that you will block out a good scheme for advertising this book. Send it to Munro with the prices marked or he will not believe our statements. It was the only way we satisfied Mr Buchan, [E.M.] Forster, and such like.'

The ingredients of Munro's first 'modern' novel – bereavement, frustration, small-town constrictions, Presbyterian morality, exile, domestic servitude – might suggest a piece of grim naturalism. Instead *The Daft Days* portrays happiness and loving kindness and incipient female emancipation. The young heroine is an American orphan living in a Scottish town with her lawyer uncle and two aunts, all of them unmarried. The younger aunt harbours unfulfilled dreams of being a schoolteacher: for her 'the years of opportunity were gone, the golden years that had slipped past in the little burgh town...' The elder aunt, when her niece shows acting talent, declares that the theatre is 'Satan's abode'. Also in the household there is a maidservant, far from her Hebridean home.

Neil knew 'all the obvious, facile and insincere devices by which it is as easily possible to secure popularity for a book as it is for a patent medicine'.[2] Far from being facile, *The Daft Days* took him three years to write. Traces of sentimentality – the 'homespun' philosophy of Daniel Dyce, say – are a small part of the whole, balanced by its 'rowan jelly humour'. And the *leitmotif* is the call of the wild geese above the roofs, 'far-fetched and undomestic', symbolising dreams and aspirations. The novel continues Neil's chronicling of Inveraray, though it can be read without suspecting so. The text is sown with clues such as Jocka's house, Divine the hawker with his oranges, the knocker in the shape of a brass man's hand, still in its place to this day. The book is set in the years round 1900, the days of Inveraray's final efflorescence under the 8th Duke. It is noticeable that Neil never dealt, in fiction, with the period between *Gilian the Dreamer* and the 1890s, which includes the years when he himself lived in Inveraray. The changes adumbrated in Gilian have already come about – 'the last of the old Highland burgh life and the raw beginnings of the new... the real *duaine-uasail*, gentry of ancient family, colloguing with the common merchants whose day was coming in'. Indeed, the Dyces' maid Kate MacNeil, who comes from the Isle of Colonsay, is the only Gaelic speaker mentioned.

The story of *The Daft Days* had been sparked off by Neil's own children's invasion, in June 1903, of the large house in Inveraray's Main Street, known to him hitherto as the abode of a childless bachelor – his own first employer, William Douglas. That first summer Neil had been able to spend only a few weeks there with his family before going on his journalistic jaunt to Canada. No prizes for guessing where he got all the Americanisms and the nonchalant independence that went to the making of Bud Dyce.

In Chapter XXVI, Bell Dyce suffers from nervous prostration at the prospect of her niece going away to school in Edinburgh. Dan Dyce discovers Bud at her aunt's bedside, '...reading aloud from Bell's favourite Gospel according to John... So had Ailie sat, a child, beside her mother on her death-bed, and, reading John one day, found open some new vista in her mind that made her then and there renounce her dearest visions, and thirl herself forever to home and [Dan] and Bell.' This passage can be contrasted with the last chapter in George Douglas Brown's book, when Mrs Gourlay, at death's door, reads aloud from First Corinthians. It confirms the impression that Neil consciously made his novel the obverse of Brown's. This can even be seen in details. For instance, both opening chapters feature a maidservant: Brown's is a 'frowsy chambermaid', Neil's the sonsy Kate MacNeill in 'her new stiff lilac print'. There is only one 'nesty body' in *The Daft Days* – Captain Consequence. Just as there is almost unrelieved pessimism and lovelessness in Brown's book, Neil's brims with optimism and charity and thus falls prey to charges of sentimentalism.

The passage about John's Gospel is also a hidden reference to the death of Neil's own mother while he was writing *The Daft Days*. In Chapter VII, Dan Dyce talks freely of his own religious views, much less strictly Presbyterian than Bell's. 'It is not sin that is eternal, it is righteousness and peace.' Then a glance from Bell makes him dry up. 'The mood that was not often published by Dan Dyce left him in a flash, and he laughed and put his arms round [Bud].' A clear echo of Neil's own reticence, this suggests there is much of himself in Dan, mingled with traits from his old employer of the warm heart and quaint manner.

Dan Dyce is the only male character drawn at any length, but there is a whole spectrum of late-Victorian womanhood. Here the light-hearted tone belies the subtlety. Contemporary reviewers who said Neil could not create female characters seem to have overlooked the women of *The Daft Days*, probably because the novel deals only glancingly with relations between the sexes.

At one end of the spectrum there are the Duff twins with their dame school, 'so prim, pernickety, and hopelessly in all things wrong'; at the other end there is Bud. In between there is Bell Dyce, content with her domestic realm. There is Kate MacNeill, who billows from the kitchen window and hears 'the whistling in the close'. And then there is Ailie, a sort of Janus figure.

'That's what I should have been, Dan, if you had let me – a teacher,' Ailie tells her brother. Perhaps, if she had not thirled herself to home as a child, she might have outfaced her brother's lack of encouragement (his motives are left unanalysed). Yet she is 'a newer kind of woman' than the Misses Duff: 'She was glad she was free, that her happy hours were not so wasted in futilities, that she saw further, that she knew no social fears, that custom had not crushed her soul, and yet she someway liked and pitied them.'

Ailie, recognising Bud's gifts from the start, gives her all the encouragement lacking in her own life. Bud has inherited great acting talent and goes forth from her loving family to triumph on the London stage. The Dyces make a special trip down to see her perform, just as Neil took every opportunity to go to the theatre on his jaunts to London.

The Daft Days is hard to classify. It could be seen as a kind of prose idyll, depicting the brief years when Bud's presence illumines the quiet Dyce household. It has been seen, by Ronald Renton, as 'confronting... the problem of the female creative artist in a society whose educational system and social and religious mores inhibit the expression of her talent'.[3] Sir Arthur Quiller Couch saw it as 'a shining book... differentiated as pure Scots by that strain of sentiment of which we Southerners fight shy... Your literature has purchased its sentiment at a fearful price – an expense of spirit in a waste of slop – but when one comes upon a book like this of Mr Munro's, with its confident, delicate handling, he has to admit that the cost has been justified.'⁴

Neil had two books published in 1907, the other being *The Clyde: River and Firth*. It remains a handsome, collectable book in which Neil's 200 pages of text are illustrated with many reproductions of paintings by John Young Hunter and his wife Mary. Neil had now cleared his plate of literary fare and could spend the summer relaxing. Financially he was secure – in June 1907 his *News* salary alone reached £400 p.a. That month he went on another journalists' tour, this time to Denmark. These jaunts were a precious restorative, devoted as he was to his family. All that is recorded of this journey is a visit to a *svineslagteri*.

On 24 July Neil was put under the microscope when *The Bailie*, Glasgow, featured him as subject No. 1814 of its 'Men You Know' series. The long article is interesting as it gives another Glasgow journalist's view of him: 'He has gained fame – and a well-deserved fame – but he maintains himself the old natural man... NEIL MUNRO, as the generation knows him now, is a novelist. But in the basis and outcome of his character he is really a journalist... He has partly lifted the veil that hides the Saxon from the Land of Mist, or perhaps the Land of Mist from the Saxon... As a work of art possibly, the BAILIE would say, *Gilian the Dreamer* is his finest realisation. Mr Munro has the years of God in his favour, and he may do something still more effectual... Scotland at the moment has need of a great novelist.'

That September the family circle at Gourock was reduced again, but only temporarily, when 17-year-old Effie went off to a Swiss finishing school near Lausanne. At the same time, Neil junior entered primary school. Perhaps the changes made his father restless, for October found him 'gingerly contemplating a very tempting proposal to pick up my tent-pegs and flit to London!'⁵ Arthur Spurgeon had written to ask if he would be interested in the post of Chief Editor of the House of Cassell. But the proposal cannot have been tempting enough – or Neil's ties to the land of his birth were too strong.

CHAPTER TWENTY-EIGHT
It's a sair fecht, a faim'ly!

NEIL had a restorative start to 1908 – a douce week at Forres Hydropathic, in the company of J.M. Smith and Dr Farquhar Macrae. Then in March came word that he was to be given the honorary degree of LL.D. by Glasgow University. He wrote to five-year-old Winifred Hodge, daughter of his friend David in London: 'If ev-er I hear you call-ing me Doc-tor (or per-mitting your Par-ents to do so, or anybody you know) I shall be quite Wild. – Neil – your young friend with the real 15/- seas-on ticket – has got an un-pleas-ant new game. When he is go-ing to bed, he cries 'Doct-or!' at me, and es-capes up stairs be-fore I can get at him with the strap.'[1] This letter was written partly for the eyes of Winifred's parents: there is a wistful postscript: 'Thank your mother and father and yourself for the post-cards. But why does your father never really write?'

At the end of March the *News* announced that the *Erchie* and *Para Handy* tales, hitherto in Monday's 'Looker-On', would now appear in alternate Saturday 'White Editions'. Presumably without Neil's knowledge his real name was given as the author. It was never again appended to the humorous tales until the posthumous edition of *Para Handy*.

Neil was capped LL.D. at Gilmorehill by Principal MacAllister on 22 April, and a week later the directors of the *News* entertained him at a complimentary dinner with the staff in the Imperial Union Club. 'In a happy speech Mr Munro thanked the company for their kind sentiments, and assured them that he appreciated very highly the good wishes of his colleagues on the *Glasgow News*.'[2] Congratulations came also from Neil's cousin Kate Turner, to whom he replied: 'A few days ago I was in the Glasgow Sailors' Home in search of copy, and was introduced by an injudicious friend as "Dr Munro" to a bluff, handsome, brass-bound English captain – the official inspector, or something of that sort of such institutions. In a little he began to describe minutely to me a severe attack of neuralgia from which he was at the moment suffering. Neither in mischief nor in malice, but out of sheer embarrassment I tacitly accepted the role of medico... asked some searching questions about his "unnards" (as Para Handy, savin' your presence, would say).

168

Then I prescribed 10 grains of phenacetine, hot fomentations and a day in bed. The gallant Captain was touchingly grateful, and followed my advice to the letter.'³

After a year at a finishing school – the Pensionnat Johnston at Vennes, Lausanne – Effie was fetched home that June by both her parents. One of her fellow-pupils in Switzerland had been Fanny Lehar, sister of the composer, who paid her fees out of his earnings from *The Merry Widow*. Effie herself was the musical member of her family: she had a beautiful soprano voice and took singing lessons. An accomplished young lady of 18, she had been happy at finishing school but was glad to be re-united with her own family and go off with them down to Inveraray.

Amid all the usual Inveraray diversions, Neil began to plan out his next novel. Again it was to be near-contemporary, light and entertaining, to follow up on the success of *The Daft Days*. He took the title from a real Fancy Farm in Greenock, of which some buildings still exist. Among the portraits in the hall of Neil's *Fancy Farm*, we are told in the eponymous novel, is 'a smaller, more pacific canvas, where the seaman, little more than a lad, in lieutenant's uniform, stood against a lichened cromlech with a trailing branch of cherry-blossom in his hand' It is a picture of Sir Andrew Schaw of Schawfield, the novel's chief character.

Outwardly Sir Andrew is a patchwork of pieces borrowed from Neil's friends and acquaintances. Like George Douglas Brown he has been engaged to the wrong one of two sisters. Like the 9th Duke of Argyll he has had to let his house to strangers (hence he resides in the dower house). Like Cunninghame Graham (who had to sell Gartmore, his ancestral estate) he is democratic and quixotic. Like Conrad he is a sailor, or rather former sailor.

But his character owes more to Neil himself. *Fancy Farm* is at once a sublimation of his lifelong dream of living in the country and an imaginary trial ground for his notions of what he would have made of being a laird, mostly put into the mouths of Sir Andrew and his protegee Penelope Colquhoun. Sympathetically portrayed as something of a 'New Woman', Penelope also has Munro elements: her father, a minister, is descended from Highland shepherds, and her mother had been a 'servant-maid'.

The location of Schawfield is left vague, but there are clues that it lies on the western coast of Argyll, somewhere about Old Poltalloch and Duntroon. The name 'Schawfield' is the same (but for a 'c') as the Islay seat of J.F. Campbell's family, but might also allude to Hayfield, a house built by one Captain Hay on the site of

Tiravadich, seat of Neil's Macarthur forebears. (Hayfield was burnt down in 1912.) The little town also called Schawfield is clearly, from its lay-out, based on Inveraray. (Sir Andrew yearns to know the 'secret inner life' of its tenements.) There is almost no overtly Highland content in the novel, reflecting Neil's pessimism about the future of the *Gaidhealtachd*. Cattanach the factor, like Kate MacNeill in *The Daft Days*, is the only Gaelic speaker in the book.

But little of this would be written that summer. Of more immediate interest to Neil was the first murder trial to be heard in the town since 1887. Effie and Hugh went to see some of the proceedings in court with their father, who well remembered how, in his own childhood, the judge had driven all the way from Edinburgh in a carriage with postillions: this time the judge, Lord Johnston, travelled by train to Dalmally and then by waggonette through Glen Aray. No doubt the Munro children went to see him being welcomed at the foot of Croit a'bhile Brae by the Provost, bailies and other dignitaries. Did the Inveraray children revive the chant their parents used to sing to the trumpeters' music, the 'Pity me' that Gilian the Dreamer heard from the Paymaster's house? Neil described the scene in 1908: 'In five-and-twenty years nothing had changed, not even the tunes of the trumpeters from Edinburgh, who, wearing the same old cocked hats and gold-laced coats and waistcoats, heralded the exit of the Judge from his hotel, and set the pace for the procession. Tradition had always ascribed to the burgh a couple of halberdiers, and when the revival of the Circuit Court was mooted, it was necessary to find them. The halberts were recovered, rusty and broken from the interregnum, to be repaired and refurbished, but the moths had apparently made prey of the old uniforms which local archaeology cleverly restored. Escorted by a company of Territorials, attended by the Lord Lieutenant, the Duke of Argyll, the magistrates and Council, the clergy, the bar and the counsel in their robes, his Lordship walked to the court-house, himself the most gorgeous figure in the procession. The town bell rang, the sun shone, one had an eerie Rip-Van-Winkle-ish feeling in reverse, and rubbed one's eyes to make sure it was not old Lord Deas again with a servant behind carrying the japanned box with the black cap.

'During the opening prayer in the Court, the Duke of Argyll sat beside Lord Johnston on the bench, but did not wait on the trials. The fact aroused some speculation – has an Argyll sat on the justiciary bench at Inveraray since the day when James Stewart of the Glen was tried and condemned for the Appin Murder? At all events there is no local memory of it, though many Dukes since then have, as Lords Lieutenant, had the privilege to do so. It was not the only incident of the Circuit that recalled *Kidnapped* and *Catriona*. David Balfour found the judges and the counsel at worship in the kirk on the Sunday when he reached Inveraray... On Sunday last Lord Johnston also could be found in Inveraray kirk, though unaccompanied by the bar, which nowadays is less attentive to the ordinances.

'The first day's Court was followed by the Judge's dinner-party, and here again the lapse of over twenty years has rendered one feature irrecoverable – there was no "Judge's port". They were "viveurs", the old Lords; you read of delectable nights on the old Western Circuit, when the Bar sat late after His Lordship had retired, and kept a messenger briskly plying between the Argyll Hotel and the Judge's cellar down the town, for the Judges of no later than five-and-twenty years ago, fastidious about their wines, kept a well-stocked cellar in Inveraray... Port was their favourite tipple long after sparkling French wines had captured the taste of the rest of the world; we shared one of the last bottles from the cellar some years ago, and found that, after a sleep of a quarter a century, it had lost no little part of its bouquet. The younger port of last Monday's dinner was infinitely better as Elchies, Kilkerran or Deas would doubtless have confessed...'[4]

Lord Cockburn, when he was in Inveraray in April 1843, had offered not port but claret 'jolted last week all the way from Leith'.

The Munros returned to Gourock and the children went back to school. Hugh, 15, Lilian, 12, Moira, 11, and Neil, 8, were all now at Greenock Academy. The family had fallen into the habit of calling Isobel 'Baby' and were just training themselves to use her proper name when she started school that September at 'Miss Comber's'. On her first day there she announced, without consulting her parents, that her name was 'Bud', after the heroine of *The Daft Days*. The name stuck to her all her life, though her parents mostly called her Isobel.

Lilian was mostly called Lala, from Moira's childish attempt to pronounce her name. Sometimes the family called her 'airy fairy Lilian', from Tennyson's poem. She was only eighteen months older than Moira, who tended however to associate more with Bud, despite the gap of five years. Moira and Bud invented private phrases such as 'shaking the brown mitt' (when making up after a quarrel) and 'sour milk secrets' (other people's). Bud once coined a good phrase: 'Laziness is a sublime.'

When the children had done something naughty they would ask

each other 'Is Maggie angry?' If they were out playing at tea-time, she rang a big handbell to summon them, and their playmates – who called her 'Maggie Munro' – knew it was time to go in, too. At a certain time of year Maggie would sniff at the girls' long, blonde plaits to detect if they had been at the burning of gorse on Tower Hill. She had a fine stock of Doric phrases which entered family tradition:

'It's a sair fecht, a faim'ly.'

'As black as the earl o' hell's weskit'

'I'd as soon keep you for a week's a fortnight.'

'You're hearty when you laugh.' (Not over generous.)

'Awa' to Freuchie in a frying pan!' (Maggie's first post had been in Abernethy, not far from Freuchie and Kingskettle.)

'They wid rin a mile doon a fir dale and scaud the de'il at the end o't.' (Of runny porridge. A 'dale' is a deal, a plank.)

'Mrs Whurramajig.' (Instead of ' thingummyjig'.)

'I've to cook, wash, mak' kail and gang to Glesca a' in the yin day.'

'It'll no' be this the morn's morn.' (After inordinate fun.)

'This'll no pey the rent and buy the weans' peenies.' (For instance, when rising to start work again after a fly cup of tea. 'Peenies' are pinafores.)

'A' the comforts o' the Sautmarket.'

'A long lie and a tea-breakfast.'

'I'm hearin', but I'm no' heedin'.'

'It wouldny cut butter on a hot stone.' (Of a blunt knife.)

With Bud now at school, the house was empty of children during the day for the first time since 1889, which should have allowed Neil to give *Fancy Farm* his full concentration. But he had nothing concrete to offer William Blackwood when he wrote in October, seeking news of the next novel, which originally Neil had hoped to complete by the end of the year. Neil had to reply that although he was 'fairly launched on it', it would take several months to complete. Part of the problem may have been that even as he struggled to

172

create an amusing story of country life, he could sense the impending catastrophe into which all Europe would soon be plunged with tragic consequences for millions, including his own family.

It is chilling now to read Neil's prophetic 'Looker-On' column of 9 November, 1908, written nearly six years before the start of the Great War. In it an imaginary character, Macdonald, is put off his golf stroke by Boy Scouts 'playing soldiers' and tells his companion: 'You're like most other people, I see; you imagine that great events are all suddenly arranged by parliaments or the newspapers, that wars are due to international misunderstandings, to something or other that happens in the Balkans, or some purely individual folly of the German Emperor... I have the Highland "flair" for those mysterious, magnetic, mental states that are bound to result in battle; we call it *roimh-eolas* in The Language... This country is swiftly drifting into war; no, not drifting, for the war is pre-destined, and we are hurling headlong into it. Not a Peninsular, Crimean, or South African war, mind you, to be fought at a comfortable distance from our comfortable semi-detached villas by hired professional soldiers, but a war on this very island, a war which will drag my boys, if they're spared, away from the business... the mimic war of the bairns has grown so hot in recent years that I, with my Highland *roimh-eolas*, know that actual terror is close at hand; and I'm sick at the thought of little Willy.'

It may not have needed the great power of *roimh-eolas* to have forebodings about war, though the phrase 'something or other that happens in the Balkans' is uncanny. On one page alone of the *News*, for instance – the very same page as this 'Looker-On' – it was reported that the Baltic entrance of the Kiel Canal was to be enlarged, that a British dreadnought had been launched and that Baden Powell had replied to a critic who said he was doing 'murderous work' in advocating preparations for war by saying: 'Let men take up arms and there will never be war, but if men go sneaking about with their hands in their pockets the enemy will come and it will be too late.' A week later, Neil imagined, in his 'Looker-On', a German attack on the Clyde – 'A Chapter omitted from Mr H.G. Wells's "War in the Air"'. A few days later, the *News* had a cartoon quoting the First Lord of the Admiralty saying in a speech at the Guildhall: 'We mean to keep our supremacy for all time.'

Towards the end of 1908, the English theatrical manager Alfred Wareing came to Glasgow, intending to found a repertory theatre. He had earlier brought the Irish Players of the Abbey Theatre,

Dublin, to tour England. Now he had an option to rent the Royalty Theatre, Glasgow, for April, May and June 1909, for £80 a week. Wareing would later recall: 'I was alone in Glasgow, but not unfriended, for Anna Henley, the widow of the poet, was living there, in Bath Street, with her sister Molly McBride and her husband Will, the notable Scottish artist. To Mrs Henley and her sister I poured out my plans, which they understood and quickly accepted. Their advice and help became my chief standby. At once they arranged a dinner party to which I was asked to meet Dr Neil Munro...

'And so we met again, after an interval of nearly ten years; for I had been introduced to him in John Smith's bookshop in Renfield Street by J.G. Wilson, who is now a famous London bookseller, presiding over the house of Bumpus.

"The night drave on... the minutes winged

"Their way wi' pleasure... the hour approaches"

when I set out to escort Neil Munro to the last train for Gourock. I well remember his first words when we got to the pavement in Bath Street. "You must have known Henley awf'lly well," and thence, to the Central Station, we talked about the poet we had both known and admired. We met again, in the *News* office, and I got from him many useful suggestions, giving in return the suggestion that he should write a play to fit my company. I will admit that I was eloquently persuasive, for I had learned that his was a name to conjure with in Glasgow. With proper Scots caution, he was fain. He promised a play to be produced that season, and neither of us had any idea what it would be about. Anyhow, it was announced: "A New Play, by Neil Munro," and expectations began to buzz.'5

Just before Christmas 1908, William and George Blackwood proposed a shilling illustrated 'clothbound' edition of *The Daft Days* for the next spring. This would do well, having a wrapper drawing by Monro Orr. *The Daft Days*, not generally considered in the front rank of Neil's novels, sold excellently – 41,118 copies of a later cheap edition were sold between 1913 and 1918 – and at the end of the year Neil had a satisfactory bank balance of £1,343.

All the family went down to bring in the New Year at Inveraray, perhaps the visit Moira would describe many years later. 'We travelled in the *Comet* to Lochgoilhead and then over Hell's Glen in the old coach. On the way we were told how [father] had walked over there many times as a young man going home from Glasgow for a week-end to his beloved Inveraray which, I think he was rejoiced to feel, was just as beloved to his children.

'That New Year when we went as children, we wakened up in the morning to find we were snowed up and had to dig a way out of our house in the Main Street. Up to the forest we walked with our father, who very seldom walked with us, and he told us how, when he was a boy, the deer would come down to the town in bitter winter frost to look for food...'[6]

CHAPTER TWENTY-NINE
My own folk are pleased with me

EARLY in 1909, Neil was able to move into a substantial hut on a levelled site in the little steep wood behind the house at Gourock. A joiner had been employed to build it as a refuge where Neil could retire to write. Once Charlie Maitland came to stay and, aided or perhaps more accurately encouraged by Neil, put in a gravity-fed system whereby the hut could be lit by gas. This contraption mystified Neil junior, who many years later would remember it clearly as consisting of a container fixed to a tree, with a length of very small-bore metal tubing issuing from the container to a lamp in the hut. For a while there was also a battery-operated amateur telephone from hut to house.

Yet despite all these refinements Neil did not find the isolation congenial, and before long he was often to be found writing in the dining room as he had always done or, when the children were at school, lying wrapped in a plaid on Neil junior's bed, thinking out plots. If the purpose of the new hut had been to accelerate production of *Fancy Farm*, it was a failure, and in March Neil cannot have been surprised to get a stiff-ish letter from William Blackwood: 'You would have heard from me sooner but your not coming up to time with your new novel threw my serial arrangements for *Maga* seriously out of gear, and it is only now that I have been able to fix matters up so far. I have managed to stave off the story which was to take up the running after yours until August 1910, and I hope to begin another within the next few months. This will leave room for you between say October or November 1909 to September 1910. It is the best I can do in the circumstances...'[1] By now Blackwoods had prepared the shilling edition of *The Daft Days* and on 17 March George Blackwood wrote to report a good start: nearly 8,000 copies ordered in London, nearly 5,000 in Glasgow and 3,616 in Edinburgh, also 'a special order for Australia of 1,000 copies'.

Neil's reply to George Blackwood reveals a further diversion that might account for the lateness of *Fancy Farm*: 'I have been intermittently at work on some new short stories lately, with a view to collecting enough for a book, and today it seems to me that you might possibly consider the enclosed "The Brooch" suitable for *Maga*.'[2] The book – *Jaunty Jock* – would not coalesce till 1918, but in the meantime William Blackwood thought the story excellent.

As a director of the new Glasgow repertory theatre, Neil went to London in April and, with Alfred Wareing, visited J.M. Barrie, presumably to ask him for a play. He also lunched with John Galsworthy (then known as a playwright as much as a novelist) at Dieudonné's Hotel, Ryder Street, and with Arnold Bennett at the Gourmet Restaurant, and saw Barrie's *What Every Woman Knows* at the Duke of York Theatre.

Having once declined the Freedom of the Royal Burgh of Inveraray, Neil now felt it churlish to reject a second offer and on Friday 21 May the honour was conferred upon him. The ceremony in the Court House started at 5 o'clock. Provost Donald McVicar presided, and Neil made a speech. Ex-Provost Guthrie, who as a councillor had seen Prince Albert made a Freeman in 1847, was of the company.

Later there was an eight-course dinner in the Argyll Arms, during which selections were played by the Inveraray Pipe Band under Pipe Major Charles Maitland, who gave up his place at the dinner table in order to play. They had turned out in full uniform by special instruction of Lord Archibald Campbell. 'At intervals during the evening songs were excellently sung by Mr J.H. Rose [the Postmaster], Inveraray, and Councillor Rankin, Oban. The singing of "Auld Lang Syne" and "God Save the King" brought the proceedings to a close,' the *Oban Times* reported.[3]

That newspaper, alas, did not print William Disselduff's 'lively reminiscences' of the days when he and Neil had been in Douglas's office. It did, however, give the full text of Neil's fairly long speech in the Court House: 'I tell you the truth when I say that I should be a much happier man at this moment if your worthy Provost, instead of presenting me with the freedom of the town in this ceremonious fashion, had quietly taken me for a walk round John Turner's

Corner, and slipped the casket unostentatiously in my topcoat pocket. (Laughter.)...I know that if I wrote about the scenes and characters of my native place for fifty years I should not exhaust its possibilities, however I might misapply them. For the things we love intensely are the only things worth writing about in poetry or romance...'[4]

At the end of May, Neil heard again from William Blackwood, who wrote to say he proposed to publish 'The Brooch' in the December or January number 'as it is just of the creepy nature which would be appropriate then'. Blackwood then added, pointedly, 'I also hope you are making good progress with the new novel, as I expect I shall have to begin it in October...'[5]

Neil should have been hard at *Fancy Farm* that summer in Inveraray. Instead, he took time out to write the first act of a stage comedy, *Macpherson*, based on Erchie – the play he had promised Alfred Wareing but had failed to deliver in time for the summer season in Glasgow. By August there was still no sign of *Fancy Farm* and George Blackwood wrote to postpone the deadline for the start of serialisation to the November or December *Maga*. Neil replied apologetically from Inveraray: 'I come here, usually, each summer, with an enchanting anticipation of seclusion, quietness, and much work to be overtaken, but I generally find that it is an illusion and that work is more difficult here than anywhere else. It has been my experience this summer again, and I leave on Friday with a bad conscience. You certainly ought to have a considerable portion of the story before you now, and I hope to let you have it very soon, as I have sent off the earlier chapters finally to the typewriter.'[6]

Neil added that he was about to go to Italy with a party of British journalists, though he would rather stay at home and finish *Fancy Farm*. The Italian trip took up the first half of September. But in the second half Neil at last got down to his new novel in earnest and on 4 October he sent George Blackwood the first six chapters of *Fancy Farm*, mentioning in his covering letter Harper's 'remarkably successful run' with *The Daft Days* in America (where it was entitled *Bud*).

Time was now running out fast for *Macpherson*, if the play was to be ready for Wareing's autumn season. Wareing had been remarkably patient following the initial disappointment that summer when 'Alas! the season ended with a deal of glory but no cash and no play from Neil Munro'. Yet Neil's promise held good, as Wareing would recount: 'The directors of the Citizens' Theatre (they had joined me partly because of Neil Munro and Mrs Henley) were so hopeful of the success that would attend the production of Munro's play that they agreed to my urgings to embark upon another season in order to produce it...

'So an Autumn Season was arranged with a new play by Neil Munro still as the *pièce de résistance*. Alas! ideas would not flow; the last week of the season was in sight, and there was no sign of the play. I pleaded and then I pressed, and at last I got the script of *Macpherson*, a comedy in three acts by Neil Munro. He had written the play in little more than a week and he had written it to fit my company. There were two important male parts; the one devised for M.R. Morand was none other than 'Erchie', a character who had figured in some of Munro's sketches of Glasgow life... The other was built for Campbell Gullan, himself a Glasgow man, who knew to the flicker of an eyelid the type of Glasgow man Munro had drawn for him to interpret. Here, indeed, an important part of my dream of Stock Company days was realised. We had found our 'stock' author! Campbell Gullan was so much in love with his part that he startled me by asking to be let off playing in W.S. Gilbert's *The Palace of Truth*, which preceded *Macpherson*. He had been a real wolf for work, eager for any part, but 'John Latimer' was too good to take risks with...'[7]

On Sunday 7 November Neil read over the play with Kempton, the stage manager, and was given '£20 down on a/c of Royalties'. *Macpherson* opened on 20 November at the Repertory Theatre and ran for a week. Neil described it in a letter to William Blackwood as 'an extraordinary success'.

The review in the *Glasgow Herald* said: 'Every seat in the house was occupied, and when the curtain went up on the "Drawing-room at Mrs Latimer's, Appin Gardens, Dowanhill", an interested murmur went round the assembly. When, two minutes later, Erchie appeared with his "'flet fit and warm hert"... the laughter began instantly – laughter of that warm, hearty quality which intimates that the joke is not merely tickling risible surfaces but goes right home. As the play proceeded, the laughs grew still heartier and more frequent, and when at length Erchie made his final exit, leaving the darkened stage empty, the applause was furious... [Mr Munro] achieves strong national comedy with an undercurrent of serious-ness and sentiment expressed in perfectly natural conversation.'

The reviewer in *The Scotsman* wrote: 'In response to loud calls from all parts of the house, the author was obliged to come to the front and acknowledge the flattering ovation. Judging by the skill and the knowledge of human nature displayed in *Macpherson*, there seems to be no reason why the author should not make his mark in play-writing even more pronouncedly than he has done as a journalist and novelist.'

Wareing, with such a money-spinner on his hands, was grieved to have to bring down the curtain down prematurely: 'We could very well have run it through the holidays to the end of January, when, instead of just saving the Glasgow Repertory Theatre, it would have restored its lost capital and set it up in funds again. The D'Oyly Carte Opera Company, however, was booked to appear, we had to give place to them, and there was no other theatre available. We revived *Macpherson*, and always successfully, but we had missed the tide that would have led us on to fortune.

'Neil Munro had no illusions about his play; it was a successful bit of hack work, that was as much as he said of it. We read some of the notices together in my office, and he was greatly amused at the way his brother journalists had treated him. The only disparaging notice of *Macpherson* appeared in the Students' Magazine, but as the writer of it found the highest pleasure in Tchekov's *The Seagull*, which George Calderon had produced for me a few weeks before, no one was surprised. I believe the Editor was admonished by the President of the Union, who is now Major Walter Elliott, M.P. for the Kelvingrove Division of Glasgow. And yet *Macpherson* contained unmistakable evidence of real gifts as a dramatist, the dialogue was easy and natural, and very lively and full of fun, and some of the characters came out sharp and clear, although he had taken trouble with only one of them, John Latimer...

'Although Neil Munro never wrote another play for us, his association with the Glasgow Repertory movement remained close; at every possible occasion, and he himself made many such, he was actively friendly.'[8]

With Neil's support as a director, the Repertory Company would at last made a profit in 1914, but it was not to survive the outbreak of war. For Neil, *Macpherson* had been an enjoyable interlude, but he chose not to abandon novels to seek his fortune with the drama, as Barrie had done before him. Just six weeks after his play's brief but glorious success, Neil made light of his talents as a dramatist in a 'Views & Reviews': 'It is quite touching now to witness the annoyance of Repertory Theatre management at the idea of being considered "intellectual". "We are just plain, ordinary people," it protests. "Our aim is to amuse: every now and then we make you laugh uproariously. Have you seen our utterly ridiculous *Macpherson*? Not a scrap of intellect about it!"

'I wonder who the miscreant was who branded the Repertory with the name of "intellectual": he could have done it no worse service, for the unintellectual loathe the word, and the really intellectual probably smile at the suggestion that the modern theatre may be looked upon as a kind of academy where the students sit in the pit and stalls, their brains all simmering with profound and unfamiliar thoughts. If the stage ever had that effect, it certainly has not got it today... For instruction, intellectual stimulation, wings to the imagination and permanence of impression, a good novel leaves the best of modern plays leagues behind.'[9]

With a world war in the offing, Neil's decision not to write for the stage was perhaps well-advised. Although *Erchie: My Droll Friend* had gone out of print, the success of *Macpherson* inspired Neil to write a fresh run of 42 more Erchie pieces which began in the *News* in January 1910. In the end he would remark that Erchie earned him more than any of his novels. Neil's income from Erchie and the Para Handy books was a vital part of his budget, supplementing his salary from the *News* and the royalties from his other books, although these would never approach the astonishing £40,000 that J.M. Barrie (with no family to support) made from *The Little Minister*.

Some years later, after seeing Barrie's play *Mary Rose*, Neil junior asked his father if he could write a play like that. The reply was: 'With one hand tied behind my back.' It was the one and only time he ever heard his father boast.

CHAPTER THIRTY

Or I'm a soused gannet

AT last, in January 1910, *Fancy Farm* opened at *Maga*, even though, once again, Blackwoods did not have the complete manuscript. Much of 1910 would be a scramble to keep up the instalments – indeed, May found Neil writing to George Blackwood: 'I enclose two chapters of *Fancy Farm*, and the third will follow tomorrow. Your instalments will be much more timeous after this or I'm a soused gannet. Yours contritely...'[1]

Meanwhile Hugh had matriculated at Glasgow University, shortly after his 17th birthday, and intended to study medicine. He would live at home and travel in to his lectures by train each day from Carnus, where his father kept busy – but not always at *Fancy Farm*. Neil was still turning out two columns a week for the *News*, and 1910 saw not only the fresh run of Erchie stories but also a steady stream of Para Handy. Even when Neil Munro was struggling over a novel, his alter ego Hugh Foulis remained prolific, to the delight of *News* readers.

Having set his hand to the plough with *Fancy Farm*, Neil managed to keep more or less to deadline, although at Inveraray, as usual, there were countless diversions. A sentence from a letter to George Blackwood, written by Neil at Inveraray at the end of August, characterises that last Edwardian summer: 'This, as you surmise, is no place for working: it is the land of eternal afternoon and idleness, and friends continually coming off steamers and yachts and motor cars and bicycles just "to dip in for a moment or two", and others who want you to fish, or picnic, or golf – oh confound them all!'[2]

It was easier to work at Gourock, where Neil at last completed his novel and posted off the final chapters to *Maga*. The children went back to school and Hugh to university to continue his medical studies, passing physics and chemistry in October but 'ploughing' in medical botany.

Fancy Farm came out in book form in November and would sell well enough for Blackwoods to bring out a cheap shilling edition in 1912. Despite being a reasonable success at the time, it remains the least well-known of Neil's novels. *Fancy Farm* has been seen as 'above all a novel of ideas'[3] and 'a representation of the author's ideal world'.[4] At the same time it contrives to be a light-hearted contemporary love story with a pervasive undercurrent of humour. Neil himself said: 'The story is one purely of manners, character, and, like *The Daft Days*, must depend on these and its humour for interest.'[5]

The humour is mostly in the lively episodes involving the folk of Schawfield, as well as Sir Andrew's aunt and his housekeeper. The ideas themselves are sometimes harder to follow. While Neil was trying to decide the plan of *Fancy Farm*, he wrote a 'Looker-On' entitled 'The Blight', about the tragic effect of an English landlord in the Highlands: in Chapter IV of *Fancy Farm* he would go further, expatiating on Sir Andrew Schaw's being unlike 'his social compeers, – Scottish lairds with ancient Scottish names, who had English mothers, and had gone to English schools' and so on. The problems of a relatively impoverished Edwardian laird are examined in some detail, without any generalising. Penelope Colquhoun and Sir Andrew's cousin Norah act as a corrective to the more deleterious effects of his 'democratic cantrips'.

Many of Sir Andrew's ideas are casually or even flippantly given in conversation. 'Dear aunt, let us be really serious when it comes to art. It's the only Faith that's left for half our fellow-creatures' is one of his remarks. Many ideas are also attributed to Penelope Colquhoun, who calls herself 'a right down Radical'. Sir Andrew insists: 'There must be progress, movement, in the arts, as in everything else, and the novelty at first is only to be appreciated by a small and shrewd minority.' But Penelope disagrees: 'There's only change.' The reader is left wondering which side Neil himself is on!

Even before *Fancy Farm* came out in hard covers, William Blackwood was once again expressing the hope that Neil's next novel would 'suit *Maga* as a serial'. Novels by Henry Newbolt and Ian Hay were to follow *Fancy Farm*, so Neil would have the best part of two years to write his novel, if he wanted to 'take up the running again' (a favourite phrase). Blackwood added: 'Of course if you did not want to tie yourself definitely to a date just yet, I might be able to meet your convenience if you kept me posted as to how you were progressing, so that neither of us might be put in a difficulty.'[6]

In his reply, Neil adumbrated the idea which would eventually become *The New Road*. He assured Blackwood: 'I can't figure myself very well anywhere else than in *Maga*, and I hope to find myself once more between the old buff covers about the time you suggest. I have been thinking, for a change, of a return... to something of the manner and adventures of *John Splendid*, and I think I could peg a lot of picturesque happenings on to General Wade's making of the great military roads through the Highlands. Those tame, domestic excursions in the last two books are all very well, but I mustn't allow my claymore hand to get stiff!'[7]

The Blackwoods were delighted to hear he was going to 'flash his claymore again', as George Blackwood put it, at the same time reviving a project that had been considered long beforehand – an illustrated edition of *The Lost Pibroch*. But in the end nothing came of it, unless it be the unsigned line drawings in a copy of the book now in my possession.

Towards the end of 1910, Neil accepted a commission from A.& C. Black to write a book 'on Ayrshire or Burns'. This was intended to be an 'artistic itinerary' of Ayrshire, illustrated by Neil's artist friend George Houston. It was 'mainly to please Houston' that Neil agreed to embark on this distraction from the *magnum opus* that lay ahead with *The New Road*.

On 7 December, he and Houston went to the dress rehearsal of *Little Red Riding Hood* at the Theatre Royal, Glasgow, Neil noting afterwards: 'Harry Lauder the famous Scotch comedian has the star part of "Sandy Shaw". I went to his dressing-room with Willy Disselduff, Dunoon, his law-agent and business man (who tells me he disburses £30 a week among Lauder's poor relatives – a comment on Lauder's reputed Scots meanness) and had quarter of an hour's talk with the great wee man, who, starting by ceremoniously calling me "doctor", came down to "Mr Munro" and finally to "Neil" in less than two minutes. "Why do ye no' come to London?" he asked. "Why do you live there?" I retorted. "To make money to come back and stay on the Firth of Clyde," he replied. "I hate London." "I'm better off than you," I said, "for I stay at the Firth all the time." He was very proud of a gorgeous Macleod tartan kilt and plaid he was wearing in the performance. A great deal of his humour, I think, is in his legs – his "close-mouth" dancing and so on, but he has a good natural singing voice... He has bought a house and a good deal of property at Dunoon through the agency of Disselduff [son of Munro's former colleague in the Inveraray law office].'[8]

Just before Christmas, Neil reported to Blackwoods that he had enough Para Handy tales to make 'another 1/- volume' if they would care to publish it. Blackwoods accepted promptly and the volume would come out early the following year, entitled *In Highland Harbours With Para Handy*. Meanwhile, during the Christmas festivities, Neil turned out a short story, noting on 28 December: 'Finished "The Tudor Cup" in three days for Northern Newspapers Syndicate. £15/15/-.' This tale would be re-printed in *Jaunty Jock*.

In February 1911, Neil lunched with Harry Lauder and his wife at the Waverley Hotel in Sauchiehall Street, where 'the great wee man' was still staying during his long pantomime run in *Little Red Riding Hood*. Neil noted: 'He has been off with a bad throat for two or three weeks and during that time read *John Splendid* of which he highly approves. Harry tells me his mother was a Maclennan of the Black Isle... and she spoke the Gaelic better than English... As a lad Harry had a great notion of joining a Highland regiment and he went to the recruiting quarters of the Black Watch where a sergeant measured him. "You're half an inch too short!" said the sergeant. "Could ye no' hit me a dunt on the heid wi' a club and raise a bump, then measure me fast again before the swellin' gaes doon?" suggested Harry to the sergeant. Dr John Macintyre the throat specialist [in whose house Neil had met Conrad in 1898] has been attending Harry, and the latter (who is delightfully naive in his conceit) tells me MacIntyre assured him he had "one of the only three perfect singing throats he had ever seen – the other two being Melba's and Patti's". (I wonder how many singers MacIntyre said that to!) After luncheon I went to Harry's dressing room where he was preparing for a matinee performance. He wears a kilt throughout the performance. His first step in putting it on is to tie a substantial 'bustle' over his hind quarters. He is bald. "I mean to live to be a hundred," he said, and he might, for he has a powerful torso, with very deep chest, great confidence, elasticity, and no very bad habits. He tells me he made two "clinkin'" songs when laid up – one "Roamin' In The Gloamin" which he sang today at the matinee and the other an Aberdeen song with the odd refrain in the chorus of "where the silver granite grows". "Granite does grow," says Harry.[9]

Throughout 1911, Hugh continued his medical studies, passing his 'first professional' in March. Yet even as he learned the skills to save life, Europe was moving towards the cataclysmic event that would destroy lives by the million. With a dark cloud forming over the future, Neil took refuge in the past. On 16 March, his 'Views & Reviews' column was about the 'Killing Time' – Richard Cameron, the Covenanters, Claverhouse – a preliminary skirmish in the series of tales he was working on to go with Houston's paintings.

In a lighter, Hugh Foulis mood, he created a third character to form a comic triumvirate with Erchie and Para Handy. The *News* of 8 May carried the first Jimmy Swan tale, 'The Adventures of a Country Customer'. Developed from a character called John Swan who had appeared a year previously, the commercial traveller took on a life of his own that would run to a book.

For George V's coronation, if 'The Looker-On' of 26 June is to be believed, Carnus was decked out overall at the instigation of the Munros' jobbing gardener, who provided a great deal of bunting of dubious provenance and used up all the rakes and hoes as flagpoles. Then the family removed to Inveraray, where the two-month break was interrupted as usual by a fishing trip. From the wilds of what was probably Bridge of Orchy, Neil wrote: 'Into this remote and lonely little Highland inn, the rain or inclination has for some days past been driving the most astonishing variety of Englishmen, and Englishmen or Englishwomen only. We have had hardly a single Scottish guest. This predominance of the English on these highways and in these hotels (for the one from which I write is typical) has greatly changed the atmosphere of our annual retreat. We are no longer far from the madding crowd: at any moment a motor-car may haul up at the door and throw into our once-exclusive smoking-room a party of men and women who have dined last night at the Savoy. Such an event dispels the mood appropriate to our situation, where the windows look upon the great bare mountains, and the wind never seems to cease from faintly piping round the house, and the burn beside the door continually cries and chatters night and day, endued with arresting and mysterious voices – of kelpies, bairns unborn, folk long dead, phantom chariots, ghostly horsemen. The wind and the burn, so old and so enduring and so unchanging, compel, in the native-born, quietness of speech and long silent lapses, upon which those high-pitched, commanding, or querulous English voices seem as impiously intrusive as if it were a church.'[10]

In September a play by Arnold Bennett, *The Great Adventure*, was put on to re-open the Repertory Theatre season in Glasgow. Neil had tea with Bennett and some others at The Picture House, a cinema in Sauchiehall Street, and in the evening went to a dinner given to a dozen people in the Art Club in honour of Bennett by John Richmond, one of the Repertory directors.

'I stayed all night with Wareing. On Sunday I motored with Bennett, Wareing and Marriatt [Bennett's friend] by Garelochhead to Tarbet and back by Loch Lomond. We meant to go to Inveraray – it was a fine day – but had some trouble with the car. We lunched at Garelochhead. I got home to Gourock in the evening.

'Bennett, who wears a white bowler hat and a fancy waistcoat, is not physically a striking personality... He slept in the car several times going past Loch Lomond... He told me he had been round the same parts of Scotland before, and liked wild moorland scenery, particularly Dartmoor!... At the dinner in the Art Club, he would not speak, even in response to the toast of his health. He played – not very well – a few accompaniments to songs by Robin Thomson of the *Record*.'[11]

Alfred Wareing, reminiscing years later, said Bennett had told him he 'considered Munro the finest journalist of that day'. Yet Wareing also observed: 'The two writers were as unlike as possible; it was exciting to listen to their comments on places, people, and events; each saw something quite different from the other, and what they saw and remarked was an index to their characters. Neil Munro was a Poet, Arnold Bennett a Man of Business.'

That same month the *News* proclaimed that it had the largest circulation in Scotland. It consisted of ten pages, cost a halfpenny and came out in seven editions daily (afternoon and evening). Its success was due in no small measure to having 'the finest journalist of that day' as a regular contributor, with readers looking forward eagerly each week to Neil's next creation.

Yet not all his projects came to fruition. A puzzling diary entry for 16 November states: 'Finished scenario of a play *Jaunty Jock*'. No more was ever heard of this play, doubtless re-cycled as the tale *Jaunty Jock* which gave its name to Neil's second collection of short stories.

CHAPTER THIRTY-ONE

Jolly decent imaginative work

THE new year, 1912, was brought in at Inveraray before Neil went down to Kirkcudbright to stay with the artist E.A. Hornel for a few days. George Blackwood wrote to ask if *The New Road* would be ready 'to take up the running' in September. Neil felt unable to commit himself to this date and replied: 'About the serial, I have been greatly hampered of late by various things, and I hesitate even to say it may be ready in September, as I am as determined as yourself this time not to start publication before it is quite complete. As soon as I see the end of it in sight, I will let you know; meanwhile I think you should make all your arrangements regardless of me.'[1]

Neil did not confess that he had not even made a start on the serial and was making more progress with the Ayrshire sketches for A.&C. Black. There were pleasant diversions also in connection with the Repertory Theatre, including a February trip to Kilmarnock with Alfred Wareing to dine with Lord Howard de Walden, who was teaching fencing to the actors for the Repertory's forthcoming *Romeo and Juliet*. In March, Neil noted that he had attended the company's performance of *Oedipus Rex* in English. This was the last entry he would make in his diary for over six years, the next being in September 1918.

There would be two more summers before the world was plunged into war and for both of them George Houston, whose family now exceeded the Munros in number, leased a hunting lodge with salmon and trout fishing at Arichastlich in Glen Orchy. This fitted in perfectly with Neil's fishing pursuits. On 10 June he wrote to Wareing: 'I have practically not been able to set foot in Glasgow during the past three weeks. Hodge was here a week... Then Mr Smith and I motored him to Glen Orchy, there depositing him with Houston, after which J.M. and I came round by Inveraray. A few days later we were back in Breadalbane again on our annual fishing expedition (possibly the last, as Breadalbane has, without in any way consulting us, leased the whole district to ane lord yclept Durham who may fail to recognise our vested interests). We were eight days at the Black Mount, and conjointly caught great store of trout but no salmon, the season being too dry to let 'em up the Orchy.'

At the end of September George Blackwood reported that Sir Arthur Quiller Couch wished to include Neil's poem 'If I Were King of France' in *The Oxford Book of Victorian Verse*. Blackwood also asked about the progress of Neil's 'new novel': a serial by Quiller Couch was just ending, to be followed by one from Ian Hay: 'Then I hope it will be Neil Munro again.'

By the end of October, the ten Ayrshire sketches were finished, in time to catch the Christmas market. The book's title, *Ayrshire Idylls*, is a mellifluous misnomer as regards the letterpress, yet Houston's fine watercolours, oils and tiny black-and-white drawings, excellently reproduced, redress the balance towards the idyllic. The handsome quarto volume was dedicated to James Murray Smith and cost 7s 6d – not an inexpensive item in those days. Neil was paid '£250 down' for his contribution.

Having learned his lesson from the arduous research that proved necessary to produce *The Clyde* for A.&C. Black, he had decided this time to accompany the illustrations with what were in effect short stories, the form in which he excelled. All are set in the past and there is little direct correspondence with Houston's pictures. Two sketches are purely fictional, the rest vivid, imagined glimpses into the lives of real people – Burns, Boswell and Johnson, Covenanters, John Galt – all with Ayrshire associations. The Scots idiom, used mostly in the dialogue, is natural and well integrated. Episodes in Burns's life, the subject of four of the stories, give something of Neil's own ideas of artistic creation. He had studied Burns to some extent already, having given the Immortal Memory to Greenock Burns Club (1903) and written a long foreword to an edition of Burns's poems (Blackie 1906). On such tasks he never stinted time or thought.

'The Making of Tam O' Shanter' is set in Dumfries-shire but

firmly roots Burns's inspiration in his native county and his early years: 'And he was come in sight of Ellisland, his farm. The place brought to his soul a pang as if the memory of an ancient sin had stung him. There it was, its steading bowered in trees, near the verge of the gravelly precipice that sank to the river's side, a poet's farm, God help him! – a visionary's choice, as if a man could harvest crops of shilfy-song or winnow a rent from evening sunshine!...From Edinburgh parlours, Highland and Border wanderings, communion with his social and intellectual betters, he had nothing learned that was not his already when he walked behind the plough, and all the fervours, all the sweet illusions and enchantments which he gave a voice in song were harvested in Ayrshire.'

'Magic Casements' is written in the first person, ostensibly by a former schoolmate of John Galt. It relates Galt's return to the Irvine of his boyhood. Neil had read Galt in Blackwoods' 1896 edition, edited by D.S. Meldrum, and himself wrote an introduction to *Annals of The Parish* for the publisher Adam Gowans in January 1913. It is interesting to read 'Magic Casements' in the light of Wittig's remark that *The House with the Green Shutters* 'was practically the first Scottish novel since Galt which dealt with nineteenth-century Scottish life as it really was'.[2]

Galt's friend relates how 'I got a peep at what lies out beyond this tolbooth of the flesh... and I got that vision through a daft man's eyes. At least he would be so reputed. But me, I cannot think of him as daft, nay, rather with the stanchions and the fetters of the spirit broken, flying where he wist!'

This recalls Gillesbeg Aotram, the wanderer, in *Gilian the Dreamer*, whom Gilian knows to be wiser than those who call him daft. In 'Magic Casements', as the old schoolmate sits with Galt in the Black Whale Inn on a wild autumn night, he is overcome by the thought that their youth is 'bye'. (Galt was only fifty when he died in 1839: Neil was almost fifty when he wrote this tale.) Enter a gaunt stranger, his garments soaking. 'The night is wild... and it is far from Talavera!' is his greeting. And he reads from a book he has with him Keats's verse that ends:

'Charmed magic casements, opening on the foam
Of perilous seas, in fairy lands forlorn.'

It is, of course, from the stranger that Galt's friend gets the 'glisk – but for a moment – at the gleeful truth behind appearance'. Galt himself has no sympathy with all this and calls the stranger crazy, whereupon his friend rounds on him: 'Ah, John, ye write a bonny book... but I'm feared ye're still far ben within the bridewell o' the body. Or ye are older, far, than me. Or ye have been ower lang awa frae Scotland!' The story ends with these words.

Although *Ayrshire Idylls* sold well, Neil would always feel that, because of the format, many of his regular readers missed some 'jolly decent imaginative work – if I say so as shouldn't'.³

Accompanied by George Houston, Neil went to Paris at the end of November for a St Andrew's Night dinner at which he was chief speaker. His theme, surely a tongue-in-cheek one, was 'the paradox that of a land of rocks and waters and moist plains its sons should have made and should guard the illusion of a paradise of terrestrial beauty'. He and Houston also took the opportunity to see an exhibition of work by the Italian Futurists and to enjoy an unexpected bout of fine weather, which Neil shared with his readers on his return:

'I think it was from one of the Erckmann-Chatrian novels – possibly *The Conscript* – read in boyhood, that I got the notion, only now dispelled, of winter Paris as more wildly bleak and cold than any British town could be in that particular season... Ignorance, innocence and illusion are good things to take abroad with you, for then at least you are sure of many surprises. Paris last week resolutely refused to be cloudy and cold to agree with my anticipations. Above her most of the time there bent a blue and cloudless sky. The café terraces were almost as busy with *al fresco* drinkers of mazagran and absinthe as if it were July; only rarely did I see the outside brazier fire which mitigates the really frigid hours of the hardened boulevardier... There is a theory, carefully fostered by the French, and innocently accepted by foreigners, that the amazing all-night cafés of Montmartre, and all the other decadent and dreary shows round the Place Pigalle, exist solely for the entertainment of the foreign visitor, specially for the spirited Briton. I don't believe it. We go there once just to make sure that it isn't worth going back again... and Montmartre, with all that it implies, is native and mainly self-supporting, as much an expression of "the sick hurry, the divided aim" of some elements of modern France as Post-impressionism or Cubism in painting".'⁴

The New Year of 1913 was brought in, as usual, at Inveraray, and Neil returned to Gourock to find a letter from George Blackwood: 'Our present serial... will run out in June or July and we must have definite arrangements for what is to follow... I hope... that you will be able to say for certain that the claymore will be ready to start clashing in July or August.'⁵ Neil was no longer in the mood to prevaricate and replied briskly: 'So far as I am concerned, you may confidently have your fiery cross ready for July... I have cleared the desk of all other impediments and the job marches gaily.'⁶

In February Neil's two columns in the *News* were reduced in length, no doubt part of the clearing away of impediments, but he had misled George Blackwood as to the progress he had made already. On 1 March he noted: 'Began *The New Road* which was plotted out during the past three weeks.' Yet from then on his output was phenomenal. On 31 March he noted: 'Did 1000 words a day of *The New Road* all this month = 39,000.'

At the end of March, Lord Archibald Campbell died. His son Niall Diarmid (afterwards 10th Duke) wrote to Neil from Ruadh na Carraig, Inveraray, saying that he and his sister had both been 'much touched by the display of affection to my father's memory... at Hallowe'en yearly when in prayers of November the Chalice and Host are uplifted I would have you as one of a Race for ages living in the friendliest [word illegible] of feudalism in Carnus of Glenaray to be not unmindful of the passing of Gilleasbuig the most affectionate of fathers to his son'.⁶

With a substantial part of his novel written, Neil wrote to George Blackwood on 4 April full of confidence about *The New Road*: 'For the first time for many years I have been able to concentrate closely on the work... I hope for the first time to have the bliss of writing "Finis" before I see a line of the story in print.' But it was not to be. Yet again, the manuscript would be incomplete when *The New Road* opened in July's *Maga*: it was not till April 1914 that Neil would finish the last three chapters.

Meanwhile, in September 1913, Neil asked George Blackwood if he was 'in the mood for another shilling "Hugh Foulis" volume... with the title *Jimmy Swan The Joy Traveller*'. This proposal was accepted with alacrity, and there was further correspondence with Blackwoods about the American edition of *The Daft Days* (published by Harper's) and Neil's negotiations for publishing *The New Road* in America.

At the end of October, Hugh joined the 8th Battalion, Argyll & Sutherland Highlanders (Territorial Force Infantry) as a second lieutenant. The world had changed since his father had drilled as a carefree 16-year-old with the 'delightfully casual' Inveraray rural volunteer company, or marched in the rain with the Glasgow Highlanders. As storm clouds gathered inexorably over Europe, it must have been clear to both father and son that in all likelihood

Hugh would be called on to fight. The old sureties would soon be swept away, symbolised that November by the withdrawal of the old *Edinburgh Castle* paddle steamer from the Gourock/Lochgoilhead run. Neil penned a lament: 'Upon her was made one's first delirious trip to Glasgow; our years of what the Language calls "*amaideachd*" and "*goraiche*" [folly] had a thousand links with Captain Barr and Archie Muir; with those loud thudding engines, that small galley, those odorous lamps and windy decks, Fitzgerald's fiddle, or the old blind player's concertina... How poignantly sad the thought of that last call of the *Edinburgh* at Lochgoilhead, Douglas, Carrick Castle, Ardentinny, Blairmore, Cove, Kilcreggan!... How melancholy her wake as she slipped for the last time down past the old shores!'[7]

As if unwilling to sail down to Inveraray in some inferior vessel, Neil broke with tradition and brought in the New Year of 1914 at Kirkcudbright, staying with his artist friend E.A. Hornel.

CHAPTER THIRTY-TWO

By the old ways north

FOR Hugh's 21st birthday in February 1914, his parents arranged a party at the Ashton Hotel, Gourock. According to family tradition, Hugh himself was too shy to attend it. In April he went with his parents and Effie to spend a week at Inveraray, but duty prevented him spending the whole week there – he had to go to Oban for a week-end camp with his regiment.

In those last precious months of peace before the Great War, Neil put the final touches to *The New Road* in book form, posting off the last proofs on 7 May. 'Let me pray that many thousands will tramp our New Road, and possibly make it worth while starting Ninian on even subtler and more thrilling deeds for another *Maga*,' he wrote to George Blackwood.

A few days later came news of the Duke of Argyll's death at Kent House in the Isle of Wight. As well as reporting the funeral at Kilmun for *The Times* and *Manchester Guardian*, Neil wrote an article, 'The Duke at Home: An Inveraray Impression', revealing almost inadvertently a genuine affection: 'For once you saw emerge from the turgid rhetoric about a fallen prince the genuine figure of a kindly, manly, gracious and accomplished gentleman... he really was more unaffected and amiable... than any other in the peerage... It was because he was an artist, with more of the artist spirit, I think, than his father... a Bohemian of the refined and elegant order...'[1]

Relieved of the burden of *The New Road*, Neil went back to Inveraray with Jessie for ten days, and worked in the garden. On 6 June he went to Campbeltown to stay for a week with his old friend Sheriff John MacMaster Campbell and his wife. While he was there *The New Road* came out in book form. Neil and MacMaster Campbell drove (or more likely were driven) to Muasdale to visit a friend, Dr Malloch, but found instead a different 'kent face', Dr John MacIntyre (the playwright 'John Brandane', not the throat specialist), who was acting as locum. Neil was much interested to find in the house a collection of miniatures belonging to the late Mrs Malloch, who had had many Inveraray connections. MacIntyre noted: 'Among the miniatures were several of people connected with the originals of the characters in *Gilian the Dreamer*. If I am not mistaken, the Paymaster himself was there.' He noted also how 'Munro revealed a new side of him, for taking out a little notebook he made a wonderful little sketch of the islands of Cara and Gigha, as seen across the Sound of Gigha.'[2]

On 15 June, back in Gourock, Neil wrote in his 'bread-and-butter letter' to Mrs MacMaster Campbell: 'On Saturday Hugh went to camp: I again foregathered on the pier here with the Oban contingent... and the Ballachulish company – some of it in "good trum" [drink taken] and likely to come in for drastic measure from Hurricane Jack whenever he got them inside the line...' ('Hurricane Jack' was the Adjutant, Jock Campbell of Jura.) Neil must have had thoughts of that summer day in 1881 when 'A' Company, Argyllshire Highland Rifles, had mustered at Greenock before the 'Wet Review'.

The New Road, Neil's last novel, was published eighteen days before the assassination of the Archduke Franz Ferdinand. The reviews, as George Blackwood wrote, were 'absolutely first rate' and a second impression was out before war was declared. *The New Road* has consistently been regarded as Neil's best novel: Francis Russell Hart calls it 'his finest work... a work of sustained art Stevenson could not manage...'[3] John Buchan, in a long *News* review, said that the novel '...seems to me one of the finest romances written in our time. Mr Neil Munro is beyond question the foremost of living Scottish novelists, both in regard to the scope and variety of his work and its rare quality. *The New Road* does not attain the imaginative height of *The Lost Pibroch* – such a pitch can scarcely be reached more than once in a man's life; it has not the bewildering rush and glow and poetry of *John Splendid*, or the austere inevitableness of *Doom Castle*, or the wonderful wedding of landscape and romance of *Children of Tempest*... With its masterly construction, its insight into character, its drama, its complete adequacy of style, *The New Road* must take high rank in Scottish fiction.'⁴

On reading this, Neil wrote to tell Buchan 'how greatly I appreciated your characteristically generous tribute to my book in the *Glasgow News*. It was a happy inspiration of the Editor to ask you to do the notice, and the more gratifying to me since I dared not suggest it myself though there is no man's approval of my stuff I would sooner have than yours.'⁵

In this return to 'something of the manner and adventure of *John Splendid*', a return so liberating to his muse, Neil also went back to the 1730s, when Wade was building the first roads in the Highlands. The original purpose was military, the bridling of the clans after the 1715 Rising, but merchants quickly perceived another use for the new roads.

One of these, Alan-Iain-Alain Og of Inveraray, is the uncle of the novel's hero, Aeneas Macmaster. He asks Aeneas to make his way to Inverness and buy salmon, timber and other goods. To Aeneas, college-educated, this sounds like 'hackles for the spirit, mean engagements' but as soon as his uncle says it is 'just a bit of an adventure' his spirit is lifted.

Another Inveraray man, Ninian Macgregor Campbell, the Duke's *beachdair*, is just then leaving for the North 'upon MacCailein's business', and it is arranged that Aeneas will travel with him. Ninian's father, said to be from 'Balwhidder' and to have 'found protection with MacCailein and a home in Shira Glen', is clearly none other than Rob Roy. Ninian himself is pure invention, described by his creator as 'a sort of Gaelic Sherlock Holmes'.⁶

And so again, as with *John Splendid*, Neil followed Stevenson and Scott in having a young hero accompanying an older man on a Highland journey. At the back of his mind was perhaps Hugh, the son who unlike himself was at university and who became a second lieutenant while his father was writing *The New Road*: in Chapter XXXI Aeneas talks of a new campaign and says: 'I must take another rank.'

The plot's chief strands are the mysterious death of Aeneas's father and the nefarious dealings of Lovat, represented by two fankled fishing lines Ninian carries about [Ch XVII]. The *leitmotif* is the new road – 'a rut that, once it's hammered deep enough, will be the poor Gael's grave!', Ninian rightly says. He and Aeneas go 'by the old ways north', not on the new road, and have thrilling adventures as they tramp through the hills. They uncover evidence of Lovat's gun-running, and in the end unravel the mystery of Aeneas's father's death. All is told with a vivid onward rush and there is no failure of imagination.

Their journey is made before the literary romanticisation of the Highlands, in the days when heather was heather was heather. James Macpherson's Ossianic fragments did not begin to appear till 1760. Neil carefully links Aeneas's 'glamoured notion of the North' with his classical learning and 'the heroes of the ceilidh tales'. Studying Blaeu's map in his uncle's house before setting out, he finds 'the climate of his mind' altering: 'He saw high-sounding names like Athole, Badenoch, and Brae Lochaber, Lorn and Spey; they moved him like a story. All his days they had been known to him, but mistily and more as things of fable than of actual nature – lands of fancy only, figuring in winter songs and tales of old revenge.' But early on their journey Aeneas and Ninian meet the blaggardly Barisdale – Col Macdonnell, a historical personage – and Aeneas begins to think 'that, after all, the heroes of the ceilidh tales – the chiefs and caterans – were, like enough, but men of wind as this one seemed'.

Interestingly Barisdale, on meeting whom Aeneas begins to be disillusioned, was mentioned by Scott in a footnote to Waverley: 'MacDonald of Barrisdale, one of the very last of the Highland gentlemen who carried on the plundering system to any great extent... a scholar and a well-bred gentleman.' That footnote may well have set Andrew Lang gathering the material about Barrisdale which he supplied to Stevenson. Neil met Lang only once – in 1899 on the steamer between Ballachulish and Oban – but thereafter Lang several times sent him 'what he considered good material for Scottish romance'.[7] Did he pass on the material about Barrisdale, unused by Stevenson? The scenario of the play *Jaunty Jock* which Neil wrote in 1911 seems to have emerged as the tale in which 'Jaunty Jock' is Barrisdale's nickname.

Duplicity such as Barisdale's and Lovat's fascinated Neil. It is found also in Duncanson, Argyll's 'doer' in *The New Road*. Yet Aeneas, whom he has greatly wronged, pities Duncanson after his death for a 'poor wretch who surely never knew what love was, and can never learn it now'. When he says this, he himself and Janet, Ninian's daughter, have just become sure of their love for one another. Janet, who rides alone to Inverness by the new roads, and the other women of the story – Annabel Macmaster, Primrose Campbell, Margaret Duncanson and, not least, the 'russet girl' at the inn in Glen Coe – are drawn with an intensity that relates them to the women in *The Lost Pibroch*.

In the closing chapters there are two discrepancies which have never been corrected. In Chapter **XXX**, Alan-Iain-Alain Og says his brother Paul wrote to him every month from France: in the next chapter he maintains that Paul never sent him so much as 'a scrape' from France. In the last chapter Aeneas finds Janet 'aloof, evasive, and yet two nights ago, she stood surrendered in his arms'. But there has been no word of their embrace – an intentional omission?

With *The New Road*, Neil set a high standard. As Buchan observed: 'Nowadays too many novels are masses of undigested observation, not art, but the raw material for art; but with Mr Munro a wealth of thought and experience is wholly transmuted by the shaping spirit of imagination. Too many modern novels, again, are concerned with matters which are practically irrelevant, which someone has decribed as "hair-brushing in stuffy bedrooms". With Mr Munro we move among the high passions and the ancient and essential drama of human circumstances.'[8]

CHAPTER THIRTY-THREE

War! Inveraray Post Office open day and night

ALL through July 1914, war with Germany loomed. Summertime Inveraray lost that vaguely monotonous aspect of perpetual afternoon. On 2 August, a Sunday, Neil thought it ominous that rural post offices were being kept open day and night for telegraphs. He got his friend John Gilmour of the Argyll Arms to drive him to the nearest railway station at Dalmally. A decade later he was ashamed to recall 'what silly patriotic and romantic elations were stirred in me when I found that already there were armed guards on every railway viaduct, on reservoirs, and the Loch Long torpedo testing station. All along the Callander-and-Oban and West Highland Railways, the fiendish ubiquity of German spies, and their readiness to start immediately blowing up culverts and railway bridges, or poisoning us at our kitchen-taps, were already taken for granted!'

The next day, Monday, he went to Glasgow via Arrochar to work at the *News* office, staying with J.M. Smith to save travelling from Gourock. It would be a long war and Neil would find himself working long and punishing hours.

The Territorials were mobilised as soon as war was declared on the 5th. Hugh hurried back from Dublin, where he was doing a stint in a maternity hospital, reaching Inveraray in time to march through the town on the 6th with A. Coy, the local part of the 1/8th Argyll & Sutherland Highlanders. They went by steamer to Dunoon, and after a week there moved to Dunblane for a day or two, then on to Bedford. (It would of course have been open to Hugh to finish his almost-completed medical studies and re-enlist as a doctor. But he wanted to be with the Inveraray boys.)

During those first days of the war, Hugh's father found time to write some verses, published as 'Evening Prayer of a People' in the News on the 9th. It was, of course, written when he still felt 'silly patriotic and romantic elations'. It was re-printed as a postcard, and sold in aid of the Prince of Wales's National Relief Fund.

> Lord, from this storm-awakened isle,
> At this dark hour on land and sea,
> 'Twixt bugle-call and Sabbath bell
> Go up our prayers to Thee...
> O had we died untried, unproved,
> And missed this hour of stress!
> Praise be to God for this last gift,
> The joy of steadfastness!

On 31 August Neil went down to London to look after the News office as David Hodge, who was in charge of it, was 'off colour'. Neil's new duties included telegraphing a 'London Letter' to Glasgow every morning.

Hugh wrote to his father from Bedford on 3 September. The reference to a 'false alarm' is unclear. 'I got your note apologising for the false alarm, but as things go at present it would almost appear as if you had only anticipated disaster; I think things look as bad as ever... There is no word of our move out of here yet. But the tents, we understand, are on their way, so that we may leave shortly... On Tuesday we had a lecture on the war from Hilaire Belloc – in the town hall. All the officers of the Division were there. Quite good, if he hadn't addressed officers of the Highland Division as "gentlemen of England" on several occasions. It annoyed Hurricane Jack very considerably!'

Next day Neil wrote to Moira from the Savage Club: 'Now it's your turn for a letter. Tell your mother I got the box of sox &c today, and her note, all right; I also got Effie's interesting letter... Last night I dined at Romano's with Mr Weir,[3] and the man who was "'Charley's Aunt" at the Weir Fancy Dress Ball... We went after dinner to the Coliseum Theatre for an hour – not a very entertaining show. I went home to my hotel [Norfolk Hotel, Surrey Street, Strand] at 10.30, and wrote my 'London Letter' for the News up till 1 a.m. A District Messenger boy was to come to my bedroom at 6 a.m. sharp and take it to the post office, but I wakened at 6.15 and he was not there. I was fully dressed, ready to go to the post office myself, when he turned up at 6.30 very apologetic... So back to bed again & I slept till 8.30. I'll have to do something like that every day now; no more long lies and breakfast in bed for your poor old pa!

'... Winifred [Hodge] will now be settled down among you, and I hope you'll all give her a happy time. I'm sure she'll say it's much better fun to be in Gourock just now than in this hot noisy and excited place... I sometimes feel that if I could pardon the Germans anything it would be their blowing three quarters of London up and turning it into country again – after they had let the residents out I mean. But I don't think there is much chance of the Germans taking or getting the chance.

'It's now 2.30 p.m. I'd like to sneak upstairs without any of you noticing, and think out a plot in Neil's room, with a rug on. But alas! no plots just now. Love & kisses to you all. Your affect. father, N.M.'

Neil expected to be in charge of the *News* London office for the duration of the war. He was working harder than he had ever done, mostly from 6 a.m. till midnight or later. Sometimes he had to be 'on the wire' at 1.30 a.m. All 'copy' had to pass the censor, and sometimes it took four hours to get a message from Fleet Street to Hope Street in Glasgow.

On 6 September, his first Sunday in London, Neil went to Bedford to spend the afternoon with Hugh, whom he found 'in good spirits and as the result of a month's incessant hard training... in fine physical condition'. Almost 20,000 Highland troops were billeted at Bedford. With most of his battalion Hugh had volunteered for foreign service and expected to be sent abroad soon, possibly to Malta, Egypt or India.

On 10 September it was Moira's turn again for a letter from her father, now at the Arundel Hotel on Victoria Embankment where his room had 'a jolly french window which looks out on the Thames... Your poor old pa is getting mighty little sleep these days – less I think than he ever got in his life before, but he's not kicking, and doesn't seem to be any the worse for it, so your mother will not see much difference in him when she comes to London... I am hopeful that I may get home sooner than I thought of last week. My love & hugs to you all. Your affect. pater N.M.'

Moira, who was almost 17 but still at school, replied to her father: 'Neil got your letter yesterday morning and he is going to write to you today or tomorrow perhaps. He is 14 today... At present Winifred, Bud, Neil and Dennis Swan are working hard with the meccanos and toy railways. Winifred is just like one of the family now – you should hear her squashing Neil when he is in one of his sarcastic moods!... On Friday morning, Effie came down to breakfast with a thrilling story about hearing a cannon being fired through the night; she got such a fright she was quite sure the Germans were coming up the Firth. None of the rest of us had heard it so we were rather doubtful if it was true or not, until on Saturday we got the [Greenock] *Telegraph* with the paragraph I have enclosed in it... We have got two war maps fastened up on the nursery wall; one is the *Glasgow Herald* wall map and the other the *Daily Mail* one. We find them rather difficult to follow though...

'P.S. The house which the shell landed at was Captain Duncan's.'[1]

The shell must have been a stray one of our own. Early in the war a boom was thrown across the Firth of Clyde from the Cloch to Dunoon, and it was never breached by any German ship or submarine. But rumours abounded. Para Handy, for one, claimed: 'The polisman assured us Kibrannan Sound was hotchin' wi' submarines.'[2] Neil himself for a good while was telephoned several times a day by a Greenock man, high up in shipping, with alarms about German submarines in the inner Firth. But in the end Neil's 'scepticism and unpatriotic calm' silenced the alarmist.

Monday 14 September brought Jessie's turn for a letter from her husband: 'This is what I have been doing this week end when not working:- On Saturday afternoon I went out to call on Dr Donald

McArthur [Inveraray] and his sister Freda. We were joined by a
Lieut. MacLaren of the Scottish Horse – a Crianlarich man who has
sung Gaelic songs at Inveraray concerts... after tea we sang Gaelic
songs till the passers by in Cadogan Place must have suspected we
were riotous Germans. At 7 in the evening I went by engagement to
Weir's flat in Adelphi Terrace & found Willie Weir, Jimmy [Weir]
(who is flying every day, and only got away for the evening) and
Jenny McConnachie just arrived safe from Dresden. The Germans
had been telling her appalling stories of how wretched and terrible
it was to be in London just now, and Wm Weir said yes, it was
frightful, & we were all reduced to starvation rations. So then he took
us all over to Romano's, & we had a very swagger dinner beginning
with oysters, and ending with peaches & liqueurs, a bottle of
champagne having also been disposed of. Thereafter we went to the
Palace Theatre, & Jimmy & Wm Weir left later for Glasgow.

'I was up till 4 a.m. on Sunday morning, rose at 10 and went to
Bedford. Hugh and his old landlord Wright met me at the station,
and we walked out to the old billet, where Mrs Wright gave Hugh
and me a good lunch and afternoon tea at which Alister [fellow
officer of Hugh's, brother of Donald McArthur] joined us.
Fortunately Hugh had the whole day to himself yesterday. I was in
his new quarters, which are quite comfortable. Alister and he share
one bedroom and one bed, and a large sitting room. They share also
one servant, a man named Livingstone who, having been a trained
valet, does his work very efficiently, even to putting their studs into
their shirts. A few doors off, all A Coy is in a large self-contained
house, sleeping on the floors meanwhile, with only a rubber mat
below them... Hugh has lent Peter Maitland his Wolseley valise – a
field sleeping-bag with stuffing... I spoke to most of the Inveraray
chaps – who seemed to be in good spirits, very tanned... Dan
Thomson [son of Neil's stepbrother John], who is ill, is acting as
Orderly Room Clerk... Every day the regiment marches several
miles out into the country & manoeuvres in a grand estate [possibly
Woburn] which is immensely larger than the Inveraray policies.
Sometimes it goes out in darkness & moves among woods & fields
noiselessly without a single word of command – but nudges &
signals with a flag...

'Hugh is looking very fit & well, & trying to grow a moustache
which as yet is pathetically feeble-looking... They don't know how
long the Highland Division may be at Bedford, but the Lowland
Division is leaving for Egypt. The Highland Division would much
rather go to France... If they went to France, their business would

not be at the Front, in all likelihood, but guarding the Army's lines of communication... Hugh gets about 5/6 a day wages for seven days a week; it is paid monthly into his bank account, & when he has paid his mess bill out of it, I think it leaves him 8/- or 10/- a week. As Alister & he are strict teetotalers (though I saw Hugh take a glass of port at Mrs Wright's) they won't spend much on drink... I'll write Isobel & Winifred tomorrow. Love to you all. Your affect. husband N.M.'

A letter to Moira on 18 September mentioned that a Captain Stewart – 'son of that Charles Stewart of Fasnacloich (and Achara) I once stayed a week with in Appin' – had been killed in action.

At the end of September Neil returned to Gourock to prepare to go to France as a war correspondent. Leaving on 14 October, he travelled via Folkestone and Dieppe and reached Paris at 9.45 p.m. the next day. The British forces were then fighting at Ypres. Many British wounded were in Paris hospitals, and Neil visited a hospital at Versailles. On 25 October he sent Moira a postcard from Senlis: 'This is how a town looks when it is shelled by the Germans. Our piano wouldn't have a chance! I was out here on Sunday. Next Sunday I go to the cemeteries – it is *le jour des morts* – & there will be great scenes. N.M.'

On 1 November he went to the cemetery of Bagneux: 'In a sheltered square of half an acre... were four hundred and thirty new-made graves, with temporary wooden crosses on them – the lairs of many Frenchmen, English, Irish and Scots "in one red burial blent".'

Neil left Paris two days later, going first to Etaples and then to Montreuil where he stayed with his old friend, the artist Macaulay Stevenson. After a further five days at Boulogne he returned to England on 12 November. He described this as being 'politely but firmly deported by His Majesty's Army!'.[4] All correspondents were considered 'in danger of seeing too much of the present state of affairs'.[5]

On Saturday 14 November, Neil went to Bedford again and stayed the night at Hugh's billet: next day they walked together to the Isolation Camp at Howbury, lunched at the Swan and heard Handel's *Messiah*. While there, Neil almost certainly showed Hugh the diary of Lieutenant W.A.T. Synge of the King's Regiment, cousin of the Irish playwright, whom he had met during his five days at Boulogne. Synge had kept a diary since the start of the war, 'a matter-of-fact, unsophisticated soldier narrative' which, with little persuasion, George Blackwood would publish in *Maga*. It is likely this led Neil to suggest to Hugh that he should start a similar diary.

On the Monday Neil returned home to Scotland, in order to take up the reins as acting editor of the *News* in place of J.M. Smith who was unable to stand the wartime pressure.

Hugh was gazetted 1st Lieutenant on 14 December. On 23 December he came home for Christmas, on three days' leave. Neil and Jessie brought in the New Year without him at Inveraray.

At the beginning of February, Neil was made a director of the *News*, and went to London to arrange for a 'private wire'. At the end of March, George Blackwood wrote, enclosing royalies and wondering if a new story was contemplated. Neil had had no time to write fiction, but replied: 'That *The New Road* should have done so well considering how abruptly the war came athwart its progress is very gratifying... It must seem odd to you to have so old a contributor and confrere who never shows himself in the Old Saloon [45 George Street]. Upon my word it's a visit I often contemplate just to prove I really have a corporal existence and am not, to look at, any different from when you saw me last a good many years ago. For some months back I have been acting as locum for the Editor of the *News* whose nerves cracked up with the stress of these times. It is rather good sport, and likely to last till July (by the way I'm now a Director of the *News* Company, if you please!) but it leaves me little or no time for literature... In these circumstances I fear I can show you no successor to Ninian Campbell for some considerable time yet. I have a story simmering though – of the same period and character, am gathering material for it, and hope before very long to plunge delightedly into its execution.'[6]

Just then *The First Hundred Thousand* was appearing in *Maga* under the name 'The Junior Sub'. Neil found it 'amazingly good' and even wrote to ask Hugh if he was the writer, because 'it was so confoundedly like his experiences, his quality of humour and with something of his style revealed to me only in letters. He wrote me back that he wished he were. The odd thing is that at least a dozen people in various parts of the country have written to me assuming that Hugh was the author, though why they should think so is beyond my comprehension since he has never published a line.'[7]

George Blackwood told Neil in confidence that Ian Hay was the author, and suggested that Hugh should send him something for *Maga*. That was not to be. But Hugh began to keep a diary on 1 May, when the 1/8th Argylls left Bedford to join the British Expeditionary Force in France.

CHAPTER THIRTY-FOUR

We went for you to the yetts o' hell

LESS than twenty-four hours after leaving Bedford on the evening of Saturday 1 May, the 1/8th Argylls came within sound of guns at Merville. Hugh had made his first diary entry on S.S. *Onward* during the two-hour night crossing from Folkestone, escorted by destroyer. They camped just outside Boulogne, went on by train to Merville, then marched ten miles in the dark to Robecq, near Bethune. Almost at once they saw cannonading and star shells, also aeroplanes being shelled over the firing line.

On 6 May they were ordered to stand by at 6.30 a.m., but this was called off. On the 8th there was a heavy bombardment towards Neuve Chapelle, where their former adjutant Campbell of Jura, 'Hurricane Jack', posted to the Gordons, had fallen in March. On the 9th there was instruction on poisonous gases: the Medical Officer explained that a gun, sent over from Bethune, was for dissipating gases. Two days later they found it was for shooting enemy messenger pigeons.

On the 11th Hugh noted that the bombardments had 'made two men funny': a sergeant in his Company – 'A Coy' – would probably go back to England. Time was divided between company training, route marches, musketry and 'interior economy'.[1] There were daily inspections of rifles, field dressings, iron rations and feet. All water had to be boiled. Hugh and three other officers slept at a farm on stone floors.

On 14 May, marching 12 miles to new billets, they saw for the first time shelled villages and churches: 'On the way to Merris our satiric CQMA cruelly ridiculed Stretcher Bearer Turner of my platoon, whom distant cannonading has made nervous of late. Both were marching in rear of Coy with us.

'McIsaac (pointing to ruin of farmhouse; ruined probably for last 100 years): Some heavy shelling there, Turner!
'Turner: My God; did you ever see anything like it?
'McIsaac (indicating some peaceful rising in the distance): There it is.
'Turner: What?

202

'McIsaac: Hill 60; we'll be at it there the night yet!
'(Silence from Turner, who begins to look apprehensive.)'

On 18 May they marched 12 miles in the rain to Vieille Chapelle, three miles behind the line, arriving at 3 a.m. Next day, while the battalion waited for dusk at a crossroads near Festubert before moving up to the trenches, they were shelled for the first time. A Coy halted at Battalion HQ at Richebourg St Vaast, a mile behind the trenches. They slept out all night in equipment and stood to arms before dawn.

At noon on the 20th, A Coy went forward to the Battalion's dressing station, 800 yards behind the reserve trenches: 'Heavy bombardment going on at time; had to fill sandbags and reinforce with them north gable of a house and windows; under fire, shrapnel and shells all time. Men very cool, and worked well; nobody hit. In afternoon at 3 p.m. we were shelled out of our field and had to march back to billets 300 yards back – in middle of heavy artillery which thundered all night. We paraded at 9.15 p.m. (A Coy) to clear battle-field between support and fire trenches, and were on our way to trenches when we were recalled... 10 p.m. In farm: heavy artillery fire from guns beside us, and heavy musketry and machine gun fire... (A distressing experience one's first shelling... One must try to get fatalistic...)'

On the 22nd, with Captain Alister McArthur and 20 men of A Coy, Hugh went out at night to bury the dead between support and fire trenches. He noted that the 1st Argylls buried more than 600 British bodies. Next day 40 or 50 'big shells' dropped into the village. Nine of D Coy were killed. On the 24th A Coy dug itself in. 'I have not made [a dug-out] yet, but slept out in the open last night,' Hugh noted on 25th. Next day they shifted into old billets of the 6th Argylls.

At 10 p.m. on the 29th, A Coy moved to the fire trench to reinforce D and C Coys. Next evening their trench was bombarded with shrapnel, but nobody was hit, and at 11 p.m. they were relieved by Ghurkas: 'We stumbled along long communication trench (stinking with half buried bodies) to Teetotal Corner... Joined rest of battalion outside Richebourg St Vaast, and marched 3 miles to Lacouture; I was very much fatigued for want of sleep. Got men into barns at a big farm, and got into a barn myself and slept from 2 a.m. (when we arrived) till 10.30 a.m.'

They moved on 1 June to Locon. There they lined the street for Mr Asquith, who passed in a car with staff officers, looking 'old but cheery'. Near Locon, Alister and Hugh found a billet in a 'splendid estaminet, and I slept in my first bed since leaving England. Scrumptious!'

On 8 June they moved into trenches: 'I moved on as covering party for workers past old German trench far up communication trench, and advanced in extended order over country for 600 yards. Searching shell holes and ditches; snipers stopped as soon as we went out... Covering party lay out till 1.45... My covering party had some shells unpleasantly close.'

At 9 p.m. on 10 June, after severe enemy bombardment of fire and support trenches, they moved forward.

'Thunder and lightning began again after we left, and heavy rain... My platoon guide – a sergeant [of 6th Argylls] was very nervous and not at all sure of the way. However we plodded off – 450 men in single file! A, C and D were for the fire trench, B in support. I shall never forget that journey to the firing lines. The paths led over awful ground, across ditches by narrow planks for bridges (7 or 8 of these). We moved very slowly but in spite of this touch was lost by rear platoons, and long halts had to be made in the open till they came up again. Many men fell headlong... into ditches... The last 600 yards was by communication trench, half full of water in parts. Everybody was soaked and plastered with mud from head to foot. We were sniped repeatedly and two men hit, delaying the whole column. A Coy arrived at the firing line about 1 a.m. Shells also gave us a nasty time. Three high explosives failed to burst after falling ten feet or so from the Coy in the communication trench. One did explode when all were lying down and half buried some men of my platoon. I took over my bit of the fire trench from a 6th subaltern. It was isolated from the rest of the Coy on the right by 60 yds of open ground. On the left I was only 50 yds off the German trench, and on the right 200 or so. When the 6th left I found only about a dozen rifles could fire, because of the mud on the journey up! These I got to exchange shots with the enemy while the others cleared their rifles of mud. On the left when flares went up we could see the sandbagged German trenches 60 yds away.'

The British fire trench was a temporary one, earth heaped against wire netting supported by two rows of poles. They were bombarded by shrapnel a few hours after reaching the trench. On the 12th there was heavy rifle fire from both sides: 'At 4 a.m. enemy dropped 10 shells from a trench mortar close to our trench; most appalling projectiles I had experienced yet.'

Four men in A Coy were killed that day. On the 14th they were relieved by Seaforths at 1.30 a.m. and Hugh had ten hours' sleep near Locon. There was a conference of officers and 'congrats. by C.O.'. But next day they moved off again to reserve trenches at 7 p.m. 'for a rumoured big attack' by the Seaforths, who 'lost heavily and gained nothing'. Hugh's fellow officer Phillimore was killed by a wound in the thigh. Another attack on 16th did not come off. Friday 18 June was sunny:

'Got word this evening at 7 p.m. that A and D are to attack in conjunction with Gordons on the right. A is to lead, and of course with no. 1 Platoon I have to lead the assault. Have to creep up a ditch towards the German line at L9, break cover and rush with the bayonet, clearing up the trench to the left as far as the machine gun emplacement. This at 3 a.m. We have only two officers – Alister and myself – no bombs – no engineers; fail to see how we are to stick to any trench that we may capture.

'After going thoroughly into the thing, got word that attack was off about 9 p.m. Had screwed up all my courage too! May come off tomorrow.'

That night the whole battalion was on fatigue, carrying rations up to firing line, and there was much shelling. Next day Hugh found time to write to his father, whose feelings about the peril in which his son now lived can only be imagined: 'The last few days have been very warm and sunny, and the trenches quite bearable, but for the plague of flies and shells: I don't know which are the worst... [We] only have to work through the cool night. Through the day it is a matter of loafing in the sun (or in dug-outs, according to the activity of the German gunners). The unfortunate thing is that no dug-out will stop a direct hit from a modern high explosive, but one has a feeling of false security in a hole, which I have not shaken off yet... I am feeling very fit just now, and have solved the secret of sleeping through the day. The secret is easily solved when you are not allowed to sleep at night!'

Next day the brigade moved up to the fire trenches again, Hugh's platoon in the same place. On 21st part of his trench had to be evacuated to let artillery bombard 'M10'. 'In the evening a fizz bang blew in parapet but no one hurt.' On 22nd a shrapnel shell – 'almost certainly our own' – burst on their parados, severely wounding Hugh's platoon sergeant. 'At 9 p.m. prolonged cheering began on the left and spread along to right in German lines; two got on to parapet and waved and shouted, jumping down before we got any aimed shots in. Strange to hear cheering in such a place. Fall of Lemberg? We got anxious and stood to arms, and I put up many flares over enemy trench on left. On being relieved, marched 4 miles to transport and had tea and bread and cheese in a field – raining and pitch dark! Then marched 6 miles to Cornet St Malo – behind Locon – many men unable for march rested at transport and reported later. Fine quiet isolated billet at Cornet St Malo; had 10 hours sleep in a bed! Also a sort of bath and change.'

Next day Hugh discovered they were in fact at Boheme. On 25th they marched to Estaires: 'Strolled through town in afternoon. At night dined with Headquarters staff in their big chateau – 1st subalterns. Fine dinner with champagne!'

On 27 June they marched to Fauquissait, and that day Hugh began writing for his father a long description of the fire trench, handed over by regulars 'scrupulously clean and intact'. They were 120 yards from the German trench. The officers' dug-outs were 'luxurious', and Hugh had 'a straw bed covered with clean white sandbags, shelves. etc.'. Enemy shell fire was between 2 and 4 p.m.: 'But there is one thing that destroys our peace of mind – at least those who are nervous, and I am not one. And that is that quietness means deep doings! Both sides are mining, and have been for months. We have three new shafts in our trench almost finished... The miners inform one diffidently that the enemy must be pretty far on with their "galleries"! And it seems to be a competition as to who gets his mines touched off first! But it is all intensely interesting... How I wish I could show you over the trench! – Quite safe, I assure you. You could spend an hour or two sight-seeing, and then have an excellent meal in my dug-out! French bread, tea or coffee, sardines, butter, jam, eggs – almost as good as at home. Graham also taps (privately) a well in the mine shaft – flowing out of blue clay – and the very cold, pure water passes description... You could watch our gillies and gamekeepers work as snipers, armed with telescopes and telescopic rifles – now callously hunting bigger game than of old, and with even greater zeal. Or through a loopholed plate you could watch our shells bursting over the German trench (they seldom reply!).'

On 29 June they were visited by the G.O.C., Bannatyne Allason. 'Allason remarked on my looking very pink and white after being two months out! I had just washed!' That night A and B Coys evacuated their trench. 'At 3 a.m. a mine was exploded; sickening vibration of earth but no explosion. Earth and sandbags thrown 50 feet above German trench. Immediately mine went off (five distinct explosions) 15 minutes' intense bombardment by our artillery – shrapnel, lyddite and high explosive; and eight machine guns

hammered from our trench and houses behind for 5 minutes...
Then silence.'

Forty feet of the German trench had been blown up. The British
trench was shelled all the next day and four men in A Coy were
wounded. 'At 10.55 we slackened off all fire on the destroyed
portion of the German trench, and very soon could hear enemy
working. Opened fire with trench mortars, machine guns and three
mortar bombs, one of which destroyed one of our mine shaft
heads...We ceased fire again and at 11.15 repeated the performance.
Enemy again sent over three bombs, none on trench fortunately.
Beautiful starry moonlit night; extraordinary experience the din of
rifles and machine guns, appalling crash of mortar bombs, clouds of
smoke; the whole lit up like day by German flares to be plunged at
intervals into darkness.'

Back home in Scotland, Neil continued to work ferociously long
hours at the *News*, trying not to worry and to keep up some
semblance of normality. At the end of June, when his son had been
in France for two months, he even wrote to George Blackwood: 'By
the way, are you still in the humour to do a 1/- *Jimmy Swan: The Joy
Traveller*? I think I wrote to you about it a year ago, but then came
chaos, and I haven't had the heart to think of it since. But the stuff's
all ready...'

On 1 July Hugh and his comrades were shelled all day. Hugh
described 3 July as 'the worst day we have had yet... Shrapnel,
lyddite, high explosives and bombs rained on and over our trench –
mostly over. The earth shook with the continuous explosions, filling
the air with black smoke and earth. In ten minutes it ceased. Alister
came along to my platoon and asked me to go along to B Coy and
find if bombardment had affected them. I went along and found Neil
Campbell, and at that moment the bombardment opened again. All
we could do was to cower in the trench and wait. Three high explosives fell just over the parados from us... In fifteen minutes
bombardment ceased again. Found on going back that our trench at
No 4 platoon had been damaged, and eight men wounded. Trench
was scattered with sandbags, earth, and debris; and here and there
pools and stains of blood... Got most of the men down to the
dressing station at once, since shells had stopped. Stretcher bearers
who came back brought news that a shell had wrecked the orderly
room and severely wounded Dan Thomson who died shortly afterwards. Had it quiet rest of day. Relieved about 10.30 p.m. by 6th.
Came down behind firing line about 1500 yards... I slept in a
haystack.'

Dan Thomson was the son of Hugh's step-uncle, and I believe he was the first Inveraray man killed in the war. The Germans a few yards away were aware of the country from which their opponents came. During this time at Fauquissait the enemy used to shout over at 2 a.m. 'Stand to arms!' or 'Are there any Clyde man there?', and 'Bonnie Mary of Argyll' was played on the cornet, perhaps by a German who had been in a Clyde steamer's band.

The battalion then began night fatigues. There were many casualties from stray bullets among fatigue parties. On the night of the 7th Hugh took out a fatigue party of 60 with rations and 2,000 sandbags to the firing line. On the 9th his platoon marched through Laventie to billets near La Gorgue, for six days' 'rest'. After a lecture on bombs Hugh found he had the gift of throwing them accurately. He was also on a machine gun course. On 13th he was at a farewell dinner given by Major T.L. Brown: 'Glorious dinner in schoolhouse... Sat beside Rogerson. and Lauder [son of Harry Lauder], and had a hilarious night; English, Gaelic and French songs (last by interpreter).'

On the 15th they heard that instead of going back into trenches they were going into reserve at Laventie. There John Lauder found an Erard piano which he played all the morning of the 17th. That night Hugh as gang commander took a working party to the trenches. On the 22nd they marched through Merville to a billet in a farm. On 25th the Brigadier General said the Brigade had lost 131 men killed and 680 wounded since coming to France. On the 27th they left La Gorgue by train at 3.30am. A 14-hour journey took them to Corbie, just beyond Amiens.

'Had hour halts at Calais and Abbeville for meals – hot water free, buffet served by English girls. At Abbeville a train of Belgian recruits in khaki arrived while we were stopped and a great interchange of greetings, souvenirs, &c took place. They sang our National Anthem, Tipperaray, &c and the Belgian and French anthems; we sang "Bonnie Scotland" and "Scots wha hae"!! In middle of this a train of French troops passed through between Belgian train and ours amid great cheers. Reached Corbie at 5pm. Civilian populace all turned out to see the kilts; left Corbie with band playing and cheering crowds, and marched five miles to village of Lahoussoye."

On 28 July the 6th and 8th Brigades were inspected by General Munro. Next day they marched ten miles to Bouzencourt, after the C.O. had superintended a practice of the 8th's pipers and drummers. 'Great reception from the French civilians and soldiers in villages we passed through; danced in and out among the band arm in arm bumping against the C.O. and Brigade Major!' Next day they marched through Aveluy and Authuille to relieve a French regiment (166th). The 8th's location was 'Hill 141, Authuille': Hugh's platoon was on extreme right of brigade, with French on the right, probably indeed at La Boisselle, for there are random notes in his diary headed "La Boiselli". La Boisselle was later taken by the Germans: eleven months later it would be at the very centre of the Battle of the Somme. The 8th Argylls were well housed: 'Magnificent trenches with huge dug-outs 10–20–30 feet deep accommodating 30–50 men.'

Back in Scotland, Hugh's family were spending the summer as usual at Inveraray, where he could never be far from their thoughts. On 5 August he received a letter from his sister Moira which for a few moments brought back the happy world he had left behind. He replied next day: 'In spite of the poor boat service to Inveraray now you seem to be as popular with visitors as ever, and I can picture father frowning in the dining room, while Maggie tells white false-hoods at the front door! I had a postcard from father yesterday, sent from Ballachulish where he had been with Mr Houston... And you say that you seem to get nothing but fish to eat just now. How I wish I were you! An occasional tin of very pale salmon is as much fish as we get. I sometimes dream of little Ballantyre trout, split open, and fried in meal! Scrumptious!' In the same letter, written in pencil in the trenches – probably at Hill 141, Authuille – he said he had not had his clothes off for a week.

Moira's letter had arrived a year to the day since the British mobil-isation. Hugh noted in his diary: 'This morning at stand-to enemy left their trench in some numbers and fired at our trench from the ridge in front. Am preparing a surprise for tomorrow morning.' But he did not mention if the surprise was carried out. At this point his diary is much briefer. Among random notes headed 'La Boiselli':

'Enemy could not get hand grenades into our trench, but we could land them in theirs – down hill. Had to crawl along front trench to visit sentries, and squirm along sap to No. 1 sentry (12 yds from enemy). Absolute silence and only listening.'

'At La Boiselli kestrel hawks and owls numerous – after mice. Chalmers in support trench shot two kestrels one on a tree and one in flight – with a rifle!'

On 13 August the Battalion was relieved and moved to billets at Millencourt. On the 16th Hugh noted: 'Strict new regime. Parades 7–8 a.m., 9–10, 11–1pm. Officers' musketry class from 3–4 and 5–6 p.m.!' On the 17th he noted: 'Had a fatigue party... to dig trenches near Albert. Had a stroll into Albert for something to eat, and visited the church; the huge figure of the Virgin Mary on top of the tower is knocked at right angles to the tower by shelling and the figure hangs over the town with outstretched hands.'

On the 20th, he was preparing to go back to the front line: 'Hear we go into trenches tomorrow, to the nasty bit at La Boisselli – enemy 15 yards off! Chalmers and I for A Coy go off at 2 to spend 24 hours in trenches before battalion takes over. Left at 2.15pm under McGregor – our packs loaded on his horse! Stayed night in trenches with 7th Black Watch; in morning visited Ilot salient; lots of torpedoes came over during night – concussion snuffing candles in dug-outs!'

Next day they moved into trenches, A Coy being in reserve. On the 23rd A Coy went into the firing line, with D Coy in Ilot salient. 'I had a platoon of K's [men of 'Kitchener's Army'] thrust on me,' Hugh noted. On the 27th A Coy moved into the salient: 'Shortly after relief enemy put over many mortar bombs, but we had no casualties. My post – Ilot – only 12–20 yards from enemy. No firing or shells – only bombs interchanged... Early in night heard enemy working on left of Ilot; got machine gun on them, stopping work. Began again, so threw over grenade into their trench; they replied by sending six back – all short. Bomb and rifle grenades all night.'

The following day 'at 4 a.m., 150 of 6th Seaforths came up on fatigue to work on salient. Got good deal of work done, our artillery keeping down enemy's bombing. This fatigue came up again in evening at 4 p.m., and immediately enemy began sending over many mortar bombs of all sizes; one fell in a squad (working) killing one and wounding four (Seaforths); everybody took cover but sentries; enemy fired salvoes of large mortar bombs, and one nearly got me, Alister and McKellar getting into a dug-out in time – blew in part of Cochereau. At night a terrible thunderstorm, and dark as pitch with blinding lightning; trench full of water; visiting sentries on hands and knees an ordeal! Enemy threw over about fifty hand grenades and rifle grenades during night – mostly short; kept putting up flares also. Guides I sent down to Coy Headquarters for Verey flares lost their way, so had to put off several big French rockets to illuminate front. McKellar and I stayed up all night.'

Next day, 'at 4.30 a.m. we withdrew from salient into Bouvier post, and engineers put up a mine – concussion, but no surface effect – to destroy enemy's galleries. Re-occupied salient immediately. Enemy made no retaliation. Later more Seaforths came up to work and did well; everything quiet but a few hand grenades. Just as I was writing just now enemy exploded a mine on our left in front of Cochereau, shaking whole salient; then followed three huge trench mortar bombs which fell over the Becourt trench; I dashed up to my sentries and found them all right. Artillery have located mortars and are firing H.E. now. Don't think mine has damaged trench... Found that two miners were entombed in Mine S2 (Maugin). Had a fatigue of 20 men on to take out sandbags, but too big a job, and had to abandon; canary lowered into mine died at once – no hope for men. At 4 p.m. we were relieved by D Coy under Sandy Mac... we going into reserve again.'

A Coy were in reserve for three days, cleaning up trenches and doing fatigues to salient. On 1 September they marched to 'practically same billets' at Millencourt. On the 5th the C.O. left the battalion – 'water on knee' (Hugh's quotation marks) – their new C.O. being 'a young major of Indian Cavalry'. Hugh noted: 'Don't know what our new C.O. thought of his new commando today! C.O. groggy – three coys went to wrong place for church parade; awful handling of arms and drilling.'

There was 'a beastly emergency move' on the 7th, but after a circular march they returned to billets. On the 11th A Coy was sent 'to garrison Becourt, Chateau, and trench round Becourt wood. Officers in Chateau (an old billiard room, riddled with bullets and sandbagged). Here also are Headquarters of 6th Seaforths. Only 800 yards or so from firing line; great rattle of musketry and machine guns all night, ruined village and station court humming with stray bullets.'

There were the usual fatigues. The 8th Argylls played the 6th at 'association', losing 4-0. Becourt Chateau was shelled, also Albert. Meanwhile letters from home brought a little relief from the constant mayhem. On September 12, Moira wrote to her brother, a week before her 18th birthday. She and Lala had just started at the College of Domestic Science in Glasgow. 'We have been frightfully busy writing up notes on laundry, household management, etc. so that you ought to find a house in *perfect* order when you return.'

It was not to be. But Hugh did read this letter, which was sent back to Carnus among his belongings. A few more diary entries chronicle his last days, as the brigade was ordered to take over again the Authuille-Thiepval line, 'which we held when we first came to this part of France'.

Saturday 18 September, Chateau Becourt. Hot day. Fatigues again. A daring Taube came over our lines very low at about

8 a.m., our anti-aircraft battery and three machine guns battered for fifteen minutes or so without effect! Relieved at night by a company of 7th Buffs (E.K.R.) Marched to Millencourt – rest of battalion had gone from Albert earlier, and arrived at 11.30 p.m.

Sunday 19 September, Millencourt. Took company to Buisi to bathe in the Ancre – muddy, weedy river at that point; had a dip myself. A service battalion of the S.W. Borderers were resting in the field by the river. Church parade at 4.30 p.m. Dined with D Coy at night, and had a 'meeting. at C mess after.

Monday 20 September, Millencourt. Early parades. Had a route march at 4.30 to Bresle via Rue Nationale, home by Henencourt, where we marched past the Divisional Staff and General Munro. Battalion looked very fine and received commendation... Lockie [Adjutant] told me to-day he had put me forward for a third star!

Tuesday 21 September, Trenches, Aveluy. Left Millencourt at 5.15 and marched via Aveluy to trenches. A Coy on right, then B.C.D. 2 platoons of Seaforths attached to A on right; on right of Seaforths 8th Sussex (K).

The next entry, dated Wednesday 22 September, was made by Private Graham, Hugh's servant:

Left trenches 8 p.m. to get Mail returning 9.30 and had paper E.N. [?Evening News] for Mr Munro. Taking over duties as Mess Cook for 10 days in Officers Mess I did not go on duty with him. He left Trench at 11 p.m. with Seaforth officer 1 Corporal 1 Lc.Cpl. on wire Patrol at the same time intending to capture German Flag stuck on Wire Entanglement. Reaching same Mr Munro tied a piece of rope round his stick (as he had suspicion of some foul play). How the accident happened remains unknown. A Bomb was attached in some manner or other and exploded causing instant Death. I received word at 11.20 p.m. and at once proceeded to the Sap where some of his platoon had already carried the remains to and then conveyed them to First Aid Post, where Captain McArthur placed a Sword along with myself. (Thursday noon) conveyed remains to Millencourt. Had grave dug.

Friday 11am. Under Lieutenant Disselduff we laid him to Rest in a little Churchyard side by side with some of his departed comrades of the 8th Argylls. A kind and thoughtful Master to [?]B. Graham.

Hugh's family learned of his death on 25 September. He died at the age of 22 and would be listed as 'Captain H.A. Munro' in the Army Officers' Service Records, his promotion having been confirmed posthumously. The cause of death is given as 'killed in action in the field, Aveluy'.

A letter his father wrote to John Macmaster Campbell on 21 October gives more details:

You have doubtless heard how our dear lad met his end: in some spirit of emulation between young officers of the Seaforths & Suffolks [?Sussexes] he went out on a night of bright full moon to get possession of a wretched German flag that had been flaunting outside the German wire for a long time, taking two men of his platoon with him to cover snipers and a machine-gun trained on the flag. Everyone knew the flag was a trap, with a bomb probably attached to it, and Hugh had provided himself with a long looped cord or wire to throw over the stuff and haul on at a safe distance. A young Seaforth sub with two men were on the same job. Half way across the ground it became more obvious that there was great hazard in the undertaking; the two Seaforth men refused to crawl any further and retired to their lines. Hugh told his two men to stay where they were and cover him, while he went on followed closely by the Seaforth officer. What exactly happened at the fatal moment we shall probably never know in this life, but when he reached the flag the opening of enemy fire on him may have made him impetuously grasp at the flag or throw his loop over it too roughly; at all events the bomb burst, and, struck on the head, he was killed instantly. At the same moment a torrent of machine-gun fire swept the spot. The Seaforth and Hugh's two men got safely back to their trenches; immediately an Inveraray man McVicar said the body must be got in at all costs, and at the utmost peril four of them went out – two unarmed. McVicar lifted Hugh on the back of McLennan, who used to be a young police-constable at Inveraray; took off his coat and covered Hugh's legs, which shone white in the moonlight, and with McVicar behind him to shield his burden, McLennan dashed for the trenches, covered by the two men with rifles, one of whom was wounded, but not seriously, I am glad to say...

We have got from various quarters (John Disselduff is a treasure) photographs and sketches of the place, the funeral, and the grave, on which there is now a wreath of Glenaray heather sent by the girls. We have got all the personal belongings which were about Hugh when he fell, including a diary he kept from the day they left Bedford till the day before he died. Quite copious and interesting, and not a single 'grouse' in it... Curiously enough, he had, on the eve of an attack – which did not come off – at Festubert, handed the watch and diary to his orderly (a splendid fellow, Graham, son of old Penny Readings Graham, who loved him like a brother and attended him like a mother) with the instruction that if he were killed, and Graham survived, the watch was to go to Effie and the diary carefully to me.

> Did I know this night where my dead son
> Walks bloody with his chief,
> Would I not put plaid on my head and run
> Through the last black gate of grief,
> To walk by his side and bring to his mind
> The darling isle and the folk so kind?

These lines from 'The Only Son' have often been taken as a lament for Hugh – but if so it was a premonition. Neil had written the poem eight years previously, in 1907. At some time after Hugh's death, Neil expressed his sense of futility and loss in a single sentence uttered by Ninian Campbell in his unfinished novel *The Search*: 'There's not a more unhandsome thing 'twixt the four brown boundaries of this world than a young man's corpse, and he a sacrifice to old men's notions he had no concern in.'

CHAPTER THIRTY-FIVE

That strange French countryside war-battered

DURING the autumn of 1915, when all the business of daily life had to continue, Neil managed to escape to Inveraray for a week-end in October. The New Year would find him there again. In January 1916, replying to a belated letter of condolence from Peter McKay, late of Glenure, he wrote: 'Looking out from my window here I can see very many houses bereaved like our own; of all Hugh's old school mates the merest fraction is left; the rest are in unmarked, unknown graves in Gallipoli, or asleep behind the lines in little cemeteries in France and Flanders... I hope you are well and happy in Australia; if one could forget the war there I'd be inclined to join you, but where on earth can one escape the influence of that horror!'

Two of Hugh's old school mates who did survive the war were George Blake and Douglas MacLeod. Blake, later a journalist and novelist, was at home on sick leave in the spring of 1916, and frequently visited the Munros.

That February Neil received his first fee as a director of the *News*, £315. He had been released from the burden of editorship with the return of J.M. Smith. A fellow journalist (not a *News* colleague) once wrote 'Not that Neil Munro was the ideal journalist or the ideal editor. He was too wild to be either, and wild enough to seem to be both.'[1]

Throughout 1916 Neil made efforts to get out to France, vainly appealing to the War Office and seeking the support of George Blackwood in his endeavour to visit the battlefields as a Scottish eye-witness. Blackwood's brother James in London took the matter up, and in April Neil heard from the War Office that he would soon receive a definite proposal. But months would pass – the months of the Battles of the Somme and Verdun – with no further word.

Meanwhile at Easter the Munros returned to Inveraray for the first time as a family since Hugh's death. Neil had had 'certain important sanitary alterations' made in the Inveraray house – 'Charlie Maitland calls it, I think, a Silent Syphon'.

He noted on 1 June that salaries at the *News* had been reduced by

215

a third 'till further notice'. His diary was petering out, and in
October he made the very last entry: '*News* becomes a Union Shop.'

That October he suggested (in vain) to George Blackwood that
Maga 'should be directly represented by a correspondent at the
Headquarters in France'.[2] Blackwood had written to ask Neil to
contribute to Maga's centenary number, due in April 1917, saying
'if you can come up with another such gem as "To Exiles" I shall be
more than delighted'.[3] Charles Whibley was to collaborate with Neil
in 'Noctes Blackwoodianae' for this *Maga*, a modern version of the
'Noctes Ambrosianae' written by Christopher North, James Hogg *et
al* in early *Maga*s.

That October also Moira started work at the Scottish Filling
Factory, Georgetown (near Paisley), where shells were filled and
packed. She became an examiner, but had to give up the job after
seven months because of adverse effects of the materials. She then
worked in the office at Princess Louise's Hospital for limbless ex-
servicemen at Erskine, where she lived in till after the Armistice.
Effie's war contribution was to run a little infants' school at Carnus,
while Lilian took up hospital cooking. Neil junior, now 16, and Bud,
14, were still at Greenock Academy.

At the end of November, Captain Neill Campbell of Inverneill
wrote to Neil to say he had been to see Hugh's grave: 'I thought you
would be glad to know that it was being well looked after. Both the
crosses are quite good & clear, also the Gaelic one.'

At Christmas-time Neil wrote to his old friend Pittendrigh
Macgillivray: 'It has been in my mind, many times, to go "ane's
errand" [specially] to Edinburgh to see you, but much as I revere
Auld Reekie, I have not been in it twice in the last fourteen years. I
should rejoice to learn that... you were on a great national
monument to Scotland's part in the present struggle. Written words
can't do it, we want stone and bronze, and you are the man.'[4]

Neil went down to Inveraray once again on Hogmanay. That
winter he was often visited at Carnus by Hugh's old school friend
George Blake. Up until now Blake had known Hugh's father simply
as a cheerful, welcoming presence at Carnus and had not yet come
to appreciate the depths of Neil's character. Years later he would tell
how 'there was [sic] in this man two men, just as his published work
proclaims, a perfect dichotomy. There was Neil Munro, the being
of delicate sensibility who felt and wrote that terrible story "War";
and there was Hugh Foulis, gay and shrewdly observant of the world
about him, who created Para Handy... It was Hugh Foulis that the
world, even his friends, encountered. For Neil Munro lurked shy

216

and sensitive behind the protective barrier of laughter and chaff set up by his alter ego.'⁵

In the grey aftermath of Hugh's death, it was not always possible for Neil to keep up a front during Blake's visits. One incident in particular would stick in Blake's mind: 'I can remember only once having seen him in plain distress, the mask of gaiety cast aside. It was in the dining-room of his house in Gourock where, the surviving friend of his dead son, Hugh... and my own small service in the Army done, I used to visit him once a week. It was a winter night of 1917, and word had just come through to him in his capacity of journalist that a great new submarine [K13] on trial in the Gareloch had sunk with all hands and that some fifty men were still alive, but almost hopelessly imprisoned within the hull. So, with the awful load of knowledge upon us, we sat in silence for the best part of two hours, and never since have I seen a man in such distress as Munro was that night. His face worked; his long fingers tore at that fine mass of hair which was so fair that, when in the course of nature it turned white, no great difference was to be observed; and when he tried to express his agony of mind, it was in a voice that broke and stuttered almost incoherently.'⁶

Blake, who wrote those words fourteen years later, certainly knew Neil well, though they were of different generations. The idea of a dichotomy can lead to futile questions such as 'which was the real Neil Munro?' – and besides, reticence was only to be expected of a Victorian Gael. Yet this account of an evening in January 1917 bears witness to the almost unbearable stress that Neil had continued to live under since Hugh's death.

In February he went to Edinburgh to see George Blackwood and discuss his contribution to *Maga*'s centenary edition. In the end Neil's input to 'Noctes Blackwoodianae' was minimal. 'Such mosaic jobs by writers far separate from each other need a lot of time to do satisfactorily,' he remarked in a letter to Blackwood. The reason he could not do more was that two days after the trip to Edinburgh he was at last given clearance to visit France. His letter to Blackwood was posted in Paris: 'I should have written sooner, but my movements in the past fortnight have been of a character to make that impossible.'⁷

He spent a month of wintry weather at the British front and French fronts, visiting Verdun and its forts and finding at Bois-le-Duc 'one of the scurviest hotels between Hell and Oban'. Neil Munro the journalist reported what he saw, but Neil Munro the man expressed his deeper feelings in a series of poems. Back at Carnus, he made early reference to them in a letter to George Blackwood: 'The "Bagpipe Ballad" stuff may be too long for you (and may even be unsuitable). If you care for it at all, I have a scheme for a series of them, all based on bagpipe tunes – their titles mainly – which I think would make a pretty book.'[8]

Blackwood thought the Ballads 'just of the very best' and put the first instalment straight into the centenary *Maga*. 'The whole will certainly make a first rate book, and we would very gladly see it on our list of publications.'[9] Sixteen of the Ballads would be printed in *Maga*, including 'Roving Lads' ['Wild Rover Lads'], written as early as 1916, but the 'first rate book' did not materialise in Neil's lifetime.

In April he sent off 'another bunch o' the braw ballants', informing Blackwood at the same time: 'The Foreign Office has at last wakened up to the obvious, and I have been asked to go out officially to the British front to write about the Scottish regiments.' In this may be seen the hand of John Buchan, now Director of the Department of Information. Neil ended his letter: 'I have sufficient ballads well under weigh [sic] to keep you going as long as you'll stand them, in my absence.'[10]

At the end of April, writing to Blackwood on money matters, he added: 'On Monday I set out for France, in a uniform in which I am assured by my household I look like a young Sub [subaltern] with a slight taint of the conscientious objector about him. "It's all in the belt ye can put round your wame."'[11]

Neil spent three weeks in France. By now, however, the censors were imposing even more drastic limitations. 'The conditions under which one is permitted to write from the Front nowadays necessarily produce very thin and futile stuff,' he wrote later. He predicted accurately that his articles would never be re-published, and they languish yet in the National Library of Scotland. In one piece, Part I of 'With The Scots In France', passed 'as censored' on 17 May, he wrote: 'I stood yesterday on the frightfully battered and malodorous ridge of Vimy, watching the shells that shrieked over my head and burst continuously round the town of Lens, and our aeroplanes like giant birds, indifferent to fate, soar over the German lines with bouquets of shrapnel bursting apparently harmlessly round them...'

Buchan had given him a letter of introduction to General Lukin, then commanding the 9th Division. Lukin was on leave, but two men Neil knew on his staff provided him with a temporary mount – the General's own douce charger Billy.

On 14 May, Neil wrote home to Moira: 'It is, if I mistake not, your turn for a letter now... M. le Curé my billeeter, his aged papa (an old retired sea-dog) and two women vigorously cultivate the garden all day, and make me speculate as to how you & Effie are getting on with yours. I wish their enthusiasm for nature extended to the dogs; they have a mongrel little cur of pathetic mien kennelled at the front of the house, another of the same at the back, and these unhappy brutes are not off the chain from one end of the day till the other. If 'twere Dougie [the Munros' fox terrier] I'd sooner have him dead first. I heard 150 pipers and about as many drums playing on Sunday all at once, under the most interesting circumstances... I hope you are all well & happy at Carnus; I'm convinced myself it's the jolliest place in the world. Love & kisses to you all. Your affect. father, Neil Munro.'

The letter makes no reference to the carnage of the battlefields, nor to what Neil must have been going through in the darker recesses of his soul, but he continued to write poetry.

> So played the pipes in Arras
> Their Gaelic symphony,
> Filled with old wisdom gathered
> In isles of the Highland sea,
> And eastward towards Cambrai
> Roared the artillery.
>
> ['Pipes in Arras']

Neil, mindful of the censors' limitations, wrote of the Scottish soldier 'making the best of an unpleasant job regarding which he has no romantic illusions'. Some notes for his own use on his last two days at the British front – 21 and 22 May – reveal a bit more. These days were spent in a car with Lieutenant Ernest Brookes, driving from Rollencourt eastwards to Arras, then towards Wancourt where they were very near the front lines:

'The road was lined by German funk-holes. Boche crumps and big shells were falling every minute in the fields round us. We drew up our car in the shelter of a pile of timber, walked a little way down the road near where the shells were falling thickest as Brookes wanted shell-burst photographs at near hand. Wounded came up from the front line trenches and passed us... Our big guns, well hidden, fired constantly over our heads...'

They went on to Bapaume and Albert, passing seven or eight tanks knocked out of action, and abandoned orchards. Then at last they went to Millencourt: 'Visited Madame Coussin Morel, in the last house on the Senlis road, saw Hugh's last billet in her house, and then visited his grave in the cemetery; also the grave of Sergt Armstrong by his father's request.'

After a night in Amiens, Neil and Brookes returned to Rollencourt via Beauquesne, GHQ during the Battle of the Somme. There, a year before, when Haig had it as his headquarters, Brookes had photographed the King, Joffre and Poincaré. Neil then returned to Scotland and continued to seek solace in poetry. The 'Bagpipe Ballads' constitute an oblique yet public farewell to Hugh:

When in that strange French countryside war-battered,
Far from the creeks of home and hills of heath,
A boy, he kept the old tryst of his people
With the dark girl Death
                    ['Lament for Macleod of Raasay']

In May the tenancy of the house in Inveraray was taken over by Neil's old school friend Robert Fraser, who now had the chemist-cum-newsagent's shop (though not himself a pharmacist) and was Registrar of Inveraray. From then on he and his wife would welcome the Munros (chiefly the younger generation) as paying guests. For some time also Neil had been contemplating a move from Carnus and had been searching for another house. Certainly the Gourock house was beginning to be a tight fit, yet I suspect that Neil's under-lying motive was the desire to be gone from all the old haunts before the war ended, and Hugh did not come marching home.

That summer Neil was on the point of nervous collapse, no doubt brought on by the aftermath of Hugh's death and the harrowing sights he had witnessed in France. He managed to send off three 'Bagpipe Ballads' in June and two more in July, but on 17 August he wrote to George Blackwood to say he had no more ready for September's *Maga*: 'For four weeks I have been very much under the weather – depressed, nervous, as weak as a kitten, incapable of working, with no physical reason that is apparent; and I take it badly since I have never had much more than a headache in my life before that I can remember. For some days back, as a result of a strict regimen and some doctors' stuff, I have been feeling better, and I hope very soon to be all right again...'

Neil was now 54. No further details of this episode survive: perhaps 'civilian shell-shock' is a likely diagnosis, now known as 'post-traumatic stress disorder'. The effect of the massive loss of young men upon their parents' generation, as distinct from indi-vidual bereavements, is incalculable.

No details survive, either, of the Munro household in that third autumn of the war, but on 23 December Neil wrote to Moira: 'I can't imagine you'll have a *Merry* Christmas in Erskine House, but at least, I hope, you'll have a happy and contented one among those poor maimed fellows. – It must be a sort of glum Christmas morning here, with you and Lal absent. Do you remember the wild noisy rush downstairs to the nursery where the stockings were hung? What a racket! – Waked me up – I mean disturbed me sadly in the process of thinking out a Plot. I hear that George Blake was expected home last night. Your mother was away all Friday evening gallivanting with Mrs Blake; I don't know what those giddy old gals are up to, unless it's picture-houses, vaudevilles and Mackay teas. Give my regards to Katie and Polly and take a few paternal hugs for yourself. Your affect. father N.M.'

CHAPTER THIRTY-SIX

This is the house for me!

THE unwontedly strong tone of a letter Neil wrote to George Blackwood early in 1918 indicates some mental recuperation. Although *Jimmy Swan The Joy Traveller* had been published by Blackwoods during the dark days of 1917, perhaps providing some welcome light relief for the young men in the trenches, Neil was not entirely satisfied with the service he was getting from his publisher. He now informed George Blackwood that a London publisher wanted to bring out cheap popular editions of his novels, if Blackwoods would be prepared to license them:

'It is certain of a considerable sale which would be helpful to my reputation and not unprofitable to your copyright. I don't know how you may regard these proposals, but they confirm a conviction I have had for a long time back that we have for a good many years failed to take much advantage of the popular market into which practically all the other fiction writers in the country put their books within two or three years of their first publication. At present, doubtless, you may have difficulties about paper supplies, and the proposals now made to me may seem to you a reasonable way out of your difficulty. I had expected *The New Road* in a cheap edition would have been out long ago, for I understand you had it set up. All the Glasgow booksellers have ceaselessly been pestering me to know when it may be expected; they tell me that since you announced it about two years ago they have had great and repeated demands for it and that its non-appearance is difficult for them to explain to many customers who continually ask for it.'[1]

Blackwood replied at once, agreeing that all Neil's books ought to be out in cheap popular editions but stressing that 'the right of publication in what we have is our property. I trust you will not blame us too severely, and will allow us to proceed with these cheap issues as we are in a position to do so.' Yet he seems to have come up with more positive proposals soon afterwards, for on 28 March Neil wrote: 'Of course I am quite agreeable to your new price and royalty arrangements for the cheap editions. I know all about the paper difficulty: we [at the *News*] are up against it every day!

'In spite of the paper shortage, may I ask if you are prepared just now, *tout de suite*, to publish a new 5/- or 6/- volume of short stories for me? About 50,000 words. They are real Munroesque Highland and Lowland romantic yarns which for the past twelve years I have published fugitively... one of the tales is called "Jaunty Jock" and that might, in the present circumstances, be an irresistible title.' Blackwood replied at once 'We shall be delighted to arrange with you for the new book you have in view,' adding a postscript: 'Is the muse not going to give us some more "Bagpipe Ballads" soon?'[2] Neil sent off eleven tales by registered post, telling Blackwood: 'I can, at a push, add one or two more if you consider it desirable.' Perhaps due to the paper shortage, only the eleven were printed.

At the beginning of May the Munros said farewell to Carnus, scene of so many happy memories, and flitted across the Firth of Clyde. Neil had at last found their new home: 'After two years of searching for a house I came, one day, upon this one, and before I had set foot within its doors I said to myself, "This is the house for me!" It was the only simple Georgian house in a community of Victorian villas, but something more than that was in my impetuous determination there and then to buy it. Outside, and in, and in its garden and outlook it had a curiously familiar atmosphere. I somehow felt at home, as I had never done anywhere since leaving my distant native village as a lad. The illusion sometimes overtook me that I had in some mysterious past lived here or knew its earlier tenants.'[3]

The house was in Craigendoran. It was on the water's edge, had two and a half acres of ground, and was very near Craigendoran pier and station where two railway lines from Glasgow diverged, one to end in Helensburgh a mile or so to the west, the other to strike off to Mallaig in the far north-west. The only un-Munroesque thing about the house was its name – Rockville – which Neil soon changed to Cromalt, after an Inveraray place, as he had changed Westview into Carnus.

Eight years later he would discover why Cromalt had seemed so familiar to him from the beginning: 'To-day the whole thing has been explained to me in a fashion which confirms my old belief that all things have an immortal spirit – even stone and lime, and planted trees, foot-worn stairs, hearths that have warmed folks dead and gone. For the first time I have been going through my title-deeds to the house and ground... They go back to 1802... imagine my surprise to find that the owner of the place 117 years ago was a merchant from my native village, an old friend of my people, with his name on a stone in our village churchyard! I had never heard of his living at any time in the Lowlands.

'Yet, between the hours of 10 and 11 a.m. on 28th February, 1809, Donald McMath, standing somewhere in front of this door of mine, was formally "infeft and seized" in this property by having handed to him a symbolic divot and stone. There was with him on that occasion a distant relative and namesake of my own, who was the "Baillie", and one of the two witnesses to the transaction was a man from the same Highland village whose grandchildren I knew well. I'll swear that even though it was yet meridian, Donald McMath took them all in and ceremoniously produced a dram. Which of the cupboards was it kept in?

'Six years later, Donald sold this house to Colin Campbell, Esquire, of Jura, then a Glasgow merchant, who lived in it for sixteen years, which accounts for my finding recently a 1771 copy of Shakespeare with his bookplate on it. Next time I meet a Campbell of Jura I shall tell him that an ancestor of his haunts my house.

'The Disposition by which Donald McMath transferred his ownership to Jura in February, 1815, was signed by him in that Highland law-office I was to become apprentice in, long years after; his witnesses were men whose grandsons I knew intimately. It is only an Extract of the Registered Disposition I have, but each of its eleven pages of stamped paper has, at its foot, a hurried signature I could not decipher till I came to the end, when I found it was the signature of "Walter Scott, Esquire" one of the Principal Clerks to the said

Court of Session. 'So here I have the "Wizard's" holograph guarantee that he was dragged away from the composition of *Guy Mannering* to attend to the affairs of my house, a very humble one compared with Abbotsford. It is not, however, the ghost of Scott that haunts my dwelling, but a band of jovial Highland spirits from my native place and my native shire, the friends of Donald McMath and Jura. No wonder that here, from the first, I felt quite at home, that the old walls whispered with a Gaelic accent, that Highland dreams so much possess me.'⁴

Before the end of May, Neil wrote a jocose letter to Winifred Hodge, the daughter of his widowed friend David, who was the same age as Bud and generally spent much of her holidays with the Munros:

I am delighted that you are to join our Seminary this summer, and just to indicate roughly what will be expected of you I set down the tentative Daily Programme as follows:-

7 a.m. Maggie rings the Big Bell – a whopper that is as big as the old *Lord of the Isles* one.

8 a.m. Bathing in good weather from the *Bathing House*, to which you can go in your pyjamahs [sic].

8.30. Porridge.

9. Elementary lessons in the culture of the Vine – Black Hamburg & Muscadine, by the Principal.

9.30. Examination in Latin, Mathematics and Early English History by Miss Munro M.A.

9.35. Study of the Poultry Farm, with Introduction to 'Lucky MacFarlane' and her 15 chicks – very amusing family group.

10. Rambles in The Grounds. No climbing of the great old Chestnuts allowed.

10.30. Practice in the Scottish Accent with Neil Munro Jr B.Litt. (Compulsory. Special fee 5/- per quarter.)

11.30. Visit to Essachosan the wild flower garden.

12. Berry-picking.

1.30. Lunch.'

Some time that year – it must have been in summer, as he was wearing a boater – George Blake applied for a job on the *News*. James Murray Smith appointed him, his salary being £4 a week. 'We were not "specialists" in those days,' Blake would recall. 'My experience during the first month or two in Hope Street included leader writing, book reviewing, gossip writing. the production of light verse, art and dramatic criticism...'[5]

Having Hugh's friend working on the *News* must have been a comfort for Neil that summer as the war moved towards its conclusion. There was no long holiday at Inveraray now. At the end of July Neil wrote to Alice Weir, whose husband had just been elevated to the peerage: 'Only one thing vexes me about your change of identity – that unless your husband does the sporting thing some day of buying Dunderave, there are but few prospects of any more pic-nics and fireworks on Loch Fyne. Ah! those were the good days, when we were care-free and heart-unwounded! I hope there are many long years before you and your husband and the children, as jolly as those simple old Inveraray ones that to me now seem almost a dream. I haven't been on Loch Fyne for nearly a year – the longest absence by far since first I left it... I look forward to a horticultural & benign old age!'

Lord Weir, who ended the war as Air Minister, did buy Dunderave, and Neil would often stay there. Meanwhile, on a September Saturday that year, he and Captain David Bone visited Cunninghame Graham (long a widower, and childless) at Ardoch, on the edge of the Firth six miles east of Cromalt. 'He gave me a demonstration of lasso-throwing, and after a few misses, which annoyed him (he becomes a little old & short of breath) he caught me neatly enough round one ankle by his loop, at a distance of about 30 or 40 feet. We had a dram, & afternoon tea, & a walk in the grounds... One old Uist housekeeper with the Gaelic... does all the house-work. G. chaffs her in Spanish, which of course she does not know. She spoke Gaelic to me, a tongue G. envies me... He recently came home from S. America where he had been buying re-mounts for the British Army, had ridden 2,000 miles & done good work generally.'[6]

Returning proof of the contents page of *Jaunty Jock* to George Blackwood later that month, Neil put in a special request: 'Are you in the not uncommon position – part pleasing, part exasperating – of having the Government interested in your Excess Profits? It is in the hope that such may be the situation that I diffidently make a suggestion with which your late uncle quite agreeably fell in once or twice – that you might let me anticipate some Royalties. My removal to a new home here has entailed some expenditure which leaves me at the moment a little short of funds, without realising some part of investments that are paying too well to be liquidated. If you can, without inconvenience to yourself, let me have £200 in advance of all Royalties it would be a great obligement. I felt this week like going to Edinburgh to tackle you on the subject, but my valour in money matters is more robust with a pen than *viva voce*... I hope almost immediately to try you again with a series of "Bagpipe Ballads", with the idea that next year we could have a volume of them resounding to our glory and eke our profit... The *People's Friend* folk are to publish a third series of Para Handy sketches, some time ago completed, instead of the In *Highland Harbours* lot they wrote to you about, and there should, with more paper available, be a new popular book in these for next year. And I have actually begun a Romance (provisionally entitled *The Search*) for you!'[7]

George Blackwood sent the requested £200 right away, to the relief of Neil who hated mortgages and had bought Cromalt outright for £3,600. It is almost bizarre to think of the Hurricane Jack stories first appearing in that ultra-couthie magazine, *The People's Friend*. It is also remarkable that, long before discovering that a Campbell of Jura had once owned Cromalt, Neil got the name 'Hurricane Jack' from the nickname of Jock Campbell of Jura, the adjutant who had been so annoyed when Belloc addressed Highland officers as 'gentlemen of England' and who now lay in a war grave in France.

On 27 September Neil himself left for France at a few hours' notice, to spend a week or so 'writing up the Australians for propaganda'. The Great War that had cost the lives of so many young men was almost over. Two weeks before the Armistice, Neil wrote to Pittendrigh Macgillivray: 'Last Friday I got to thinking on the subject of War Memorials in Scotland, and gloomily visualised every shire, city and village with its trumpery Iona cross or tasty bit of monumental sculptor's art, for that is what it will come to unless responsible people with a sense of the solemn greatness of the occasion and the way to realise it in art take the elected buddies by the scruff of the neck and lead them the way they should go. Next morning I saw from the newspapers you had been speaking in Paisley on that very topic. I know, intuitively, we are in agreement...'[8]

At the end of the war James Murray Smith retired and Neil took over the editorship of the *News*, in the fond supposition that it was merely a temporary job. Blackwoods published *Jaunty Jock* before the end of the year. Cunninghame Graham wrote to Neil from Stirling, where he was standing for Parliament: 'In the midst of this infernal folly of the election, I have gone back for an hour into real life amongst real people, in reading some of your new stories. Ah laochain, you have the real touch.'[9]

On Christmas Eve Neil wrote from the office to Moira at Erskine Hospital: 'The Editor sends his Love and many Kisses to Miss Moira Munro, and wishes her a Merry Xmas and a Happy New Year, with the hope that he may have her company to Inveraray, Lochfyne, Argyll, next week.' Lilian and Moira were home for the first Christmas at Cromalt when there was (as Neil wrote to Alice Weir) 'a crowded house of young folk most of the time – 18 at table generally. My dancing, I assure you, remains robust, but I am advised by the family that a once majestic vocal organ cracks sometimes now in song. Nevertheless I *shall* sing if I have a mind to it; I am not old enough yet to be bullied.'

CHAPTER THIRTY-SEVEN

My imaginative faculty has been lying fallow

PERHAPS it proved too cumbersome for all the Munros to go to Inveraray (the plan implied in Neil's letter to Moira), or perhaps they decided to combine the first Cromalt Hogmanay with the first New Year's Day of peace-time. At any rate, on 1 January 1919 Neil made a solitary pilgrimage to Inveraray, travelling by hired car over the Rest and Be Thankful. He spent a quiet evening with his old friend John Gilmour of the Argyll Arms, and returned home the next day. This first visit after an unprecedented absence of eighteen months to an Inveraray where – by his own choice – he no longer had a hearth of his own was surely carried out with gritted teeth.

Towards the end of January, George Blackwood reported that *The New Road* was 'selling steadily in its original form and was again reprinted recently'. The first impression of *Jaunty Jock* (4,000) was exhausted, and a reprint was in hand. As soon as more paper was available he meant to bring out a cheap edition of *The New Road*.

When May 1919 came, the Munros had completed their first year at Cromalt. Neil wrote again to Winifred Hodge, hoping that she would be coming to Cromalt for her holidays:

'Let me warn you... that you and Bud will be carefully watched during the green-gage season. With all else in the garden a reasonable amount of pilfering will be winked at, but Mr Andrew Vallance (our Head Gardener) is to be instructed to shoo you off the green-gages at all costs, as I fancy them for myself... You will *not* be required this summer to weed, or mow, or sweep up leaves, the said Andrew does all these things when nobody is looking. There is a profusion of cherry, plum, apple & pear blossom on the walls; our first green peas are up and there are *millions* of daffodils, tulips and narcissi [he is mocking Winifred's manner]. In the greenhouse there is a wonderful display of *cineraria stellata*... Neil has resumed Botany & Physics in the University... Lilian is home, I hope for good. Bud is immersed in Mathematics, for which, as you remember, she always had a perfect craze. Maggie has ten new Rhode Island Red chickens that look very picturesque on the Paddock, has saved £12 on the sale of eggs since November, and intends, I understand, to buy us a silver tea-service when she has about £25. It has always been a real grief to her that we have not had a silver tea-service... I was at Inveraray last week, and found it just as usual, with real sweeties in Mary Ann's window. Last night Bostock & Wombwell's circus was on the other side of the railway from this house, and throughout the early watches of the night we could hear the lions roar. I hope you are well. Your loving uncle, NEIL MUNRO.'[1]

Vallance the gardener had been employed by the previous owners of Cromalt: Neil kept him on, doubling his wages. Bud was now at St Bride's, a private girls' school in Helensburgh, and Neil junior had begun medicine in Glasgow as his brother had before him. Here it should be noted that although their father would have liked his daughters to go to university, none of the Munro girls did so.

George Blackwood, writing on 1 July about a Braille edition of *Jaunty Jock*, enquired about 'the new novel' and the possibility of more 'Bagpipe Ballads'. Neil's reply was evasive, alluding ominously to 'the curse of active journalism – merely temporary I assure you'.[2]

A new pattern of summer was forming for the Munros. Though Neil, thirled once more to the *News*, could no longer spend two months at Inveraray, Cromalt with its large garden edging the Firth was partial recompense. On briefer visits to Inveraray he generally stayed at the Argyll, perhaps fishing with George Houston who now spent much of the year with his large family at Cuil, a house near the head of Loch Fyne which he had rented since 1914. Jessie was mostly content to stay at home in Craigendoran, with Maggie. The younger generation made independent arrangements to stay with the Frasers. George Blake also stayed frequently at the Frasers', or perhaps next door at the George.

Effie had celebrated her 29th birthday in December 1918, and Bud her 17th in January 1919. The four Munro girls did not lack for admirers, a situation perhaps not unconnected with the composition of Neil's poem 'The Tocherless Lass':

Drumore has a leash of daughters,
And wants men for the three...

One poor fellow who rowed all the way across Loch Fyne to call on Effie was fobbed off by the white fib that she was 'out'.

The Scottish poet Charles Murray, now living in South Africa, was in Scotland that autumn, and Neil wrote to him at Duff House, Banff: 'I'm much pleased that there is a likelihood of meeting you soon in Glasgow... Send me a postcard... or walk right into the News office & kick open the most obvious doors. You will then observe a pallid, emaciated Child of the Hills – that will be me! For the past year my imaginative faculty has been lying fallow. I am, as you perhaps know, editing the *News* at present, and – between ourselves – daily discovering that the larkish spirit in which I passed through a long apprenticeship to the damnable trade of journalism is no longer recoverable after more than twenty years of a glorious interregnum of liberty and more or less fine letters. However! there is the consoling thought that I can always chuck it when I like.'[3]

That last sentence was a streak of bravado. It must be borne in mind that Neil was still supporting a household of eight souls. Could he realistically have afforded to 'chuck it'? The flow of royalties was dwindling, though Blackwoods kept all his fiction in print, and a two shilling edition of *John Splendid* proposed by George Blackwood that December sold well (9,957 copies in 1920). In December also George Blackwood wrote: 'I conclude I should have heard from you if you had been able to do any more "Bagpipe Ballads".[4] Are you making any progress with the new novel?' Neil's reply was characteristically coy about actual progress: 'As yet, unhappily, I am being held up...'[5]

Unwilling or unable to press ahead with the sequel to *The New Road*, Neil tried in the January of 1920 to begin a modern novel set after the war, with the tentative title *The Windfall*. He seems to have got no further than the first two pages of Chapter I, 'The Newcomer', now reposing in the National Library of Scotland.

Three weeks into January 1920 came a heartening letter from Charles Murray, now in London and about to sail back to South Africa: 'This is just a line to say I had a fine long talk with John Buchan, we got on to you and it was good to me to hear him on your work, especially I was glad to hear him quote "To Aliens" ["To Exiles"] amongst other things. He couldn't speak high enough of *The New Road* – "the best Scots novel for generations", &ca &ca. He laments that you can't chuck the work and do nothing but your own. Reckons you are the biggest Scot in literature, and I entirely agreed tho' perhaps I should out of politeness have put him first, I didn't; but it was so good to hear his wholehearted admiration of your work both prose and verse that I felt I must tell you. I have met many other Scots your admirers here... Oh yes Buchan spoke of Barrie as one who has taken the easy lower road and in no way to be compared to you.'[6]

But back at the *News*, Neil was fully occupied with the 'jawbox' of journalism. He travelled up to Glasgow by train, arriving at Queen Street Station instead of Central as in the old Gourock days, and jinked through back-street lanes to reach nearby 97 Hope Street without being recognised and waylaid (it's a trial for the shy, being kenspeckle). He was the most affable, if unconventional, of editors and his staff loved him. George Blake said that under Neil's editorship 'Number 67 Hope Street, Glasgow was the happiest newspaper office in the world...

'Our content and cheerfulness and success were mainly due to the lightness of the hands on the reins that guided us. No editor was ever less solemn in his sense of importance, more blithe in his disdain of the grimmer sciences like politics and economics. Politically speaking, Munro's editorship was nothing more than a joke. He had a touching habit of appealing to his leader-writer for an explanation of the existing situation, then he would wink at the rest of us behind the back of our grave colleague. "Fine, Bal! Give them it hot!" he would cry, grinning. "Make a firm stand for liberty. Britons never will be slaves." It seemed to us that he could take no aspect of newspaper work quite seriously, and for that very reason the office in Hope Street was a grand training ground for the apprentice in journalism. He let us go our way, provided we stopped short of folly; – and if we seemed to be in danger of being too industrious, Munro would saunter into the room, humming, profess to be astonished and impressed by our absorption in work, and beg us to come out for a coffee.

'I remember he once took a fancy to entertaining a group of us daily to a species of cider which, got up elaborately to look like champagne, Munro insisted was as delicate and brisk as any product of Rheims. It was nothing of the sort, and he knew as much, but humorous pretences of the kind were the breath of life to him. "The bouquet!" he would insist. "Such finesse – a je ne sais quoi..." This joke lasted him fully a month, and then he invented another one. The professional psychologist can perhaps reconcile this sublime contempt for the profession of journalism with the ability to make to journalism as fine a contribution as any man ever made. He could be positively bitter in his expressed opinion of the trade that had absorbed so much of him. "The jawbox," he kept on calling it; and that was not one of his jokes. Perhaps he resented having had to give so much to it that might have gone into serious literature. Perhaps he did not know the true value of his own journalistic creations, Para Handy and the rest. Certainly he behaved in these later years as if the whole newspaper business was a preposterous enterprise, not one that a rational human being should take seriously.

'He could be as wilful as a child in what he wrote, and the man in charge of a gossip-column would look twice at any paragraph handed him by his own Editor; so reckless was he sometimes in his disregard for the solemnities. There would have been some pretty upsets in the social life of Clydeside had Munro always been left to go his own gay, careless way. But he never for a moment resented your suggestion that this or that might be toned down. "Oh, well, maybe you're right," he would say carelessly; then, assuming the accent of Para Handy, "Man, but you young fellows iss terrible tumud nowadays," and he would stroll away, and one would catch a faint echo of "Give me a Little Cosy Corner..." [Neil's favourite song, which he had taken an age to learn note-perfect]

'I am sure Munro was happy among us. He always loved to be with young people – another form of escape from pomposity. Even on his grave fellow directors he could play boyish tricks. One of these centred on a bottle of fine old Madeira that was brought in to a solemn meeting of the Board one Thursday afternoon. It was apparently a Madeira of unique rarity, and its virtues were very gravely discussed by the old gentlemen who controlled our destinies. At the end of the meeting, what was left in the bottle was reverently decanted, and the decanter was left with Munro to keep against the next week's *sederunt*. I think I can now divulge the fact that all the Madeira had disappeared by noon next day, thanks to Munro's hospitality to his staff. He was left then with the certain knowledge that the decanter would have to be produced on the following

Thursday, but he was in no way daunted by the prospect. It was filled up again to the proper level with cheap brown sherry bought by Munro in a grocer's shop – and the great jest was crowned by the fact that the elders in due course tasted it prayerfully and agreed, Munro struggling with the imp of mischief within him, that there is after all nothing like a fine old Madeira.'[7]

In 1920 the supply of newsprint had still not returned to pre–1914 levels: 'Reduced size of newspapers is playing the Dickens with us all at present,' Neil wrote to Pittendrigh Macgillivray in April 1920 from the Langham Hotel on one of the business trips to London he could not evade. That time there was at least a bit of jollity in the prospect of returning to Scotland 'by motor-car with a friend, going slowly'.

The hiring and firing part of being editor was one he especially did not relish. Once Joe Campbell, a friend of Neil's, brought a young woman called Mary Grieve to the office for advice about getting a job on a Glasgow paper. She wrote of the interlude years later: 'English readers may not know the respect and affection which Scotland bestowed on Neil Munro. His novels *John Splendid* and *The New Road* made a much deeper appeal to Scottish hearts than the anglified and somewhat snobbish Pall Mall club atmosphere of John Buchan's novels. Buchan got the respect and admiration due to a boy from the manse who had made himself an important figure in the great world. But Neil Munro was our own man, and his stories were of our own place and people. I stopped thinking about myself and looked in veneration round the oak-panelled room for the great author. I found him at last, rather small, neat and unimportant-looking in a grey sort of way...'

This aptly suggests the sense that Neil – now in his late fifties, besides – felt himself somehow in eclipse, latterly, in his journalistic role. The gist of his advice to Mary Grieve was that journalism was not a career for women: '"A waste of time, my dear. Unless, of course, you were to write the bits about weddings and the ladies' dresses"... Dear Neil Munro, a greater novelist than a prophet...'

Mary Grieve, future editor of the magazine *Woman*, 1940–62, ends this passage in her autobiography, *Millions Made My Story*: 'By one of those odd happenings which, trivial in themselves, bestow a sort of pattern on life, Alison Munro, old Neil's granddaughter, was the newest recruit to the staff of *Woman* when I left the paper.'

In June 1920 Neil went to the Baltic in a ship from Hull, presumably on a journalistic jaunt. He was much intrigued by the Scandinavians who took up all the steerage, emigrants on their first visit home from America. Observing many of the women 'furtively weeping, as if on a second emigration' he concluded that although perhaps their nostalgia was not so persistent as with Scottish emigrants, much of the latters' sentiment 'is based on sheer romantics, if not less worthy considerations'.[8]

An unspecified date in 1920 saw publication of the very last piece of serious fiction completed by Neil, a short story entitled 'The Oldest Air in the World'. It appeared in a miscellany, *The Pipes of War*, edited by Sir Bruce Seton, who intended any profits to go to Scottish military philanthropy. The tale links back intriguingly to *The Lost Pibroch*, Neil's very first book, and brings to mind a sentence from one of that book's tales – 'The beginnings of things are to be well considered – we have all a little of that art; but to end well and wisely is the gift of few.' Though 'The Oldest Air in the World' has a post–1918 setting, the manner is the same as that of *The Lost Pibroch*, the plot, slight as it is, even has to do with piping.[9]

Towards the end of 1920 C.M. Grieve – the future Hugh MacDiarmid, no relation of Mary Grieve – published his first volume of *Northern Numbers*, a selection of contemporary Scottish poetry chosen by the poets themselves, and dedicated 'with affection and pride' to Neil Munro. Grieve, then 28, included some of his own poems. In his foreword he explained 'for the most part the contributors... are close personal friends, and... this is rather an experiment in group publication than an anthology'.

Northern Numbers was reviewed in the *News* in the 'Views & Reviews' of 23 December. The writer opines that five of the eleven poets – John Buchan, Violet Jacob, Joseph Lee and T.S. Cairncross – 'have contributed verses of genuine distinction... Finally – and unmistakably – the truest poetry in *Northern Numbers* has come from the pen of him to whom the collection is dedicated. Mr Munro contributes five poems, brief, sombre, and moving... They have unique atmospheric quality; they "tell" – inevitably, as it were: and though they are so distinctively "Highland" in inspiration, they are, at the same time, the truest possible expression of the Scottish spirit.'

The reviewer, ominously, did not include C.M. Grieve in his short-list but took exception to a passage in Grieve's foreword (signed 'C.M.G.') which stated 'If this venture is successful, subsequent volumes... will be published at convenient intervals. No new contributor will, however, be admitted without the approval of the majority of the present group.' Here the reviewer sniffed a rodent odour which he seemed to recognise: 'This, you observe, carries the

"Group" idea still further – and this "Group" business is precisely what I do not like about *Northern Numbers*. Indeed I find it difficult to believe that there is any such Group at all. That two of the foremost Scottish litterateurs of the day should be associated with a number of young poets of, at least, questionable promise is a state of affairs my imagination is incapable of conceiving. I cannot help regarding this "Foreword" as misleading, unconsciously misleading, but still phrased in such a way as to create a wrong impression in the mind of the non-professional reader, who may be led to believe that Messrs Munro and Buchan are members of an ambitious coterie. My point is, that Messrs Munro and Buchan should not be graded quite as low.

'But that by the way. The chief argument against a poetry Group is that it imposes limitations to which no free artist will ever submit. Just so is *Northern Numbers* imperfect. It includes Munro and Buchan – it excludes Charles Murray. The "Foreword" gives a sort of reason for omissions of this kind – "that for the most part the contributors…are close personal friends". C.M.G. will have to find a better reason for the absence from his pages of the verses of the most distinguished Scottish poet of the day.'

Who wrote this unsigned piece in 'Views & Reviews'? I am pretty certain it did not come from Neil's pen. I cannot think that he would have written of his own poems in those terms, and I also find that the style is not just his. Of course the column was unsigned, and it is far too late to find out who did write it. It might have been George Blake, or Robert MacLennan. But undoubtedly much of it reflects Neil's views, in particular about poetry groups, and as Editor of the *News* the ultimate responsibility was his.

On the day the review appeared, Neil wrote a Christmas letter to Lady Weir. It can safely be left to round off 1920.

'I am, for ordinary, a very grumpy person when I get up in the morning, but this morning I awoke with a silly old song in my head, and scandalised my wife by singing *before breakfast* (a bad omen as you know).

Down from their mountains in their squadrons & platoons,
Came five-and-twenty fighting men & a couple of stout
gossoons –

'I've been marching about to that chorus all day, and on reflecting why it should have surged up out of the past wherein it has been so long buried, I realise it is because your Christmas card was about the

234

last thing I saw last night! And now "Slattery's Light Dragoons" begins to alternate in my humming with "The Lum Hat Wantin' a Croon", "The Pawky Duke", and the luscious "dying fall" of "Jock McGraw". I don't suppose you sing them now... Well I don't care – I loved Slattery, and have had quite a jolly revival of old emotions today over the head of him... Well, all this is just by way of a Christmas card, guaranteed hand-done. I hope you and Lord Weir and all your household are well – it is so with us at Cromalt...'

CHAPTER THIRTY-EIGHT

Inveraray is as gorgeous as ever

IT was in March 1921 that Neil, so rarely self-revelatory, alluded for once to less happy aspects of his own early life. He had been reading a book called *An Ulster Childhood* by his Irish friend Leslie Montgomery ('Lynn Doyle', 1873–1961) and was now writing a letter of thanks. 'I've tonight finished the little book, having read every word of it with interest and appreciation. It's the more pleasant to me because it's of your boyhood, and because for you that seems to have been a jolly good time, even if it be an illusion of retrospect. I fancy I shall never write the story of my own childhood, though there were tragic and pathetic elements in it which would make a dozen novels of the grimy sort in vogue. I sought escape from them in the imagination, for so long, and so ardently, that I couldn't help becoming a romancer in the end.'[1]

This tiny outburst in throwaway style is clearly a response, written on impulse for one sympathetic ear. Montgomery rightly did not throw the letter into his waste-paper basket and so was able to send it over to Scotland when, after its writer's death, there was an aborted idea of publishing a volume of Neil's correspondence. Neil might also have said that he found refuge in humour, surely true. But then, humour and romance make strange bedfellows.

He was seriously ill for the first time in his life that June, 'a bad chill to the loins, with agonising complications of my whole

235

abdominal economy'.[2] He had to stay in bed for twelve days. If this was, as he claimed, his first serious illness, he must have considered the incapacity he had suffered in 1917 to be purely psychological. On his recovery he sent a wedding present to George Blackwood – 'a Barograph which, having no delusive legends of "Storm", "Set Fair" etc. as in a barometer, is, I always fancy, the most discreet form of weather-glass for a newly married couple!'[3]

Cromalt continued to be a full and busy household, though Lala was absent 'housewifing in a Hospital in Arbroath in – apparently – interludes between dances and dinners'.[4] Lala was able to go to Inveraray with Effie, Moira and Bud in September. Moira wrote back to 'Dearest wee Magee' [Maggie]: 'We are having a ripping time and Inveraray is as gorgeous as ever. Yesterday Bud, Effie, Alan, Tom [the Davidson brothers, distant cousins] and I went over to St Catherine's in the Ferry and motored back round the head of the Loch in McDonald's car. Lala didn't come as she wasn't feeling up to the mark and had to lie down. It was simply great and we laughed and talked until we were tired! At night the boys came in and we played games and had supper together. Alan and Tom are awfully jealous because George [Blake] is coming and say they'll go to St Catherines Hotel to get out of the way!...We have been bathing a lot and it's great but awfully cold to get in at first... Everyone is so pleased that Father and the others are coming down...'[5]

In another letter to Maggie, Moira wrote: 'I expect you and Tess [her mother] are still working as hard as ever in spite of the fact that we aren't there to cause work!' The letter consists largely of Inveraray gossip and ends: 'This is just for the eyes of you and Tess!' Neil junior was either at Cromalt, causing work, or in digs in Glasgow, and apparently hard up, as he sent a typed notice to 'The Misses Munro' at Inveraray -

Preliminary Announcement
of
SALE
to be held in the rooms of Mr N. Munro Jr. at Cromalt,
Helensburgh, early in the first week of October 1921.
Articles in the sale include:-
Books in general lit.,
Pictures... [and so on]

One glimpse of a surgical operation in progress had made Neil give up medicine and try the arts faculty instead. He had two very hard acts to follow in his brother Hugh and his father, and into the bargain he resembled his father amazingly both in looks and temperament, forby being his namesake. In the end he decided to follow him into journalism.

On 8 November Neil senior met W.B. Yeats. 'I was asked by Raeburn Middleton, a Glasgow artist, who said he was a cousin of Yeats, to dine with him and the poet (on a lecturing tour in Glasgow) at the Art Club at night. I declined to spend the night in town & was then asked to come to Middleton's studio in West Regent Street at 4 o'clock, when Yeats would be present. I went, & found in the studio Professor Magnus Maclean & three ladies, one of them the very young new Mrs Middleton. Soon after Yeats joined us. (I had met him for a moment years ago when he came here with the Irish Players.) Physically he looked very fit, and contrary to the usual account of him he proved quite unaffected, speaking freely, but not in any mandarin fashion & apparently as ready to be a listener as a talker. He had a slight Irish accent, but not exactly a "brogue" as Strang [the artist William Strang] gave me to understand... He wore big horn-rimmed eye-glasses (bi-focal), but seemed far from getting as blind as Strang predicted. His attire was a conventional lounge suit of brown, & he wore a green knitted necktie. At first he did not know who I was, but a little later identified me as the author of *John Splendid* & *The Lost Pibroch*, both of which he seemed to have read.

'The Middleton woman turned out to be one he had known as a girl visitor to Sligo when he was a boy, & she reminded him that he had taken her & her sister on that occasion on a butterfly hunt. He recalled to her many places in the neighbourhood of the place he had met her in, including some ruin he called "Shanwalla!" (sean bhalla) regarding which he narrated quite seriously that he had once, with some others, seen mysterious bright lights hovering over it at night. Apparently he believes, or professes to believe in fairies.

'We got on to talk of "Fiona Macleod". He knew Wm Sharp & his wife well, & was amusingly ironical in his references to Sharp's so-called "double personality". Yet there seemed to be a desire to regard sympathetically Sharp's mystic inspiration by this phantom being "he was in love with". Sharp had apparently written to him (as he did to me) in the role of "Fiona", "who was always going to call, but putting it off". On one occasion, he said, he saw Sharp (ordinarily a very sober man) get drunk, & explain it as a result of his remorse at his infidelity to "Fiona"! Mrs Sharp gallantly kept up the "Fiona" mystification. On one occasion Sharp brought to Meredith a very beautiful young lady & identified her as "Fiona Macleod".

Meredith talked most respectfully to her of the Celtic muses &c and was most indignant when it came out that there never was an earthly "Fiona".

'Yeats had come into the studio when it was dusk, & Middleton at once lit the gas, which the poet approved of, as he said he was like his father, & could not talk in the dark. "It's like speaking into a telephone," he said...

'Speaking of the Dalriadic invasions of Argyll, which I had said struck me as effected curiously without any fighting on the part of the natives, he said it would be just a colonisation on the same lines as we colonised America – a suggestion that Ireland at the time was in civilisation as far ahead of Caledonia, as England was of Red Indian America.'[6]

Earlier that day Neil had written to ask George Blackwood if he had 'any use for a third volume of adventures of the Vital Spark under some such title as *Hurricane Jack*'. Blackwood replied by return, delighted that the book, being a reprint, was 'practically ready'. He proposed a selling price of two shillings, royalites to be '10% on the published price, 13 copies being accounted as 12'. Yet again he enquired after Neil's progress with the novel and poems.

Not long before Christmas came the announcement of Effie's engagement to Jack Bruce, who worked in Glasgow in the firm of his father, a shipowner. I have it on the best authority that Jack, who lived in Helensburgh, had first set eyes on Effie in the street – 'I did but see her passing by, but I shall love her till I die,' he used to say, truthfully. How he then managed to make her acquaintance I know not. At Larchfield School in Helensburgh he had been a contemporary of the actor Jack Buchanan and John Logie Baird, pioneer of television. Jack Bruce had been in the army during the war, and was about the same age as Effie, whose 32nd birthday fell that December.

It seems Neil had now given up spending Hogmanay at Inveraray. He saw in the New Year of 1922 at Cromalt. As he wrote to his old friend John Macmaster Campbell: 'The weather is too boisterous for the "Rest" journey, and anyhow I find the old place too melancholy at this season, with so many old friends gone, with nothing flourishing there save MacCailein's private chapel with its costly new chime of bells.' He meant All Saints, the Scottish Episcopal church in the avenue, built in 1886, and the bell tower next it which the 10th Duke was erecting as a war memorial to all Campbells fallen in the recent war. A peal of ten bells, cast in Loughborough, had been brought to Inveraray in 1921 and was kept in a wooden hut till it was hung ten years later. In his New Year letter to Macmaster Campbell, Neil also mentioned some article about the current revival of Irish Gaelic, which led him into a rather revealing sentence: 'It will be the moral and spiritual salvation of the country; both Scotland and Ireland are being not only provincialised but vulgarised and degraded by English influences of which the Press is perhaps the most vicious.' His long experience – forty years of journalism, the last four as an Editor – would suggest this judgment was percipient rather than jaundiced, and certainly not just attributable to personal feelings anent the 'jawbox'. The *News* was still an independent paper, unusual in that it had no connexion with a morning paper. But the big London-based newspaper syndicates were looming up like thunder clouds to the south: the Rothermere group had even started a Scottish morning paper, the *Record*.

That February Neil had to work extra hard at the *News*, as half the staff was 'laid up'. As a result, by April he was recognisably 'run down', enough so to be persuaded to spend a month away from work, on a ship owned by his prospective son-in-law's family. Jack's father 'Pa Bruce' accompanied him on the voyage. On 2 May Neil sent Moira a postcard from Rome (Hotel Continental): 'Have just been at the Colosseum... and since lunch have walked as far as from Cromalt to Row [Rhu].' On the 30th he wrote to Alice Weir: 'I have just returned from a month's cruise in the Mediterranean – in a fruit ship; am still redolent of oranges, so brown my children laugh at me, and, generally speaking, Robust to a Degree! Have you heard that Effie is getting married: the other daring adventurer is a neighbour of ours here – Jack Bruce... (Shipping; Mediterranean trade; – which accounts for my trip in the fruit-boat); everybody's very pleased about it, more particularly as after her marriage at the end of September, she takes up house in Helensburgh, not far from us...' The voyage on the fruit boat prompted an article that George Blake would select for the book *The Looker-On*. In it Neil describes as 'very fine and unforgettable the shores of the Mediterranean, but orange groves and prickly pears, stone-pines and olive-trees less frequently uplift the spirit to the key of spring than Rosneath in a brisk sou'-wester, all emerald with May.'

Shortly before this cruise, Neil had signed an agreement with the producer Kenelm Foss granting rights 'to produce cinematograph films illustrative of... *The New Road*', but in the end this project would come to nothing.

Having been off work for so long, Neil did not go down to Inveraray that summer and was thus spared from witnessing the erection of the war memorial (as distinct from the Campbells' bell tower). By one of those odd conjunctions that affect our lives, the memorial was to be unveiled by the Duke on 20 August, a month before Effie's wedding. Hugh's name is among the list of the dead. The dignified and realistic full-length figure of a Highland soldier standing at ease was designed by Kellock Brown, who had sculpted a bust of Neil in 1898. It is more than likely that Neil had a hand in Brown's being given the commission and also in the choice of subject, so very far from the 'trumpery Iona cross or tasty bit of monumental sculptor's art' he had deprecated to Pittendrigh Macgillivray in 1918. The memorial is very well placed, at the edge of the loch, on the Cross Green, and facing the entrance to the Avenue. Donald Mackechnie in his booklet *The Inveraray of Neil Munro* (c.1985) wrote that Neil 'felt the occasion too poignantly personal for him to take part in the ceremony. His friend, Sir Donald MacAllister, the famous principal of Glasgow University, spoke on his behalf and on behalf of the relatives of "the Young, Loved, Lamented".'

On 21 September Neil reported himself 'only now able to get out for a little daily after two or three weeks in bed'.[7] The nature of his incapacity is not known, but I am pretty sure that thoughts of Hugh and of the finality of Effie's impending departure from the household had something to do with it.

Effie Munro and Jack Bruce were married at Cromalt towards the end of September and then set off an a protracted honeymoon. On 1 November her father wrote to Kate Turner in Lincoln to thank her for a wedding present to the absent Effie: 'At the moment she is somewhere in Italy, or in Sicily, and unless the Fascisti arrest her and Jack Bruce, we expect them back about the middle of next month... It's an age since I saw you last. Me, you must now figure as a staid old buffer with grey locks... All the three "surviving"girls are at home at present – Lilian who has been a cook for some years, and was till recently at King's College Hospital, Denmark Hill – a devil of a job for a fragile little chip of a thing such as she is – is now "resting". Neil, who is determined on journalism, and I think has some of the qualities necessary for that abominable profession, is now being coached in the same by me...'

CHAPTER THIRTY-NINE

A soul imprisoned!

EARLY in 1923, Neil received a letter from the Duke of Argyll, written at Inveraray Castle. The two of them seem to have been delving into early records of the Macnorovichs, from whom the Lochfyneside Munros are held to descend. The Duke listed five Macnorovichs from Glen Aray whose names he had found in a 1677 'Roll of those appointed to go on the 9th Earls Hosting to Toppirmorrie in Mull'. But the only name from Carnus, which Neil believed to be the early home of our branch of Munros, was Findlay McNabb. The Duke ended his letter: 'I am very glad to have discovered your lair in Glasgow.'[1]

In March there began a flurry of correspondence between Neil and George Blackwood. Three of Neil's books were due to be reprinted, and Blackwood proposed to use the opportunity to start a new uniform edition, reviving the 3/6 format but in a green cover. He added forlornly: 'I am always hoping – indeed as you know have been hoping for several years – for a new story from you, or even word of "Bagpipe Ballads", but nothing matures.'[2] Neil's response casts a pinpoint of light on his situation as he saw it, or at any rate as he wished his correspondent to see it:

'I am very glad you are reprinting these books. For a year or two back I have been pestered on all hands by people who could not get copies anywhere, and the personal recriminations of the Glasgow booksellers on this point have, honestly, driven me from going into their shops! I had seriously begun to think you were turning me down and consigning me to your mortuary, which seemed to me the more distressing since two or three Glasgow booksellers have been assuring me they could, between them, sell an expensive limited edition of said works – a project not unworthy of your attention.

'You don't mention which three books you are reprinting. I fancy more than three are out of print. I have a novel (provisionally entitled *The Search*) blocked out and partly written which should suit you to a T, and every time I read *Maga* I lament that it is not ready for you. At the same time I am brimful of "Bagpipe Ballad" stuff, and [illegible] a noble volume to knock all other Scottish bards since Burns out of time! The cursed thing is that editing a daily paper

241

makes any consistent and steady preoccupation with Literature impossible.

'Strictly between ourselves, I took on this editing job with the impression that it would be of brief duration, and it has lasted longer than I expected or desired. There has always been, in the past two or three years, an agreeable prospect of my being able to quit the newspaper with a little capital which would render me independent of all journalism for the rest of my days. A few months ago the thing seemed settled, and I rejoiced at the immediate prospect of getting out of the "jawbox" of journalism and back to a vastly more agreeable job for you. But the change is postponed for the moment, though I have every reason to hope it may take place this summer. The prayers of the congregation are earnestly requested for the relief of a soul imprisoned!'[3]

Naturally Blackwood was delighted with this news, and he wrote back that the idea of a limited edition was 'a project well worthy of attention... and I shall not lose sight of it... Never again doubt our loyalty to you. Nothing short of the impossibility of keeping reprints going during War time would have led to your books being o.p.' But the limited edition never took shape.

Learning in March that Joseph Conrad was soon to pass through Glasgow on his way to America, Neil alluded covertly to their joint pebble-tossing exploit 25 years before in an Erchie story about the removal of Gladstone's statue. Erchie says: 'The only yin [statue] in George Square that attracts attention noo is Mr Oswald wi' the lum hat, for it has never occurred to anybody to put a lid on the had to keep the boys frae pappin' stones in't.'

On 20 April Neil met Conrad for the second and last time: 'Conrad came to Glasgow (St Enoch Station) in the evening; put up at the St. E. Hotel, and left next day for New York by Anchor Line *Tuscania* (captain David W. Bone). With John Bone [brother] I awaited his arrival on the platform, and we werre photographed by *Bulletin* [newspaper]. Richard Curle came from London with J.C.

'I found Conrad greatly aged since I saw him last in 1898... by speech obviously foreign in a way not apparent at that time. Grasps your hand in both of his; says "my dear" frequently. He knew me at once on the platform. We dined with him in a private room in St. E. His visit to Glasgow in 1898 was, he tells me, the first he ever made. He had been back here only once since – for two days during the war, interested in some cruisers. Also [saw] Lithgow, Port Glasgow, who had been commander of a battery in which was his (J.C.'s) son Boris... Suffers from gout. Took hardly anything at dinner – morsels of food and spoonfuls of sherry. We had champagne, but he drank Perrier...'[4]

A third Bone brother, the artist Muirhead, accompanied Conrad to America. Conrad stayed with his publisher Doubleday on Long Island. There – a tiny eddy in the cross-currents of literature – Scott Fitzgerald and Ring Lardner danced tipsily *al fresco* as an act of homage, but were ejected without Conrad seeing them.

In May Neil suggested to Blackwood the idea of re-printing the tales in *Ayrshire Idylls* (1912), this time sans George Houston's illustrations. Blackwood took this up and bought from A. & C. Black, who had paid Neil 'a sum down for the job', the right to re-print the tales as part of their uniform edition of Munro, making it up to ten volumes. The right cost £50, which Blackwood set down as an advance to Neil. He had *Ayrshire Idylls* printed using 'a very blown-out page', to bulk it out.

Blackwood also wrote that there had been enquiries about including the Hugh Foulis books in the uniform edition, but added: 'I do not know that this is really feasible. Some of the books would be very thin for a 3/6 issue, and then we should have to give your name to them.'[5] Neil agreed it was not a feasibility yet. But there was now more Para Handy: 'I have never sent you, by the way, the Hurricane Jack series by Foulis which I wrote to you about last year. May I do so soon?'[6] Blackwood immediately welcomed this addition to the series and Neil produced the artist for the jacket – W. Douglas MacLeod, Hugh's schoolfriend.

An article on 'The Novels of Neil Munro' by J.F. George, in *The Bailie* of May 9, betrays partial inside knowledge of Neil's situation: 'It has been asserted with truth, I believe, that no really great novel of Glasgow life and character – a novel on something like the scale of *Vanity Fair* – has yet been written. Munro, in collaboration with Foulis, is the man to write it. Will he? Possibly not. A busy working journalist, even if only middle-aged, is always a sad and weary man by evening.'

The fact of the matter was that Neil would be sixty in a few weeks' time.

That July saw the death of another old acquaintance, Lady Archibald Campbell, the Duke's mother. Neil wrote a letter of condolence to which the Duke replied: 'My dear Dr Munro, I am greatly touched at your kind message of sympathy to me and my sister in our Mother's passing from what had long become for her a Land of Dreams and Shadows... her death is a severing of very old links in the History of my Clan, on whose lands you *Mac an roichs*

[sic] have dwelt for so many generations in affectionate intercourse and loyalty...'[7]

For three weeks of August Neil was 'meandering all over the West Highlands' (surely not on matters unpiscatorial) and thus had to apologise to George Blackwood for the late return of proofs of *Hurricane Jack of the Vital Spark*, which was published in the autumn.

In October came an invitation from Lady Weir, which Neil declined: 'Fancy you trying to tempt two douce old buddies to a masquerade ball! Something might be done for us in the roles of Dr Samuel Johnson and Mrs Thrale (except that I'm not yet fat enough), but I should certainly want to dance, and as I can't, in public, dance anything more recent than "La Va", the Guaracha Waltz & Circassian Circle, Petronella, and The Nut, it's out of the question. We had arranged that Neil and one of his sisters should go, but it seems a Tennis Club dance they were booked for is on the same evening.'[8]

The only record of the closing days of 1923 is an enigmatic letter from Neil to Archibald MacIntyre, farmer at Drimlee in Glen Shira: 'I am much obliged to you for the trouble you took in sending the young tup to me here. It arrived all right on Wednesday evening. I enclose £1 note, with all good wishes...'[9]

Neil had been editor of the *News* for far longer than he wished and was determined to make 1924 the year he gave the job up. Characteristically, he let word of his resignation from the post filter through to George Blackwood in a roundabout way. During the early months of 1924 he wrote more than once to Blackwood on minor publishing matters without mentioning that the longed-for deliverance was to be at the beginning of April.

In late March, with a party of twenty or so other journalists (including Seton Gordon), Neil went to Lochboisdale in South Uist in a Canadian Pacific liner, the 'Marloch', to report the embarkation of 300 Hebridean emigrants, nearly all being Roman Catholics. In his subsequent article he took a realistic rather than a sentimental view: ''Tis Uist that should grieve, losing those who love her! For a thousand years a race who will take a hillock or a stream to their bosom like a sweetheart, spent their dreams, their inarticulate passions, on this Uist of the sheldrakes, and all they every got from her was a passing smile. They asked but for bread, and she gave them stone and water. So good luck to Red Deer and Alberta! I know them. Forty bushels to the acre. A good frame house with a pianola. Free fishing in the creek, and no gamekeeper for the prairie chicken...'[10]

When April came, Neil's old colleague Robert MacLennan – who had once posed as Erchie for photographs – took over the editorial chair. Soon after that, Neil was down in London. On 26 April Blackwood wrote: 'I have just heard from my brother of his happy meeting with you in a London Pot-House of ancient fame. He reports that you told him you had now given up your onerous editorial duties... I hope you enjoyed your experience at Wembley...'

Neil took three weeks to reply: 'Your brother James didn't tell you, I fancy, that for a little I failed to identify him and Lobban when I met them in the Fleet Street pot-house... Rather a shock, not to know your own publisher! But it's so long since I saw James last (and it must be twenty years since I saw Lobban) that there was some excuse for my failing at first to recognise in those two settled-down men of affairs the sparks of yore! I have ever had the illusion, in spite of my grey hair, that I and my contemporaries are mere youths yet.

'Some months ago I told Sillars of Arran to tell you I was resigning the *News* editorship. – The property changed hands – mainly through my engineering – and is now controlled by Lord Weir's step-bother Richmond. I took the opportunity, long anticipated, of relinquishing a job I never had much inclination for, and am now content to be a contributor, and a Director on the Board... now that I feel my own master again I hope before long to show you I have still some imagination and invention left. A few left-over mechanic tasks will occupy me for the next two months, after that I shall plunge into a new adventure of Ninian Campbell's which was begun a good while ago, and had to be suspended for sheer lack of time just when I had convinced myself it was going to be a jolly good yarn and was getting the greatest of pleasure out of its construction. And there *are* some more "Bagpipe Ballads" in existence, though I want to hold on to them till I can get enough to make a second series.'[11]

Blackwood replied at once: 'I shall look forward to packets of MSS pouring in from you in due time... your 3/6d series... has done remarkably well in Scotland. Somehow or other the Sassunach is not so appreciative as he ought to be.'

Towards the end of Neil's editorship of the *News* he had a curious visitor: 'In the early part of this summer a youngish man with a startling resemblance to R.L.S. came into my room at the *News* office with a suggestion that he should write special articles for the paper. I identified him at once as the Robert Stevenson who, according to the Scottish newspapers, was described as a "cousin of R.L.S. newly come from California". We had indeed, the same day, a short interview with him by one of our reporters in which he black-guarded the Americans and their ideals heartily.

'The young man spoke with me for about 10 or 15 minutes. He had an east coast of Scotland accent, gave out vaguely that he was a painter and writer. A gentle sort of soul; I formed the opinion he was a little "soft".

'"You're astonishingly like R.L.S.," I said to him. "You are his cousin, aren't you?" He replied that he was & then hurriedly said something about certain sordid elements in the situation & changed the subject. Later on Ralston in our office told me the young man had been in his room too, & in reply to Ralston's expression of surprise at his likeness to R.L.S. had said: "I may well be like him, for he was my father." To Ralston, in proof of his claim, he showed personal correspondence with the Osbornes, in which he was addressed as "Dear Bob".

'Some months after, a film picture with R.L.S. scenes & woodcuts [? – word not legible] was produced in Edinburgh under the auspices of Councillor MacLaren an old acquaintance of R.L.S. and it was boldly given out that "a son of R.L.S." was in the cast. This was Robert Stevenson... the son of a Margaret Stevenson and born at Alva in 1879. In J.A. Steuart's Life of R.L.S. (1924) he mentions Margaret Stevenson as one of three Edinburgh women Stevenson knew intimately, but says nothing about Robert Stevenson though I know he knew about him.'[12]

There is nothing here as to whether or not anything by Robert Stevenson ever appeared in the *News* – it seems highly unlikely.

The delicious sense of release Neil experienced on relinquishing the *News* to Robert MacLennan was short-lived. As he explained to George Blackwood: 'I plunged into *The Search* (tentative title) with much eagerness, and found myself getting on with much satisfaction to myself. I had, however, only three weeks of it when my successor took Sleeping Sickness, and I had to go back to the office and take up the tiller again.'[13]

MacLennan was not able to return to work for five months, but despite this Neil still carried out a plan which he had, I feel sure, long been cherishing. With Jessie, Lala, Moira, Neil junior and Bud, he set out for France that June. He had not returned to Hugh's grave since 1917, and Jessie, who like the rest of the family had never been there, must have been wearying to go. On Thursday 19th Neil sent Maggie a postcard from Paris saying that they were leaving for Amiens, en route for Millencourt, the next morning at 8.45.

An unsmiling photograph of the family standing round the grave, apparently taken by Neil senior, is the only record of that time. Neil had chosen two lines from Walter Scott's 'Coronach' to be put on Hugh's gravestone –

He is gone on the mountain,
He is lost to the forest

The Munros returned to London the very next day to be greeted by the heaven-sent news that Effie had given birth two days previously to a daughter – Jessie and Neil's first grandchild. She was christened Margaret Moira, but always known as 'Moira'. The baby had arrived early, to judge by a letter one of her new aunts wrote to Maggie from the Charing Cross Hotel:

'Magee, darling old thing, I'm sure you'll be thinking I'm a fine one for not writing to you before this... We are all as bucked as can be about Effie & Jack's wean. It is really too great for words! Poor Tess is simply stunned at it arriving during her absence!...I hope you are getting along happily and not forgetting your weans. Poor old Dougie will be missing us, I should think. He'll knock us all over when we get back! We've got a great deal to tell you. All about Hugh's grave and a great deal more. Best love old dear, Moira.'[14]

Neil junior was now working as a journalist on the *News*. He was in the office late on the evening of 3 August, a Sunday, when word that Joseph Conrad had just died came over the wire. Neil telephoned his father to tell him of this. When he got back to Cromalt next day he was astonished to find how dejected his father was by the news.

A few weeks later, Robert MacLennan returned to the editorial chair, and Neil senior wrote to George Blackwood: 'Once more I am on the trail with Ninian Campbell. I have every confidence that I can finish with him in four or five months.'[15] Blackwood was sanguine enough to think he could start serialising the new novel in January's *Maga* – but the end of the year came without another word from Neil.

CHAPTER FORTY

Startles me like a hare

IN the first week of 1925, Neil received a long letter from Macaulay Stevenson the artist, who lived in Montreuil-sur-Mer. Most of the letter is a tirade about the present state of art: 'Artistically now, Paris is all to the devil... I am never more proud of my own dear people than when I go to Paris to look for art. I bless my own dear countrymen's clean puritanism – puritan, yet romantic...' The letter ends splendidly: 'Art is long – too long to go on with any more for it is just on post-time. Bless you, my dear dear old friend – Bless you and yours – And tell the boys in *The News* that my heart warms to them every time I take up the dear old paper. Wish them all, from Jack Richmond right round, A Happy New Year, from Old Friend R. Macaulay Stevenson.'[1]

The said Richmond's brief tenure as owner of the *News* was even then drawing to an early close. By April it was bruited abroad that both the *News* and the *Daily Record* (which was part of the Rothermere syndicate) were being sold to the Allied Newspapers Syndicate of Messrs Berry. As a director Neil inevitably got caught up in the upheaval. This may in part excuse his lack of progress with *The Search*. Despite the good start, he would not mention the novel again to Blackwood for nearly a year.

At the start of April Neil had further contact with the mysterious Robert Stevenson, who wrote to him from digs in Edinburgh at 52 Chesser Grove: 'Well my dear friend, at the present moment I'm really stuck in the mud... I told [my landlady] today if nothing turned up, she could look after my few belongings and I would take to the road...' This thinly disguised appeal for funds seems to have elicited a typically generous response from Neil, for a week later Robert wrote again to thank him for his 'very kind letter. I really couldn't suppress the tears. – it was indeed a heaven sent ray of sunshine... I never even dreamt that anyone would think a poor straggler like me worth helping...'[2]

Later that month Robert made a trip to Glasgow and called in at the *News* office, only to find Neil was not there. So he wrote to him again: 'I promised to return & see your son, but the friend I had with me was seemingly too tired & in the multiplicity of Glasgow streets, lost our bearings... I regret I haven't got any writing done to send you...'

At this time Neil had a letter from Edinburgh from his friend Donald A. Mackenzie, the poet and folklorist, who had taken an interest in Robert Stevenson's wellbeing and was convinced he was the son of R.L.S. (Eventually his claims were investigated by the Robert Louis Stevenson Club which concluded they were false. On a different tack Mackenzie, who had contributed poems to C.M. Grieve's first *Northern Numbers,* lamented to Neil: 'I'm not printed now-a-days... I can't "jazz" apparently. Even the *Glasgow Herald* returned my stuff. And they print rubbish by H. McDiarmid (who is that cad Grieve) about

"The worms will soon be chowing
"Anither braw man"

Mackenzie underlined 'chowing' and added '(?with teeth)'.[3]

Dr John MacIntyre – the playwright 'John Brandane' – wrote also that April, asking Neil for 'a word of encouragement to the Scottish National Theatre Society, which we might publish in our programmes'.[4] Neil replied, revealingly: 'All my best wishes are with the National Theatre Society. I confess I was a little pessimistic about it at the start, as the result of our experience with the Repertory Theatre, as I generally am in the case of any National Scottish movement that is not obviously going to interest the Income Tax Commissioner right away. Unless I see the Monied Interest crowding up in their Ford Sedans to get in before allotment I am apt to withdraw into my native Celtic Gloom and – strictly to myself – predict an imminent epidemic of cold feet. But the S.N.T.S. has done marvellously well; there seems no reason why, on the lines you are going on, it should not be more permanent than St Enoch's Kirk [demolished that year]. It has discovered to the playgoing public of Glasgow a sense of Scottish drama that is not written merely for the delectation of the Englishman – I mean something different from the galloshans vein of "Rob Roy" or the pawky sneevle of "Jane of the Jawbox, a Comedy of the Tenements". I wish now it would break out on a new plane; neither romantic-historical in your line and my line, nor "Glasgowish" & peasant, but exploiting a loftier kind of social life, if only to prove that we had and have some kind of nobocracy in Scotland. I see, for instance, exquisite comedy suggestions in old County families of, say, sixty years ago when that caste had still really racial characteristics and was intellectually by no means to be despised – far from it.

'For God's sake don't ask me for a "message" to anybody; a suggestion like that with its implication that I am a grave and reverend seigneur whose "messages" are expected to do good to anybody startles me like a hare and paralyses my pen. But if any few lines in this personal note to yourself look to you like something you want, well use 'em, but don't let me know!'[5]

In May *The Scottish Educational Journal* began publishing a series of essays by C.M. Grieve (Hugh MacDiarmid) on contemporary Scottish authors (these appeared as the book *Contemporary Scottish Studies*, First Series, the following year, and were re-printed as late as 1995). Having sand-blasted John Buchan and J.M. Barrie, MacDiarmid turned his attention to Neil Munro in the issue of 3 July.

In it Neil was arraigned as 'not a great writer… not even a *good* writer… His persistence in remaining a journalist instead of devoting himself entirely to letters is illuminating. It argues, perhaps, self-criticism of an uncommon penetration… unless it were sheer economic necessity, or an incurable hesitancy to "burn his boats behind him". Inhibitions! That is the fault of all his writing – the inability to let himself go; a defect of temperament, and, perhaps, an infirmity of will… His reticence, a certain high, if narrow integrity, an aversion to log rolling, to being classed with any school, and so forth – qualities not without their value in contemporary letters, and which must certainly be acknowledged here – are, after all, comparatively unessential matters when a "house is divided against itself and cannot stand".

'Neil Munro is the lost leader of Scottish Nationalism. He has chosen to be without following and without influence. That he has carried off his spiritual unsuccess with a certain air, a melancholy reserve, goes without saying in a Celt, touched as he has been, however ineffectually, to the higher things. He is a promise that has not been kept and while it is not permissible to enquire too closely into just why or where it came to be broken, I may speak perhaps of such a thing as a disabling fear of life, a soul-destroying tyranny of respectability… So I think that unworthy hesitations – whatever their nature, economic, moral, psychological – have made Neil Munro "unequal to himself". All men have spoken well of him. He has preferred the little wars of Lorn to the conflict of real life in which he ought to have engaged. His literature is a literature of escape – and, in so far as it has succeeded in escaping, in being a sort of antithesis of self-expression, a substitute for it, it is without life – for life cannot escape from its destiny…'

250

MacDiarmid poured scorn on George Blake's description of *The Lost Pibroch* as 'short story perfection',[6] protesting: 'That forces some impossible comparisons – with Maupassant, Poe, Chekhov, Bunin, Katherine Mansfield, and several scores of others: but Munro cannot be thought of in comparison with any of these: he must – to do justice to him – be compared (to his great advantage) with Ian MacLaren, Barrie, Galt (and I still think to his advantage but slightly) with Stevenson, Fiona MacLeod, and even Cunninghame Graham, though he is an inferior stylist to either of the two last named, and lacks entirely MacLeod's amazing powers of word-painting and of spiritual insight, even if he *is* more faithful to the scenic facts and psychology of his chosen region and types.'

MacDiarmid, however, was prepared to concede: 'Neil Munro's novels and short stories, although even now they have begun to "date" badly, are documents in our literary history. He will be remembered as having been in some ways the greatest of his contemporaries amongst our countrymen: and his books will retain a Scottish – even when they have lost all literary – interest. Nothing that I have said impugns their eminent readability: there are certain elements of the Scottish spirit – certain elements of the Scottish tradition – nowhere else reproduced or nowhere else so well; for the true Scotsman, savouring his heritage, he is indispensable, and for the Scottish literary student at all events he will remain so. I have read and re-read almost all that he has written, and brooded long hours over it. I could write pages of keen appreciation about each of his books. What I have said here would be unconscionably mean and ingrate were my scale forgotten. Let me repeat I am here regarding him from the standpoint of world literature... Neil Munro remains, on the whole, one of the six best short story writers Scotland has yet produced, the others being R.L. Stevenson, 'Fiona MacLeod', John Buchan, R.B. Cunninghame Graham, and (to count them as one) the Misses Findlater.'

Finally, while praising 'John o' Lorn', MacDiarmid dismissed most of Neil's poems, finding that they bore 'a curious vague impression of having been *translated*. Perhaps here we stumble upon a real clue. Had Neil Munro never learned English – and lived quietly in an entirely Gaelic-speaking community – he might have come to his true stature as an artist. Is the cardinal flaw that vitiates all his work, so easy to detect and so difficult to explain, really the product of a species of mental miscegenation?'

Whether or not Neil read any of this, or took it to heart, we will never know, although right away John MacIntyre wrote to him, offering to launch a counter-attack on his behalf. MacIntyre was right to be cautious and seek Neil's permission before sharpening his pen, as the reply he received makes clear. Neil revealed: 'I intended to look out for the *Educational Journal*, having got a circular which indicated that Mr Grieve was to give me his critical attention, but I forgot about it and have not yet seen the paper. That he should find little – or perhaps nothing – to approve of in me or my work is only to be expected... Between what he may have to say of me in the *Educational Journal* and many too laudatory articles on me that have already appeared in that paper, the readers may perhaps get a fair average impression of what I may be worth!...I hope no friends of mine will waste a line on him.'[7]

MacDiarmid had said too much, and said too little – too much that was personal and often ill-founded, too little by way of literary criticism to support his judgments. Neil, an old hand at the criticism himself, was well able to 'take it'.

In November Neil was appointed Literary Editor of Associated Scottish Newspapers Ltd and J.M. Smith Ltd, the new name for the Scottish end of the Berry Syndicate, on a salary of £920 per annum inclusive of director's fees.

During the year the American publishers Doubleday, Page & Co. had published a limited memorial edition of Conrad's works: Neil supplied the introduction to *The Nigger of the 'Narcissus'*. There was, however, still no sign of a new novel of his own, as George Blackwood would remind him at the end of December: 'I should like to hear that the New Year is going to bring me something from the pen of a certain old and valuable contributor... Can you give me a word of definite hope to buck me up for the New Year?'[8]

CHAPTER FORTY-ONE

I miss my Swiss

DESPITE the lack of progress on the novel, Neil's creative talent did not lie fallow. At the start of January 1926 he penned what would be his final Jimmy Swan tale for the *News*, mostly a monologue by the Joy Traveller about the new method of measuring feet by X-ray, now being adopted in shoeshops. Hearing of this device had no doubt reminded Neil of that night when he had stood in front of a Röntgen machine, observed by Joseph Conrad. About this time he completed an article on Conrad for the *Encyclopaedia Britannica* (14th edition, not published till 1929).

There is a mixed tone of forbearance and quiet exasperation in a brief letter from George Blackwood, written on 1 March to enclose a fan letter which had come for Neil to Blackwoods' office. The current *Maga* serial would end in May, said Blackwood, and 'if there is any chance of your taking up the running in June, I shall be happy to keep the opportunity open for you. But you must let me know soon. Perhaps you did not get a letter I wrote a little time ago.'

It took Neil a week to compose his long reply, which gives a clear insight into his relationship with his long-term publisher and the numerous demands on his attention made necessary by having a large family to support:

'Nothing but a bad conscience, and a poltroon's reluctance to face the music, has made me put off, so long, replying to your letter of two months ago. I have a real sense of sin that oppresses me every day, for not having given you, before now, some evidence of my intention to resume the work I ought to be doing – work I really long to be at. Can there be any other writing man with a publisher so patient as you, or any other publisher with such an impractical author? I'm a fool in many respects, but I'm not ungrateful for the evidence that you put some value on our old association – the only one I am now very likely to make with a publisher, and one that I'm always proud and contented to have made.

'The cursed thing about the trade of Journalism is that once you have got deeply immersed in it, it is mighty hard to extricate yourself – and a wife and family – from dependance on its too-easily earned and immediate income. I thought I was practically giving it up for good when I resigned the Editorship of the Glasgow News with the intention of concentrating wholly on fiction and verse, but here I am still shackled with £1000 salary as "Literary Editor" and Director of the Company and condemned yet to hack jobs for which I have no heart; and which up till now have left little opportunity for work I should much prefer to be engaged on. I anticipate a considerable relief from the News work this year, for much of it arises from the amalgamation of the journal with the Berry Syndicate, which hitherto has kept me cruelly close to the grindstone.

'Despite all my present toils of putting so much, every other day, down the "jawbox" (as I call daily journalism), I seize what opportunity I can of indulging my real fancy for fiction and verse, in which alone I am happy. *The Search* proceeds, but too intermittently for me to venture on its serial publication yet, though I have far more completed than you used to have in hand before starting any of my former stories. Once, I could gaily start with no more than three instalments ready, quite confident the remainder would be timeously in the printer's hands, but so many other trivial engagements turn up unexpectedly that now I dare not venture on it. Now and then I manage a "Bagpipe Ballad", but I'd want at least one a week to make sure I could keep it up, and it would be folly to start again without a good supply in hand.

'Another thing (between ourselves) is that last year, very reluctantly, on the pressure of a friend who is a Director of the Royal Bank of Scotland, I undertook to prepare a History of the Bank for private circulation on the occasion of its forthcoming second centenary. I shall not be finished with it for a for a few months yet. It involves a lot of research and reading little to my inclination; and one thing is certain, I shall never be seduced from fiction by history of any kind again.

'There! That's off my chest! Do not lose your divine patience with me. With no more than two undistracted months to myself, I could easily finish the novel. Let me once get out of the present mess I'm in and you'll have, I hope, no further reason to despair of me.'[1]

Blackwood replied by return: 'Very many thanks for your kind letter... I am glad to read into it the hope that there is a chance of something coming from you... I can quite understand what a tie [journalism] must be.'[2]

Writing the Royal Bank history, an arduous and complicated task, took rather longer than 'a few months yet'. Neil went about it very conscientiously, even finding a certain interest and enjoyment in the work. He now had Moira's assistance: using the typing skills acquired at Erskine Hospital, she had taken over as his amanuensis after Effie's defection. At the end of March Neil reported to Sir Alexander Kemp Wright, general manager of the bank: 'In my first draft... I have now got to the stage at which, having cut my way through the very tangled undergrowth of Scots politics at the period and the complications of Darien... I see a fairly clear landscape ahead. Now that I have got pretty well into the operations of the Bank itself and have become familiar with its guiding characters, the job becomes much more interesting: indeed I carry on from day to day just now with as much fervour as if it were a novel I was at! My early training in a lawyer's office has always left me with a great respect for absolute accuracy about business affairs, figures, dates, &c, and I have already discovered that many old published accounts of the Royal Bank's beginnings are wholly misinformed...

'Next month I hope to have finished, in my draft, with the 18th Century. What I have drafted so far has been carefully done, and will require no re-writing except such as involved in the discovery of new cognate material... In all probability I'll find myself at the last with too much draft material, and have to consider a drastic cutting down for the final copy. Before that I shall have to see you, and get some idea of what you lay most stress on in the History – its purely factual and financial details, which an erudite student of the subject might prefer, or narrative which by its most general human and romantic interest and its treatment of *men* and *events* more than dry figures would be more likely to entertain far more readers...'

In June Neil could not resist taking time off from banking history to turn out one more Erchie tale exploiting a promising seam – the link between Erchie's coal merchant friend and the miners' strike, which was still continuing though the rest of the country had gone back to work after eight days of the General Strike. In 'The Coal Crisis – Duffy Explains', Erchie says provokingly 'Ye must be makin' your fortune, Duffy,' at which the coalman exclaims: 'I'm sick o' the whole business and wish I could start a wee green-grocery. I'm only keepin' on this business for the sake o' my horse. What would he do if I was shuttin' up the ree?'

This was the last Erchie story of all. Although Neil had written more than fifty Erchie stories since his 'droll friend' first appeared in book form in 1904, he does not seem ever to have considered putting the remainder out between hard covers – unless he was keeping them up his sleeve for his old age.

That summer Neil had to do without his amanuensis for a few weeks. Towards the end of July, Moira and Bud went off on a walking tour in Switzerland with two friends. May Smith was a friend of Moira's from Greenock Academy days, while Alice Webb, a little older than the other three, was an English nurse whom Lala had got to know at Arbroath: she had some experience of walking in Switzerland. A few of the long letters that Moira and Bud wrote home most days, in pencil, have survived. They followed their father's tradition of writing to members of the family in turn, although all letters would be passed around the breakfast table.

Thus Neil learned (from a letter to Jessie) of Bud meeting a boyfriend in London – 'I had dinner at his digs (I suppose this is rather modern!!!). His landlady had prepared a sumptuous repast...' – and of the girls' ferry crossing to Dieppe and on to Paris. They took the train to Montreux and crossed the Col de Baumes to see their first glacier. 'The walk through the forest of Mignon reminded me of Inveraray – there was a real Cherry Park smell about the pines – but it was real, hard, stiff climbing all the way – & we spoke little – but felt our rucksacks much... You would scarcely recognise us if you did see us – short skirts, sunglasses, spiked boots, stockings rolled over knees, and no hats...'

On 30 July Moira wrote to her mother from Les Contamines, after two nights at Chamonix. They had been to see the Mer de Glace. 'Most people go up on an electric railway but we preferred to walk it. We got a guide to take us across to the other side of the glacier... but we decided afterwards that it wasn't at all necessary to have one. Some of the people were simply terrified and clung on to the guide's arm and slid about... On the way back we lost our way and met two Dutch boys who had done the same thing. They took our rucksack and after a great hunt we found the path again. They were awfully nice boys and walked all the way back with us. Then we all had tea outside a brasserie... '

August found them in Italy, from which Bud's 'Dearest Pop' received a letter: 'We are now resting on the roadside on the St Bernard Pass. A 6000 ft climb in hot Italian weather is rather exhausting. It is well seen that we are getting hardened as we are all lying by the roadside on hard bricks with ants crawling over us... Four Italian roadmen have just been laughing at me smearing cream on my face. My nose is pale petunia now and all skinned...'

At the monastery at St Bernard they stayed in a barrack-like room, from which Bud wrote: 'I wish you could see Moira. She has two of every article of clothing on and still her nose is blue. We can still see the humour of it all. Alice so far is still rather glum. We had to take her boots off and give her a bigger spot of brandy...'

The last surviving letter is from Bud to Lala on 10 August. They had walked to Kandersteg over the Gemmi Pass and were leaving for Bern the next day. 'I can scarcely believe it is time to go home. Sometimes we do not even know the day it is and have great old arguments about it. I am sure you cannot imagine what sights we now are. We all have scarlet noses, dresses stained with sardines, butter and cold cream. We wear sun glasses, have our washings (stockings) hanging out of our rucksacks to dry, & we put cold cream lavishly on our faces – no powder. As for our hair – it is dank, greasy & straight. But to be otherwise out here leading the life would be quite wrong. Everyone looks funnier than the last. I saw one sedate looking, prim Scots spinster (a headmistress I should say) at the top of the Gemmi in knickerbockers, puttees, gaiters, a jumper and a straw hat with roses on it. No one looks beautiful or chic. When I get home I'm going to have a good old burst at a beauty parlor, & wear all my best clothes & I'll really feel the most colossal nib that ever honoured the Burgh of Helen!... Tell Pop that we are going to start making him walk 10 miles a day when we get home. We are stunned by the men and women well over 70 who walk and sclim [climb] like mountain goats out here. (Not insinuating that Pop or Mop are verging on old age.)... We have just heard of one woman who is walking round the British Isles – she started at 60 and is now 72.'

In reading these vivacious letters, so different from Hugh's harrowing accounts of life at the Front a decade ago, Neil must have laughed out loud. He enjoyed his daughters' dispatches so much that he turned them into a 'Looker-On' column, 'I Miss My Swiss – A Letter from the Alps'. ('I Miss My Swiss' was a song title of the day.)

Meanwhile Neil junior sent the girls news from Cromalt in his own comic style: 'Dear Swiss Misses, I have been thrilled to hear of your adventures in the wristlet watch and spaghetti countries. Great stuff that snow and Swiss milk for building up fine big bouncing blondes (whom all gentlemen prefer)...'

After telling his sisters of various steamer trips he had taken to Rothesay, Greenock and Gourock, he concluded with 'Latest News from All Quarters (by private wire, bicycle, aeroplane, and sea)':

Mrs McNiven (Lady Dalry) [facetiously meaning Maggie's aunt] arrived on Tuesday at Cromalt. She is one of the world's greatest fruit pickers.

Dr Munro leaves for Dunderave Castle with Lord Weir and Mr Neville Chamberlain to-morrow (Sunday).

Mr LEE PU (famous contortionist and bone splitter) [Lala's pekingese] has got rid of his nasty cough.

James Bostock [a relation of Alice Webb's], noted man-about-town and Shoe King [Lotus & Delta], arrives at Cromalt from Arran to-night.

Mr Jack Crawford [cousin], ship's officer and Indian rug conooser, called at Cromalt y'day leaving one black feather fan (to be fought for).

This was all enclosed in a letter to the girls from 'Tess' – 'You will have a lot to tell us when you get home. Walking round Arran will be nothing to you now. Love to all, J.M.'

Their father was indeed at Dunderave with the Weirs, and Neville Chamberlain, going on to spend a weekend at Machrie in the Isle of Arran with an old friend, the solicitor Hugh Buchanan. By the end of August he was back at the banking history, and three months later felt within reach of completing the book. Once it had all been typed out and Sir Alexander Wright had read it, Neil proposed going through to Edinburgh to discuss any 'dubious points', portraits, format &c.[3]

That autumn a certain son of Helensburgh by the name of John Logie Baird asked Neil for an introduction to Lord Weir, hoping to inveigle him on to the board of a company to exploit television. Neil wrote first to John Richmond, Weir's half-brother, to sound him, but seems to have received a negative response. The age of technology had, however, reached Helensburgh with the arrival of mains electricity, so the electric plant at Cromalt could be sold.

It was indeed a new world, and Neil expressed his own sense of this in a 'Views & Reviews' column: 'Between that studio world of [Henry James's] in which were no real windows, only roof-lights, and the world as it seems to us to-day, is the abyss of Armageddon.'[4] The old world in which Neil had written his novels was receding into the past.

And so yet another year closed with *The Search* no further forward and the history of the Royal Bank still on the stocks. The only note of finality was struck sadly by the death of James Murray Smith.

CHAPTER FORTY-TWO

No more hack work for me

THE absolute necessity of Neil's income as a director and literary editor of the *News* is illustrated by the size of Blackwoods' cheque for 1926 royalties – just £128. He would of course also be paid for his articles in the *News* and *Record*, and for occasional articles in periodicals such *T.P.'s & Cassell's Weekly* and *John o' London's Weekly*. In the February of 1927, for instance, he turned out a charming *Daily Record* column about the robin which had frequented Cromalt kitchen for several winters, coming in and out through the scullery window and flitting about silently.

There was also the honorarium due for the Royal Bank history, of which he had just three more chapters to complete. But the royalties from Blackwoods were not to be sneezed at, and George Blackwood continued in his attempts to coax a novel from Neil. In a letter accompanying the royalties cheque he reported steady sales of the uniform 3s 6d edition and also quoted from a letter he had received from Stanley Weyman, the historical novelist: 'Your Neil Munro's *New Road* is valued, but it is not valued as it should be. I have read it again and again with increased admiration.' Yet again Blackwood lamented: 'I suppose you are still too busy to get on with the various projects which you had in hand for *Maga*. You know that this is always a source of much regret to me, and the above extract from a very good source shows that there are many others who share my view.'[1]

Neil sent the usual apologetic reply, in which he trusted 'that in a month or two I should be able to get on with Ninian Campbell who has been imploring my attention in vain for two years. The Bank book was a tough job, sir – no more hack work for me... Stanley Weyman's appreciation of *The New Road* I much appreciate. Let me confess to you I was in Edinburgh yesterday by engagement to meet Sir Alexander Wright of the Royal Bank; sneaking past 45 George Street with a guilty conscience, longing to go in and see you if I could have done so; but also afraid of your blameful eye! At the University Club, I met several men who depressed me (and Sir Alexander) by their unanimous agreement that what they wanted from me was not a banking book but a new novel!'[2]

259

The typescript of the bank history must have been virtually complete by then, although it was not published until the following year. This delay was perhaps necessary so that an appendix of almost fifty pages could be taken in, reporting verbatim all the speeches made at the bicentenary dinner on Friday 3 June 1927 (including the toast of 'The Guests' proposed by Lord Haig). It also lists the names of the 300 guests, among them 'Neil Munro LL.D' and his friend Hugh Buchanan, whose firm McGrigor Donald had acted as the Royal Bank's lawyers in Glasgow for over a century.

The History of the Royal Bank of Scotland, 1727–1927, contrives to interweave the disparate elements Neil had mentioned in his March 1926 letter to Sir Alexander Wright – 'purely factual and financial details' and 'treatment of men and events'. The chapter entitled 'The 'Forty-Five' is a vivid example, relating among much else how, with Prince Charlie as far south as Blair Atholl, the Royal Bank directors destroyed £10,600 in notes.

The next item on Neil's agenda, dear reader, should have been *The Search*. But when was he ever able to give his undivided attention to writing novels? Certainly not in June 1927. Bud was now engaged to Alice Webb's relative Jimmy Bostock, and they were to be married in Glasgow Cathedral at the end of July. In the weeks beforehand Cromalt was besieged by visitors, Sasunnach and otherwise. Bud and Jimmy spent their honeymoon in Sark, in the Channel Islands, before settling in Stafford. Lala and Moira went down for their homecoming.

Neil's Inveraray visits were becoming more and more sporadic. Earlier in the summer he had been there for the funeral of his old friend John Gilmour of the Argyll Arms. In mid-August he spent a few days with the Weirs at Dunderave, when they dined at Strachur Park with Lady George Campbell. In his bread-and-butter note to Alice Weir he wrote: 'I got home all right last Sunday, spiritually uplifted and refreshed. I begin to look on myself now, in virtue of having in a sense invented Dunderave, as one of the fittings which summer tenants simply *have* to take over –

'Scene – Dunderave 1936
'Who is that doddering old creature who lurks about the place?
'In the Inventory he is merely mentioned as part of the mediaeval atmosphere. One of the original ghosts of the Castle we suspect. Quite inoffensive. In the old days he is said to have kept the house awake all night shouting out the battle-cry of Freedom.'[3]

Another contribution to Dunderave lore – apart from the novel *Doom Castle* – was Neil's poem 'MacNaughton's Bath'. When Dunderave, anciently the seat of Clan MacNachtan, was 'restored' early in the century, Lorimer the architect had devised a somewhat primitive system of securing the bathroom door on the inside with a wooden peg to stop the latch being lifted from the outside. This lent a certain insecurity to having a bath.

He hadna snibbed the bathroom door!
He hadna heard the din!
And o! but he was unco vexed
When the Cawmell Clan cam in,

For even the chief o' a Hielan' clan
Hooever sturdy built
Looks fearsome gaunt in a washin' byne
Withouten coat nor kilt!

...But ever since, in Shire Argyll,
MacNaught-on's what we ca' them.

For Armistice Day that November, Neil wrote 'With Some Reflections', a piece that reflects something of his own internal re-adjustment to Hugh's death: 'It is curious to note how each recurring Armistice Day celebration at the Cenotaph becomes more and more a great gesture to humanity at large rather than a rite of purely national significance... Of all who take part in such celebrations with any poignant feeling, one moment of the Silence is now for personal loss; the remainder for humility and an inarticulate yearning for release from that impersonal Devil in us all who wears a uniform, wields a sword, wins his recruits with the aid of bard, sennachie and piper who were always inveterate liars.'[4]

In a letter to Alice Weir at the start of December, Neil said: 'There is every prospect that on Hogmanay the scattered remnant of the Clan Munro will assemble at Inveraray and shout again the battle-cry of Freedom, an ancient ceremony of the tribe, neglected for six or seven years back. Ever your affectionate Uncle, Niall Mac an Rothaich.'

This plan did not quite come off, but Neil managed to assemble a goodly gathering of young folk about him at Cromalt. Bud and Jimmy Bostock came up to spend Christmas and New Year in Scotland. On 20 December Neil wrote to Winifred Hodge in London: 'You are confidently expected to appear at Cromalt for the dancings and things to take place next Tuesday. Pay no attention to your ruffian employer if he insists on your being back to business on Tuesday. I know things about him which, if revealed, would blight his whole career... The fellow's past has been lurid and would make a thrilling series of stories for the *News of the World*...

Podger Blake's Poisonous Past
by John MacPepys

Chap.1   The Stickit Lawyer
    2   The Chaucer Forgeries
    3   Clydeside Echoes
    4   A Seat in the Plumbers Club
    5   Cajoling Mary Ann
    & so on

'Podger Blake' was of course George of that ilk, now editing *John o' London's Weekly*.

On Hogmanay the Munros – '*toute la famille*' – were at the Falls of Lora Hotel in Connell Ferry to bring in the New Year. This hotel belonged to a relation of Neil's old friend John Macmaster Campbell, which may explain the abandoning of the Inveraray project.

January 1928 was an eerie month to be a former editor of the *News*, judging by a letter Neil sent to Sir John Richmond: 'Our Chief Reporter, Davy Robertson, met Herries, Edinburgh Chief Reporter of *The Scotsman*, the other day, who casually remarked, "By the way I had a long talk with your old boss the other evening". "Which old boss?" asked Robertson. "Oh, J.M., of course," said Herries. "Man! J.M. has been dead for months!" exclaimed David. "So to speak," admitted Herries, "but he 'comes through' every now and then at our seances... and I often have a crack with him." Robertson... betrayed no surprise but asked what J.M. generally talked about. "Oh, about the ethics of Journalism and the syndicate trend," answered Herries, and this was so unmistakably what a discarnate J.M. *would* talk about, that Robertson blenched. "By God!" he said, "I hope the old chap's not hanging round 97 Hope Street much, and watching us just now, for he'll get a hell of a fright."'[5] Five days after this letter was written, Robert MacLennan, then editor of the *News*, died in Nice, where he had been convalescing from a serious illness.

James Blackwood, writing from London to relay an enquiry about *Erchie* from New York, could not resist remarking: 'The gloom of our climate is increased by the continued unfruitfulness of your

262

pen.'[6] Neil replied that he was 'convinced *Erchie* would never sell in America... Though I have no wish to see *Erchie* revived anywhere, it may interest you to know I am continually pestered by enquiries as to where copies can be got – the result, I fancy, of sketches from it being now frequently broadcast by the B.B.C. at a guinea a time!... Strictly between ourselves, I'm sick of newspapers and journalism, and have decided to abandon them altogether at the beginning of June.'[7]

But before June came Neil suffered what he himself styled 'a rather disquieting nervous breakdown'.[8] The exact nature of his malady that spring cannot now be established. To recuperate he went to Vence, inland from Nice, to stay for a month with Scottish friends, George and Pearl Adam, who lived there. 'I was somewhat run down, and in need of super-violet rays, whereof I laid in large stores by sun-bathing in Vence and at Cap d'Antibes.'[9] After that he spent another month of 'comparative idleness' at home.

Enforced idleness disagreed with Neil. He described his long break to William Power, the journalist and writer, as 'stravaiging far from home from the first of May till last night... The effect of any holidays – longer than a few days at a time – is to give me, usually, a feeling of frustration and futility... Today I've been going over copies of the *Scots Observer* [edited by Power] which have accumulated in my absence, and have the same feelings I used to have when Henley was struggling away with the original "S.O." – that if you're not making a fortune, you're at least making a tradition, and have already created a standard in "national" journalism which no sober Scotsman need be ashamed of...'[10]

Even now Neil did not abandon journalism 'altogether'. He gave up being Literary Editor of the *News* and virtually ceased his occasional contributions to the old paper. It was more than thirty years since he had begun his two columns, 'Views & Reviews' and 'The Looker-On', and it must have felt strange to give them up. But he retained his directorship in the Berry syndicate, necessitating one trip to Glasgow per week.

In June Lord Weir wrote from Holm Foundry, Cathcart: 'Dear Munro, Before his departure for London on Sunday evening 1st July, His Royal Highness The Prince of Wales has agreed to meet a small party of West of Scotland men at an informal dinner at Eastwood Park [the Weirs' Glasgow house]. I will be glad, therefore, if you will give me the pleasure of dining with me at Eastwood that evening at 7.30pm sharp to have the honour of meeting His Royal Highness. With kind regards, I am, Yours sincerely, WEIR. Dinner

Jacket – Black Tie. R.S.V.P.'[11] Neil duly went to this dinner, but no record of his impressions has come down to us.

Towards the end of July he agreed to write a 1500-word review/analysis of Conrad's *The Rescue* to appear in an American publication described as 'this unique catalog' by George T. Keating, New York, who made the arrangement. The commission was £25 and Keating had to receive the manuscript by 15 September.

On 29 July Effie and Jack Bruce had a second daughter, Jean. The proud grandfather then spent most of August as 'a gangrel body in the Hielan's'. After a tour through recently planted State forests he went to stay with Hugh Buchanan in Arran. Perhaps it was on this visit to Arran that he was induced to read a Para Handy story aloud, chose 'The Wet Man of Muscadale' which he had all but forgotten, and could scarcely get through it for laughing. After that he went on to stay at Dunderave. During this visit he 'was at the inauguration of the first hydro-plane or "speed-boat" on Loch Fyne, and saw the Duke and Lady Elspeth dash around in a cockle-shell craft at about 30mph – very different from the old Blue Barge or Birlinn of MacCailein Mor which was more deliberate in its movements.'[12] Shortly after Neil returned home from his wanderings, Effie came to stay at Cromalt with her two daughers, while Jack was sojourning in Elie, Fife.

None of this was conducive to the writing of fiction. All had been quiet on the Blackwood front since Neil wrote to James Blackwood in February, and he must have cast an apprehensive eye over a short letter from James's brother George at the end of October. 'A real Neil Munro novel for 1929 would be the very thing for *Maga*,' was the familiar refrain.

Neil had quite a different project on his mind. He was feeling well enough again to strike out in a new direction. Thinly disguised as 'Mr Incognito', he was on the verge of starting a new series of articles in the *Daily Record*, the first of which appeared on 6 November. At first the rubric 'Random Recollections' was used, in allusion to the 'Random Reminiscences' published in the *News* just after the war. Later the heading 'Past and Present' was substituted. The articles, each about 1,500 words long, appeared twice a week. Some of them are guardedly autobiographical, others tackle subjects ranging from a potted history of Queen Street Station to the artist Muirhead Bone, from pearl fishing to 'Scotland's First Electric Railway' (planned and installed near Carstairs by John M.M. Munro, Neil's cousin, in 1888–89). A very early one was about R.B. Cunninghame Graham, just then involved in establishing the Scottish National

Party. Cunninghame Graham wrote from London: 'Many thanks for your far too flattering article.'[13] In it Neil had written: 'Were there seven good durable forty-year-old Cunninghame Grahams in Scotland, I'd be sorely tempted to pitch my hat over the moon and join the National Party at whatever cost to the shop-keepers.'[14]

When a selection of these articles and others was made into the book *The Brave Days* (1931) by George Blake, he would write of Neil: 'To us who knew him, they perfectly reflect his personality. To the world at large they must stand for what they are – a picture in cheerful mosaic of Glasgow in particular and, in general, of an era now closed.' *The Observer* said: 'These delightful pages, disjointed as they are, really represent the better way of autobiography: they give incident and humour without self-consciousness and without formality.'

CHAPTER FORTY-THREE

And this becomes a lonely house

DURING January 1929 the whole Munro household went down with influenza. By the end of the month Neil had recovered sufficiently to attend to George Blackwood's letter, which he had left unanswered for three months. He told Blackwood, somewhat disingenuously, that he had given up all journalism except for his Berry directorship, and explained that he had been unwell. 'Up till Christmas it was only intermittently I found myself able to resume any wanderings with Ninian Campbell, and his story has moved but slowly... There is finished more than you used to have in hand before starting previous serials of mine, but nowadays I cannot trust myself to let you have any MS not absolutely finished. If I could secure two or three months' seclusion and complete release from any connection with newspaper work, which in its modern aspects I despise and loathe, you would have the novel by midsummer and the 'Ballads' by Christmas. And that is what I aim at...'[1]

That spring Maggie McNiven was gravely ill. In April she underwent a hysterectomy in the Western Infirmary, Glasgow. She kept the letters Moira wrote her, a good source of word-pictures of Cromalt life: 'We have had Mr [Alexander] Proudfoot the sculptor here to lunch and he and Pop are out in the greenhouse and have been out for hours this morning. The head is getting on very well and looks like Father – especially the side-view... I hope you have plenty to read. Just let Ronald know and he can tell me... Vallance is busy planting out lettuces. He is greatly interested in Pop's bust...'[2]

'My own dear wee Meg, We've just heard from Effie that she found you looking cheery today and we are all rejoicing. Ronald also phoned and he says you are getting on wonderfully... Father is just home from town.... He started out for the 2 o'clock train – missed it and came back and then we had a job getting him away for the 4 o'clock train... I suppose Ronald would tell you he was down. He stayed till this morning... The Buchanans – Mr and Mrs – came in on Saturday afternoon but Ronald and I were up at Effie's for tea...'[3]

'I expect you'll be sitting up in your bed with the sun streaming in *and* the smuts. It was great to see you looking so cheery and chirpy. Ronald was grinning away at you being so perky and like yourself again.'[4]

'Mother has heard of a maid. Mrs Fraser [wife of Neil's school-friend Robert] wrote and said that she isn't keeping one after 22 May and she can recommend her. She is about 17 and comes from Furnace and is a very good worker... Her name is Jessie Bell...'[5]

'Lala and I are sitting at the drawing-room fire. We haven't had the dining-room one on since it was cleaned. Lipu is snoozing on the rug and Dougie is in his bed. He came home this morning absolutely black... One of the hens died last night... I got all my typing done early today and took it along to the train... I expect Bella [one of Maggie's sisters] will be in to see you tomorrow and she'll be telling you about how much we've got cleaned. I *did* miss you tho' – somehow spring-cleaning isn't spring-cleaning without you there as gaffer...'[6]

Maggie made a good recovery, and by the autumn was her old self, now with Jessie Bell to help her. The 'Ronald' mentioned in Moira's letters was Ronald Lendrum, her future husband. They had met at a dance in the Art Club in Glasgow, introduced by Hugh Buchanan. He actually worked in the Western Infirmary, as assistant to Professor Munro Kerr – hence his frequent appearances at Maggie's bedside – and was also in private practice in the

Dowanhill/Hillhead district. The typing mentioned by Moira
would have been one of her father's articles, which were sent up to
the *Record* office by train, not chapters of *The Search*. Message boys
used to ask if they could take Dougie (the second Dougie: Dougie I
had been run over in Gourock) for walks up the hill behind
Helensburgh, and perhaps that is why he came home that morning
'absolutely black'. In the end he was shot by a farmer for worrying
sheep.

Neil's 'Mr Incognito' article (his 71st) on 20 August was subtitled
'Simplified Gaelic?'. It was a spirited and detailed defence of the
spelling of Gaelic against those who say it should be more 'phonetic'.
It elicited an adulatory letter to the *Record* from Angus Henderson
of 100 Bothwell Street. ' "Mr Incognito" clinches it! His article... is
one of the finest pronouncements on a disputed subject that I have
ever read – wise, cautious, well-informed and superlatively kind and
tolerant to his opponents... No one could write it but a master hand,
and fortunately for Gaelic, there is still one master hand in Scotland
that can guard its privileges and insist upon its rights being duly
acknowledged, from a scholarly point of view. I lay a chaplet of good
wishes at his feet and say with sincerity and reverence, God bless
you, "Mr Incognito" (not an "incognito" at all but a shining light
placed on a hill!)... To say anything of the case made out so brilliantly by your self-effecting correspondent would savour of
impertinence on my part, or on the part, perhaps, of any man in
Scotland, with only one or two exceptions. To criticise it is impossible, for it is based on the solid rock of knowledge and erudition...
he has said everything that could possibly be said within the limits
of his space... Again, I say, God bless "Mr Incognito", and may he
live long and happily to be a credit to Gaeldom, which, alas, has too
few literary champions to accept challenges when offered by
outsiders.'

How greatly Neil must have been heartened by this letter! He was
now leading a very quiet life indeed, describing himself as 'such a
recluse body on the outskirts of the burgh [Helensburgh] that I'm
not in it oftener than once a month'.[7] During August he and Jessie
spent a fortnight in Strath Nairn, Inverness-shire. But his health still
gave cause for concern: in December he wrote to his theatrical friend
Alfred Wareing, who wished to go for a recuperative trip on one of
Jack Bruce's fruit ships: 'Myself, I too have been off colour a bit for
many months. Dr Harrington, a specialist, "vetted" me two months
ago, traced my indisposition to eye-strain; I had been using the same
prescription by Dr Freeland Fergus for glasses [myopia] for 35

years! never in my life used glasses for reading or writing, though I ought to have started doing so at forty! and was naturally putting an unholy strain on my whole visual and nervous system. That has been amended. Further, 25–30 cigarettes per diem accounted for a slight blood pressure, and the issue is now reduced to twelve with good results.'[8]

He also told Wareing of Moira's imminent wedding: 'Thus I lose an invaluable amanuensis and secretary! Those young people have little consideration for the aged. And this becomes a lonely house. Only Lilian left. We nearly lost Maggie in the spring-time... but I rejoice to say she pulled through and is again her old self, and bossing us as heartily as ever... Neil we expect to see on Saturday, in a hurried dash home... He likes London much better than Glasgow and seems pretty well satisfied with his job at Northcliffe House...'

Neil junior was engaged to be married, but in the end this did not come to anything. Meanwhile Bud had given birth to a daughter, Elspeth. By December, Neil senior was fit enough to fulfil several engagements in Glasgow. At an Art Club dinner he met O.H. Mavor – the playwright James Bridie. Winifred Hodge came to stay at Cromalt, but it could not be like the merry Christmases of yore. On 27 December Moira went to Brechin to stay with the Lendrum family. There was no word now of the Munros bringing in the New Year at Inveraray, nor shouting 'the battle-cry of Freedom...'

Nor shall we ever know what it was that Ninian Campbell wanted Hannibal Lamont to tell him, for the typescript of *The Search* peters out with the words: 'Tell me this, Hannibal –'. It is safe to say that this stump of a novel – ten and a bit chapters, perhaps a third of the whole envisaged – was already in existence by the end of 1929 or the early months of 1930. (It was Moira who typed it out, and her wedding was due at the end of March 1930.) Much of it probably existed, at least in manuscript, considerably earlier. As sequel to *The New Road* it is essentially 'more of the same' and, so far as it goes, 'equal to sample'. A novelty is the introduction of an Englishman, Derry, as one of the principal characters, and it is his arrival at Inveraray that opens the first chapter in typical Munro-esque fashion.[9]

Why, it may be asked, did Neil persist with his two 1500-word articles a week for the Record, rather than making a space in his life in which to complete *The Search*? No doubt he thought he could still juggle both, as in the old days. But his vitality was ebbing – and his journalism was always far more fluent than his fiction. It is unlikely he had added much at all to the manuscript of *The Search* during 1929, despite hinting at midsummer completion to George Blackwood at the beginning of the year. Who was he trying to kid?

A year later his state of mind, betrayed in a rare outburst, suggests a gloom that would make completion of *The Search* more problematical than ever. 'Keep off daily or evening journalism at any cost! That way, too long pursued, lie disillusion, despair, intellectual and spiritual death!' he admonished George Blake. 'You... are still young enough, and with a small enough family, to put your fortune to the touch on the strength of your abilities and reputation. If you were in Scotland I'd swop with you tomorrow – no, that's not what I mean exactly; all it means is that at 66 I am painfully conscious of having frittered away by far the greater part of my life from timidity and laziness.'[10]

This is scarcely rational. Arguably, here, Neil's physical condition was influencing his thoughts unduly. Another clue lies in the next sentence of the letter: 'This summer all my family will be married, save Lilian, and I'm half inclined, myself, to look out for that desirable cot and garden.'

George Blake seems to have heeded Neil's advice. He became a director of Faber & Faber, his special charge being the Porpoise Press, Edinburgh, as well as writing novels set in contemporary Scotland. Nevertheless, for a short period in the early Thirties, he was one of a triumvirate editing the *Glasgow Evening News*, the other two being William Power and Robins Millar.

Jonathan Cape wrote to Neil early in 1930 suggesting that 'a very attractive book' could be made from a selection of the Mr Incognito articles. 'Would you care to do this? If so, I would be glad to make you a proposal...'[11] Neil replied: 'It may be that sooner or later I may be glad to submit such a selection for your consideration, but meanwhile the great majority of those which have appeared are only of local interest, and I have no intention of reprinting them.'[12]

On 19 March Moira was married to Ronald Lendrum in Glasgow University Chapel. Neil did not feel up to walking up the aisle with his daughter. Instead he sat in the choir stalls and joined her there. It was a large wedding – only the second in the chapel, recently completed as a war memorial – and the reception was in the Bute Hall. (Remarkably, the first bride married there had been Sheila MacLennan, daughter of another former *News* editor.) Moira and Ronald travelled round England on honeymoon, at one point staying at Hyde Lea near Stafford with Bud and Jimmy. Neil wrote to Moira *chez* Bud, informing her pointedly that he'd had his old

Oliver typewriter cleaned. 'Bless you my children! When are you coming home? Li-pu, while this house was simply crawling with human offspring in recent weeks, could not conceal his annoyance that those brats should monopolise so much of the attention of his beloved Lilian. The first day they disappeared he went romping about the place with his tail joyously uplifted. But ever since, he has been nosing around in search of 'em. *When* are you coming home? Don't drive me to send a telegram. Isn't two or three months of holiday quite enough for a honeymoon? *I have pawned all the presents & am back in the library. My gowk!* You had forgotten it was All Fools' Day. Love to everybody. Assure Ronald that this incoherent scrawl has no pathological significance. Your abandoned parent, N.M.'"[13] (Part of the letter was typed on the old Oliver.) On Ronald and Moira's return to Scotland, assuredly not after three months away, they began married life in Glasgow in the house Ronald had hitherto shared with his brother Alan at 3 Ashton Road, just off Byres Road.

It was time now for Neil to have some recuperation. Towards the end of April he went over to Ireland with Jessie and Lilian, sailing from Greenock to Dublin. Neil visited the Dail, and they stayed with Leslie Montgomery (the writer Lynn Doyle) and his wife at Blackrock. On returning, Neil found a lot of pressing work awaiting him, and the flow of visitors could not be stemmed. He was still going up to Glasgow once a week. William Power was at one of these latter day occasions: 'There was a lunch at which David Anderson, Lady Margaret Sackville, Sir Hugh Roberton, and the late Sir John Foster Fraser were present. The question arose – a delicate one in a company where poets are present – who was the best living poet in Scotland? We discussed the subject for a while, coming to no definite agreement, naturally, since each of us had his or her own idea of what a Scots poet in the fourth decade of the 20th century ought to be. At last Munro, who had kept silence, broke in: "Undoubtedly Charles Murray!" It was a fine tribute from one great Scotsman to another.'[14]

Early in June, Neil and Lilian went for a motor run to Inveraray with Mrs Blackie, wife of Walter Blackie the publisher (for whom Charles Rennie Mackintosh built the Hill House in Helensburgh). On 12 June, Neil was 'vetted' by a doctor who put him on a regimen. '... for a time at least [it] will necessitate my strict abstinence from some deep-rooted habits. It appears I have an abnormal blood pressure, and some dilatation of the heart. For the past year I have been reducing my writing to one article a week, but even that is now forbidden to me, as well as one business meeting a week which took me to Glasgow. I am now prescribed an absolute rest from reading, writing, smoking, gardening – all the worth while things in life – with the hope that a few months' change will see me right again..."[15]

In fact Neil had often written more than one article a week right up to May 1930, but on 24 June his very last 'Mr Incognito' – No.144 – appeared in the *Record*. It was about the funeral of a girl that he had witnessed in Italy many years before.

At the beginning of July, Jessie and Neil spent ten days with George Houston and his family at Cuil, near the head of Loch Fyne. Sadly there was no fishing for Neil during this period of enforced rest. Just after their return to Cromalt came a letter from J.M. Barrie, who was to be installed as Chancellor of Edinburgh University on 25 October: 'I am writing informally, but with the authority of the Senatus, to ask you to grace the occasion by being present at 10 a.m. and receiving the honorary LL.D. degree. I very much hope that you will do us this favour.'[16]

In August, Neil sailed in pursuit of better health to New York in the R.M.S. *Transylvania*, whose captain was his friend David Bone. They had fine weather for both crossings, but in New York the heat and humidity and the roaring traffic oppressed Neil, who had to spend a night or two alone in an hotel and did not feel at all well. Just then John Munro (an Inveraray man, but no relation) happened to arrive in New York from the West Indies. He worked on a ship and invited Neil on board for lunch 'preceded by a very light cocktail known as "Orange Blossom"'.

Neil was glad to get home to cool Craigendoran. Not long after his return, he wrote briefly to George Blackwood requesting permission to have *The New Road* reproduced as a serial in the *Scottish Motor Traction Magazine*.[17] Blackwood, agreeing to this by return, enquired after Neil's health and reiterated the old plea: 'I am always, as you know, hoping to hear from you about the new novel or about more "Bagpipe Ballads", or anything else that your pen may find to do that will be suitable to *Maga*.'[18] Neil's letter of thanks was yet briefer: 'I have just lately got back from America where I was for a hurried sea voyage by doctor's orders – with some improvement on my health I think.'[19] This final letter to George Blackwood was the end of another auld sang, more than forty years after Neil had first submitted a poem to *Maga*, *sub regno* William Blackwood.

Early in October Neil's forthcoming honorary degree was officially announced, and there were letters of congratulation which had to be acknowledged. Neil told William Power how 'my first reflection was that there must be some mistake or that [Barrie] must have forgotten, or never heard I already had the honorary degree from Glasgow. I had to look at *Who's Who* to assure myself that another "bar" to the LL.D. is always possible and many greedy people make collections. It is 22 years since I had the "bonnet" first put on my humble head by Principal D. MacAllister – I can hardly credit it! Barrie is aye Barrie, and Embro's aye Embro, however...'[20]

On 25 October, a Saturday, Neil travelled through to Edinburgh by train to attend the ceremony in the Macewan Hall. There were five other honorary graduands, including Arthur Quiller Couch and the composer Granville Bantock. Moira was at Queen Street station to meet her father when he changed trains at Glasgow on his way home, and she used often to tell us how tired and frail he looked.

On 12 November Neil visited George Houston at West Linn, his house at Dalry, Ayrshire. It was the last meeting of two old friends. Six weeks later, Neil died at Cromalt. The end came at three o'clock in the morning of Monday, 22 December. It fell to Neil junior, summoned north in the last days by a telegram from Ronald Lendrum, to register the death. In his confusion he invented a father for his father – a fictitious farmer called 'John Thomson Munro'.

Neil was buried, wrapped in a plaid of Munro tartan, on Christmas Eve. After a private service at Cromalt, a group of relatives and close friends travelled by car to Inveraray. Jessie and Lilian remained at home. The coffin was taken to Inveraray parish church, where the funeral service was held at noon, then the funeral procession, in which by tradition only men walked, formed at the church door and followed the hearse to the old graveyard of Kilmalieu, a mile along the loch. Effie, Moira and Bud stood on the church steps and watched the procession pass slowly out of sight round the Factor's Corner. The Duke of Argyll, arriving late, offered his sympathy to Neil junior on the way back from Kilmalieu.

CHAPTER 44

Cha Till Mi Tuilidh

PRIVATE or public, practical, poetical, even polemical, the reactions to Neil Munro's death were many and varied. The swiftness with which the family organised the sale of Cromalt and found a Glasgow house for Jessie, Lilian and Maggie was very much in the spirit of Neil's own way of doing. Of the family's grief, the only traceable record is a letter from Effie to Kate Turner, written six months later. She thanks Kate belatedly for her letter 'with all its loving and understanding appreciation of dear, dear father... You understand and appreciate what mother is, too. She has always been so good and true, so conscientious in everything. You speak of her courage, but I'm afraid she hasn't so much of that now – and can one wonder at it! She can't bear to be alone now, and must have constant backing. She has been fortunate in her sons-in-law and indeed, in all her friends and connections, for everyone has wanted to help; nobody has forgotten her. I never saw anyone so crushed as she was when father had to go; it was pitiful. But she is much better now, and beginning to feel more settled in her Glasgow flat which is a very nice one and full of her and father's possessions, gathered up in years... I never waken up to look out on a fine morning but I think of father's invariable remark, "It'll be a fine day up Loch Fyne today..." I think father enjoyed his life, and got a lot out of it. It comforts me to think that.'[1]

Jessie's new abode was a large flat on the first floor and at a corner, so that some windows overlooked the trees and grass of Athole Gardens and some looked down on Ruthven Street. Moira and Ronald's house was only five minutes' walk away, across busy Byres Road with its excellent shops and subway station. Towards the end of Effie's letter to Kate Turner, she mentions the forthcoming book of her father's poems and says also that the Rest and Be Thankful had been chosen as the site for a commemorative cairn and stone seat (this site was subsequently rejected). 'It all doesn't seem to matter very much to me, but I suppose my children and my children's children will thrill and be proud at the sight of it.'

By the same token, it is likely all the effusions of praise poured out in newspaper obituaries did not 'seem to matter very much' at the time to Neil's family. But Moira, for one, kept many newspaper cuttings and stuck them in a large scrapbook years later.

At least six elegies were composed in Neil Munro's honour. Only eight days after his death, Lewis Spence's outpouring, 'A Lament for Neil Munro', was printed in the *Daily Record & Mail*. Of its 96 lines, some bear repeating.

> December is the white dirge of his passing,
> The ghost of the year is his ghillie,
> Following him soundless into the silence...
> Can the fingers of grief awake the strings
> Of his widowed *clarsach*?
> Even in the gloaming
> Left by the gleam of his garments we faint,
> Little singers sitting in twilight,
> Mourning our Master...
> So through the generations all these hearts
> Shall raise for him a cairn of lasting love...

A Gaelic *cumha*, *Clach air Carn Niall Mac an Rothaich* [A Stone on the Cairn of Neil Munro], unsigned but dated January 1931, was found long after by one Neil McPhedran, whose family came from Port Sonochan, among his father's papers. It is seventeen verses long.[2]

> *Chan fhaicear thu tuilleadh*
> *A'tuineach mar b'abhaist*
> *Measg do chàirdean aig baile*
> *No taobh Abhainn Aora.*

> > [You will be seen no more
> > Sojourning as was your wont
> > Among your friends in the town
> > Or on the banks of the Aray.]

> Ach cho fad 'sa bhios grian
> Anns an iarmailt a'deàrrsadh,
> Bidh do spiorad gach latha
> A' tadhal Bail' Inbhir Aora.

> > [But as long as a sun
> > Will shine in the heavens
> > Your spirit each day
> > Will be visiting Inveraray.]

Charles Brodie (1861–1933), a fellow member of the Glasgow Ballad Club, read his elegy to the club 44 years and a day after Neil himself had first attended one of its meetings. A poem entitled `At Kilmalieu` by J.G. MacNair appeared in a so-far unidentified newspaper:

Chieftain he was, not less that he was landless,
Chieftain more surely than by right of birth...

The *Glasgow Herald* printed 'The Brave Days (A Tune for Neil Munro)' by 'W.L.R.', also an elegy by 'W.J.' – presumably William Jeffrey – entitled 'In Memoriam'. Neil Munro is not named in this poem, whose least extravagant verse comes at the end.

By the sealochs, Gaelic Scholar, when the mews are loud in cry,
Or in Aros of the cuckoo, by the shielings old,
We shall meet thee and may know thee, gentle spirit,
                                    primrose-shy.
A wanderer with AEngus and his birds of shining gold.

Neil's former colleagues on the *Evening News* expressed their feelings in a short article: 'We loved the man, and reverenced him this side idolatry... he was the best of comrades, a chief who won from us not so much obedience as affectionate devotion, a friend whose ever-ready sympathy and wise counsel were reckoned on confidently by the humblest member of his staff. It is hard to think of that gay and gallant spirit quenched in death, to realise that the debonair figure and friendly bantering voice will no more be part of our little world... Yet it is needful and seemly that we, who have not only admired the writer but have known and loved the man in the intimacy of long years of daily work and social intercourse, should bring our humble tribute to his memory.'[3]

In the same number of the *News* there was an article by Cunninghame Graham, 'The Inspiration of Neil Munro', with the sub-title *Cha Till Mi Tuilidh* (I return no more). 'The exigencies of life bound him to journalism, but in all he wrote, there was a literary tang... Still, I deplore that a talent meant to have produced so much enduring work should have been cramped by the necessity of fate... Some of his work should live, and that is all the best of us, the wielders of the brush or pen, can hope to be our lot.'

In the *Bulletin*, J.M.Reid struck a new note: 'Neil Munro helped to keep Scotland alive. That was, perhaps, the greatest work of his life. And, like so many other parts of his work, it had the air of being a sort of splendid accident, the by-product, as it were, of a very great talent which never seemed quite to succeed in getting its fullest expression anywhere – unless, perhaps, in the daily enterprise of journalism, which he at least made a fine and adventurous thing. Simply by remaining among us and producing work whose quality no one could dispute, he reminded Scotland, at a time when, with R.L. Stevenson gone, she had least to offer the world, that she possessed a literary life and tradition of her own. Now that a time has come when Scottish writers are more conscious of themselves and their country, his successors – so few of them, as yet, of anything like his own stature – should hold his memory in special reverence. Some of them have been at pains to show that they do not.'[4]

No prizes for guessing whom Reid had in mind. Yet at this time Hugh MacDiarmid wrote an interesting article that partly redresses his earlier onslaught in the *Scottish Educational Journal*: 'Neil Munro was undoubtedly the greatest Scottish novelist since R.L. Stevenson, but... in manner and matter he remained too much in the shadow of that master craftsman... From a contemporary standpoint, his work seems to have three main faults... it is definitely *fin-de-siècle*... he confines himself for the most part to short stories, or even sketches, instead of soaring into the full structure of a novel... he confined himself to a particular region of Scotland... Despite the moving character of many of his verses, he failed to penetrate into a poetic region of his own, probably because of the difficulty under which he always laboured of translating his essentially Gaelic thought into English terms... Neil Munro continued to be *par excelsis* a Scottish writer, but at the same time he had little or no practical sympathy with the new Scottish movement. In his conduct of the *Glasgow Evening News* he influenced many of the younger writers who are now bulking large in the recent developments of Scottish letters, but he did so indirectly rather than directly, and in my own contact with him he repeatedly emphasised that "he travels fastest who travels alone"... The idea of resuscitating Scotland as a nation in the fullest sense of the term was one with which he seemed to have little sympathy, and yet, in the balance, it may prove that his work has had a very strong influence in the opposite direction. When all is said and done, there has been no greater and more versatile Scotsman since the death of R.L. Stevenson and his maintenance of a certain high dignity and intellectual integrity was undoubtedly one of the mainstays of Scotland during the decades which perhaps represented the lowest ebb of our distinctive national tradition.'[5] (By the phrase 'instead of soaring into the full structure of the novel' MacDiarmid meant, perhaps, that he found Neil Munro's novels insufficiently grandiose.)

The *Irish Times* published an appreciation by Lynn Doyle: 'I have been asked to write something about my friend, Neil Munro, who is dead... There is no one living who knew Neil Munro but was the happier for having known him... The word "charm" has been abused; but there is no other word possible for the intangible magic that radiated from his personality. He was humorous without being a mocker; he was sympathetic without being sentimental; he saw life clearly, and was not embittered... He was a Gael of the Gaels... but he was also of a Puritan simplicity and austereness; his pleasures were of the home and the hearthside, the neighbourly "crack", the friendly glass. He was a creative artist; but his greatest creations were his friendships... Neil Munro had a high sense of romance. His world is not this costermonger earth. But it is a creation clear, finite, having its own laws, its own people...'

When Neil's works were brought together by Blackwoods in the *New Inveraray Edition* of 1935, the collection was reviewed at length (anonymously, as was then the custom) in the *Times Literary Supplement*:

'...it is noteworthy that, although the last of these eleven [sic] books...appeared in 1918... they have almost without exception run through more editions since the War than before it, and it is likely that two, perhaps three, of them will eventually assume the status of classics... If any of his work has the stuff of endurance, it is *John Splendid*, *The New Road* and possibly *Children of Tempest*... Their foreground figures move against a broad panorama of place, community and lively action, not studied ad hoc for a novelist's purposes, but naively known to his imagination: he writes of the Highlands for the only valid reason, because through circumstances and temperament they gave him the natural subjects to embody his themes. He has, of course, been accused of romanticizing them, since he did not present them as unrelievedly squalid. The charge will not stand... Indeed, when he is drawing the Highlands as such he tends if anything to under-colour what to current taste is their "romantic" side...'[6]

Three months later came the unveiling of the Munro monument, built of local stones on the rocky knoll of Creag Dhubh at the top of Glen Aray. Ironically enough, the site was made available to An Comunn Gaedhealach by Major R.W.D. Fellowes of Inistrynich, the ancestral estate that Neil's great-great-grandfather Patrick

McArthur had been forced to sell in 1771. Neil's old friend John Macmaster Campbell gave an address. Among those present were R.B. Cunninghame Graham and Harry Lauder, a piquant contrast. At the top of the monument is a Gaelic *cumdach* or book-shrine inscribed *Sar Litreachas* – true literature.

Neil's work has endured and speaks for itself, but very few who met the man are now alive to recall him. I hope something of his essence has emerged from these pages. One of his innumerable friends, the theatrical Alfred Wareing, might have spoken for them all when he wrote: 'Of his kindnesses it would amount to a profanation to speak. They were always touched with loving thoughts. He will remain an abiding memory with all who knew him, a beacon and a guide; for he was one of those rare men who make you a better one because of the friendship they bestow.'[7]

Munro In Print

ALL Neil Munro's books were in print at the time of his death. Shortly afterwards the Baroness Orczy approached his family with an offer to write his biography. They gave her no encouragement. The following year Blackwoods published a selection of his poetry (with a preface by John Buchan) and an omnibus volume of his tales of Para Handy, Erchie and Jimmy Swan, for which Neil Munro junior wrote the foreword, the author being boldly declared as 'Hugh Foulis (Neil Munro)'. Also during 1931, The Porpoise Press, Edinburgh, published *The Brave Days*, a book of Neil Munro's journalistic reminiscences, chosen and introduced by George Blake. Described in an *Observer* review as 'a sort of skeleton for an autobiography', it is a selection from articles originally entitled 'Random Reminiscences'. *The Observer* further characterised them: 'These delightful pages, disjointed as they are, really represent the better way of autobiography: they give incident and humour without self-consciousness and without formality.'

The Brave Days was followed in 1933 by *The Looker-On*, another selection by Blake, and in 1935 by Blackwoods' *New Inveraray Edition*, comprising the eight novels and a ninth volume containing *The Lost Pibroch*, *Ayrshire Idylls* and *Jaunty Jock*. 'Jus Primae Noctis', the tale originally excluded by William Blackwood as too *risqué* for inclusion in *The Lost Pibroch*, was reinstated.

Ironically the first scholarly treatment of Neil Munro's work was not by a Scot but a German. In 1937, Dr Herbert Wernitz published *Neil Munro und die nationale Kulturbewegung im modernen Schottland* [Neil Munro and the National Cultural Movement in Modern Scotland]. Furthermore, the next serious study, though in English, was also by a German, Dr Kurt Wittig, whose masterly survey *The Scottish Tradition in Literature* has three Munro pages.

In 1978 Francis Russell Hart – an American, for a change – dealt with Neil Munro very sympathetically in *The Scottish Novel: A Critical Survey*. Identifying *The New Road* as his finest work, he described it as 'a work of sustained art Stevenson could not manage'.

Before the millennium had drawn to a close, two scholarly theses were completed – Dr Hermann Völkel's *Das literarische Werk Neil*

Munros (1996) and Ronald W. Renton's *The Major Fiction of Neil Munro: A Revaluation* (1997). A third is due from the pen of Beata Kohlbek.

Ronald Renton is a double star in the Munrovian firmament, for since 1996 he has been president of the Neil Munro Society, founded a century after *The Lost Pibroch* was published, with an inaugural ceremony at Inveraray Castle. The Society's journal, *ParaGraphs*, comes out twice a year and contains much that supplements this biography. Brian D. Osborne, Secretary of the Society since its inception, has performed with Ronald Armstrong great feats of Erchie/Para Handy/Jimmy Swan scholarship. The Society has also fostered the re-publication of several Munro books by House of Lochar, while others have been re-published by Birlinn.

As long ago as 1928, the BBC broadcast, in Scotland, some of the Erchie stories 'at a guinea a time'. In 1949 *The New Road* was broadcast as a radio play, and a few years later it was made into a television serial, as was *Doom Castle*. And then, in 1959, BBC Scotland made a television series entitled *Para Handy – Master Mariner*, from scripts by Duncan Ross 'based on the stories of Neil Munro'. Duncan Macrae played Para Handy. In two subsequent series the role has been taken by Roddy McMillan and Gregor Fisher.

On 16 January 2005, Para Handy will be a hundred years old.

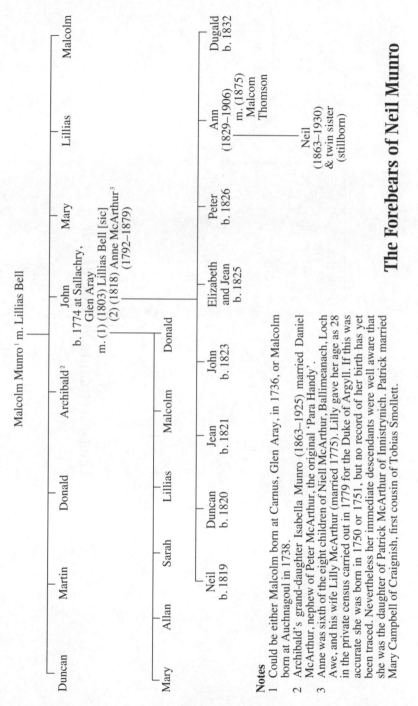

Malcolm Munro[1] m. Lillias Bell

Duncan | Martin | Allan | Sarah | Lillias | Malcolm | Donald

Archibald[2]

John
b. 1774 at Sallachry,
Glen Aray
m. (1) (1803) Lillias Bell [sic]
(2) (1818) Anne McArthur[3]
(1792–1879)

Donald | Mary | Lillias | Malcolm

Mary

Neil
b. 1819

Duncan
b. 1820

Jean
b. 1821

John
b. 1823

Elizabeth
and Jean
b. 1825

Peter
b. 1826

Ann
(1829–1906)
m. (1875)
Malcom
Thomson

Dugald
b. 1832

Neil
(1863–1930)
& twin sister
(stillborn)

The Forebears of Neil Munro

Notes

1. Could be either Malcolm born at Carnus, Glen Aray, in 1736, or Malcolm born at Auchnagoul in 1738.
2. Archibald's grand-daughter Isabella Munro (1863–1925) married Daniel McArthur, nephew of Peter McArthur, the original 'Para Handy'.
3. Anne was sixth of the eight children of Niell McArthur, Ballimeanach, Loch Awe, and his wife Lilly McArthur (married 1775). Lilly gave her age as 28 in the private census carried out in 1779 for the Duke of Argyll. If this was accurate she was born in 1750 or 1751, but no record of her birth has yet been traced. Nevertheless her immediate descendants were well aware that she was the daughter of Patrick McArthur of Innistrynich. Patrick married Mary Campbell of Craignish, first cousin of Tobias Smollett.

281

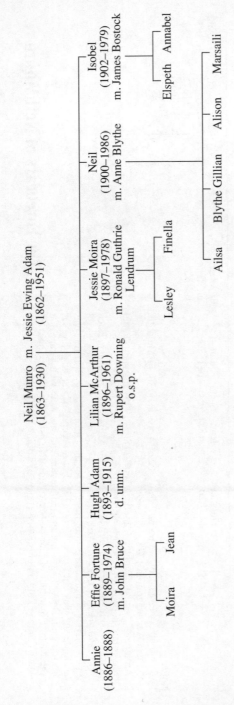

The Descendants of Neil Munro

References

Abbreviations
N.M.   Neil Munro
News   *Glasgow Evening News* (also known as *Glasgow News*).
Diary   Neil Munro's diary, National Library of Scotland, MS 26925.
        ('Retrospective diary': manuscript held privately.)
Renton Ronald W. Renton, *The Major Fiction of Neil Munro: A Revaluation*
        (unpublished M.Phil. thesis, University of Glasgow, 1997).

Introduction
1. *Times Literary Supplement*, 14 March 1935.

Chapter 1   The Oe from Ladyfield
1. Sir Iain Moncreiffe of that Ilk to the author, 8 February 1973.
2. Neil Munro junior to the author, 17 January 1978.
3. Boboon's Children, *The Lost Pibroch*.
4. *Gilian the Dreamer*, Ch.I.
5. N.M. to Leslie Montgomery (Lynn Doyle), 10 March 1921.
6. *Gilian the Dreamer*, Ch.I.
7. Ibid., Ch.VI.
8. Ibid., Ch.IV.
9. Ibid., Ch.V.
10. *The Complete Works of John Keats*, ed. H.Buxton Forman, Vol.IV (Glasgow 1901).
11. Duncan Beaton, 'The Notable Descendants of John Munro' in *The Kist* (Magazine of the Natural History & Antiquarian Society of Mid-Argyll), No. 45, Spring 1993.
12. *Gilian the Dreamer*, Ch.II.
13. Ibid., Ch.II.
14. Diary.
15. *John Splendid*, Ch.XIII.
16. *News*, 26 June 1902.

Chapter 2   Those lovely, unperplexed and simple days
1. *The Brave Days*, pp 25–26.
2. *News*, 7 July 1898.
3. *Oban Times*, 29 May 1909.

Chapter 3 Blythe were the seasons
1. George Blake, *The Brave Days* (1931), Introduction, p.16.
2. *News*, 22 August 1910.
3. *The Looker-On* (1933), pp 58–59.
4. *News*, 29 July 1907
5. *News*, 29 July 1907
6. *The Daft Days*, Ch.XVIII.
7. *News*, 26 December, 1904.
8. Ibid.
9. Lady Frances Balfour, *Ne Obliviscaris* (n.d.)
10. Ibid.
11. *News*, 25 July 1904.

Chapter 4 The key of the street and the freedom of the seashore and the forest
1. *News*, 21 March 1901.
2. Ibid.
3. Ibid.
4. Ibid.
5. Ibid. 9 February 1899.

Chapter 5 My earliest impressions of a prison
1. *The Looker-On*, pp 105–106.
2. *The Brave Days*, p.30.
3. Ibid., pp 30–33.

Chapter 6 A burgh most large and wonderful
1. *News*, 10 September 1906.
2. Ibid., 29 July 1907.
3. Donald Mackechnie, *Inveraray Notes* (privately published 1986)
4. *The Brave Days*, p.39.
5. Blanche E.C. Dugdale, *Family Homespun* (London 1940), pp 6–7.
6. *News*, 15 January 1906.
7. Ibid.
8. *Gilian the Dreamer*, Ch.I.
9. *The Brave Days*, p.98
10. *News*, 6 January 1898.
11. *The Brave Days*, pp 49 ff.
12. Ibid.

Chapter 7 This roaring city of our exile
1. Speech after receiving freedom of Burgh of Inveraray, *Oban Times*, 29 May 1909.
2. *The Brave Days*, pp 102–108.
3. *The Looker-On*, pp 99–101.
4. *News*, 26 April 1906.

5. *The Brave Days*, p.75.
6. Richard Lovett, *James Chalmers of New Guinea* (London 1902).
7. *The Brave Days*, p.80.
8. *News*, 16 March 1903.
9. Ibid.
10. Ibid.

Chapter 8   An awfu' peely-wally yin!
1. *News*, 28 August 1905.
2. *The Brave Days*, p85.
3. Ibid,, p.86.

Chapter 9   All alone on Greenock quay
1. *News*, 3 August 1912.
2. Ibid., 19 November 1903.
3. John Macmaster Campbell, *An Gaidheal*, February 1931.
4. Alfred Wareing, 'Neil Munro and the Glasgow Citizens' Theatre' in *Queue* [magazine], early 1931.
5. N.M. to John Macmaster Campbell.
6. *News*, 4 October 1900.
7. Joseph Conrad, *The Shadow-line* (1917), p.4.
8. W.B.Yeats, *Four Years: 1887–1891* (1921).
9. *News*, September 1902.
10. *The Brave Days*, p.209.
11. Ibid., pp 210–211.
12. *News*, 29 April 1912

Chapter 10   The jawbox of journalism
1. *The Brave Days*, pp 143 ff.
2. Ibid., p.316.
3. *News*, 9 January 1888.
4. N.M. to Marie Ballantyne (Mrs W.S. Ballantyne), Glasgow.
5. *News*, 23 May 1898.

Chapter 11   I believe I know the heart of the highland people

1. Diary, 21 November 1890.
2. *The Brave Days*, pp145–6.
3. William Blackwood to N.M., 17 November 1892.
4. N.M. to William Blackwood, 28 November 1892.
5. *News*.
6. Holbrook Jackson, *The Eighteen Nineties* (1913, new edition 1976), p.228.
7. William Blackwood to N.M., 8 July 1893.
8. N.M. to William Blackwood, 11 July 1893.
9. William Blackwood to N.M., 28 August 1893.
10. N.M., Retrospective Diary. 18 & 19 November 1903.

11. N.M. to William Blackwood, 26 February 1894.
12. Alan Bold, *Modern Scottish Literature* (1983), p.106.
13. William Blackwood to N.M., 26 February 1894.

Chapter 12   The said Celtic glamour
1. *News.*, 29 August 1895.
2. Wm. Blackwood & Sons to N.M., 22 February 1896.
3. William Blackwood to N.M., 19 November 1895.
4. *News.*, 1 November 1895.
5. Ibid., 5 December 1895.
6. A. Conan Doyle to N.M., n.d.
7. N.M. to Pittendrigh MacGillivray, 5 February 1896.
8. *News.*, 29 October 1903.
9. Ibid., 5 March 1896.
10. Ibid., 12 March 1896.

Chapter 13   Aora mo chridhe tha mi seoladh
1. N.M. to Pittendrigh MacGillivray, c.5 September 1895.
2. *News*, 19 August 1895.
3. Ronald Black, *Scottish Historical Review*, No.178.
4. Kurt Wittig, *The Scottish Tradition in Literature* (1958), p.271.
5. *News*, 10 June 1914.
6. *The Looker-On*, p.278.
7. N.M. to Kate McArthur (Mrs Turner, Lincoln), 11 June 1896.
8. N.M. to George Murray, 28 September 1896.

Chapter 14   First day in the house as a Literary Man
1. *News*, 28 January 1897.
2. Ibid., 22 August 1897.
3. *Evening Citizen*, Glasgow, 17 January 1957.
4. *News*, 23 August 1897.
5. Ibid. 11 October 1897.
6. William Blackwood to N.M., 28 March 1898.
7. Ibid. 23 April 1898.
8. N.M. to William Blackwood, 29 April 1898.

Chapter 15   The happy manner with Romance
1. J.M.Barrie to N.M., 15 September 1898.
2. Donald Mackinnon to N.M., 15 October 1898.
3. George Blake, *The Brave Days*, Introduction.
4. *The Looker-On*, p.298.
5. Ibid., p.297.
6. *The Brave Days*, p.113.
7. Joseph Conrad to Edward Garnett, 29 September 1898.
8. Ibid.
9. N.M., Retrospective Diary, 1904.

10. N.M. to Donald Macleod, 21 October 1898.
11. John Campbell to N.M., 16 November 1898.
12. N.M., Retrospective Diary, 20 April 1907.
13. R.B. Cunninghame Graham to N.M., 14 December 1898.

Chapter 16   I burned my journalistic boats
1. Pittendrigh Macgillivray to N.M., 7 March 1899.
2. N.M. to Pittendrigh Macgillivray, 8 March 1899.
3. William Blackwood to N.M., 30 January 1899.
4. N.M. to William Blackwood, 31 January 1899.
5. *The Looker-On*, p.63.
6. Ibid., pp 68–9.

Chapter 17   The manner of his message
1. N.M. to William Blackwood, 12 October 1899.
2. *Gilian the Dreamer*, Ch.I.
3. Fionn MacColla, *The Albannach* (1932), Foreword to 1971 Edition.
4. *Gilian the Dreamer*, Ch.IV.
5. Ibid., Ch.I.
6. N.M., *The Paymaster's Boy* (serial in *Good Words*, 1899).
7. *Gilian the Dreamer*, Ch.XXIX.
8. Renton, p.110.
9. *News*, 11 August 1898.
10. C.M. Grieve, *Contemporary Scottish Studies, First Series* (1926), p.34.
11. Duke of Argyll, *Scotland As It Was and As It Is* (1887), p.482.
12. David Storrar Meldrum, *The Bookman*, July 1915.
13. William Blackwood to N.M., 26 October 1899.
14, N.M. to Kate McArthur (Mrs Turner, Lincoln), 5 December 1899.

Chapter 18   The slave of two serials
1. N.M. to William Blackwood, 26 February 1900.
2. *The Looker-On*, p.245.
3. R.B. Cunninghame Graham to N.M.
4. Andrew Lang, *Pickle the Spy* (1897), p.299.
5. N.M. to William Blackwood, 31 January 1898.
6. N.M. to William Blackwood, 3 October 1900.

Chapter 19   I got about 2 doz trout.
1. *News*, 6 May 1901
2. William Blackwood to N.M., 27 May 1901.

Chapter 20   The pause of the morning, when time stands
1. N.M. to William Blackwood, 2 July 1901.
2. 'The Duke at Home: An Inveraray Impression' by Neil Munro [unattributed cutting, probably *Oban Times*, c. May 1914]
3. Ibid.

4. N.M. to Pittendrigh Macgillivray, 17 June 1901.
5. Ibid.
6. *Doom Castle*, Ch.III.
7. *The Looker-On*, pp 46–7.
8. Ian G. Lindsay & Mary Cosh, *Inveraray Castle and the Dukes of Argyll* (1973), pp 98 & 363.
9. Francis Russell Hart, *The Scottish Novel* (1978), p.166.
10. William Blackwood to N.M., 1 July 1901.

Chapter 21   They are saying the old wife is gone!
1. *The Looker-On*, p.201.
2. N.M. to unknown correspondent [addressed as 'Dear Sir'] 4 July 1903. The letter was found in a copy of *Children of Tempest* in the National Library of Scotland.
3. *The Brave Days*, p.303.
4. Ibid., p.305.
5. Ibid., pp 307–8.
6. N.M. to S. Muir, quoted by the latter in lecture to Lawson Memorial Literary Society, probably between 1903 and 1907.
7. G.K. Chesterton, *Robert Louis Stevenson* (1927), pp 42–57.
8. *News*, 2 June 1898.
9. John H. Lobban to N.M., 10 December 1901.
10. Renton, p.90.
11. Father Allan MacDonald to N.M., 29 October 1901.
12. N.M. to David Storrar Meldrum, 29 November 1901.

Chapter 22   I could see Inveraray – if it weren't for the mountains in between
1. *The Looker-On*, p.280
2. Ibid., p.279.
3. *The Looker-On*, p.280.
4. Ibid., pp 281–2.
5. N.M. to Kate McArthur (Mrs Turner, Lincoln), 7 January 1902.
6. N.M. to W. Turner, n.d.
7. *News*, 17 January 1898.
8. Ibid., 10 February 1902. First published in full in book form in *Erchie, My Droll Friend* (2002), ed. B.D. Osborne & R. Armstrong.
9. N.M. to William Blackwood, 6 September 1902.
10. George Blake, 'Remembering Things Past', in *Greenock Academy 1855–1955* .
11. *Glasgow Herald* , c.11 October 1902.
12. Maimie McGillvray to Donald Mackechnie, 18 March 1976.

Chapter 23   I hope to finish this yarn by April
1. N.M. to Kate McArthur (Mrs Turner, Lincoln), 16 March 1903.
2. N.M. to George Blackwood, 15 June 1903.

3. Neil Munro junior to the author, 8 February 1977.
4. *News*, 18 January 1904.

Chapter 24   Not in the kailyard, but up tenement closes
1. Fionn MacColla, *The Albannach* (1932), foreword to 1971 edition.
2. William Wallace, *The Bookman*, February 1900.
3. *News*, 8 February 1900.
4. *The Looker-On*, p.278.
5. C.M. Grieve, *Contemporary Scottish Studies, First Series* (1926), p.302.
6. *News*, 29 April 1906.
7. Peter Keating, *The Haunted Study* (1989) p.331.
8. Norman Bruce, 'Neil Munro – The Eleven Year Gap', *The Scotsman*, 7 September 1963.
9. William Blackwood to N.M., 2 October 1903.
10. N.M. to William Blackwood, 9 October 1903.
11. William Blackwood to N.M., 12 February 1904.
12. N.M. to Kate McArthur (Mrs Turner, Lincoln), 16 September 1904.
13. *News*, 23 May 1904.
14. Ibid., 15 August 1904.
15. N.M. to William Blackwood, 14 September 1904.
16. *The Looker-On*, p.278.

Chapter 25   The bugles of the mind
1. *The Daft Days*, Ch.XXV.
2. Brian D. Osborne & Ronald Armstrong, *Para Handy* (First Complete Edition, 1992), p.54.
3. Renton, p.99.
4. George Blackwood to N.M., 26 June 1905.
5. Ion Smeaton Munro, *Glasgow Herald,* 11 October 1969.
6. N.M., Retrospective Diary. 26 August 1905.
7. *Glasgow Herald*, c.June 1935.
8. William Blackwood to N.M., 10 October 1905.

Chapter 26   Blythmeat and breadberry in the house of Daniel Dyce
1. George Blackwood to N.M., 18 April 1906.
2. N.M. to Butler Wood, Skipton, 3 October 1927.
3. Neil Munro junior, *Para Handy & Other Tales* (1931), Foreword.
4. *Evening Times*, Glasgow, 3 December 1931.
5. Norman Bruce, *Glasgow Herald,* 30 May 1963.
6. *News*, 6 September 1906.
7. All the reminiscences in this chapter were transcribed from a tape made by Neil Munro junior, c.1984.

Chapter 27   Ailie's geese
1. N.M. to George Blackwood, 26 April 1907.

2. *News*, 25 January 1906.
3. Renton, p.130.
4. A.T. Quiller Couch, G.E.N., 6 May 1907.
5. N,M, to Walter Jerrold, 14 October 1907.

Chapter 28   It's a sair fecht, a faim'ly!
1. N.M. to Winifred Hodge, 11 March 1908.
2. News, April 1908.
3. N.M. to Mrs Turner (Kate McArthur), 8 May 1908.
4. *News*, 27 August 1908.
5. Alfred Wareing, 'Neil Munro and the Glasgow Citizens' Theatre' in *Queue* [magazine] c.January 1931.
6. Moira Lendrum, *New Scot*, September 1948.

Chapter 29   My own folk are pleased with me
1. William Blackwood to N.M., 3 March 1909.
2. N.M. to George Blackwood, 25 March 1909.
3. *Oban Times*, 29 May 1909.
4. Ibid.
5. William Blackwood to N.M., 31 May 1909.
6. N.M. to William Blackwood, 23 August 1909.
7. Alfred Wareing, *Queue*, c.January 1931.
8. Ibid.
9. *News*,. 10 February 1910.

Chapter 30   Or I'm a soused gannet
1. N.M. to George Blackwood, 11 May 1910.
2. Ibid., 29 August 1910.
3. Renton, p.132.
4. Hermann Völkel, *Das literarische Werk Neil Munros* (Peter Lang, Frankfurt am Main 1996), p.61.
5. N.M. to William Blackwood, 4 October 1909.
6. William Blackwood to N.M., 28 October 1910.
7. N.M. to William Blackwood, 3 November 1910.
8. Retrospective diary, 7 December 1910.
9. Ibid., 8 February 1911.
10. *News*, 31 July 1911.
11. Retrospective diary, 16/17 September 1911.

Chapter 31   Jolly decent imaginative work
1. N.M. to George Blackwood, 6 January 1912.
2. Kurt Wittig, *The Scots Tradition in Literature* (1957), p.264.
3. N.M. to George Blackwood, 29 May 1912.
4. *News*, 9 December 1912.
5. George Blackwood to N.M., 9 January 1913.
6. Niall Campbell to N.M., 3 April 1913.

Chapter 32 **By the old ways north**
1. See note 2, Chapter 20.
2. John MacIntyre, 'Notes explanatory of a series of letters from Neil Munro to myself between 1905 and 1929', c.1931.
3. Francis Russell Hart, *The Scottish Novel*, (1997/8), p.165.
4. *News*, 10 June 1914.
5. N.M. to John Buchan, 15 June 1914.
6. N.M. to John Macmaster Campbell, 17 July 1913.
7. *News*, 24 July 1912.
8. Ibid., 10 June 1914.

Chapter 33 **War! Inveraray Post Office open day and night!**
1. Moira Munro to N.M., 13 September 1914.
2. 'Under Sealed Orders', first published in book form in *Hurricane Jack of the 'Vital Spark'* (1923).
3. William Weir (b.1877) of the Glasgow engineering firm J.&G. Weir. His wife Alice McConnachie was the daughter ot the *News*'s solicitor. Weir was made Scottish Director of Munitions in 1915 and ended the war as Director-General of Aircraft Productions. He was created a viscount in July 1918.
4. N.M. to George Blackwood, 21 November 1914.
5. Ibid., 27 November 1914.
6. Ibid., 5 April 1915.
7. Ibid.

Chapter 34 **We went for you to the yetts o' hell**
1. Hugh Munro's diary, from which the quotations in this chapter are taken, is now in the Imperial War Museum, London.

Chapter 35 **That strange French countryside war-battered**
1. E.B. Osborne, 'Letters to Gog and Magog', in *John o' London's Weekly*, 28 November 1931.
2. N.M. to George Blackwood, 23 October 1916.
3. George Blackwood to N.M., 12 October 1916.
4. N.M. to Pittendrigh Macgillivray, 26 December 1916.
5. *The Brave Days*, p.10.
6. Ibid. pp 10–11.
7. N.M. to George Blackwood, 6 March 1917.
8. N.M. to George Blackwood, 19 March 1917.
9. George Blackwood to N.M., 28 March 1917.
10. N.M. to George Blackwood, 11 April 1917.
11. N.M. to George Blackwood, 28 April 1917.

Chapter 36 **This is the house for me!**
1. N.M. to George Blackwood, 21 January 1918.
2. George Blackwood to N.M., 24 January 1918.
3. *News*, 24 April 1926.

4. Ibid.
5. *Glasgow Herald* , 16 November 1957.
6. N.M., Retrospective Diary, 14 September 1918.
7. N.M. to George Blackwood, 21 September 1918.
8. N.M. to Pittendrigh MacGillivray, 28 October 1918.
9. R.B. Cunninghame Graham to N.M., 2 December 1918.

Chapter 37   My imaginative faculty has been lying fallow
1. N.M. to Winifred Hodge, 9 May 1919.
2. N.M. to George Blackwood, 9 July 1919.
3. N.M. to Charles Murray, 14 October 1919.
4. George Blackwood to N.M., 5 December 1919.
5. N.M. to George Blackwood, 8 December 1919.
6. Charles Murray to N.M., 18 January 1920.
7. *The Brave Days*, pp 20–23.
8. *Daily Record*, 25 February 1930.
9. 'The Oldest Air in the World' was to be included in House of Lochar's centenary edition of *The Lost Pibroch*.

Chapter 38   Inveraray is as gorgeous as ever
1. N.M. to Leslie Monrgomery (Lynn Doyle), 10 March 1921.
2. N.M. to John MacIntyre (John Brandane), 16 June 1921.
3. N.M. to George Blackwood, 25 June 1921.
4. N.M. to Ion Smeaton Munro.
5. Moira Munro to Maggie McNiven, 8 September 1921.
6. N.M., retrospective diary, 8 November 1921.
7. N.M. to John MacIntyre (John Brandane), 20 September 1922.

Chapter 39   A soul imprisoned!
1. 10th Duke of Argyll to N.M., 30 January 1923.
2. George Blackwood to N.M., 13 March 1923.
3. N.M. to George Blackwood, 19 March 1923.
4. N.M., retrospective diary, 20 April 1923.
5. George Blackwood to N.M., 25 May 1923.
6. N.M. to George Blackwood, 29 May 1923.
7. 10th Duke of Argyll to N.M., 24 July 1923.
8. N.M. to Alice Weir, 31 October 1923.
9. N.M. to Archibald MacIntyre, 23 December 1923.
10. *News*, 31 March 1924.
11. N.M. to George Blackwood, 19 May 1924. James Blackwood ran the London end of Blackwoods, and Lobban was a publisher's reader. 'Sillars of Arran' must remain a mystery figure.
12. N.M., retrospective diary, 1924.
13. N.M. to George Blackwood, 1 September 1924.
14. Moira Munro to Maggie McNiven, 22 June 1924.
15. N.M. to George Blackwood, 1 September 1924.

Chapter 40   Startles me like a hare
1. R. Macaulay Stevenson to N.M., 6 January 1925.
2. Robert Stevenson to N.M., 11 April 1925.
3. Donald A. Mackenzie to N.M., 14 April 1925.
4. John MacIntyre (John Brandane) to N.M., 23 March 1925.
5. N.M. to John MacIntyre (John Brandane), 18 April 1925.
6. *The Book Monthly*, June 1919.
7. N.M. to John MacIntyre (John Brandane), 6 April 1925.
8. George Blackwood to N.M., 29 December 1925.

Chapter 41   I miss my Swiss
1. N.M. to George Blackwood, 8 March 1926.
2. George Blackwood to N.M., 9 March 1926.
3. N.M. to Sir Alexander Kemp Wright, 29 November 1926.
4. Review of *Henry James, Man and Author*, by Pelham Edgar, *News*, 9 December 1926.

Chapter 42   No more hack work for me
1. George Blackwood to N.M., 21 March 1927.
2. N.M. to George Blackwood, 23 March 1927.
3. N.M. to Alice Weir, 20 August 1927.
4. *News*, 14 November 1927.
5. N.M. to Sir John Richmond, 11 January 1928.
6. James Blackwood to N.M., 13 February 1928.
7. N.M. to James Blackwood, 14 February 1928.
8. N.M. to George Blackwood, 29 January 1929.
9. N.M. to the artist John Young Hunter, 28 August 1928.
10. N.M. to William Power, 16 June 1928.
11. Lord Weir to N.M., 22 June 1928.
12. N.M. to John Young Hunter, 28 August 1928.
13. R.B. Cunninghame Graham to N.M., 11 November 1928.
14. *The Brave Days*, p.24.

Chapter 43   And this becomes a lonely house
1. N.M. to George Blackwood, 29 January 1929.
2. Moira Munro to Maggie McNiven, 17 April 1929.
3. Ibid., 23 April 1929.
4. Ibid., n.d.
5. Ibid., n.d.
6. Ibid., 27 April 1929.
7. N.M. to John Mac Intyre [John Brandane], 23 August 1929.
8. N.M. to Alfred Wareing, 5 December 1929.
9. The completed chapters of *The Search* were published in *That Vital Spark: A Neil Munro Anthology* (2002), ed. Brian D. Osborne & Ronald Armstrong.
10. N.M. to George Blake, 29 January 1930.

11. Jonathan Cape to N.M., 20 February 1930.
12. N.M. to Jonathan Cape, 28 February 1930.
13. N.M. to Moira Lendrum, 1 April 1930.
14. William Power, *Should Auld Acquaintance* (1935).
15. N.M. to J. Arnold Fleming, Helensburgh, 14 June 1930.
16. J.M. Barrie to N.M., 13 July 1930.
17. N.M. to George Blackwood, 9 September 1930.
18. George Blackwood to N.M., 11 September 1930.
19. N.M. to George Blackwood, 29 September 1930.
20. N.M. to William Power, 21 October 1930.

Chapter 44   **Cha Till Mi Tuilidh**
1. Effie Bruce to Kate McArthur (Mrs Turner, Lincoln), 14 June 1931.
2. 'Clach air Carn Niall Mac an Rothaich' is printed in full in *ParaGraphs* (The Neil Munro Society Journal) No. 8, Winter 2000.
3. *News*, 23 December 1930.
4. *The Bulletin*, Glasgow, 23 December 1930.
5. From a newspaper cutting, source as yet untraced.
6. *Times Literary Supplement*, 14 March 1935.
7. Alfred Wareing, 'Neil Munro and the Glasgow Citizens' Theatre' in *Queue*, early 1931.

Index

Adam, Agnes (Mrs Crawford), 40, 50, 54
Adam, Andrew, 40, 42, 45, 48, 49
Adam, Effie, 40
Adam, George, 263
Adam, Hugh senior, 40, 42
Adam, Hugh, 40, 45, 48, 49, 51, 54, 126, 128
Adam, Jessie (see Munro, Jessie)
Adam, Pearl, 263
Adam, Phemie (Mrs Effie Craig), 40, 42, 50, 91
Albert, Prince, 15, 176
Alexis, Grand Duke, of Russia, 31
Allan, William, 69
Allason, Bannatyne, 296
Allen, Grant, 52
Anderson, David, 270
Argyll, Duchess of, 24
Argyll, 3rd Duke of, 113
Argyll, 4th Duke of, 113
Argyll, 7th Duke of, 5
Argyll, 8th Duke of, 1, 7, 13, 14, 15, 21, 50, 87, 96, 99, 100, 135, 137, 165
Argyll, 9th Duke of, 13, 14, 15, 24, 45, 110, 111, 116, 134, 139, 160, 191, 192
Argyll, 10th Duke of, 2, 74, 160, 190, 238, 240, 241, 243, 264, 272
Argyll, 11th Duke of, 2
Armstrong, Ronald, 150, 280
Armstrong, Sergeant, 220
Asquith, Lord, 203

Baird, John Logie, 238, 258
Ballantyne, R.M., 16
Balzac, Honore de, 141
Bantock, Granville, 272
Barrie, J.M., 59, 60, 82, 131, 141, 176, 179, 180, 230, 250, 251, 271, 272
Beaton, Duncan, x

Bell, Calum, 158
Bell, Mary Ann, 158, 228
Bell, J.J., 143
Bell, Dr Joseph, 58
Bell, Lillias, 5
Belloc, Hilaire, 197
Bennett, Arnold, 176, 185
Bentley, E.C., 158
Black, Ronald, 68
Black, William, 60, 123
Blackie, Walter, 270
Blackie, Mrs, 270
Blackwood, George, 101, 134, 135, 142, 143, 146, 153, 156, 157, 164, 174, 176, 177, 180, 181, 182, 186, 187, 189, 190, 191, 192, 200, 201, 207, 215, 216, 217, 218, 220, 221, 222, 225, 226, 227, 228, 229, 236, 238, 241, 242, 243, 244, 245, 245, 247, 248, 253, 254, 259, 264, 265, 269, 271
Blackwood, James, 101, 215, 245, 262, 264
Blackwood, William, 55, 56, 57, 59, 60, 61, 63, 71, 75, 76, 78, 79, 81, 90, 93, 96, 98, 101, 103, 104, 107, 108, 110, 111, 114, 130, 131, 137, 139, 140, 143, 144, 147, 155, 156, 172, 174, 175, 176, 177, 178, 271
Blake, George, 83, 131, 158, 215, 216, 217, 221, 223, 229, 230, 231, 232, 234, 236, 251, 262, 265, 269, 279
Blake, Mrs 221
Bone, Captain David, 225, 242, 271
Bone, John, 242
Bone, Muirhead, 243, 264
Bostock, Elspeth, 268
Bostock, James, 258, 260, 261, 269
Boswell, James, 187
Boyd, A.S., 80
Brandane, John (see Dr John Macintyre)

Bratton, Kenneth x
Breton, Frederic, 124
Bridie, James (see Mavor, O.H.)
Brodie, Charles, 274
Brookes, Lieutenant Ernest, 219, 220
Brown, George Douglas ix, 69, 123, 124, 125, 128, 130, 141, 165, 169
Brown, William Kellock, 90, 240
Brown, Major T.L., 208
Bruce, Jack, 143, 238, 239, 247, 264, 267
Bruce, Margaret Moira, 247
Bruce, Jean, 264
Bruce, Norman, 143, 157
Buchan, John, 69, 89, 164, 192, 193, 218, 230, 232, 233, 234, 250, 251
Buchanan, Hugh, 258, 260, 264
Buchanan, Jack, 238
Bunin, Ivan Alexeievich 251
Bunyan, John, 17
Burns, Gilbert, 64
Burns, John, 46
Burns, Robert, 187, 241

Cairncross, T.S., 233
Calderon, George, 179
Cameron, Richard, 184
Campbell, Lord Archibald, 10, 38, 67, 71, 74, 110, 116, 176, 190
Campbell, Lady Archibald, 74, 243
Campbell, Lord Colin, 24, 25
Campbell, Colin, of Glenure, 92
Campbell of Jura, Colin, 223
Campbell, Lady Elspeth, 2, 74, 110, 264
Campbell, Lord George, 163
Campbell, Lady George, 260
Campbell of Islay, J.F., 4, 45, 62, 67, 68, 169
Campbell, Joe, 232
Campbell, John, 87, 89
Campbell, John Macmaster, 192, 213, 238, 239, 262, 278
Campbell, Mrs Macmaster, 192
Campbell of Jura (Hurricane Jack), 192, 197, 202, 226
Campbell of Kilberry, Marion, ix
Campbell of Blythswood, Miss, 111
Campbell, Neil, 207
Campbell, Captain Neill, 216

Campbell, Niall (see Argyll, 10th Duke of)
Campbell, Lady Victoria, 13, 110
Campbell of Blythswood, Walter, 111
Canton, William, 79
Carmichael, Alexander, 65, 118
Cecil, Lord Lionel, 91
Chamberlain, Neville, 258
Chalmers, Revd James, 22, 31, 61
Chalmers, Miss, 64
Chalmers, 210
Chekhov, Anton, 251
Chesterton, G.K., 120
Clark, Robert, 10
Coates, Professor, 28
Cockburn, Lord, 171
Cody, Buffalo Bill, 54
Comber, Miss, 171
Comrie, Alexander, 49
Conrad, Boris, 242
Conrad, Joseph, 42, 61, 71, 78, 84, 85, 86, 87, 89, 104, 153, 169, 184, 242, 243, 252, 253, 264
Cooper, J. Fenimore, 17
Cosh, Mary, 113
Couch, Sir Arthur Quiller, 166, 187, 272
Craig, William, 91
Crane, Stephen, 78
Crawford, Dr, 148
Crawford, John, 48
Crawford, Jack, 258
Crockett, S.R., 59, 60
Curle, Richard, 242

Davidson, Alan, 236
Davidson, Tom, 236
Dean, Stansmore R.L., 52, 104
Deas, Lord, 170
Derechef, Paul, 99
Dewar, Johnny, 159, 161
Dickens, Charles, 17
Disselduff, Lieutenant John, 212, 213
Disselduff, William, 151, 176
Disselduff, Willie, 183
Doubleday, Mr, 79
Douglas, Revd John, 48, 50
Douglas, William, 22, 23, 24, 27, 134, 136, 137, 165
Doyle, Lynn (see Montgomery, Leslie)

Index

Drummond, Dr W.H., 129, 137
Duncan, Captain, 198
Dunn, J. Nicol, 59, 61, 99

Edward VII, King, 108, 110
Elliott, Major Walter, 179
Ewing, John, 103, 116, 117
Ewing, Juliana Horatia, 163

Fellowes, Major R.W.D., 277
Ferdinand, Archduke Franz, 192
Fergus, Dr Freeland, 267
Ferguson, James, 13
Fergusson of Kilkerran, Sir James,
    105, 106, 107, 110
Findlater, The Misses, 251
Fisher, Gregor, 280
Fitzgerald, F. Scott, 243
Footles, 23
Ford, Ford Madox, 86
Forster, E.M., 164
Foulis, Hugh, 140, 143, 144
Foss, Kenelm, 239
Fraser, Sir John Foster, 270
Fraser, Robert (Bob), 10, 48, 72, 142,
    146, 162, 220

Gailford, William, 70
Galsworthy, John, 176
Galt, John, 187, 188, 189, 251
Garnett, Edward, 85
Gaunt, George, 58
Geddes, Patrick, 47, 63, 64, 66
Gemmell, Alexander, 130, 131
George, J.F., 243
George V, King, 184, 220
Gilbert, W.S., 178
Gilmour, John, 195, 260
Gladstone, William, 24, 51
Glasgow Boys, The, 52, 68, 75, 77
Godwin, William, 17
Gowans, Adam, 188
Graham, Private, 212, 214
Graham, R.B. Cunninghame, 42, 84,
    85, 87, 88, 89, 90, 169, 226, 251,
    264, 265, 274, 278
Grant, James, 17
Grieve, C.M. (see MacDiarmid,
    Hugh)
Grieve, Mary, 232

Gullan, Campbell, 178
Guthrie, Arthur, 145, 162, 163
Guthrie, Jessie, 145, 162
Guthrie, Ex-Provost, 176

Haig, Earl, 220, 260
Ham, Colonel George, 138
Hambrough, Cecil, 58
Hardie, Keir, 46
Hardy, Thomas, 56
Harrington, Dr, 267
Hart, Francis Russell, 192, 279
Harvey, John, 54
Hay, Captain, 169
Hay, Ian, 182, 187
Hedderwick, James, 39
Henderson, Angus, 267
Henley, Anna, 174, 177
Henley, William Ernest, 56, 59, 63,
    93, 106, 174, 263
Henry, George, 52
Herbert, Philip G., 53, 54
Hereford, Mrs, 145
Herries, Mr, 262
Hobhouse, Georgina, x
Hodge, Albert, 108
Hodge, David, 60, 119, 131, 142, 145,
    146, 187, 196, 223
Hodge, Lizzie (see Wallace, Lizzie)
Hodge, Winifred, 142, 146, 168, 197,
    198, 200, 223, 227, 228, 261, 268
Hodges, Jeremy, x
Hogg, James, 216
Hohenlohe, Prince, 153, 154
Hohenlohe, Princess, 153, 154
Hornel, E.A., 52, 186, 191
Houston, George, 77, 156, 159, 182,
    183, 186, 187, 189, 209, 228, 243,
    272
Hunter, John Young, 167
Hunter, Mary, 167
Hurricane Jack (see Campbell of Jura)

Irving, Sir Henry, 71, 104, 119

Jacob, Violet, 233
Jacobs, W.W., 148, 152
James, Henry, 258
Jeffrey, William, 274
Jerome, Jerome K., 152

Jewel, Jack, 46
Joffre, Marshal Joseph Jacques, 220
Johnson, Dr Samuel, 187, 244
Johnston, Lord, 170, 171
Jones, Sir Henry, 71
Jones, Kennedy, 47

Kailyard School, 60
Keating, George T., 264
Keats, John, 4, 5, 188
Kelvin, Lord, 83, 98
Kempton, Mr, 178
Kipling, Rudyard, 56, 89, 93
Kohlbek, Beata, 280
Kow, Lee Mong, 138

Lang, Andrew, 72, 92, 93, 101, 194
Lardner, Ring, 243
Lauder, Sir Harry, 55, 183, 184, 278
Lauder, John (son of Harry), 208
Lee, Joseph, 233
Lemon, Kate (Mrs Charlie Maitland),
    61, 132
Lendrum, Alan, 270
Lendrum, Ronald, 266, 269, 270, 272,
    273
LeSage, A.-R., 17
Lewis, Matthew Gregor, 17
Lindsay, Ian G., 113
Lipton, Sir Thomas, 123, 134, 153,
    154
Livingstone, David, 96
Lobban, John, 122, 245
Lorimer, Sir Robert, 113, 261
Lorne, Marquis of (see Argyll, 9th
    Duke of)
Louise, Princess, 13, 24, 111, 154
Lowis, Mr (Chamberlain of Argyll),
    110
Lukin, General, 218

MacAllister, Principal Sir Donald,
    168, 240, 272
McArthur, Alexander, 151
McArthur, Alister, 109, 199, 200, 203,
    205, 210, 212
McArthur, Charles, 40
Macarthur, Donald, 160
McArthur, Dr Donald, 198, 199
McArthur, Eoin, x

McArthur, Freda, 199
McArthur, Isabella, 3, 27, 94
MacArthur, John, 8
McArthur, Kate (Mrs Turner), 70, 97,
    109, 110, 125, 133, 135, 145, 151,
    168, 240, 273
McArthur, Lilly, 5
McArthur of Inistrynich, Patrick, 5, 277
McArthur, Peter, 151
Macaulay, Thomas Babington, 59
McBride, Molly, 174
McBride, Will, 174
MacColl, Evan, ix, 95
MacColla, Fionn, 94, 140
McConnachie, Jenny, 199
MacDiarmid, Hugh (C.M. Grieve), ix,
    95, 141, 233, 249, 250, 251, 252,
    276
MacDonald, Father Allan, 117, 118,
    122, 124
Macdonald, Alexander, 68
MacDonald of Barrisdale, 194
Macdonald, General Sir Hector, 134
McEwan, Sir William, 48
McGillvray, Maimie, 132, 151
Macgillivray, Pittendrigh, 52, 53, 62,
    64, 67, 77, 90, 111, 112, 115, 216,
    226, 232, 240
McGregor, Neilina, 104, 109
MacGregor, Rae, 11
MacGregor, Rob Roy, 161
MacHaffie & Colquhoun, 30
Macintosh, William, 139
MacIntyre, Archibald, 244
Macintyre, Duncan Ban, 68
Macintyre, Dr John (throat specialist),
    84, 85, 183, 184
MacIntyre, Dr John (John Brandane),
    155, 192, 249, 251, 252
Macintyre, John (son of Peter), 158
Macintyre, Nicol, 132
Macintyre, Peter, 16, 87, 158
McIsaac, 202, 203
McKay, Peter, 92, 215
McKellar, 210
MacKellar, Archie, 10, 27, 31, 32, 33,
    34, 40, 48
Mackenzie, Donald A., 248
Mackenzie, Fergus, 60
Mackinnon, Professor Donald, 65, 82

Mackintosh, Charles Rennie, 107, 108, 270
McPhail, Colin, 10, 134, 150
MacLaren, Charlie, 11
Maclaren, Ian, 59, 60, 128, 251
MacLaren, Lieutenant, 199
MacLaren, Wilson, 246
Maclean, Professor Magnus, 237
MacLennan, Bailie, 124
MacLennan, Lizzie, 125
MacLennan, Robert J., 144, 234, 245, 246, 247, 262
MacLennan, Sheila, 269
MacLeod, Dr Donald, 71, 79, 87
Macleod, Fiona (see Sharp, William)
Macleod, Norman, 66, 67
MacLeod, W. Douglas (Willie), 158, 159, 215, 243
McLullich, Duncan, 132
McMath, Donald, 223
MacMillan, Archibald, 127
McNabb, Findlay, 241
McNab, John, 23
MacNair, J.G., 274
McNiven, Maggie, 83, 108, 136, 139, 159, 172, 209, 223, 228, 236, 246, 247, 265, 266, 268, 273
McNiven, Mrs, 257
McMillan, Revd Donald, 91
McMillan, Roddy, 280
McPhedran, Neil, 274
Macpherson, James, 194
Macrae, Duncan, 280
Macrae, Dr Farquhar, 168
Mactaggart, Scipio, 27
McVicar, Provost Donald, 176
Mac, Sandy, 211
Maitland, Charlie, 10, 39, 48, 54, 61, 64, 87, 100, 116, 132, 142, 146, 151, 152, 162, 175, 176, 215
Maitland, John, 108, 109, 119
Maitland, Peter, 160, 169
Malcolm of Poltalloch, John Wingfield, 24, 34
Malloch, Dr, 192
Mansfield, Katherine, 251
Marriatt, Mr, 185
Maude, Cyril, 148
Maupassant, Guy de, 251
Mavor, O.H., (James Bridie), 268

Meikle, Revd Gilbert, 22, 49
Meldrum, David Storrar, 60, 71, 75, 76, 78, 79, 84, 96, 101, 123, 124, 130, 131, 141, 188
Meredith, George, 237, 238
Middleton, Mrs, 237
Middleton, Raeburn, 237, 238
Millar, Robins, 76, 269
Mitchell, Rosslyn, 157
Moncreiffe of that Ilk, Sir Iain, 1, 2
Monson, Alfred, 38
Montgomery, Ellen, 16
Montgomery, Leslie (Lynn Doyle), 235, 270, 277
Morand, M.R., 178
Morel, Madame Coussin, 219
Morris, Old Tom, 46
Munro, Alison, 232
Munro, Ann (Mrs Thomson), 1, 2, 3, 4, 5, 18, 27, 41, 54, 94, 104, 115, 134, 135, 136, 163
Munro, Ann (Mrs John), 2, 3, 5, 20, 25, 32
Munro, Annie, 42, 48, 49
Munro, Christina, 107
Munro, Donald, 29
Munro, Dugald, 5
Munro, Duncan, 5
Munro, Effie (Mrs Jack Bruce), 41, 50, 51, 54, 70, 71, 80, 83, 93, 99, 110, 119, 125, 129, 130, 131, 133, 134, 135, 136, 137, 143, 145, 158, 167, 169, 170, 191, 197, 198, 214, 216, 219, 229, 236, 238, 240, 247, 255, 264, 266, 272
Munro, Elizabeth, 160
Munro, General, 212
Munro, Hugh, 56, 70, 80, 81, 83, 93, 99, 129, 130, 131, 133, 135, 145, 153, 158, 170, 171, 181, 184, 190, 191, 192, 193, 196, 197, 198, 199, 200, 201, 202, 203, 204, 205,206, 207, 208, 209, 210, 211, 212, 213, 214, 215, 216, 217, 219, 220, 225, 237, 249, 246, 247, 257, 261
Munro, Ian, x
Munro, Ion, 153
Munro, Isabella, 151
Munro, Isobel (Bud), 80, 126, 129, 135, 142, 146, 171, 198, 200, 216,

223, 228, 229, 236, 246, 255, 256, 257, 260, 261, 268, 269, 272

Munro, Jessie, 40, 42, 49, 50, 51, 54, 56, 64, 70, 77, 80, 83, 97, 98, 99, 101, 103, 104, 110, 119, 125, 126, 129, 133, 135, 136, 137, 139, 143, 145, 147, 192, 201, 221, 228, 236, 246, 247, 258, 267, 270, 271, 272, 273

Munro, John, 4, 5, 68, 271

Munro, Lilian (Lala), 64, 80, 133, 135, 162, 171, 211, 216, 227, 228, 236, 240, 246, 256, 257, 260, 268, 269, 270, 272, 273

Munro, Moira (Mrs Lendrum), 77, 80, 98, 100, 133, 135, 162, 171, 174, 198, 200, 209, 211, 216, 221, 227, 236, 246, 247, 254, 255, 256, 260, 266, 267, 268, 269, 270, 272, 273, 274

Munro, Neil:
born, 1
family and early childhood, 1–6
school, 7–9
friends, diversions, visit to see castle Christmas tree, 10–15
boyhood reading, 16–18
mother's marriage to Malcom Thomson, first visit to Glasgow, Inveraray prison, 18–21
leaves school, farm-work, 21–22
enters law office, 22
witnesses Castle fire, 23–24
lawlessness at by-election, 24–25
grandmother's death, 25
joins rural volunteer company, 26
joins Mutual Improvement Society, 26
writes article on Inveraray fishing fleet, 26
skates on frozen Loch Fyne, 26
goes to Glasgow, 27
'diagnosed' by phrenologist, 28
works as potato merchant's clerk and ironmongery cashier, 29–30
seance with landlord, 31–31
stays in lodgings, 33–34
takes part in Wet Review, 34–37
writes verse and short articles for *Oban Times*, 35

starts as junior reporter,*Greenock Advertiser*, 39
moves to *Glasgow News*, lodges with Adam family, 40
marries Jessie Adam, 40
moves to *Falkirk Herald*, 41
mother-in-law dies, 42
daughter Annie born, 42
returns to *Glasgow News*, 45
leaves Scotland for first time to report shooting meeting in London, 45
writes first leader, on decline in Gaelic speaking, 46
appointed chief reporter of *Evening News*, Glasgow, 47
daughter Annie dies, 48
first trip abroad, to Paris Exposition, 49
daughter Effie born, 50
reports speech by Gladstone, 51
meets Macaulay Stevenson, Pittendrigh Macgillivray and other Glasgow Boys, 52
gets notion to live in country and make living by fiction, 53
has two short stories published in *Newcastle Weekly Courant*, 54
step-father Malcom Thomson dies, 54
starts writing humorous articles for London *Globe*, 55
son Hugh born, 56
Ardlamont scoop, 58
promoted to 'extra special literary work, reviews, leaders', etc., 59
skates on Loch Lomond with David Hodge, 60
starts 'Views & Reviews' in *News*, 61
Shadow-flyting with 'Fiona Macleod', 62
daughter Lilian born, 64
social life, clubs, 70
edits *Saint Mungo*, 72
attends dinner of Highland Society, London, as guest of Lord Archibald Campbell, 73–74
visits Holland with D.S. Meldrum, 75
goes freelance, 76
daughter Moira born, 77
begins 'The Looker-On', 77
moves to Waterfoot, 79

congratulated on *John Splendid* by J.M.
Barrie and John M.M. Munro, 82
employs Maggie McNiven, 83
meets Joseph Conrad, 84
declines Freedom of Inveraray, 87
meets R.B. Cunninghame Graham, 87
meets John Buchan, 89
his bust by Kelloch Brown exhibited in
Royal Scottish Academy
lost in hills above Loch Etive, 92
meets Andrew Lang, 92
reports Queen Victoria's visit to
Dublin, 99
at Paris Exposition, 99
reports funeral of 8th Duke of Argyll,
100
goes on cycling tour in France, 103
Neil junior born, 103
Sits for portrait by Stansmore Dean,
104
contretemps with Sir James Fergusson
re *Doom Castle*, 105
lunches with 9th Duke of Argyll, 110
visits Pittendrigh Macgillivray, 115
goes to Barra, 116
meets Father Allan MacDonald, 117
reads *The House with the Green Shutters*,
123
visited by George Douglas Brown at
Waterfoot, 124
daughter Isobel born, 126
buys house in Gourock, 126
creates Erchie, 126
step-son Hugh Adam emigrates, 128
flits to Carnus, Gourock, 129
D.S. Meldrum visits Carnus. Death of
George Douglas Brown. Effie and
Hugh start at Greenock Academy,
130
sits next to J.M. Barrie at Whitefriars
Club dinner, 131
takes over tenancy of Douglas's house
in Inveraray, 134
his mother tells Maggie McNiven his
father was a ghillie, 135
goes to Canada, 137
sits for portrait by William Strang, 139
goes to Italy, 145
officiates at Institute of Journalists
conference in Glasgow, 147

creates Para Handy, 149–152
on Sir Thomas Lipton's yacht, 152
on car reliability tour, 158
visits Sweden, 158
visited at Inveraray by 9th and 10th
Dukes of Argyll, 160
annual family picnics, 161
takes down sermons in shorthand, 161
mother dies, 163
featured in The Baillie, 167
sends daughter Effie to Swiss finishing
school, 167
awarded honorary doctorate by
Glasgow University, 168
takes Effie and Hugh to Inveraray
murder trial, 170
prophesies Great War, 173
meets Alfred Wareing, 174
unsuccessful attempts to write in hut at
Gourock, 175
awarded Freedom of Inveraray, 176
visits Italy, 176
his play Macpherson is a smash hit,
178
meets Harry Lauder, 183
creates Jimmy Swan, 184
meets Arnold Bennett, 185
trip to Paris with George Houston, 189
son Hugh joins Argyll and Sutherland
Highlanders, 190
laments loss of Edinburgh Castle
steamer, 190
reports death of Duke of Argyll, 191
publication of his last novel, The New
Road, 192
excited by outbreak of war, 195
takes over London office of the News,
196
visits Hugh's billet, 199
goes to France as war correspondent,
200
sees Hugh for last time, 201
returns to Scotland to edit News, 201
learns of Hugh's death, 213
attempts to get to France, 215
distressed by submarine sunk in Clyde,
217
second wartime trip to France, 218
visits Hugh's grave, 220
suffers nervous collapse, 220

moves house to Cromalt, 222
solitary New Year pilgrimage to
  Inveraray, 227
post-war editor of the News, 230
upsets Hugh MacDiarmid by running
  critical review of Northern
  Numbers in the *News*, 233
tells Leslie Montgomery of 'tragic and
  pathetic' elements in his childhood,
  235
meets W.B. Yeats, 237
takes recuperative trip on fruit boat, 239
not present at unveiling of Inveraray
  war memorial, 240
final meeting with Conrad, 242
reports on emigrants leaving Hebrides,
  244
meets Robert Stevenson, alleged son of
  R.L.S., 245
first grandchild born, 247
leaves *News*, 247
attacked by Hugh MacDiarmid in The
  Scottish Educational Journal, 251
persuaded to write history of Royal
  Bank, 254
hears from daughters in Switzerland,
  256
writes 'With Some Reflections' on
  Armistice Day, 261
suffers nervous breakdown, recuper-
  ating at Vence near Nice, 263
health deteriorates, ordered to cut back
  smoking and wear spectacles, 267
grand-daughter Elspeth born, 268
daughter Moira marries, 269
health trip to Ireland, 270
health trip to America, 271
awarded honorary doctorate by
  Edinburgh University, 272
death at Cromalt, 272
funeral at Inveraray, 272
praised posthumously by Hugh
  MacDiarmid, 276
Works of:
'A Fine Pair of Shoes', 63
'Anapla's Boy', 55–56
Ayrshire Idylls, 182, 187, 189, 243
'Bagpipe Ballads', 218, 220, 222, 226,
  228, 229, 241, 245, 254, 271
'Castle Dark', 63

Children of Tempest, 109, 122, 124,
  125, 130, 131, 133, 134, 135, 137,
  140, 143, 152, 157, 193, 277
Doom Castle, 93, 97, 98, 99, 101, 103,
  105, 106, 108, 109, 110, 112, 113,
  114, 115, 120, 121, 129, 193, 261,
  280
'Dr Everton Sharp's Experiment', 54
Erchie: My Droll Friend, 126, 143, 144,
  146, 147, 148, 152, 155, 156, 168,
  180, 262
'Evening Prayer of a People', 196
Fancy Farm, 169, 172, 175, 176, 177,
  180, 181, 182
Gilian the Dreamer, 5, 16, 80, 91, 93,
  94, 95, 96, 122, 123, 153, 167,
  188, 192
'How the Jeweller of Alnbury was
  Duped', 54
Hurricane Jack of the Vital Spark, 238,
  243, 244
'If I were King of France', 187
In Highland Harbours with Para Handy,
  183, 226
Jaunty Jock and Other Stories, ix, 143,
  176, 183, 225, 226, 227, 228
'Jaunty Jock', 222
Jaunty Jock (play), 186
Jimmy Swan, The Joy Traveller, 190,
  207, 221
John Splendid, 5, 72, 75, 76, 78, 79,
  81, 82, 83, 86, 87, 88, 92, 93, 98,
  110, 121, 182, 183, 193, 229, 232,
  237, 277
'Jus Primae Noctis', 63
'Lament for Macleod of Raasay', 220
Macpherson, 177, 178, 179, 180
'McNaughton's Bath', 261
'Magic Casements', 188
'Pipes in Arras', 219
'Roving Lads', 218
'Shudderman Soldier', 56, 57, 58, 68
'The Adventures of a Country
  Customer', 184
'The Afton Moor Mystery', 58
The Brave Days, 154, 265, 279
'The Brooch', 177
The Clyde: River and Firth, 153, 167,
  187
'The Coal Crisis – Duffy Explains', 255

The Daft Days, 27, 41, 153, 155, 156, 157, 162, 164, 165, 166, 169, 170, 174, 176, 177, 181
'The Fell Sergeant', 68
The History of the Royal Bank 1727–1927, 260
The Looker-On, 92, 239, 279
'The Lost Pibroch', 56
The Lost Pibroch and Other Sheiling Stories, ix, 61, 63, 64, 65, 67, 68, 69, 70, 71, 73, 82, 83, 85, 89, 91, 98, 128, 140, 152, 182, 193, 194, 233, 237, 251, 280
'The Making of Tam o' Shanter', 187
The New Road, 143, 182, 183, 186, 190, 191, 192, 193, 194, 201, 222, 227, 229, 230, 232, 239, 259, 277, 279
'The Prisoner that Puzzled a Prince', 55
'The Red Hand', 56, 57, 59
'The Sea-Fairy of French Foreland', 68
The Search, 214, 226, 241, 246, 248, 254, 260, 267, 268
'The Secret of the Heather Ale', 55–56
'The Sgeul of Black Murdo', 60, 61, 64
The Shoes of Fortune, 100, 101, 104, 110, 115, 119, 120, 121, 122, 123, 126, 140, 153
'The Tocherless Lass', 229
'The Tudor Cap', 183
The Vital Spark and Her Queer Crew, 155, 156, 157
'The Wet Man of Muscadale', 264
The Windfall, 229
'Thumb Hero', 60
'To Exiles', 216
'War', 216

Munro, Neil junior, x, 2, 4, 80, 103, 104, 109, 125, 133, 135, 136, 156, 158, 162, 171, 175, 180, 197, 198, 216, 223, 228, 236, 240, 246, 257, 272
Munro, Neil (uncle), 19
Munro, Peter, 5, 51
Murray, Charles, 229, 230, 234, 270, 229
Murray, George, 71

Nash, Eveleigh, 104
Neill, Colonel Duncan, 153, 154
Newbery, Francis, 108
Newbolt, Henry, 182
Newlands, Duncan, 150
Niven, Forrest, 139
North, Christopher, 216

Orczy, Baroness, 279
Orr, Jack 156
Osbourne, Brian D., 150, 280
Oscar, King of Sweden, 158
Oswald, James, M.P., 85

Phillimore, 205
Pirret, Revd David, 40
Poe, Edgar Allan, 251
Poincaré, Raymond, 220
Powell, Lord Baden, 173
Power, William, 157, 263, 269, 270, 271
Primrose, George, 157
Primrose, Sir John Ure, 148
Primrose, Lady, 148
Proudfoot, Alexander, 266

Radcliffe, Mrs, 17
Ralston, Mr, 246
Reid, Revd D.A. Cameron, 111
Reid, J.M., 274, 276
Renan, Ernest, 62
Renfrew, Daisy, x
Renton, Ronald W., x, 95, 101, 122, 152, 166, 280
Richmond, Sir John (Jack), 185, 245, 248, 262
Roberton, Sir Hugh, 270
Robertson, Davy, 262
Rogerson, 208
Rose, J.H., 176
Ross, Duncan, 280
Rossetti, Dante Gabriel, 63

Sackville, Lady Margaret, 270
Scott, Sir Walter, 96, 112, 193, 247
Seton, Sir Bruce, 233
Sharp, Elizabeth, 65, 66, 74
Sharp, William ('Fiona Macleod'), 47, 52, 62, 63, 64, 65, 66, 67, 72, 73, 74, 87, 148, 237, 238, 251

Shelley, Mary 17
Shelley, Percy Bysshe, 17
Sillars of Arran, 245
Smith, Alexander, 30
Smith, Henry, 81
Smith, Henry Dunn, 7, 8, 9, 11, 12, 24, 26, 81
Smith, James Murray, 45, 47, 50, 51, 54, 72, 76, 83, 91, 99, 103, 104, 123, 126, 129, 131, 143, 145, 147, 148, 153, 158, 168, 187, 196, 201, 215, 223, 226, 258, 262
Smith, Mrs James Murray, 83, 145
Smith, Lillias, 7, 10
Smith, May, 256
Smollett, Tobias, 17
Spence, Lewis, 274
Spurgeon, Arthur, 167
Stanley, Henry, 50
Steuart, John A., 246
Stevenson, Margaret, 246
Stevenson, Robert Louis, ix, 11, 38, 56, 60, 61, 82, 93, 96, 120, 122, 193, 194, 245, 251, 276
Stevenson, R. Macaulay, 52, 76, 103, 104, 200, 248
Stevenson, Robert, 245, 248
Stewart, Captain, 200
Stewart, Charles, 91
Stewart, Dr, 159
Stewart, James, of the Glens, 170
Stewart, John (Tarry), 13, 25
Stewart, J. Shields, 47, 48, 51
Stoker, Bram, 71
Storey, Principal Henry, 133
Straight, Sir Douglas, 148
Strang, William, 139, 237
Swan, Dennis, 198
Swinburne, Algernon, 56
Synge, Lieutenant W.A.T., 200

Terry, Ellen, 104
Thom, Wallace, 43, 44
Thomson, Dan, 81, 199, 207, 208
Thomson, Flora, 108
Thomson, John, 19
Thomson, Maikie, 19
Thomson, Malcom, 18, 20, 27, 54, 94
Thomson, Susan, 19
Thrale, Mrs, 244

Turner, 202, 203
Tweeddale, John, 60
Tynan, Katherine, 62

Vallance, Andrew, 228, 266
Verne, Jules, 17
Victoria, Queen, 7, 13, 15, 34, 36, 99, 106, 111, 118, 135
Völkel, Dr Hermann, x, 120, 279

Walden, Lord Howard de, 186
Wales, Prince of (Edward VII), 50
Wales, Prince of, (Edward VIII), 263
Wallace, Lizzie (Mrs Hodge), 119, 142, 146
Wallace, Dr William, 103, 104, 119, 141
Walpole, Horace, 17
Wareing, Alfred, 173, 174, 176, 177, 179, 185, 186, 187, 167, 268, 278
Webb, Alice, 256, 258, 260
Weir, Jimmy, 199
Weir, Lady (Alice), 227, 234, 239, 244, 260, 261
Weir, Lord (William), 197, 199, 225, 235, 245, 257, 258, 260, 263
Weir, Mr & Mrs, 31, 32, 33
Wells, H.G., 56, 85, 173
Weyman, Stanley J., 259
Whibley, Charles, 216
Wicks, Frederick, 40, 51
Wilhelm II, Kaiser of Germany, 111
Wilson, David, x
Wilson, Finella, x
Wilson, J.G., 174
Wittig, Dr Kurt, 68, 279
Wood, Alexander, 65, 98, 106, 107, 132
Wade, General George, 182, 193
Watt, Mary, 136
Wernitz, Dr Herbert, 279
Wheelhouse, M.V., 163
Wright, Sir Alexander Kemp, 255, 258, 259, 260
Wright, Mr, 199
Wright, Mrs, 199, 200

Yeats, William Butler, 42, 56, 62, 131, 237, 238

Zola, Emile, 59, 141